YUKI SHIMIZU

LOVE MODE ②

The Men of Love Mode

TAKAMIYA

KATSURA

A longtime friend of Aoe. Takamiya is madly in love with Izumi. They've been having a lot of fun lately…

AOE

REIJI

Owner of the male escort service known as B&B.

"IZUMI"

The "other" Izumi and B&B's number one host. He's been having some health problems as of late.

SAKASHITA

IZUMI

Normal kid whose life has been turned upside down because of his relationship with Takamiya. If only he'd loosen up…

LOVE · MODE
The Story So Far...

What was supposed to be a pleasant day turns into the blind date from hell when regular high school kid Sakashita Izumi finds himself going out with a man! Not having the smarts to just say no, Izumi is wined and dined by his older suitor, Takamiya. Surprised by the fact that he finds himself enjoying the company of another man, Izumi has a few too many drinks and suddenly realizes he's in Takamiya's bed and his clothes have disappeared! It turns out that Takamiya had assumed Izumi was the male escort he had ordered from his friend Aoe's dating club, B&B. But this offers no solace to poor Izumi who feels like he's been violated in the worst way. And to top it all off, Takamiya wants their relationship to continue further than that one wild and crazy night. As the two get to know each other better, Izumi finds that maybe Takamiya isn't so bad and love begins to bloom. Of course, a box of powerful aphrodisiacal chocolates never hurts when it comes to getting the juices flowing...

Editor's Note:

In order to maintain as much authenticity as possible, *Love Mode* retains the original Japanese name order for all names. Thus family name comes first, followed by the given name. The series will also retain all honorifics.

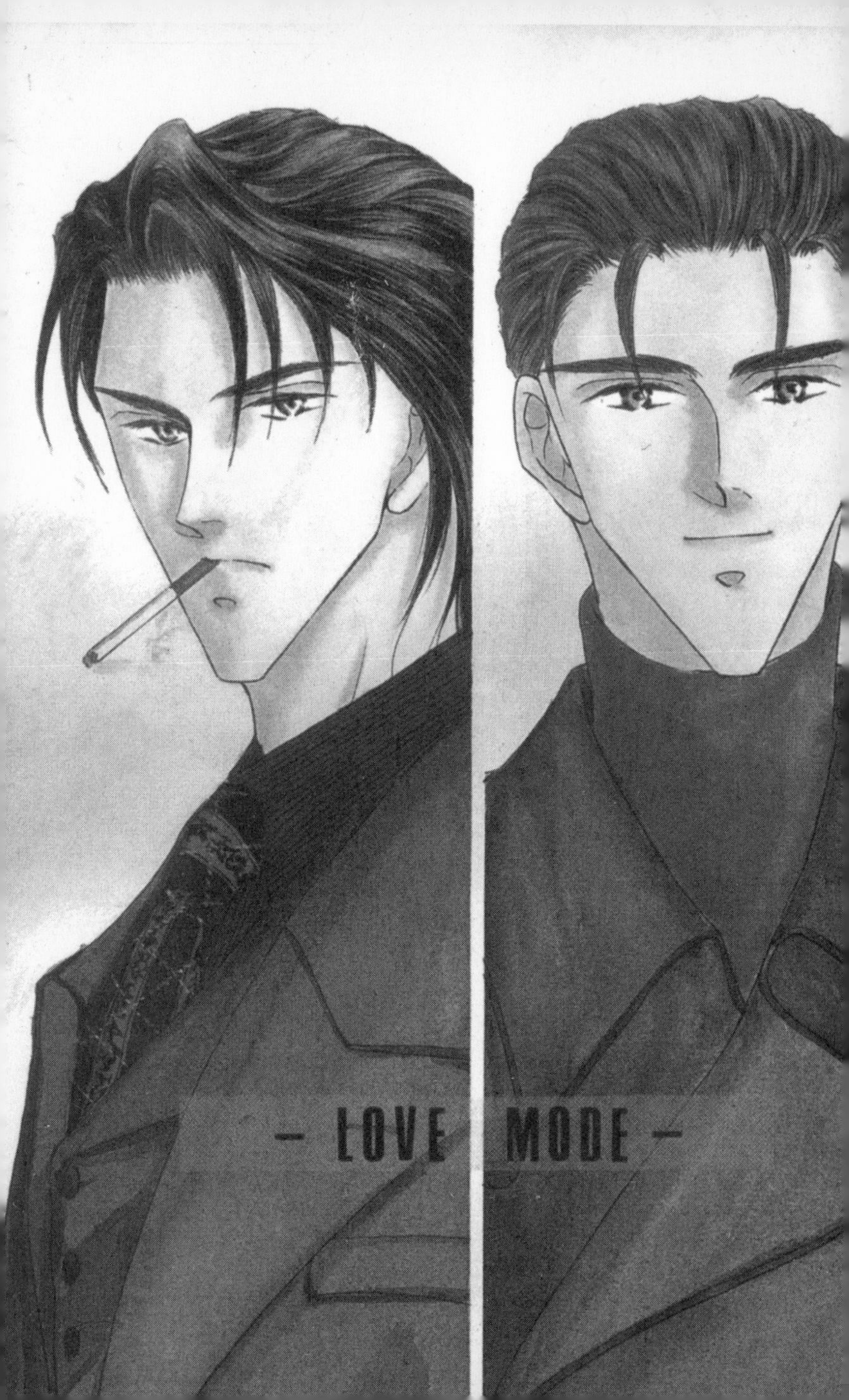
- LOVE MODE -

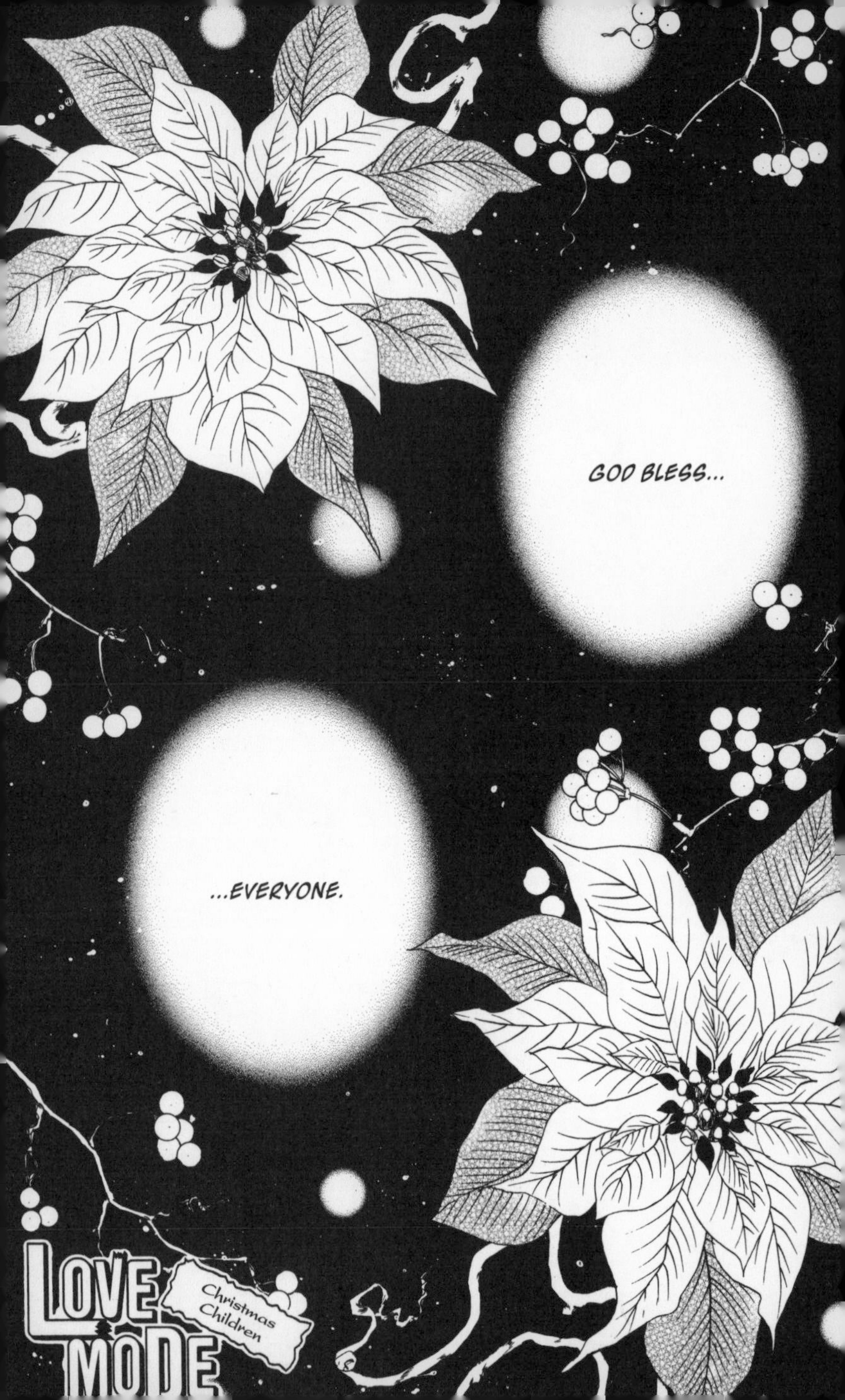
GOD BLESS...
...EVERYONE.
LOVE MODE
Christmas Children

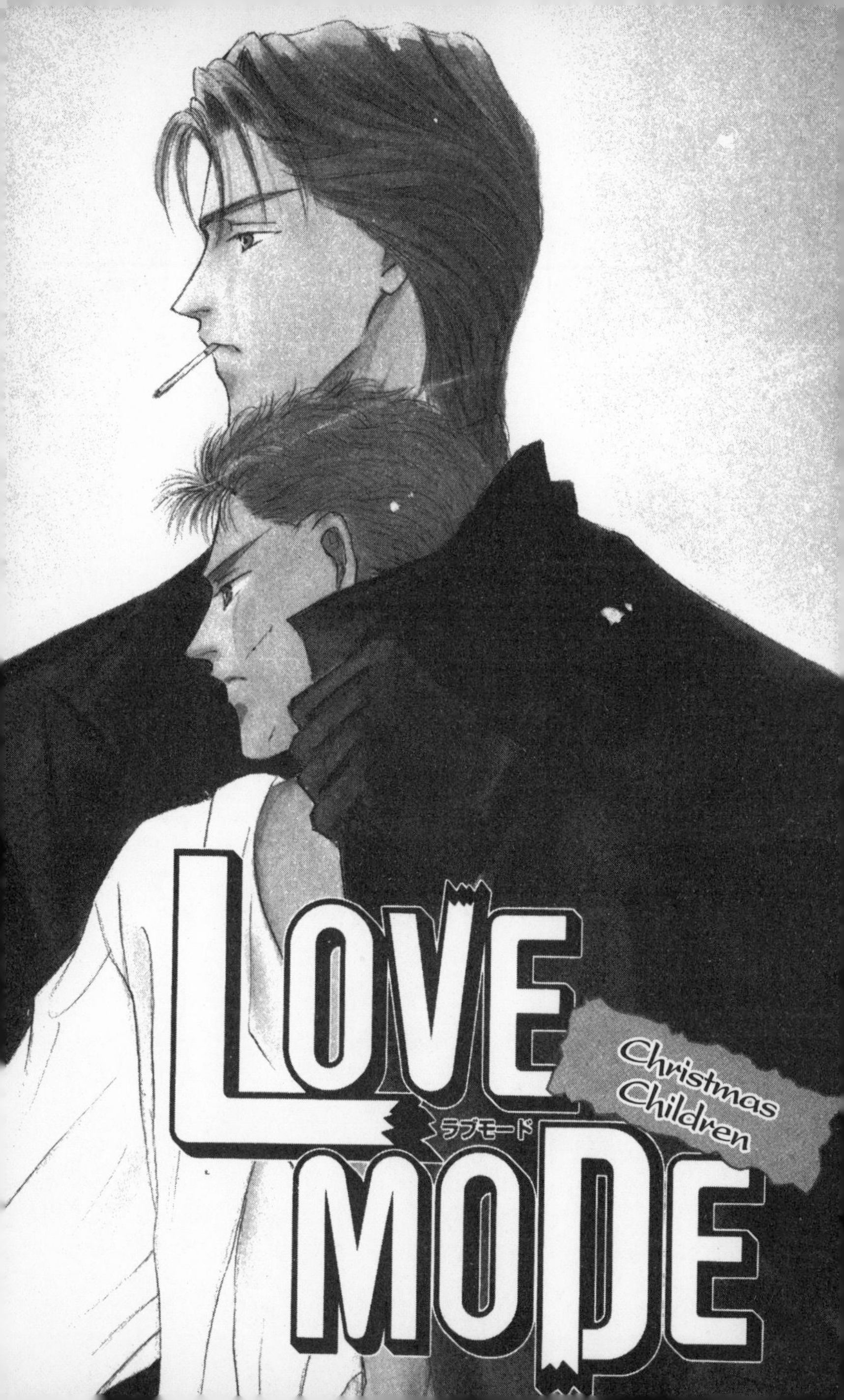
LOVE
ラブモード
MODE
Christmas Children

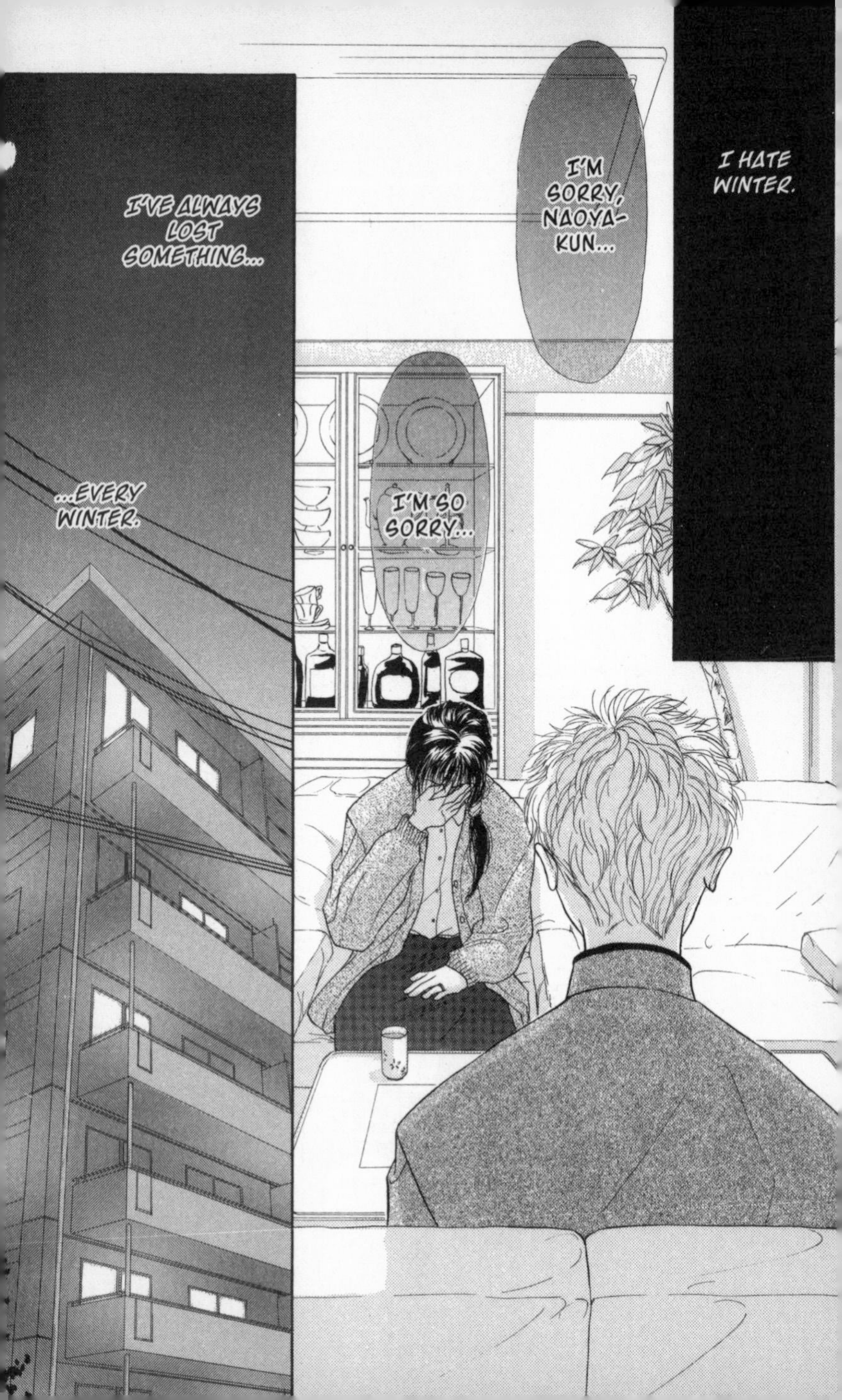
I HATE WINTER.
I'M SORRY, NAOYA-KUN...
I'M SO SORRY...
I'VE ALWAYS LOST SOMETHING...
...EVERY WINTER.

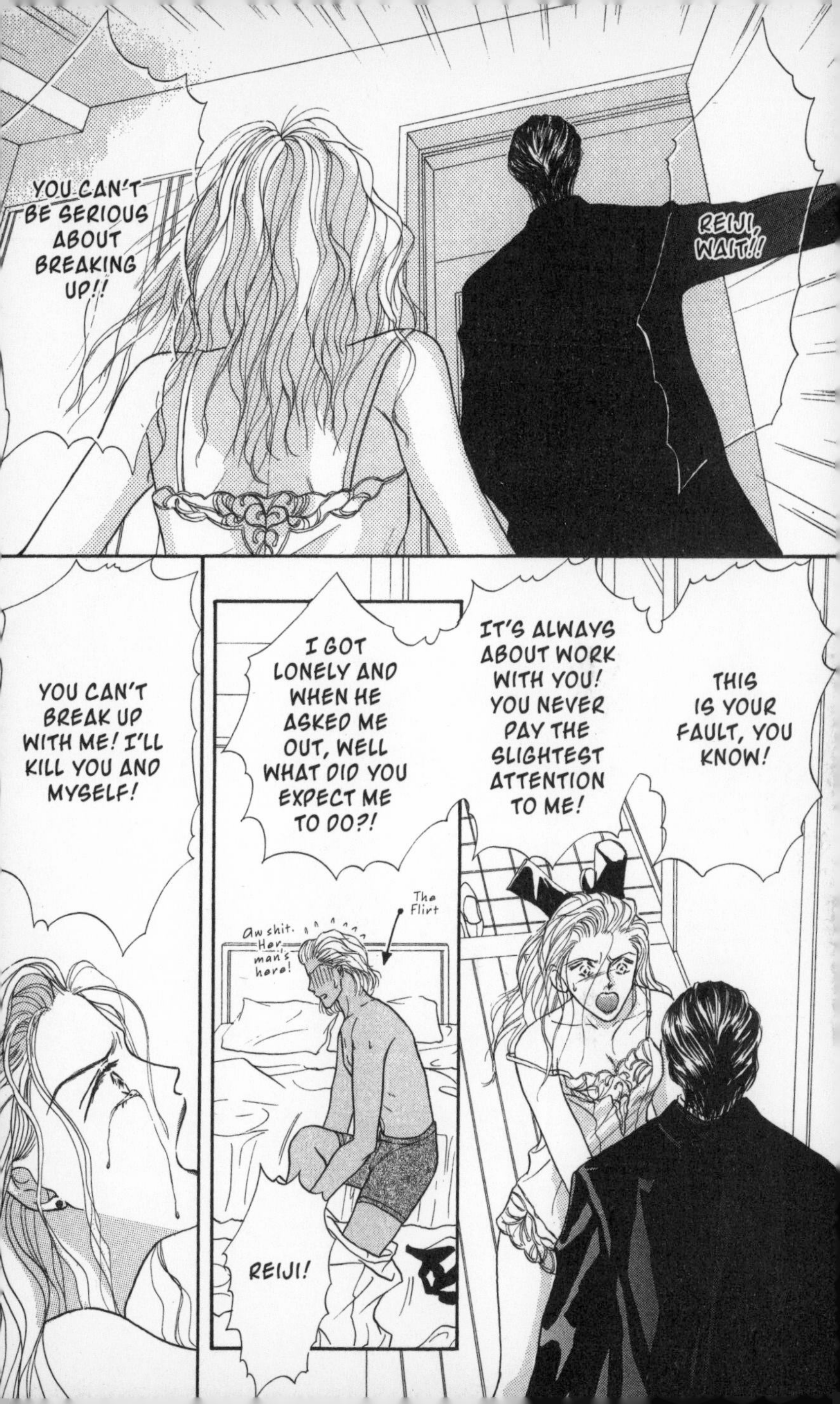
REIJI, WAIT!!
YOU CAN'T BE SERIOUS ABOUT BREAKING UP!!
THIS IS YOUR FAULT, YOU KNOW!
IT'S ALWAYS ABOUT WORK WITH YOU! YOU NEVER PAY THE SLIGHTEST ATTENTION TO ME!
I GOT LONELY AND WHEN HE ASKED ME OUT, WELL WHAT DID YOU EXPECT ME TO DO?!
The Flirt
Aw shit. Her man's here!
REIJI!
YOU CAN'T BREAK UP WITH ME! I'LL KILL YOU AND MYSELF!

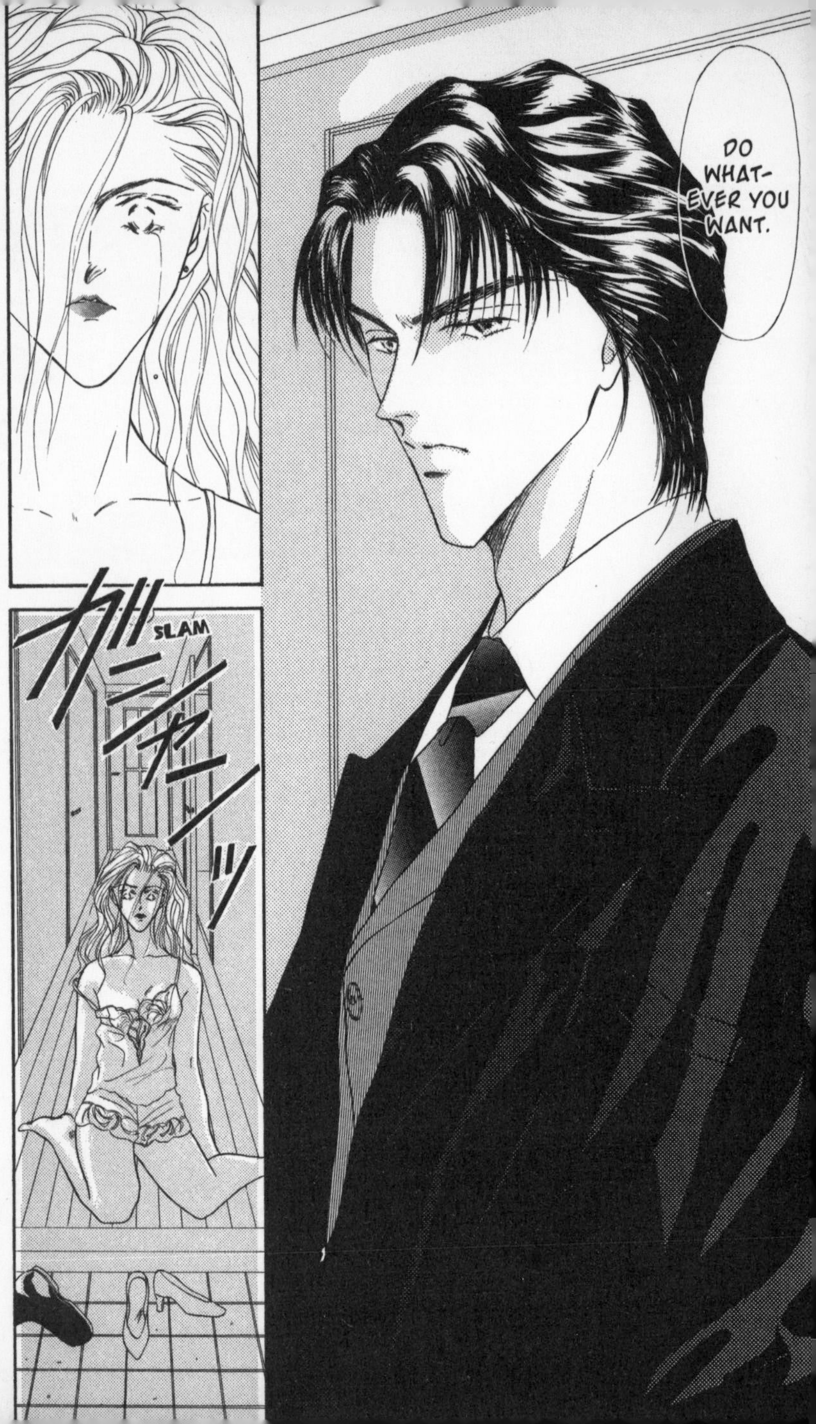
DO WHAT-EVER YOU WANT.
ガシャーンッ
SLAM

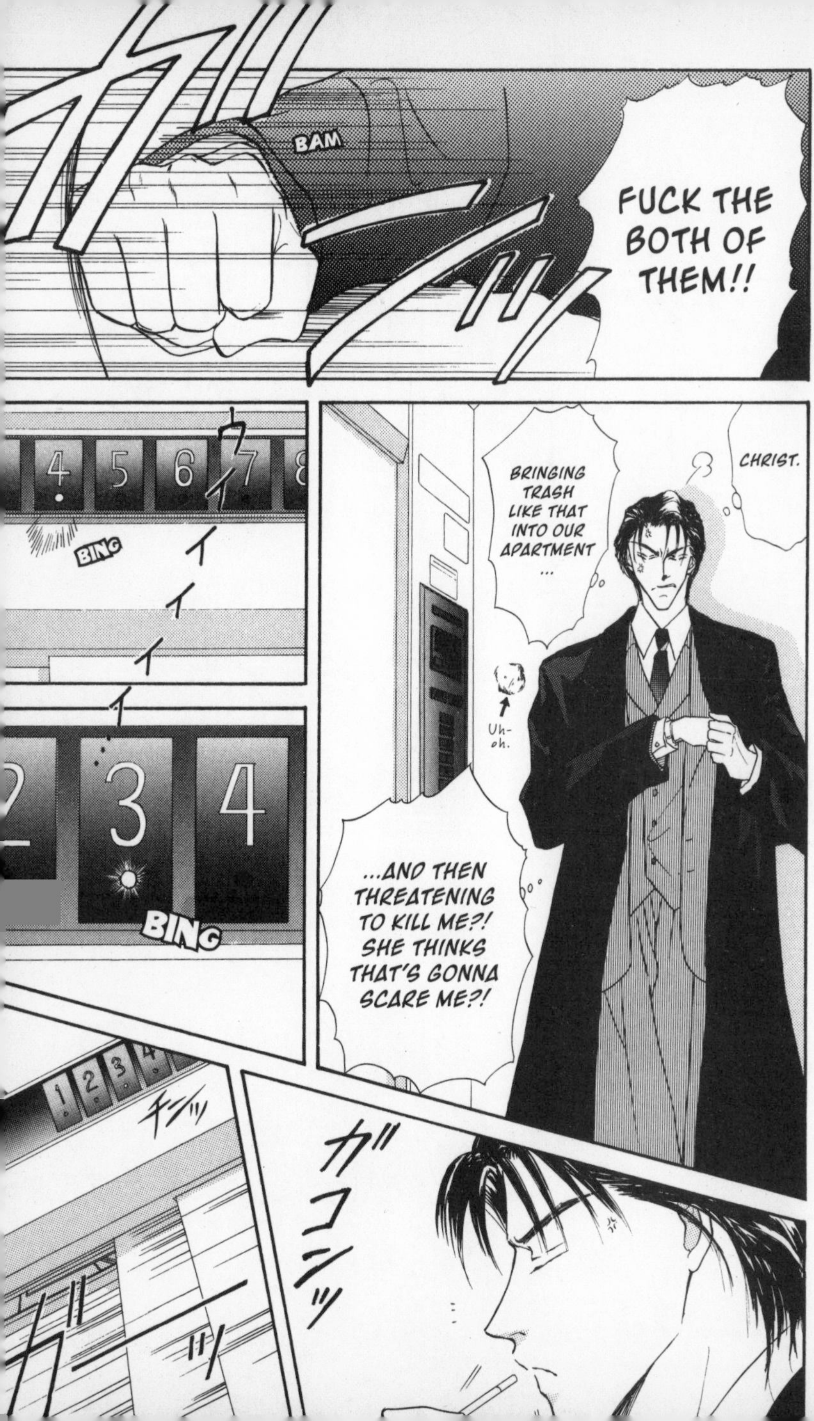
FUCK THE BOTH OF THEM!!
BAM
CHRIST.
BRINGING TRASH LIKE THAT INTO OUR APARTMENT ...
Uh-oh.
...AND THEN THREATENING TO KILL ME?! SHE THINKS THAT'S GONNA SCARE ME?!
BING
BING

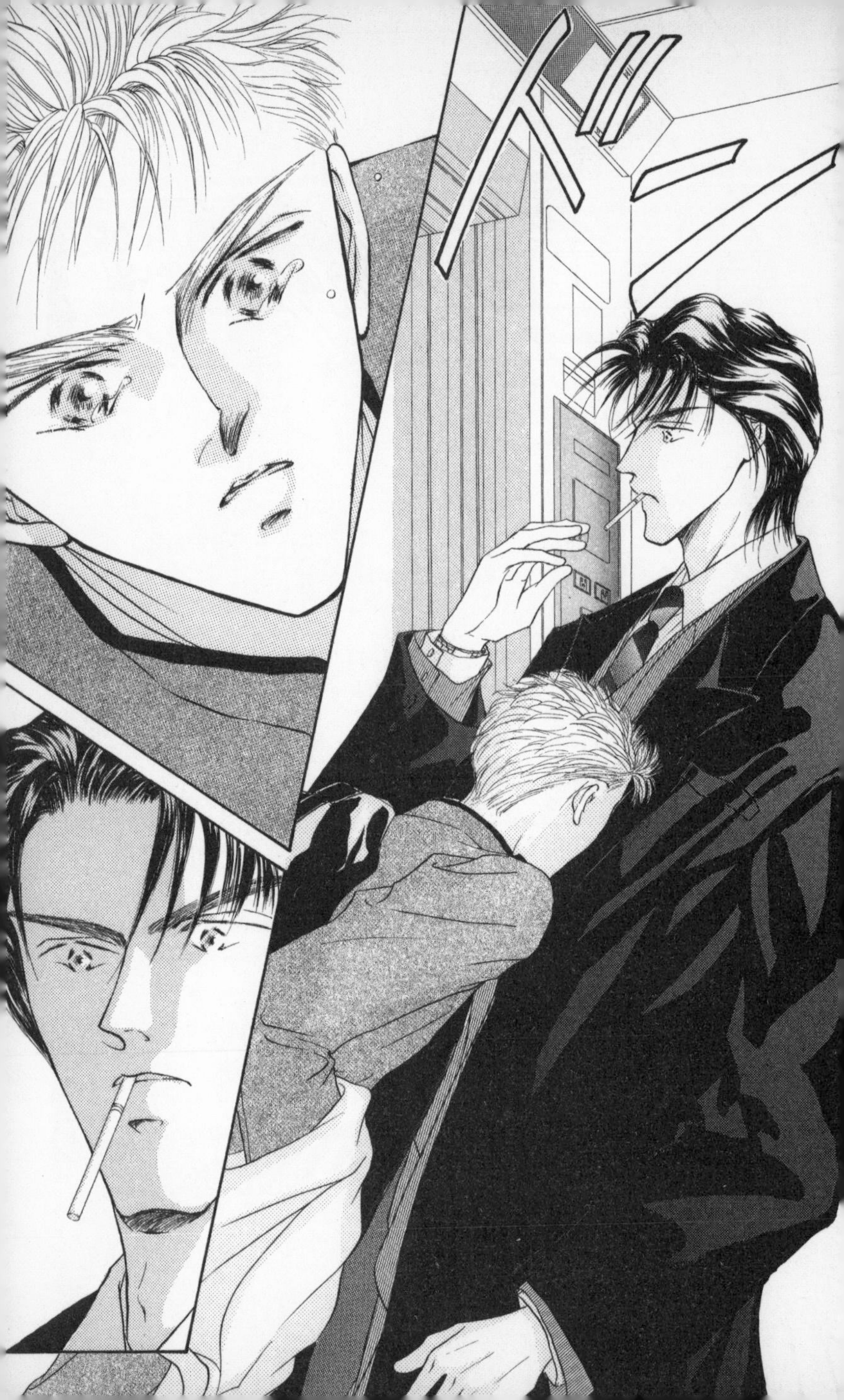

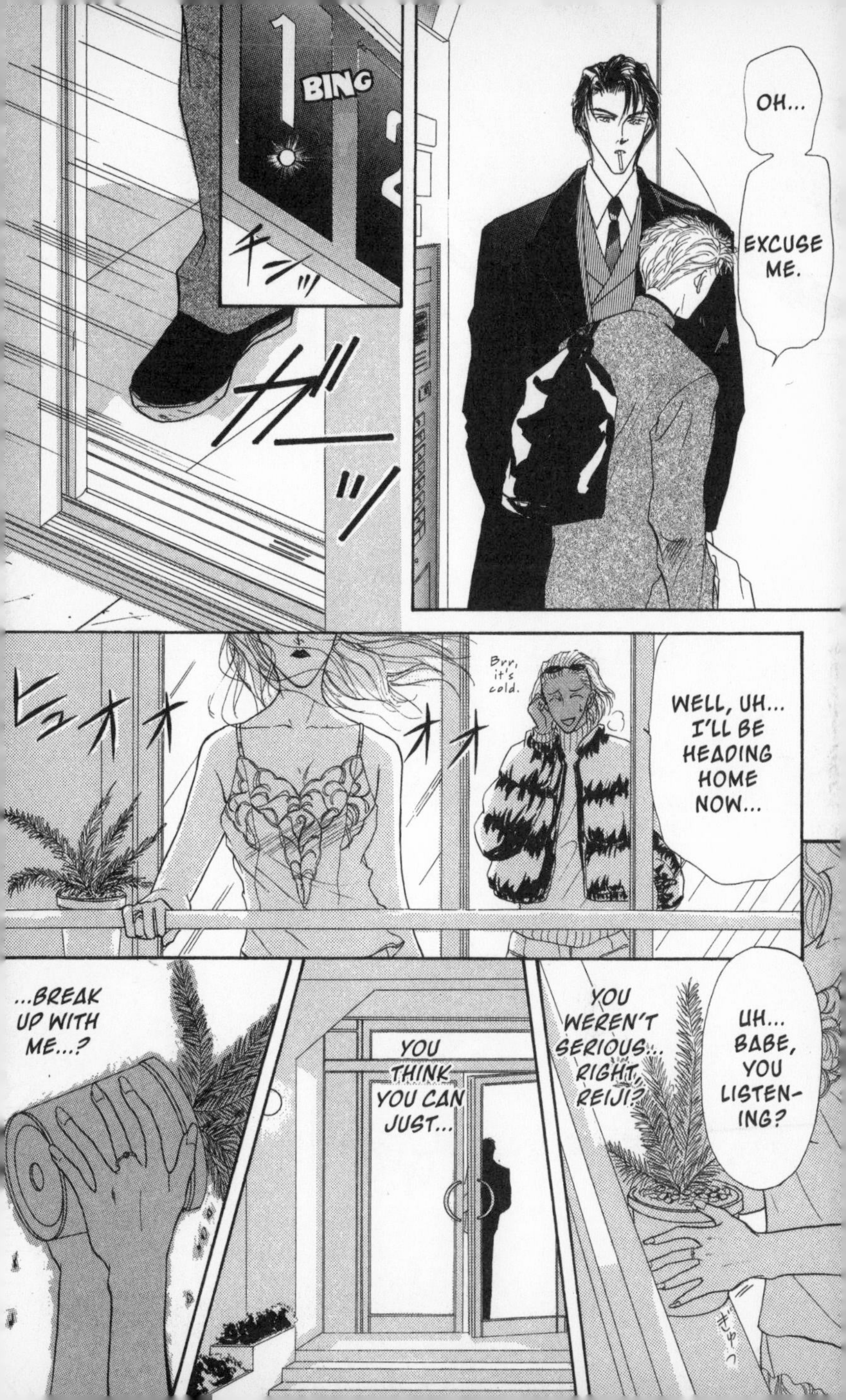
OH... EXCUSE ME.
BING
チンッ
ガーーッ
WELL, UH... I'LL BE HEADING HOME NOW...
Brr, it's cold.
ヒュオオオ
UH... BABE, YOU LISTENING?
ぎゅっ
YOU WEREN'T SERIOUS... RIGHT, REIJI?
YOU THINK YOU CAN JUST...
...BREAK UP WITH ME...?

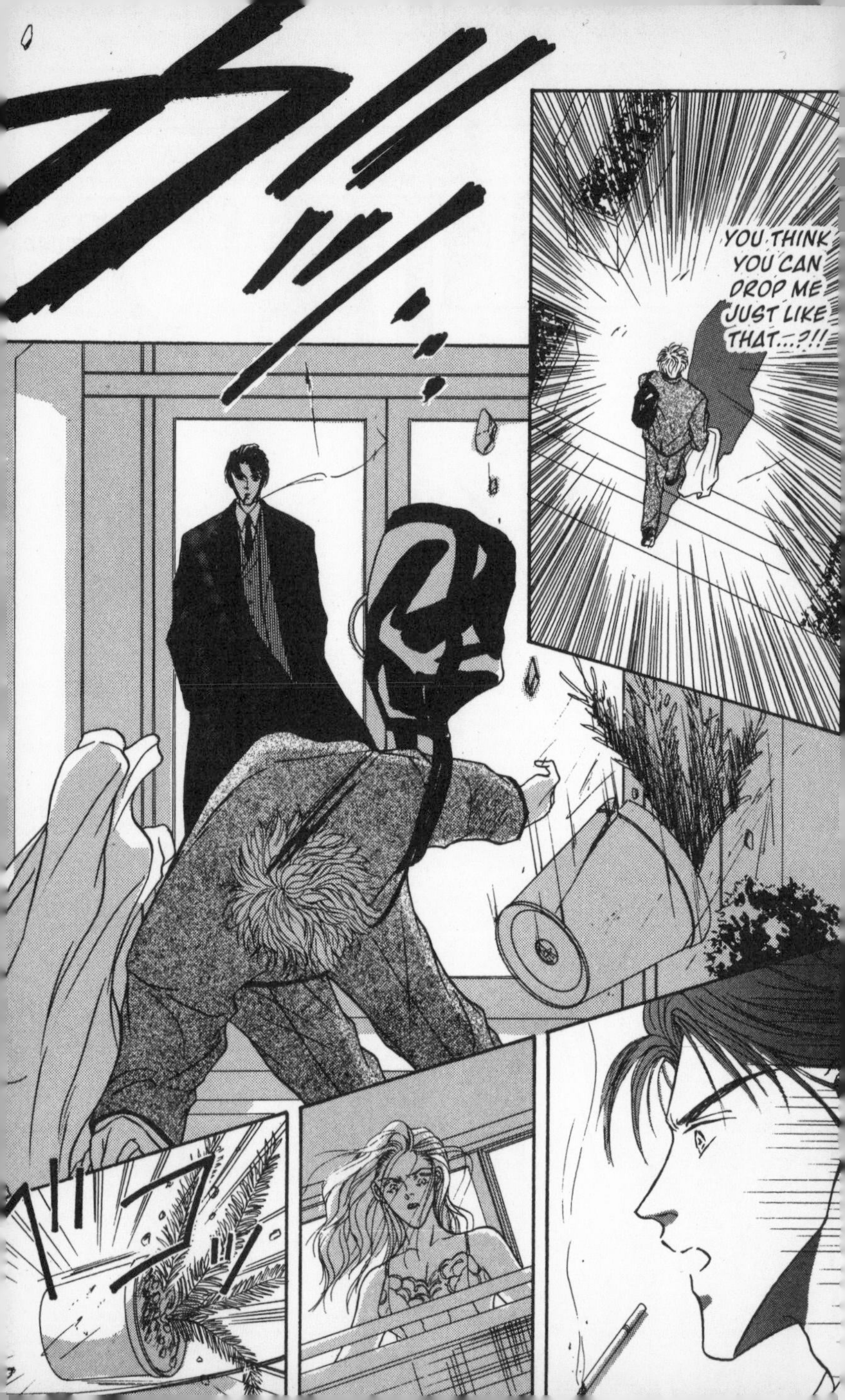
YOU THINK YOU CAN DROP ME JUST LIKE THAT...?!!

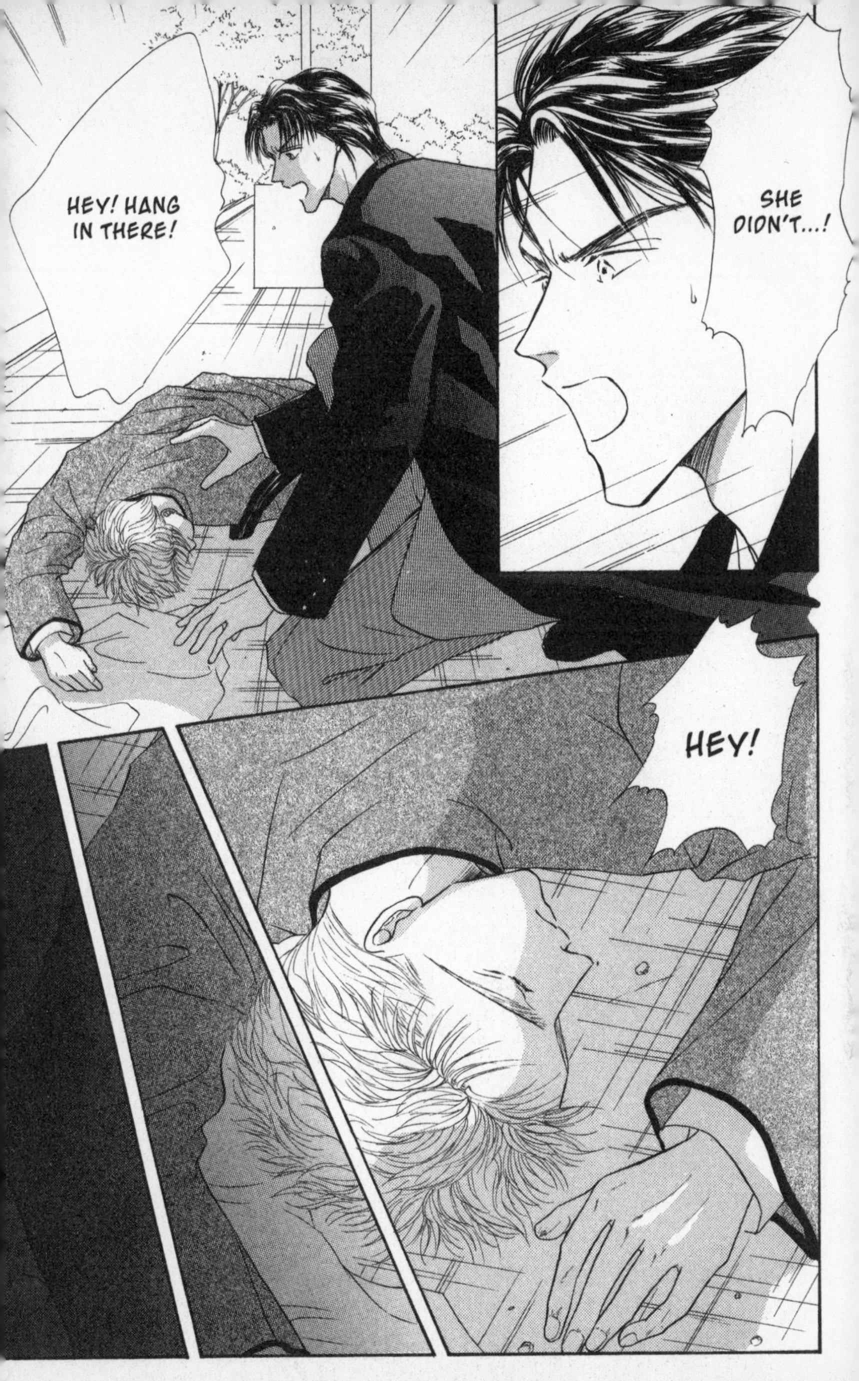
SHE DIDN'T...!
HEY! HANG IN THERE!
HEY!

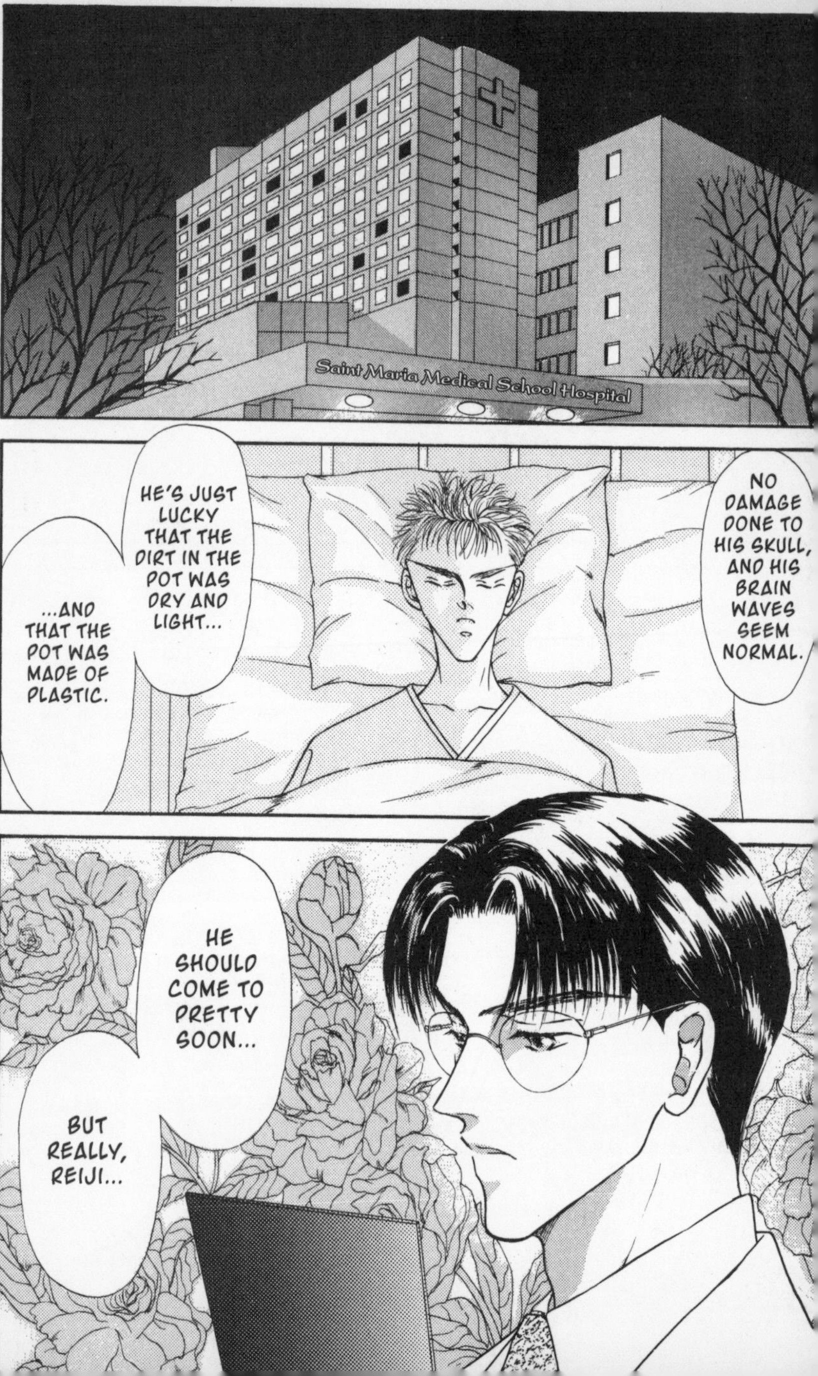
Saint Maria Medical School Hospital
NO DAMAGE DONE TO HIS SKULL, AND HIS BRAIN WAVES SEEM NORMAL.
HE'S JUST LUCKY THAT THE DIRT IN THE POT WAS DRY AND LIGHT...
...AND THAT THE POT WAS MADE OF PLASTIC.
HE SHOULD COME TO PRETTY SOON...
BUT REALLY, REIJI...

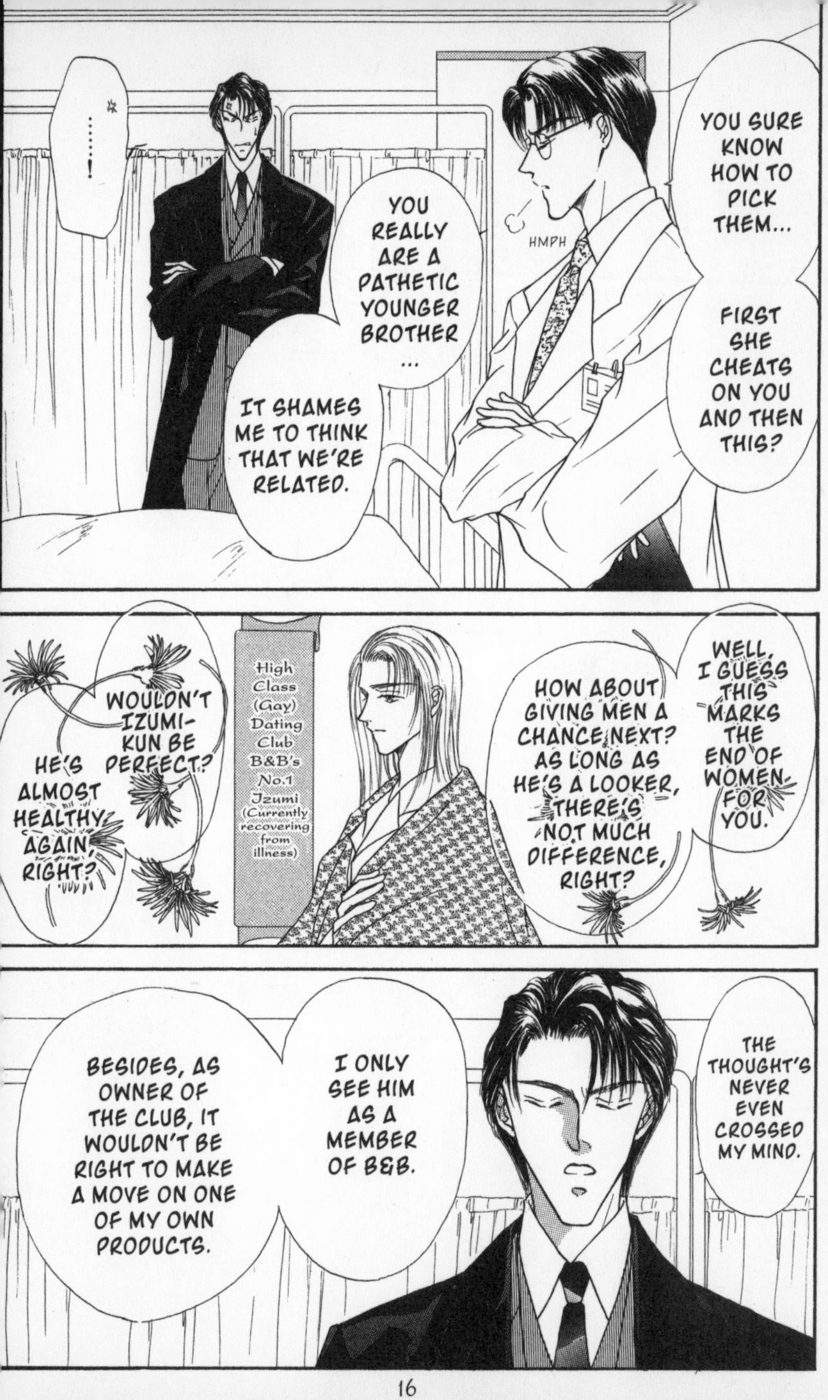
YOU SURE KNOW HOW TO PICK THEM...
FIRST SHE CHEATS ON YOU AND THEN THIS?
HMPH
YOU REALLY ARE A PATHETIC YOUNGER BROTHER ...
IT SHAMES ME TO THINK THAT WE'RE RELATED.
......!
WELL, I GUESS THIS MARKS THE END OF WOMEN FOR YOU.
HOW ABOUT GIVING MEN A CHANCE NEXT? AS LONG AS HE'S A LOOKER, THERE'S NOT MUCH DIFFERENCE, RIGHT?
High Class (Gay) Dating Club B&B's No.1 Izumi (Currently recovering from illness)
WOULDN'T IZUMI-KUN BE PERFECT?
HE'S ALMOST HEALTHY AGAIN, RIGHT?
THE THOUGHT'S NEVER EVEN CROSSED MY MIND.
I ONLY SEE HIM AS A MEMBER OF B&B.
BESIDES, AS OWNER OF THE CLUB, IT WOULDN'T BE RIGHT TO MAKE A MOVE ON ONE OF MY OWN PRODUCTS.

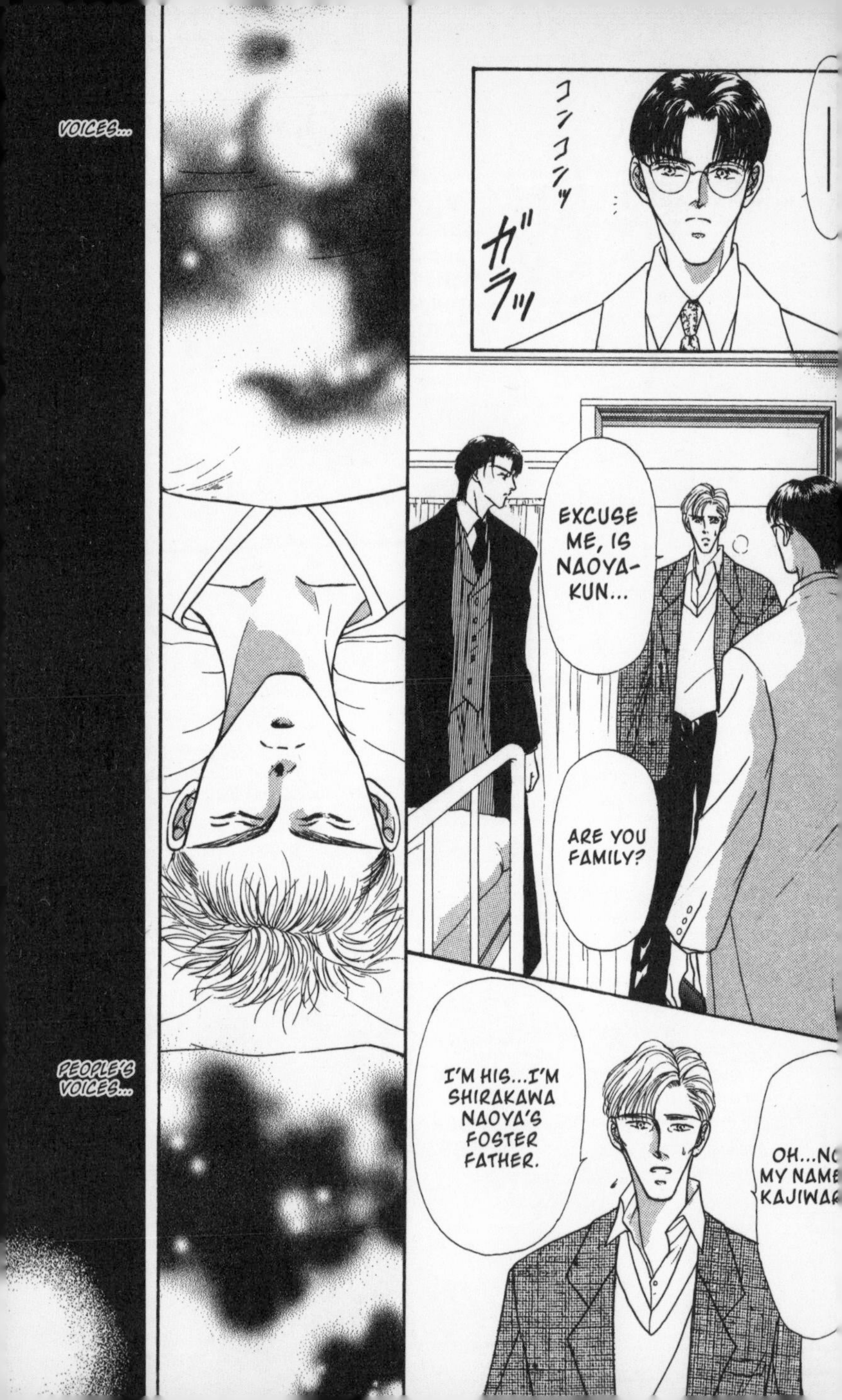
コンコンッ
ガラッ
—
EXCUSE ME, IS NAOYA-KUN...
ARE YOU FAMILY?
OH...N MY NAME KAJIWAR
I'M HIS...I'M SHIRAKAWA NAOYA'S FOSTER FATHER.
VOICES...
PEOPLE'S VOICES...

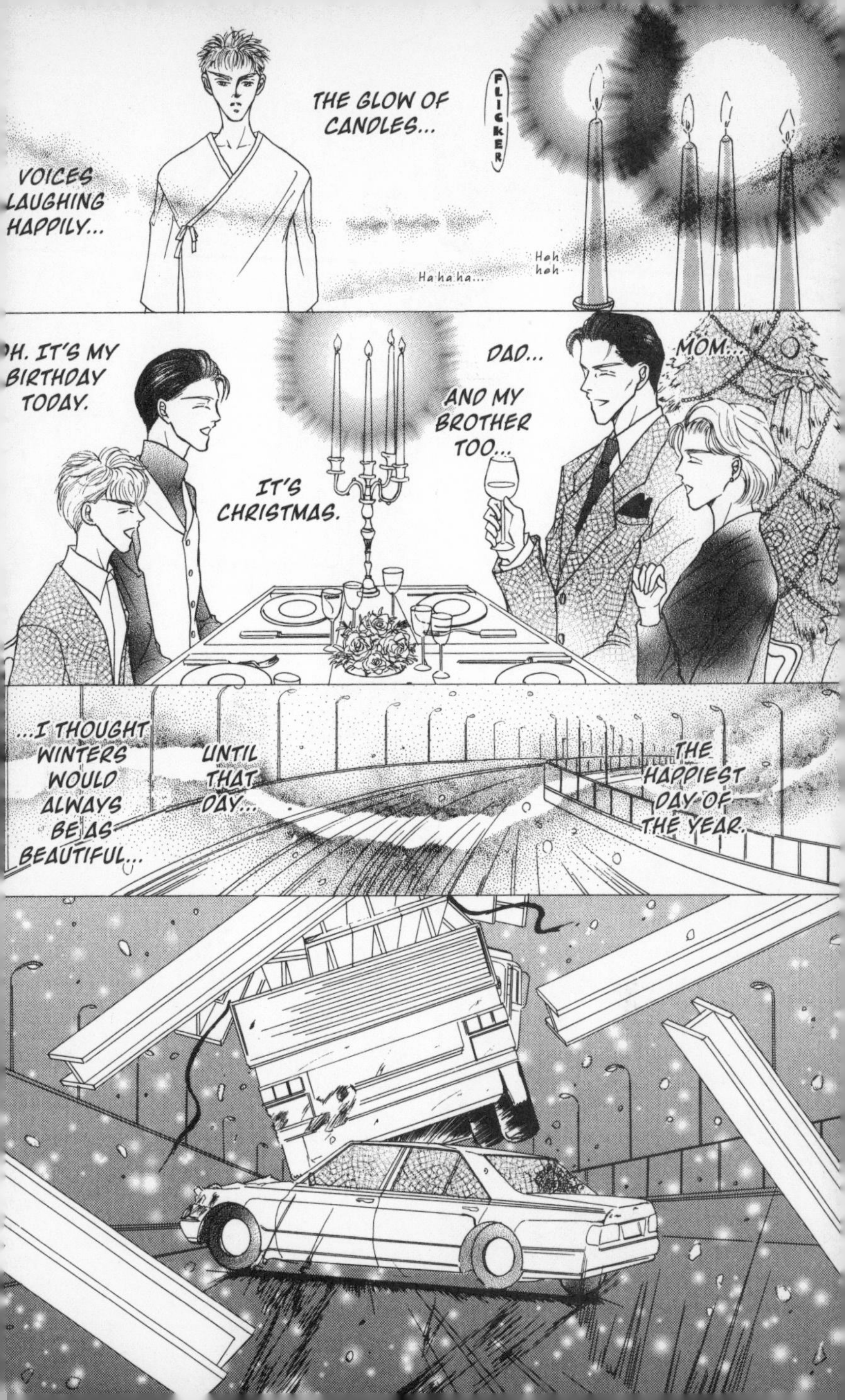
FLICKER
THE GLOW OF CANDLES...
Heh heh
Ha ha ha...
VOICES LAUGHING HAPPILY...
MOM...
DAD...
AND MY BROTHER TOO...
IT'S CHRISTMAS.
H. IT'S MY BIRTHDAY TODAY.
THE HAPPIEST DAY OF THE YEAR.
UNTIL THAT DAY...
...I THOUGHT WINTERS WOULD ALWAYS BE AS BEAUTIFUL...

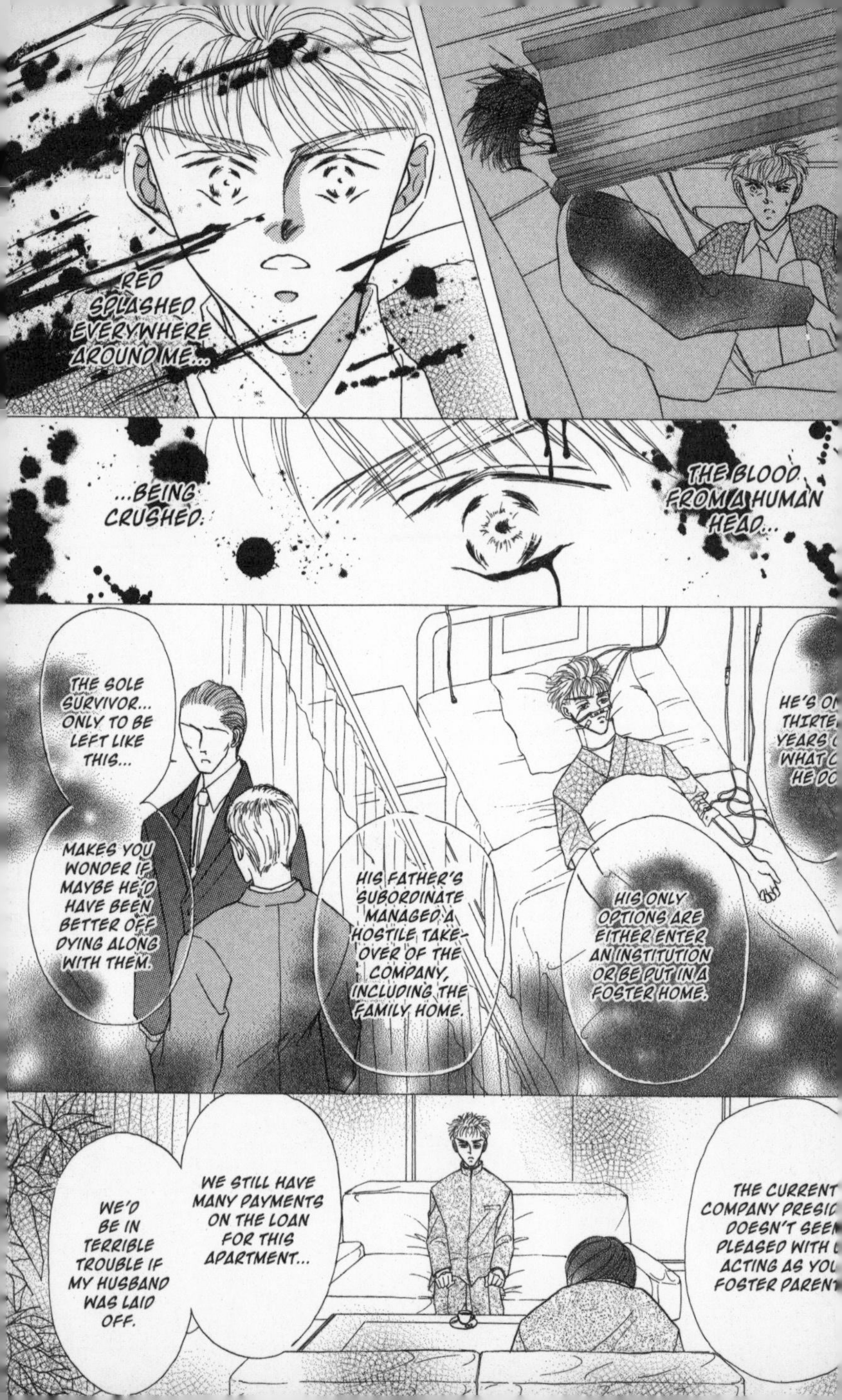
RED SPLASHED EVERYWHERE AROUND ME...
THE BLOOD FROM A HUMAN HEAD...
...BEING CRUSHED.
HE'S ON THIRTE YEARS WHAT C HE DO
HIS ONLY OPTIONS ARE EITHER ENTER AN INSTITUTION OR BE PUT IN A FOSTER HOME.
HIS FATHER'S SUBORDINATE MANAGED A HOSTILE TAKE-OVER OF THE COMPANY, INCLUDING THE FAMILY HOME.
THE SOLE SURVIVOR... ONLY TO BE LEFT LIKE THIS...
MAKES YOU WONDER IF MAYBE HE'D HAVE BEEN BETTER OFF DYING ALONG WITH THEM.
THE CURRENT COMPANY PRESID DOESN'T SEEM PLEASED WITH ACTING AS YOU FOSTER PARENT
WE STILL HAVE MANY PAYMENTS ON THE LOAN FOR THIS APARTMENT...
WE'D BE IN TERRIBLE TROUBLE IF MY HUSBAND WAS LAID OFF.

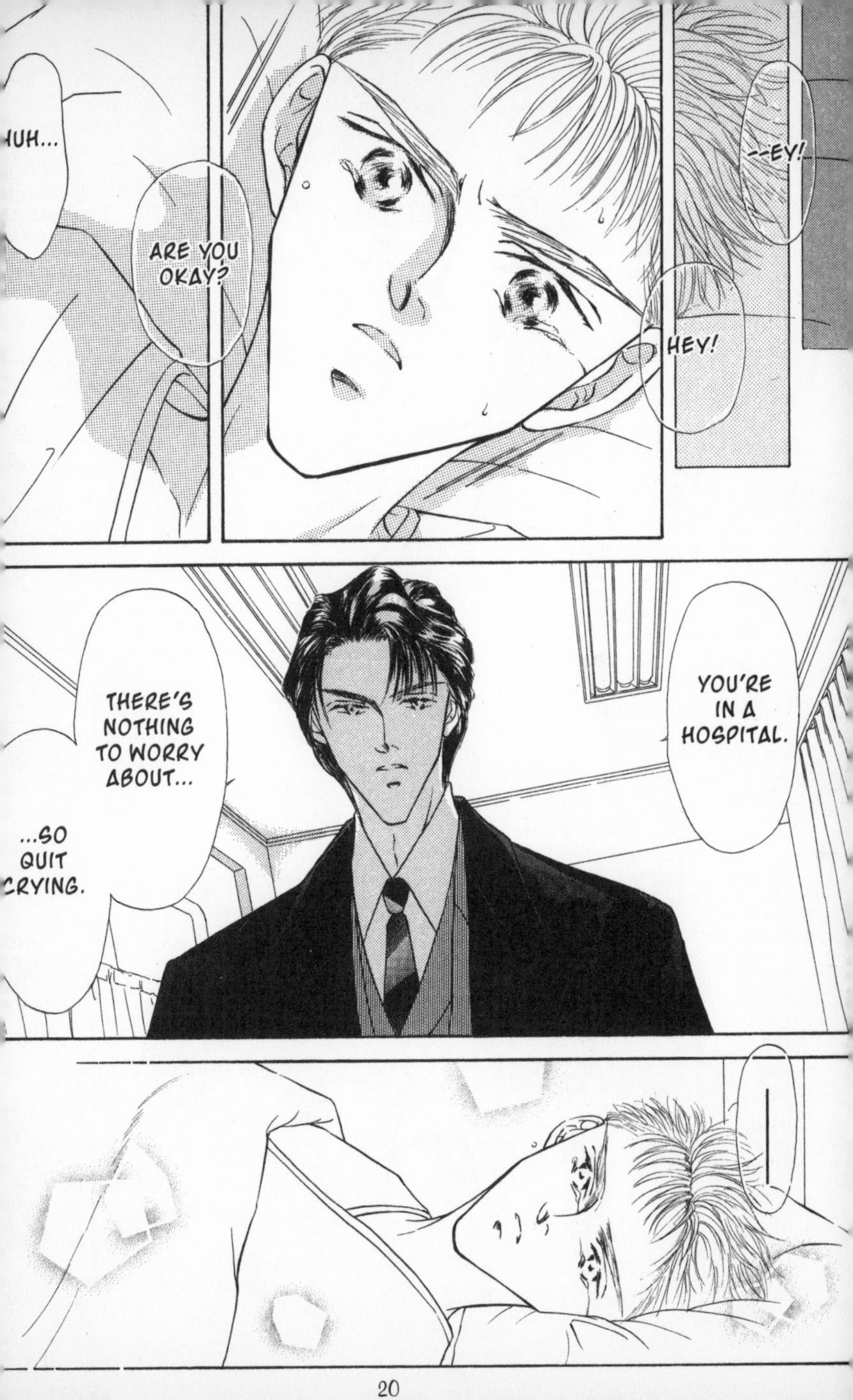
--EY!
HEY!
ARE YOU OKAY?
HUH...
YOU'RE IN A HOSPITAL.
THERE'S NOTHING TO WORRY ABOUT...
...SO QUIT CRYING.

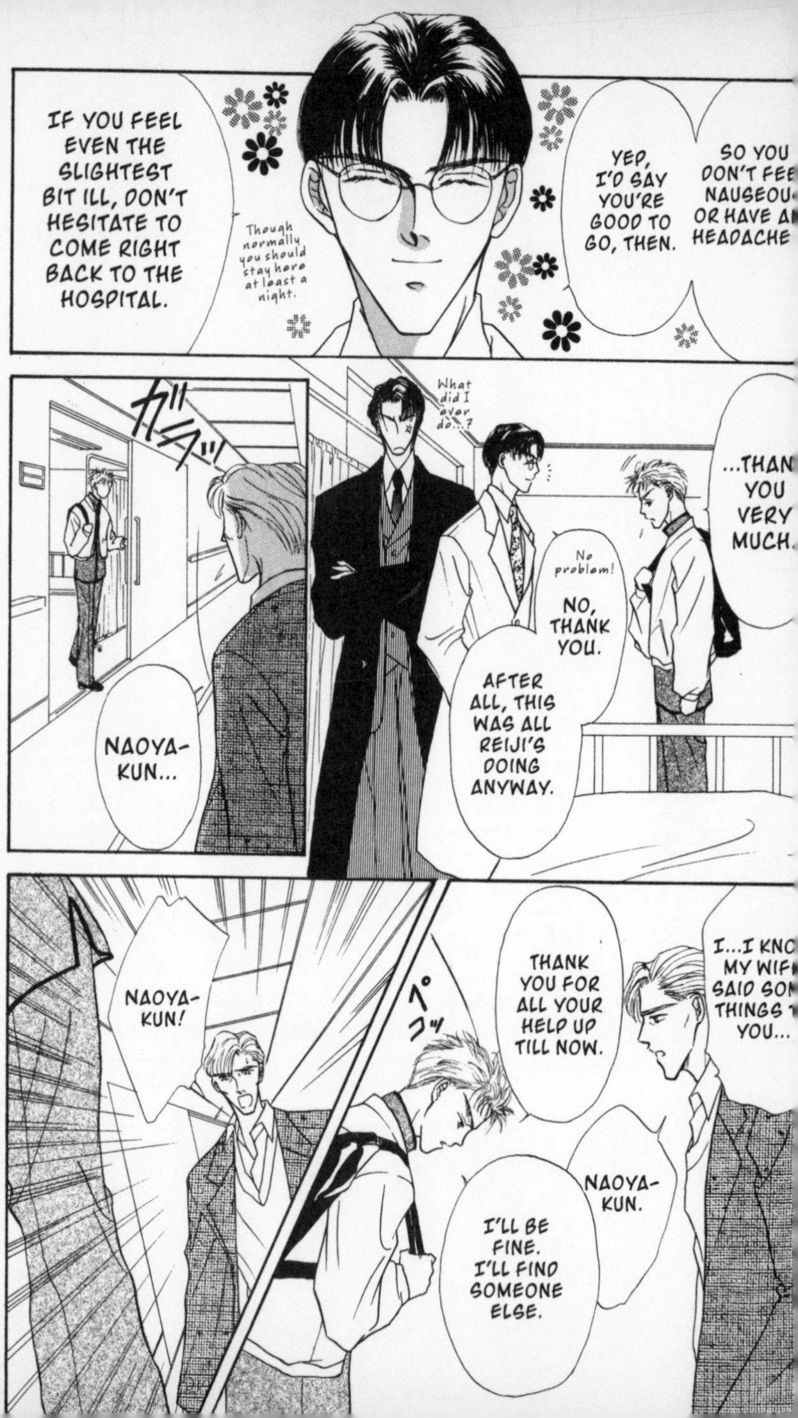
SO YOU DON'T FEE NAUSEOU OR HAVE A HEADACHE
YEP, I'D SAY YOU'RE GOOD TO GO, THEN.
Though normally you should stay here at least a night.
IF YOU FEEL EVEN THE SLIGHTEST BIT ILL, DON'T HESITATE TO COME RIGHT BACK TO THE HOSPITAL.
...THAN YOU VERY MUCH.
No problem!
NO, THANK YOU.
AFTER ALL, THIS WAS ALL REIJI'S DOING ANYWAY.
What did I ever do...?
ガラッ
NAOYA-KUN...
I...I KNO MY WIF SAID SO THINGS YOU...
THANK YOU FOR ALL YOUR HELP UP TILL NOW.
NAOYA-KUN.
I'LL BE FINE. I'LL FIND SOMEONE ELSE.
ペコッ
NAOYA-KUN!

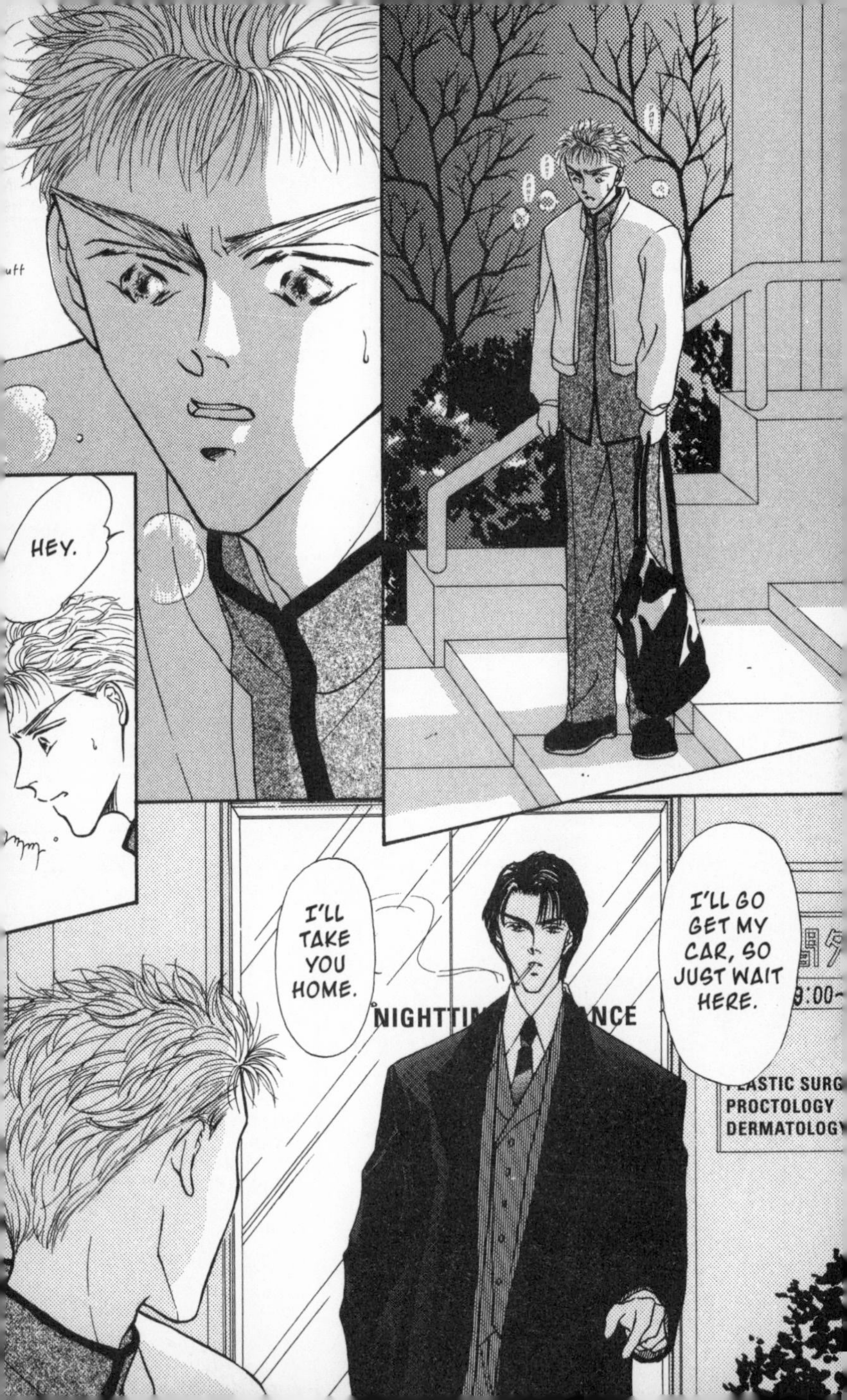
PANT
PANT
HEY.
I'LL GO GET MY CAR, SO JUST WAIT HERE.
I'LL TAKE YOU HOME.
PROCTOLOGY

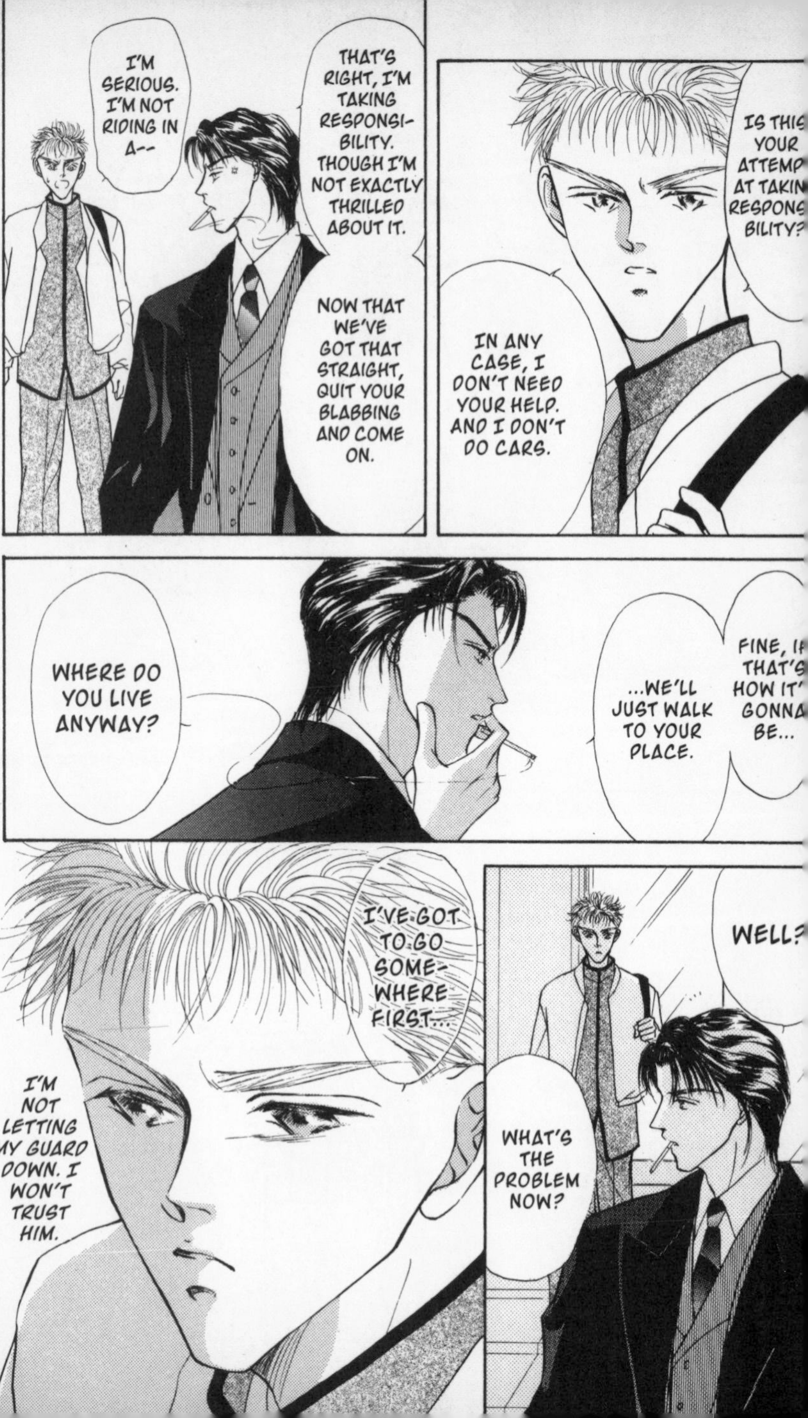
IS THIS YOUR ATTEMP AT TAKIN RESPONS BILITY?
IN ANY CASE, I DON'T NEED YOUR HELP. AND I DON'T DO CARS.
THAT'S RIGHT, I'M TAKING RESPONSIBILITY. THOUGH I'M NOT EXACTLY THRILLED ABOUT IT.
I'M SERIOUS. I'M NOT RIDING IN A--
NOW THAT WE'VE GOT THAT STRAIGHT, QUIT YOUR BLABBING AND COME ON.
FINE, I THAT'S HOW IT' GONNA BE...
...WE'LL JUST WALK TO YOUR PLACE.
WHERE DO YOU LIVE ANYWAY?
WELL?
WHAT'S THE PROBLEM NOW?
I'VE GOT TO GO SOMEWHERE FIRST...
I'M NOT LETTING MY GUARD DOWN. I WON'T TRUST HIM.

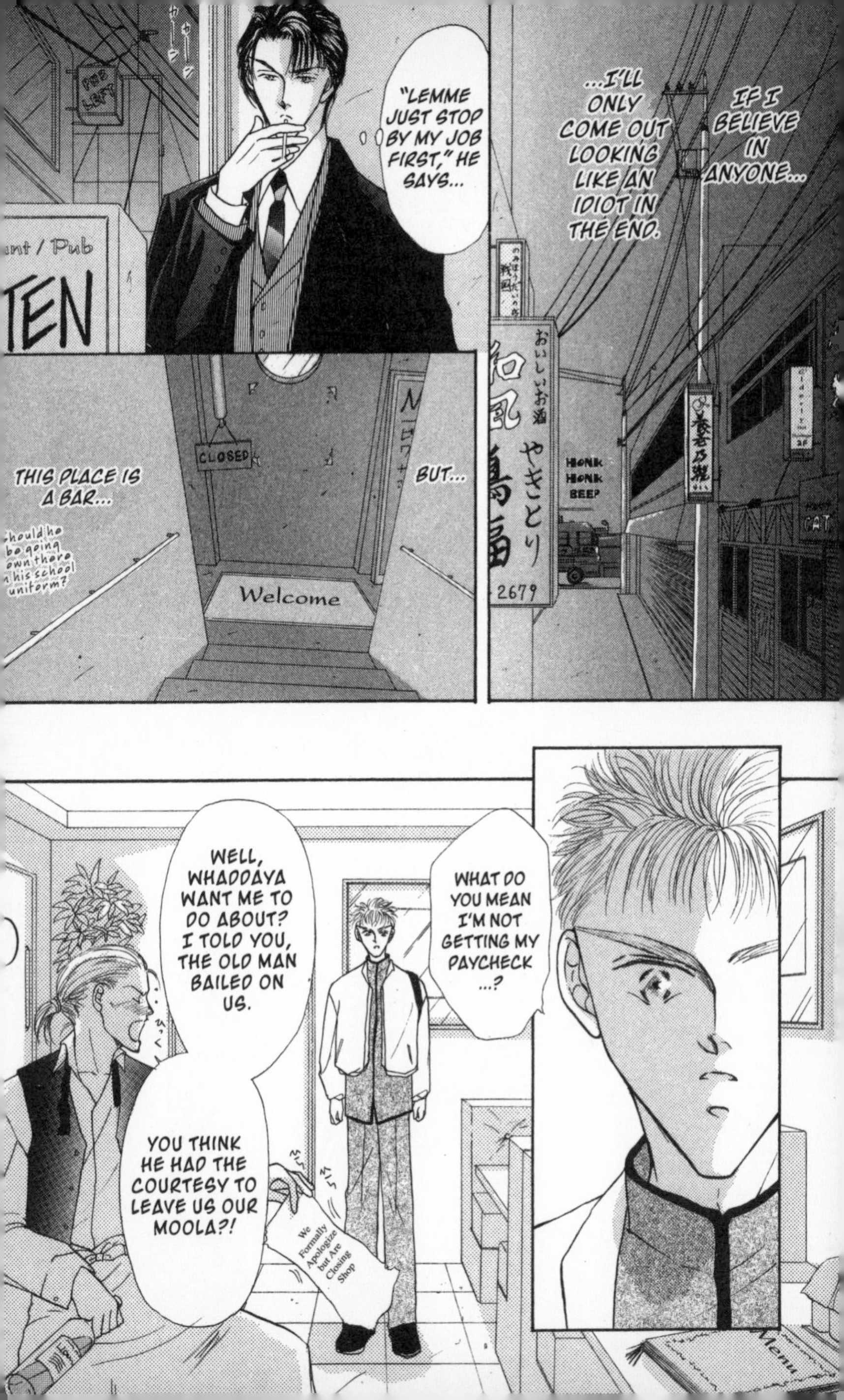
IF I BELIEVE IN ANYONE...
...I'LL ONLY COME OUT LOOKING LIKE AN IDIOT IN THE END.
HONK HONK BEEP
2679
"LEMME JUST STOP BY MY JOB FIRST," HE SAYS...
TEN
THIS PLACE IS A BAR...
Should he be going down there in his school uniform?
CLOSED
Welcome
BUT...
WHAT DO YOU MEAN I'M NOT GETTING MY PAYCHECK ...?
WELL, WHADDAYA WANT ME TO DO ABOUT? I TOLD YOU, THE OLD MAN BAILED ON US.
YOU THINK HE HAD THE COURTESY TO LEAVE US OUR MOOLA?!
We Formally Apologize but Are Closing Shop
Menu

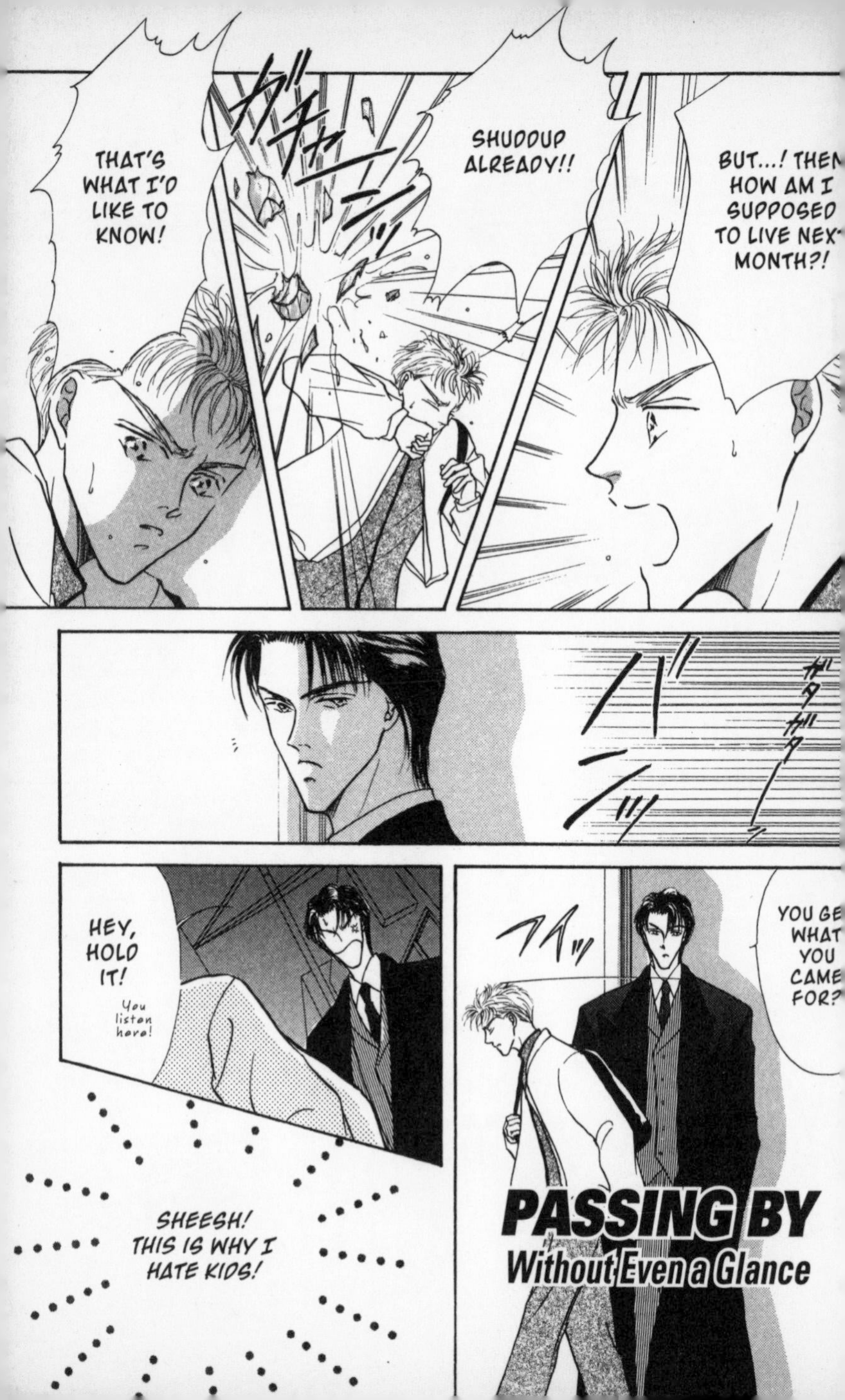
BUT...! THEN HOW AM I SUPPOSED TO LIVE NEX- MONTH?!
SHUDDUP ALREADY!!
THAT'S WHAT I'D LIKE TO KNOW!
YOU GE WHAT YOU CAME FOR?
PASSING BY
Without Even a Glance
HEY, HOLD IT!
You listen here!
SHEESH! THIS IS WHY I HATE KIDS!

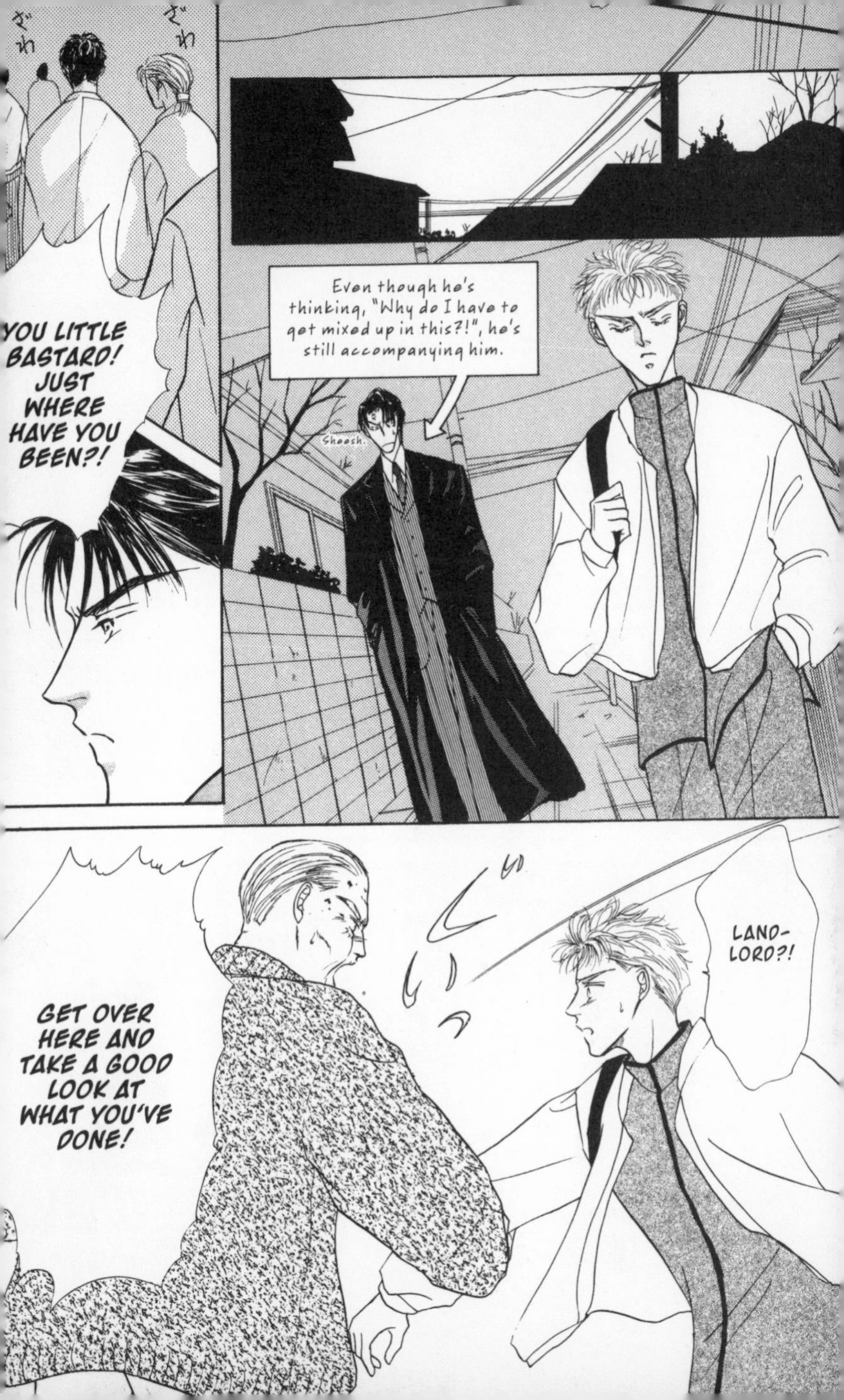
Even though he's thinking, "Why do I have to get mixed up in this?!", he's still accompanying him.
Shoosh.
ざわ ざわ
YOU LITTLE BASTARD! JUST WHERE HAVE YOU BEEN?!
LAND-LORD?!
GET OVER HERE AND TAKE A GOOD LOOK AT WHAT YOU'VE DONE!

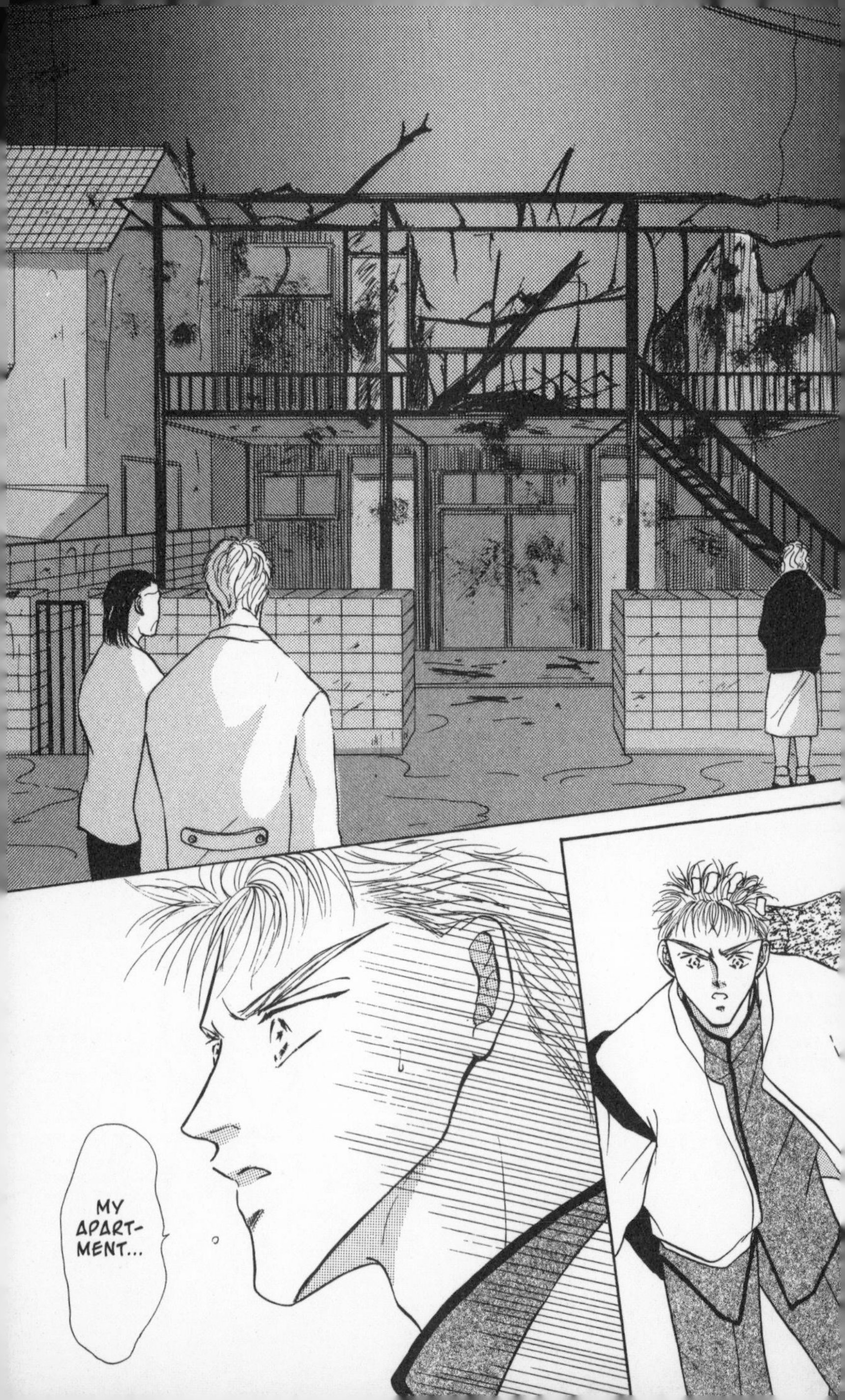
MY APART-MENT...

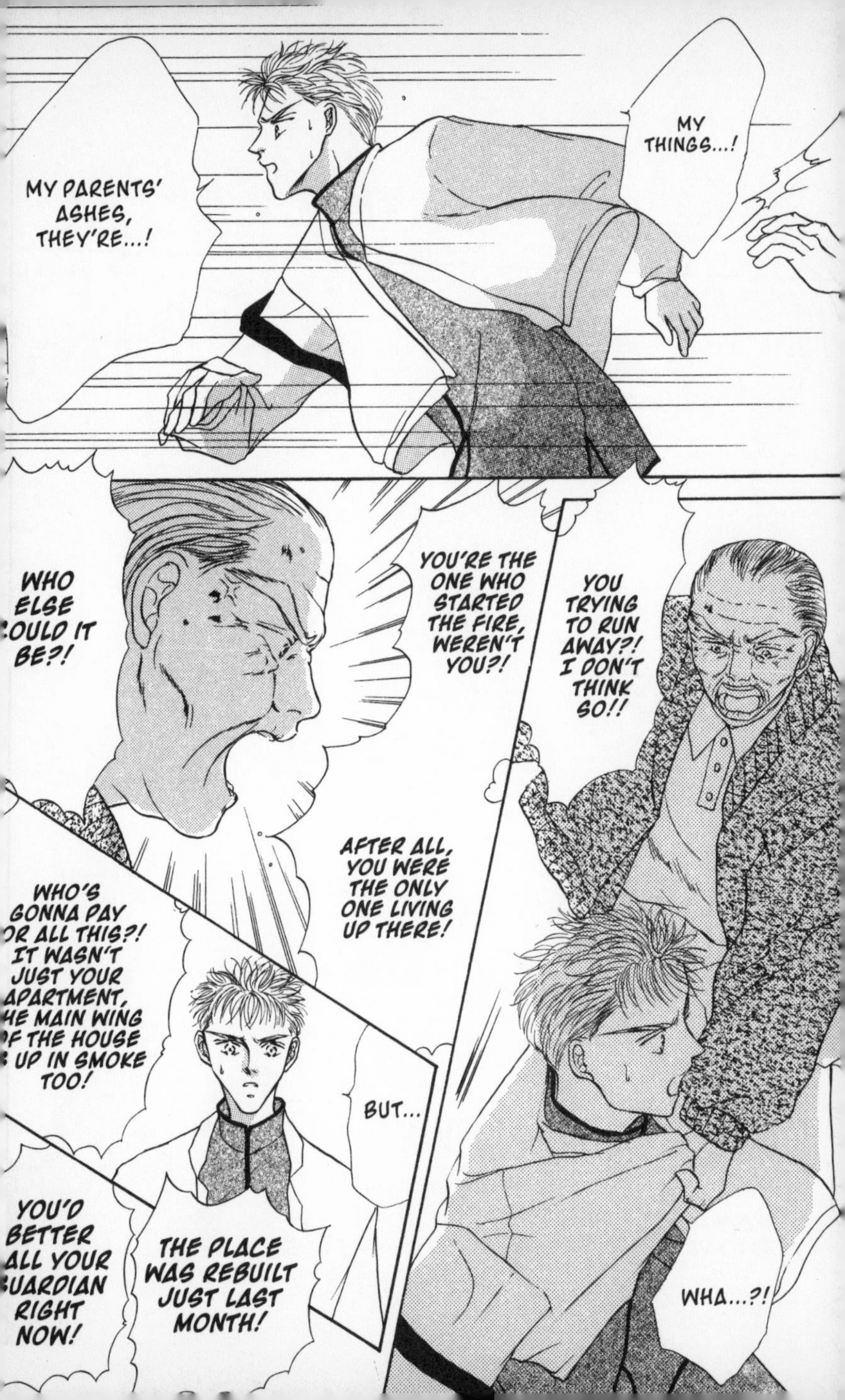
MY THINGS...!
MY PARENTS' ASHES, THEY'RE...!
YOU TRYING TO RUN AWAY?! I DON'T THINK SO!!
WHA...?!
YOU'RE THE ONE WHO STARTED THE FIRE, WEREN'T YOU?!
WHO ELSE OULD IT BE?!
AFTER ALL, YOU WERE THE ONLY ONE LIVING UP THERE!
BUT...
WHO'S GONNA PAY OR ALL THIS?! IT WASN'T JUST YOUR APARTMENT, HE MAIN WING F THE HOUSE UP IN SMOKE TOO!
THE PLACE WAS REBUILT JUST LAST MONTH!
YOU'D BETTER ALL YOUR UARDIAN RIGHT NOW!

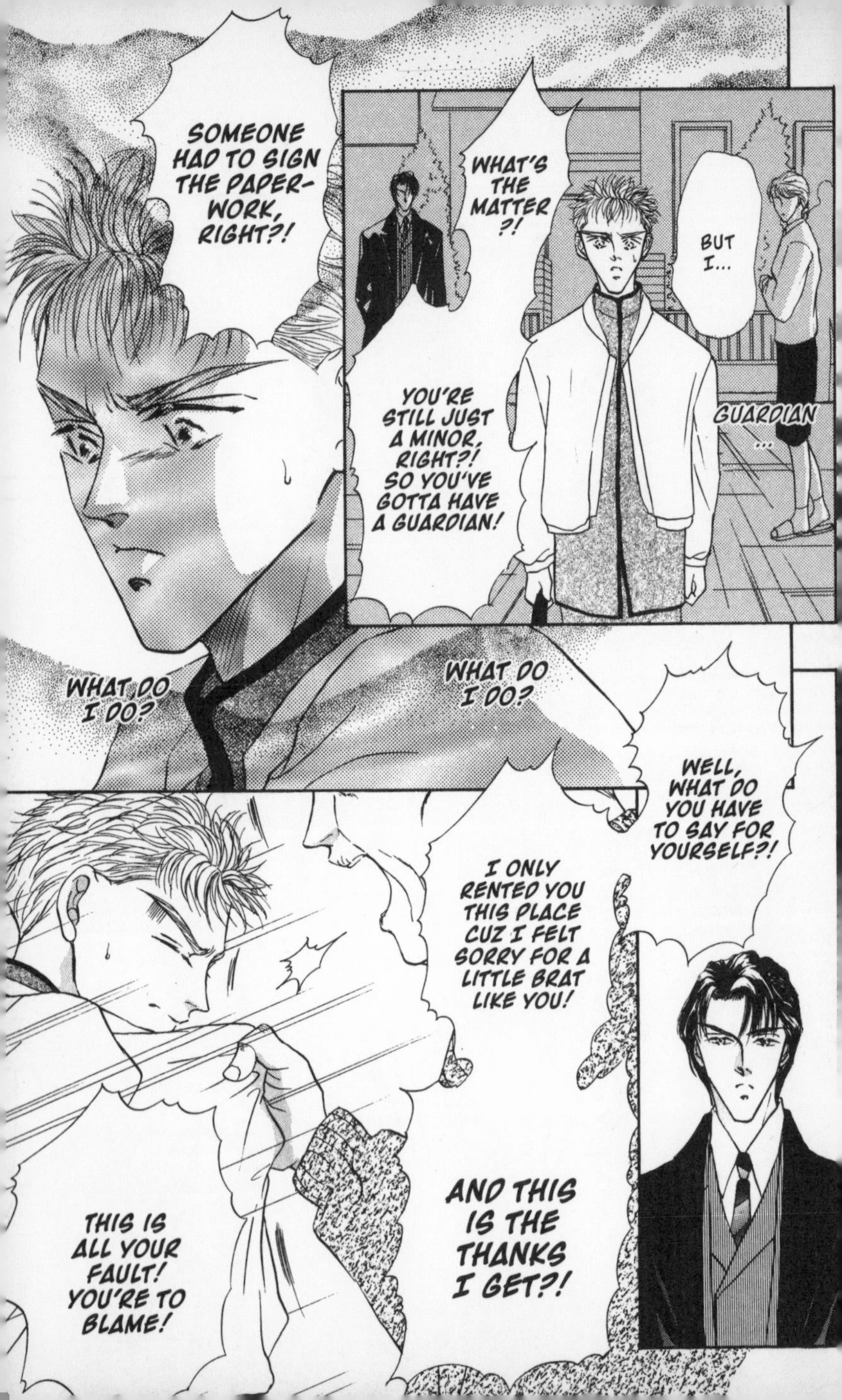
WHAT'S THE MATTER?!
BUT I...
GUARDIAN ...
YOU'RE STILL JUST A MINOR, RIGHT?! SO YOU'VE GOTTA HAVE A GUARDIAN!
SOMEONE HAD TO SIGN THE PAPER-WORK, RIGHT?!
WHAT DO I DO?
WHAT DO I DO?
WELL, WHAT DO YOU HAVE TO SAY FOR YOURSELF?!
I ONLY RENTED YOU THIS PLACE CUZ I FELT SORRY FOR A LITTLE BRAT LIKE YOU!
AND THIS IS THE THANKS I GET?!
THIS IS ALL YOUR FAULT! YOU'RE TO BLAME!

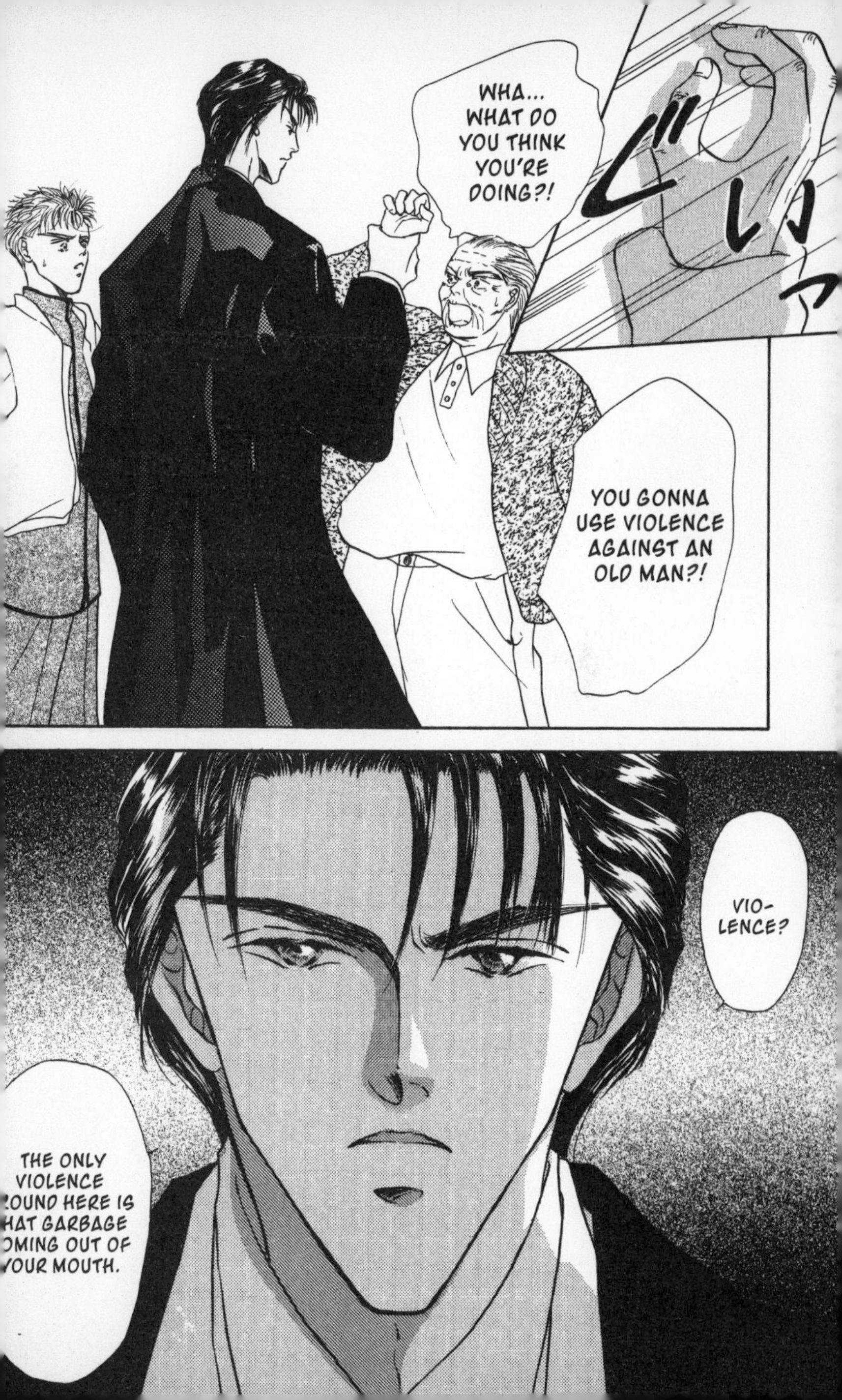
WHA... WHAT DO YOU THINK YOU'RE DOING?!
YOU GONNA USE VIOLENCE AGAINST AN OLD MAN?!
VIO-LENCE?
THE ONLY VIOLENCE ROUND HERE IS HAT GARBAGE OMING OUT OF OUR MOUTH.

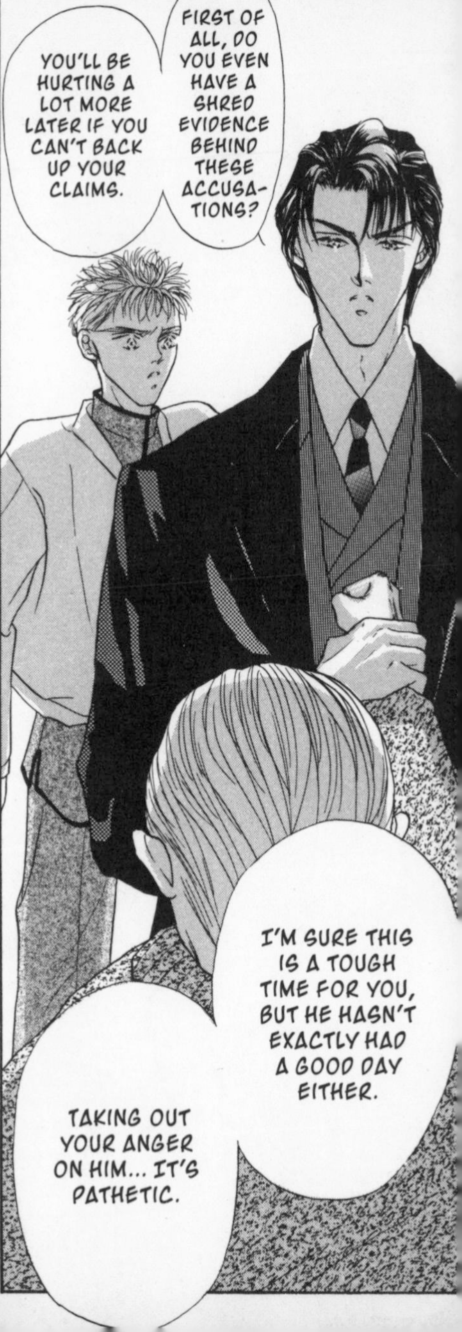
FIRST OF ALL, DO YOU EVEN HAVE A SHRED EVIDENCE BEHIND THESE ACCUSATIONS?
YOU'LL BE HURTING A LOT MORE LATER IF YOU CAN'T BACK UP YOUR CLAIMS.
I'M SURE THIS IS A TOUGH TIME FOR YOU, BUT HE HASN'T EXACTLY HAD A GOOD DAY EITHER.
TAKING OUT YOUR ANGER ON HIM... IT'S PATHETIC.

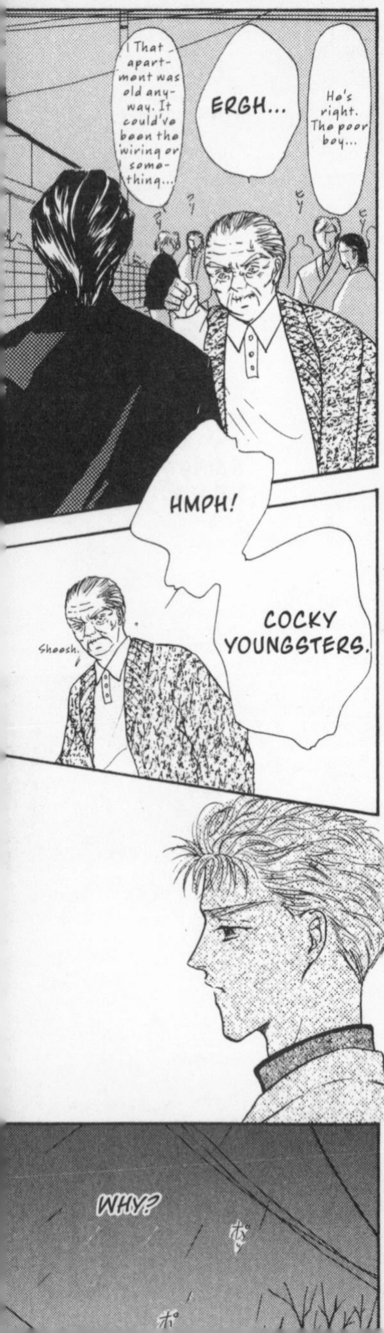
He's right. The poor boy...
ERGH...
That apartment was old anyway. It could've been the wiring or something...
HMPH!
COCKY YOUNGSTERS.
Shoosh.
WHY?

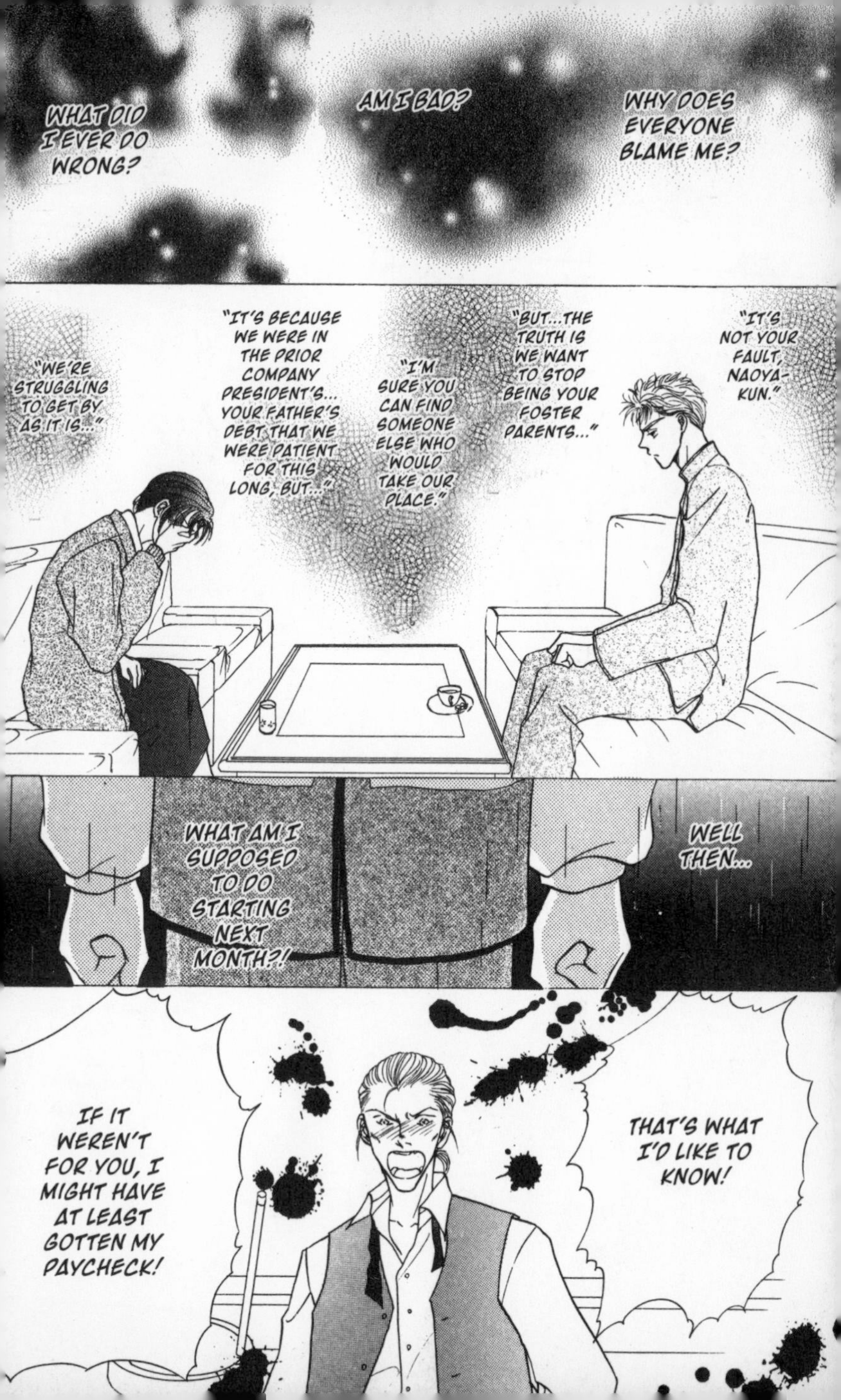
WHY DOES EVERYONE BLAME ME?
AM I BAD?
WHAT DID I EVER DO WRONG?
"IT'S NOT YOUR FAULT, NAOYA-KUN."
"BUT...THE TRUTH IS WE WANT TO STOP BEING YOUR FOSTER PARENTS..."
"I'M SURE YOU CAN FIND SOMEONE ELSE WHO WOULD TAKE OUR PLACE."
"IT'S BECAUSE WE WERE IN THE PRIOR COMPANY PRESIDENT'S... YOUR FATHER'S DEBT THAT WE WERE PATIENT FOR THIS LONG, BUT..."
"WE'RE STRUGGLING TO GET BY AS IT IS..."
WELL THEN...
WHAT AM I SUPPOSED TO DO STARTING NEXT MONTH?!
THAT'S WHAT I'D LIKE TO KNOW!
IF IT WEREN'T FOR YOU, I MIGHT HAVE AT LEAST GOTTEN MY PAYCHECK!

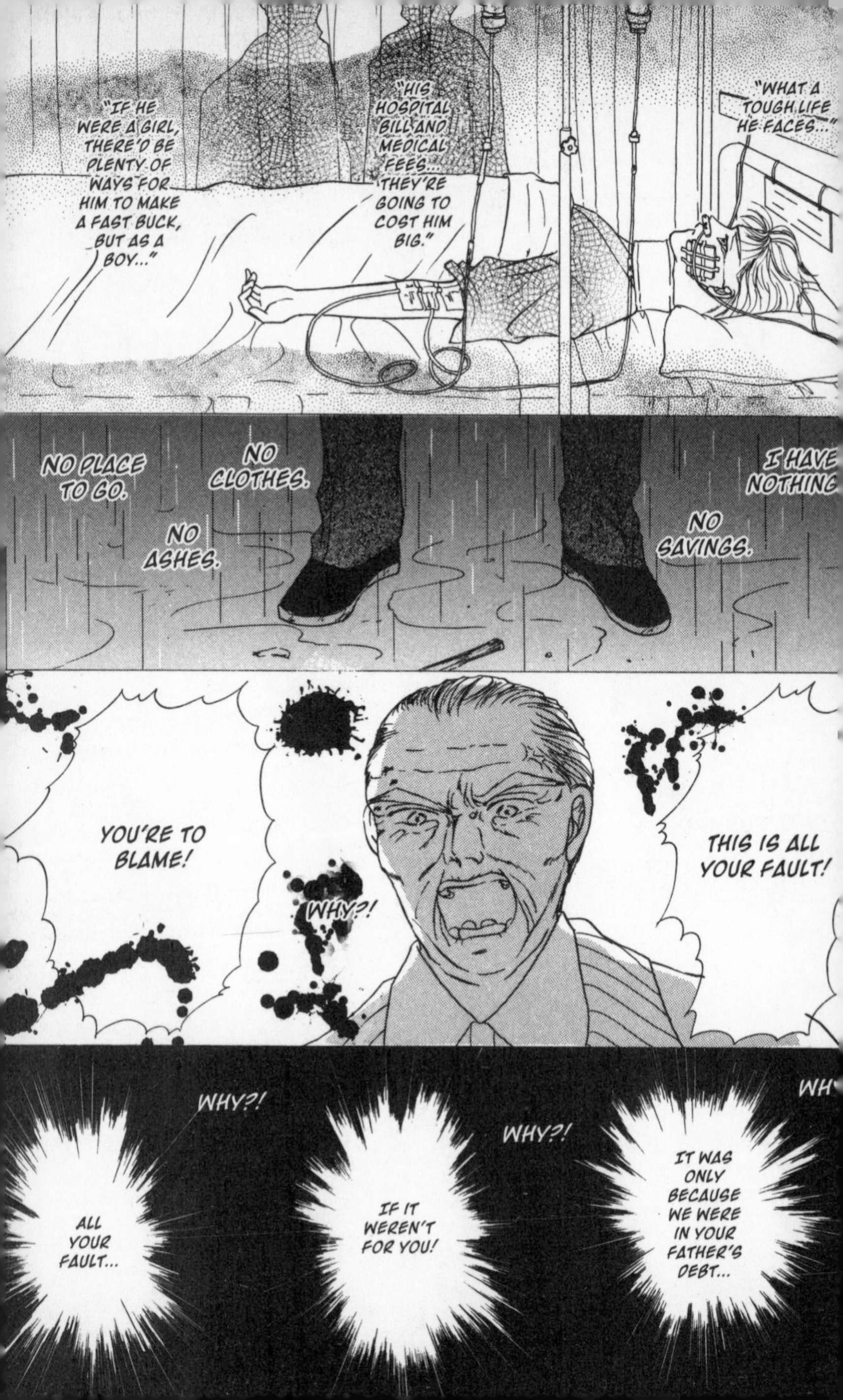
"WHAT A TOUGH LIFE HE FACES..."
"HIS HOSPITAL BILL AND MEDICAL FEES... THEY'RE GOING TO COST HIM BIG."
"IF HE WERE A GIRL, THERE'D BE PLENTY OF WAYS FOR HIM TO MAKE A FAST BUCK, BUT AS A BOY..."
I HAVE NOTHING
NO SAVINGS.
NO CLOTHES.
NO PLACE TO GO.
NO ASHES.
THIS IS ALL YOUR FAULT!
WHY?!
YOU'RE TO BLAME!
WH
IT WAS ONLY BECAUSE WE WERE IN YOUR FATHER'S DEBT...
WHY?!
IF IT WEREN'T FOR YOU!
WHY?!
ALL YOUR FAULT...

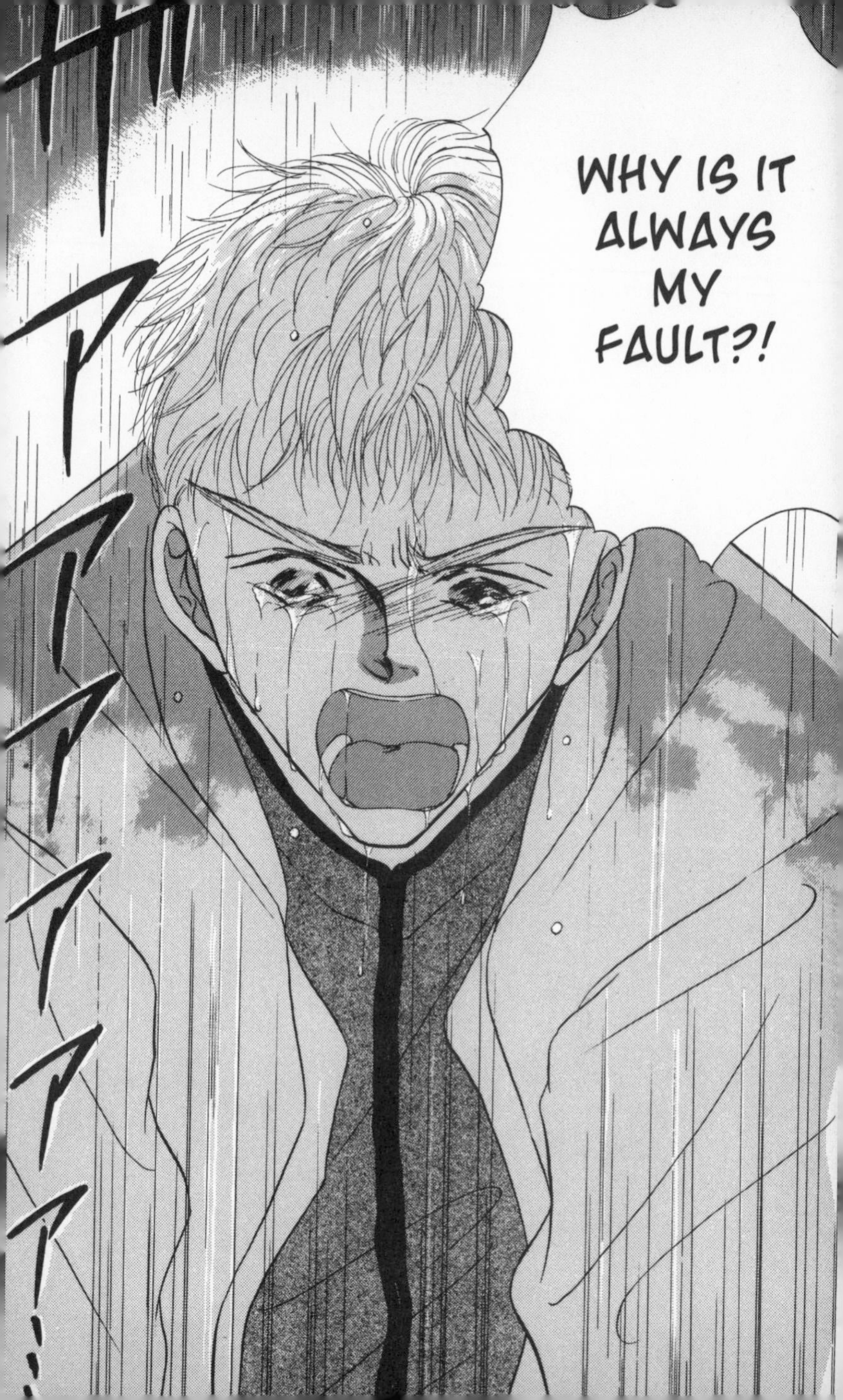
WHY IS IT ALWAYS MY FAULT?!
ササアアアアアアア…

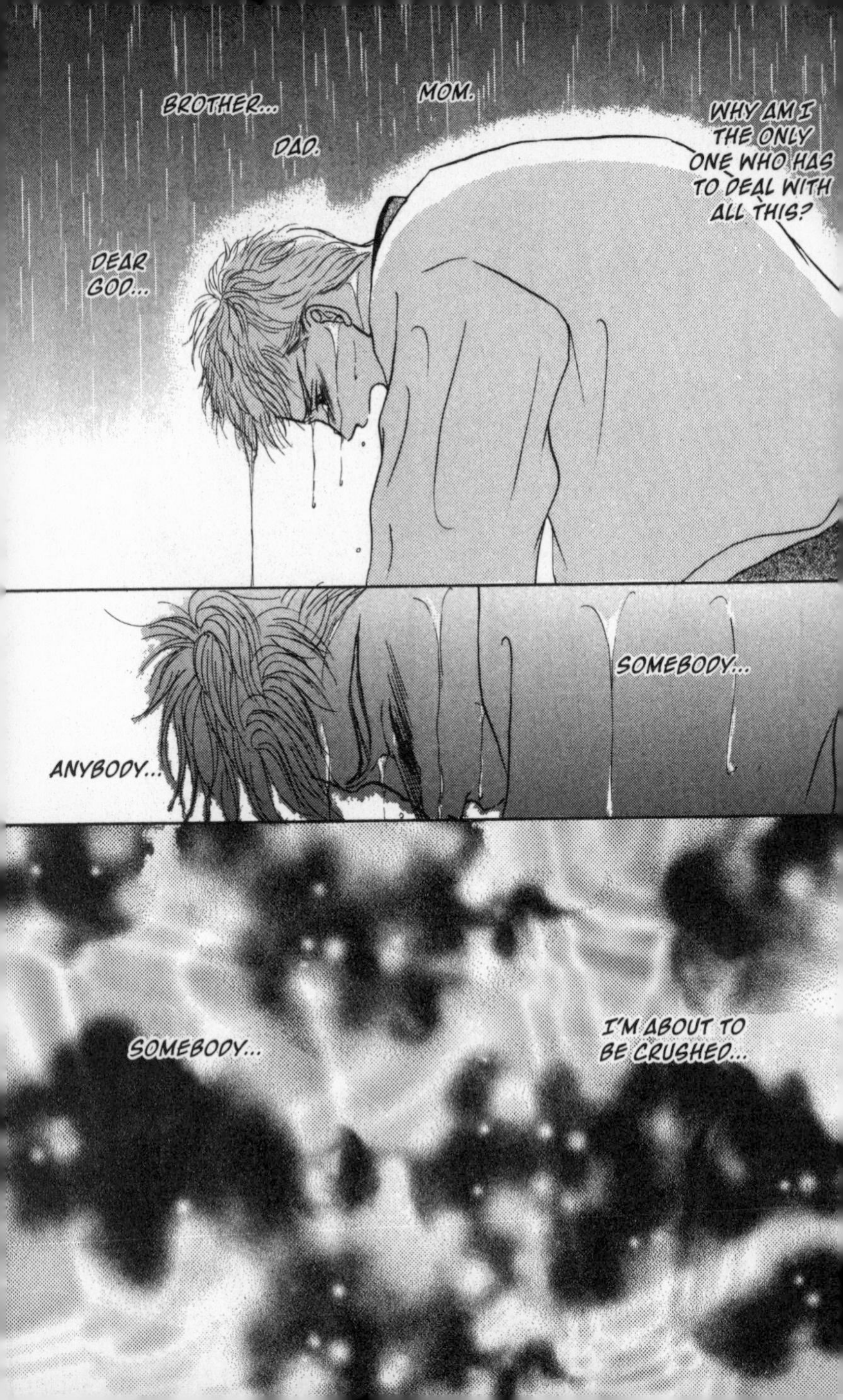
WHY AM I THE ONLY ONE WHO HAS TO DEAL WITH ALL THIS?
MOM.
DAD.
BROTHER...
DEAR GOD...
SOMEBODY...
ANYBODY...
I'M ABOUT TO BE CRUSHED...
SOMEBODY...

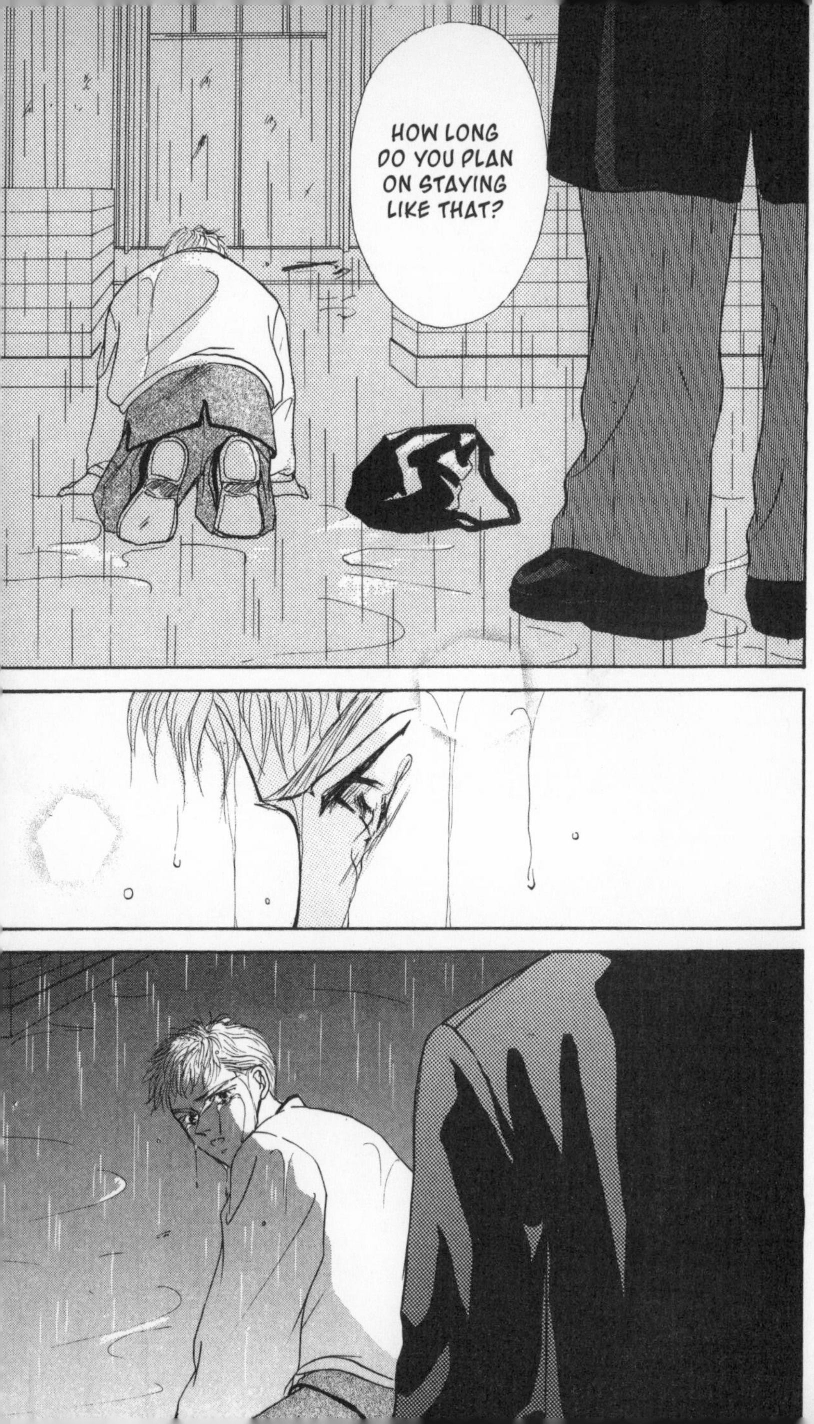
HOW LONG DO YOU PLAN ON STAYING LIKE THAT?

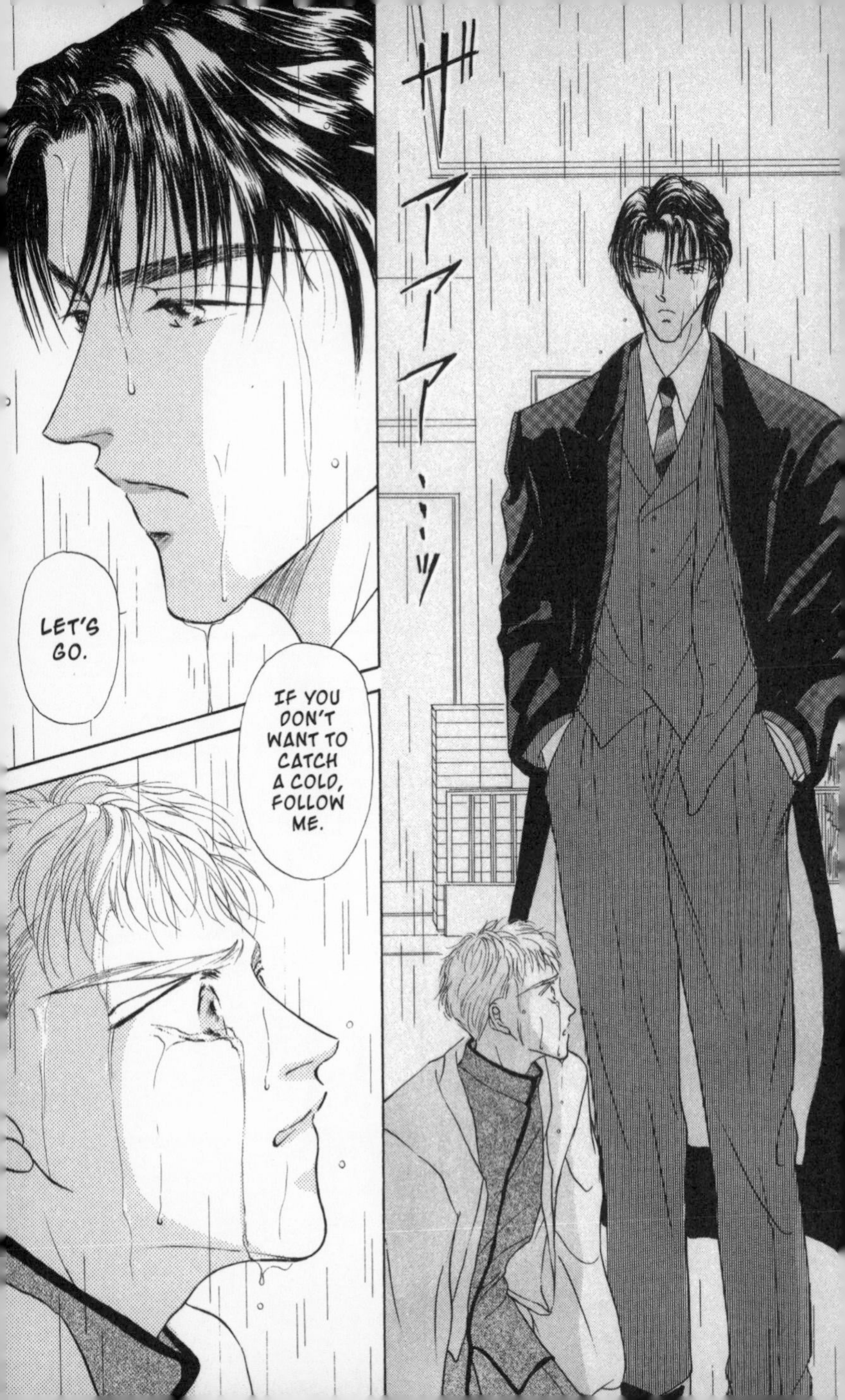

ザァーアア…ッ
LET'S GO.
IF YOU DON'T WANT TO CATCH A COLD, FOLLOW ME.

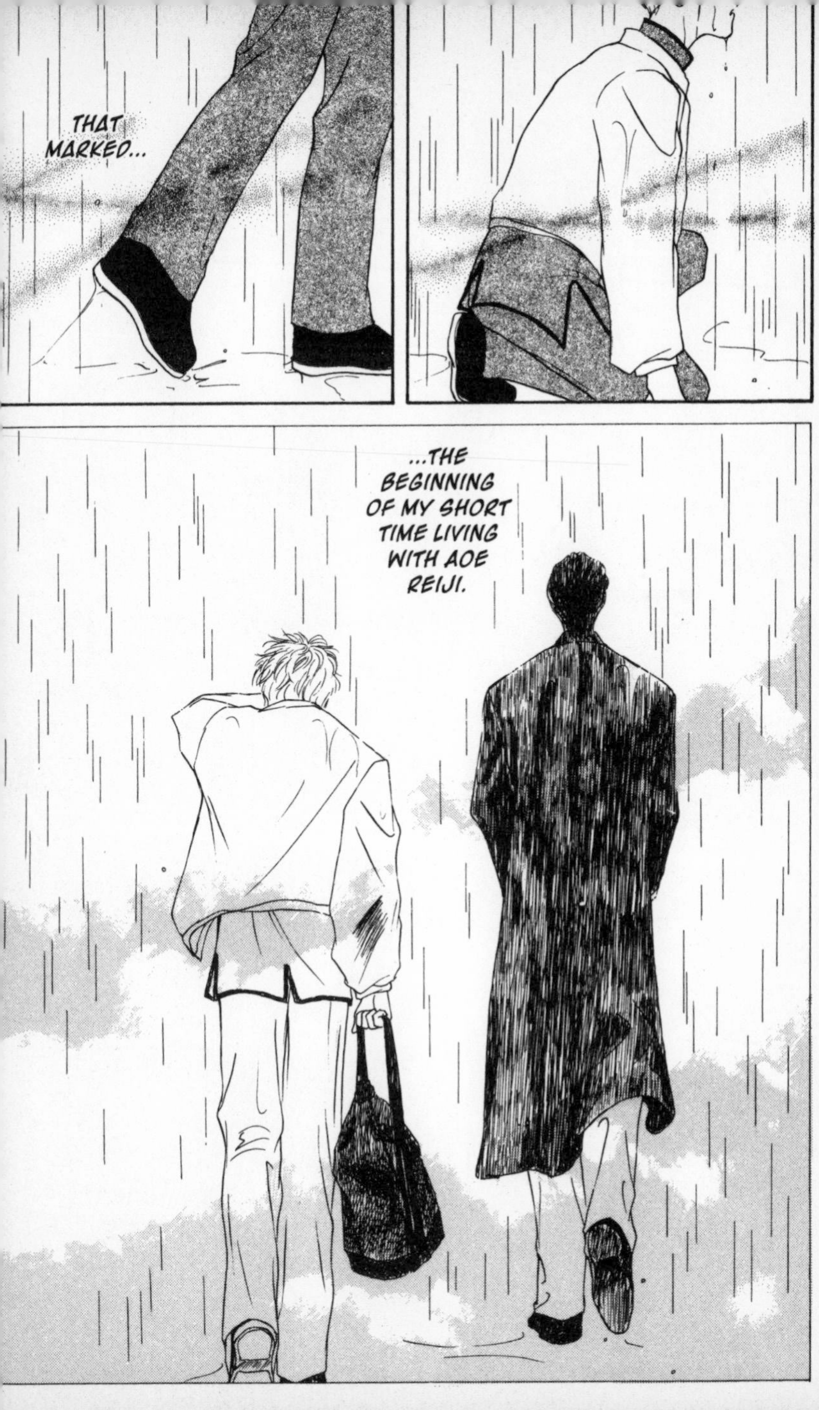
THAT MARKED...
...THE BEGINNING OF MY SHORT TIME LIVING WITH AOE REIJI.

Christmas Children

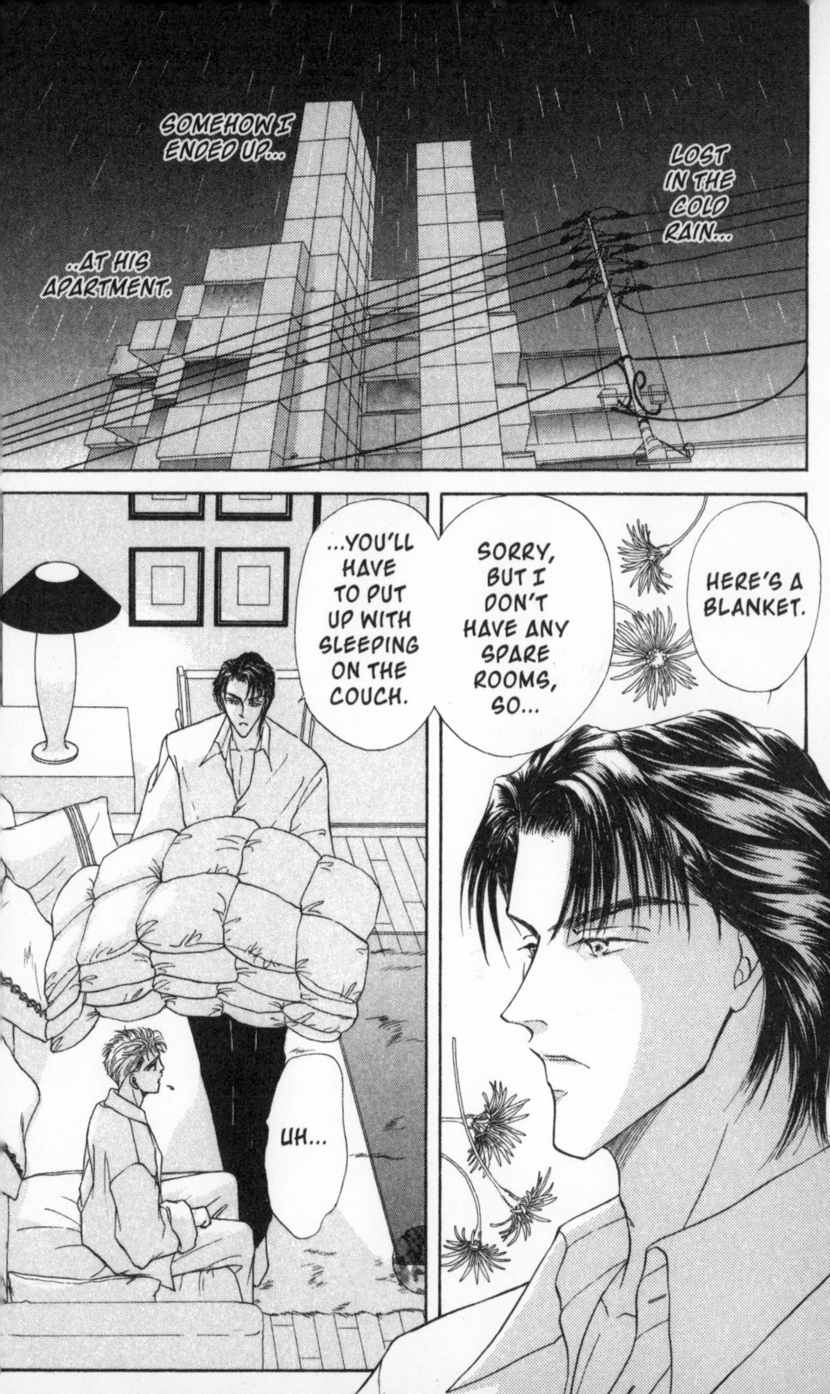
LOST IN THE COLD RAIN...
SOMEHOW I ENDED UP...
..AT HIS APARTMENT.
HERE'S A BLANKET.
SORRY, BUT I DON'T HAVE ANY SPARE ROOMS, SO...
...YOU'LL HAVE TO PUT UP WITH SLEEPING ON THE COUCH.
UH...

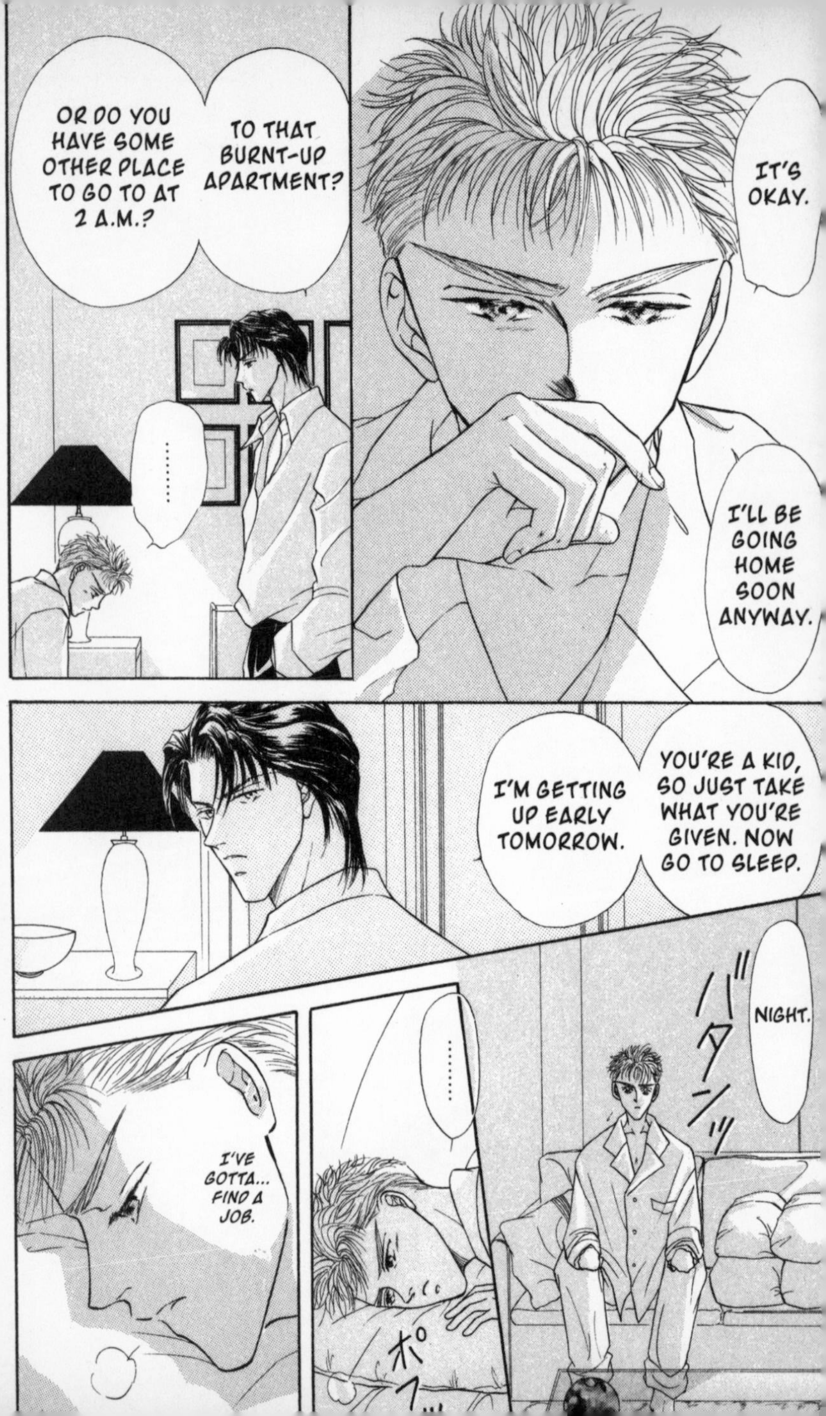
IT'S OKAY.
I'LL BE GOING HOME SOON ANYWAY.
TO THAT BURNT-UP APARTMENT?
OR DO YOU HAVE SOME OTHER PLACE TO GO TO AT 2 A.M.?
......
YOU'RE A KID, SO JUST TAKE WHAT YOU'RE GIVEN. NOW GO TO SLEEP.
I'M GETTING UP EARLY TOMORROW.
NIGHT.
バタンッ
......
ポフ…
I'VE GOTTA... FIND A JOB.

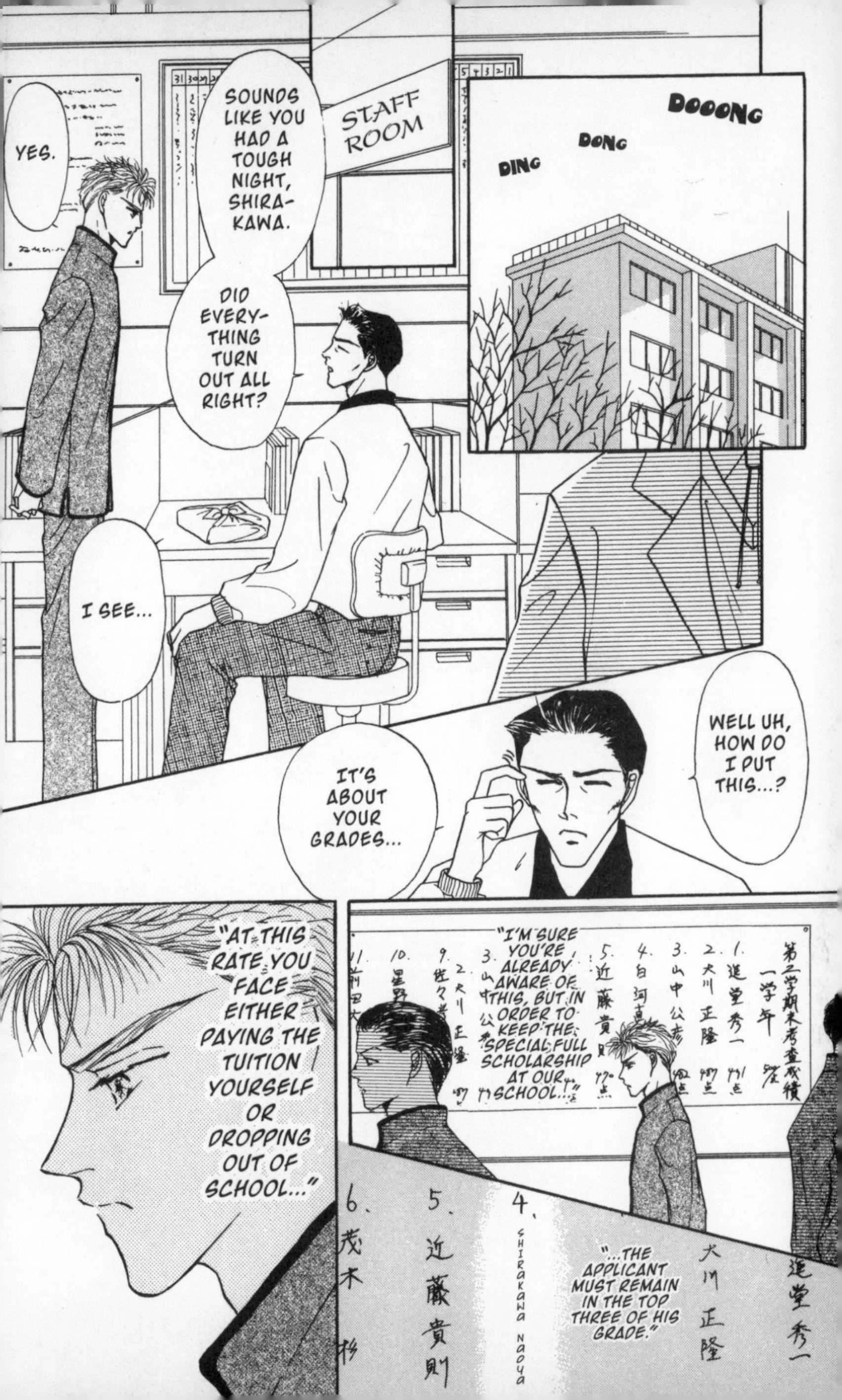
DING
DONG
DOOONG
STAFF ROOM
SOUNDS LIKE YOU HAD A TOUGH NIGHT, SHIRA-KAWA.
YES.
DID EVERY-THING TURN OUT ALL RIGHT?
I SEE...
WELL UH, HOW DO I PUT THIS...?
IT'S ABOUT YOUR GRADES...
第二学期末考査成績
一学年
1. 進堂秀一
2. 犬川正隆
3. 山中公彦
5. 近藤貴則
"I'M SURE YOU'RE ALREADY AWARE OF THIS, BUT IN ORDER TO KEEP THE SPECIAL FULL SCHOLARSHIP AT OUR SCHOOL...!"
進堂秀一
犬川正隆
4. SHIRAKAWA NAOYA
5. 近藤貴則
6.
"...THE APPLICANT MUST REMAIN IN THE TOP THREE OF HIS GRADE."
"AT THIS RATE YOU FACE EITHER PAYING THE TUITION YOURSELF OR DROPPING OUT OF SCHOOL..."

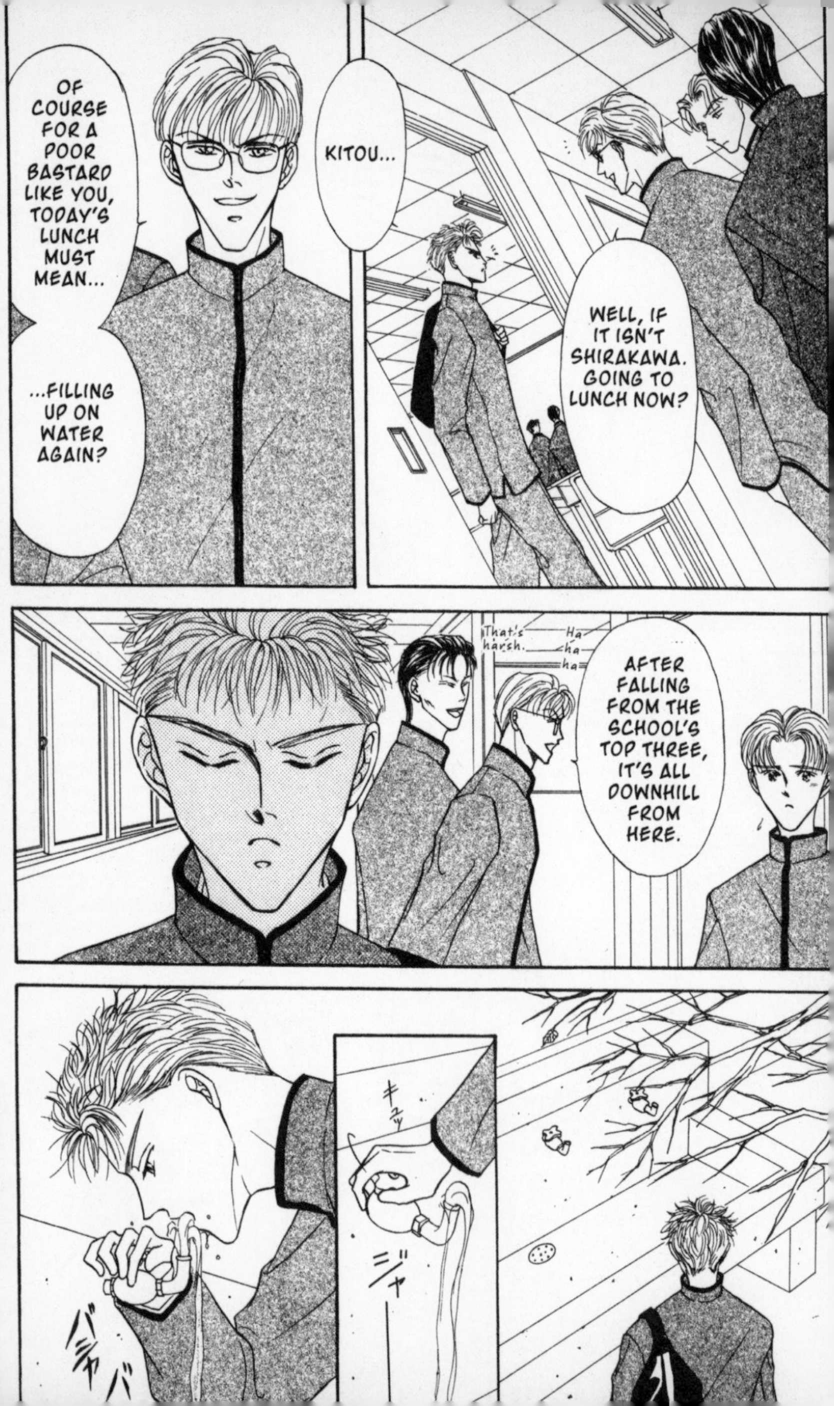
WELL, IF IT ISN'T SHIRAKAWA. GOING TO LUNCH NOW?
KITOU...
OF COURSE FOR A POOR BASTARD LIKE YOU, TODAY'S LUNCH MUST MEAN...
...FILLING UP ON WATER AGAIN?
AFTER FALLING FROM THE SCHOOL'S TOP THREE, IT'S ALL DOWNHILL FROM HERE.
Ha ha ha
That's harsh.
キュッ
ジャ
バシャバ

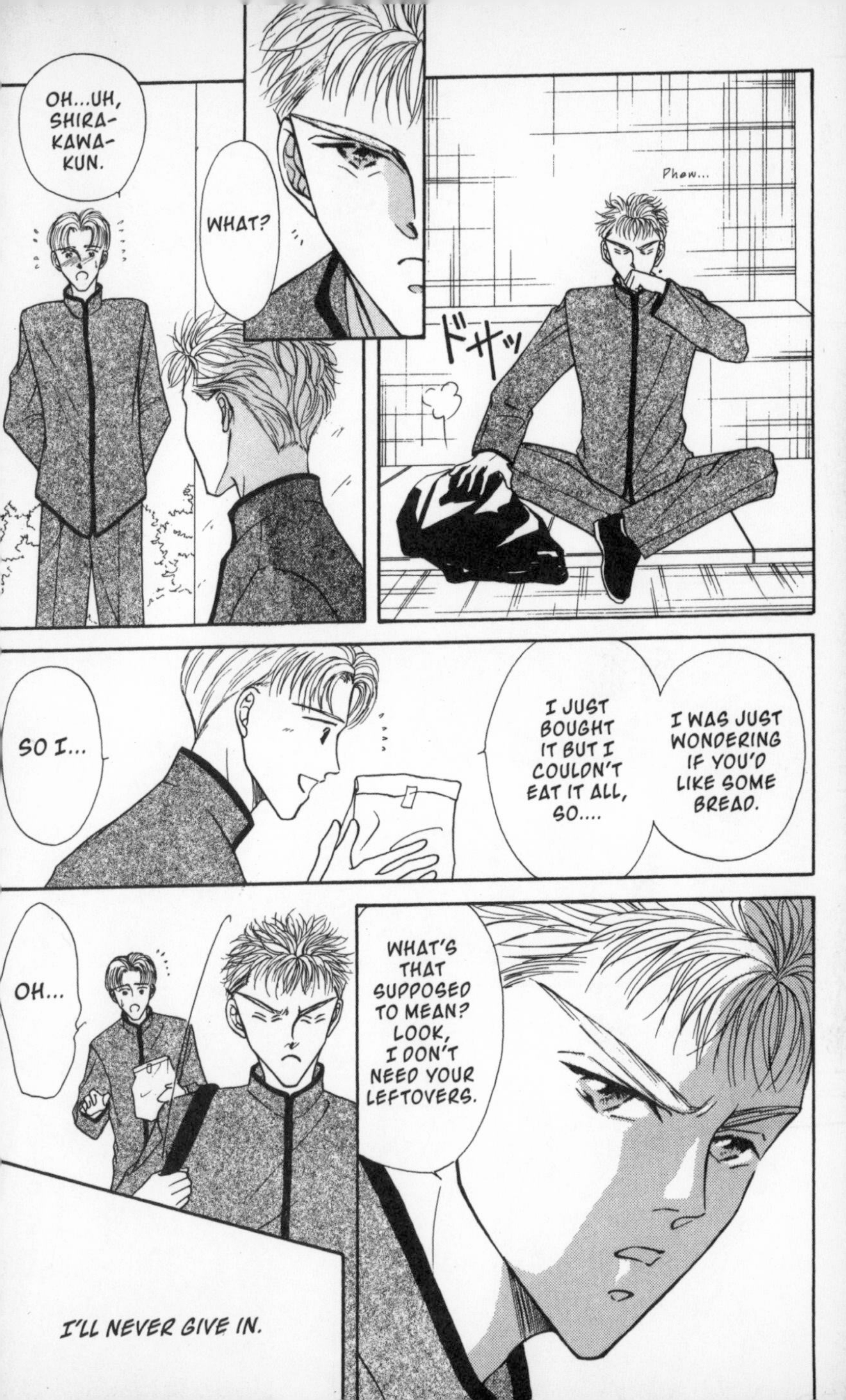
Phew...
ドサッ
OH...UH, SHIRAKAWA-KUN.
WHAT?
I WAS JUST WONDERING IF YOU'D LIKE SOME BREAD.
I JUST BOUGHT IT BUT I COULDN'T EAT IT ALL, SO....
SO I...
WHAT'S THAT SUPPOSED TO MEAN? LOOK, I DON'T NEED YOUR LEFTOVERS.
OH...
I'LL NEVER GIVE IN.

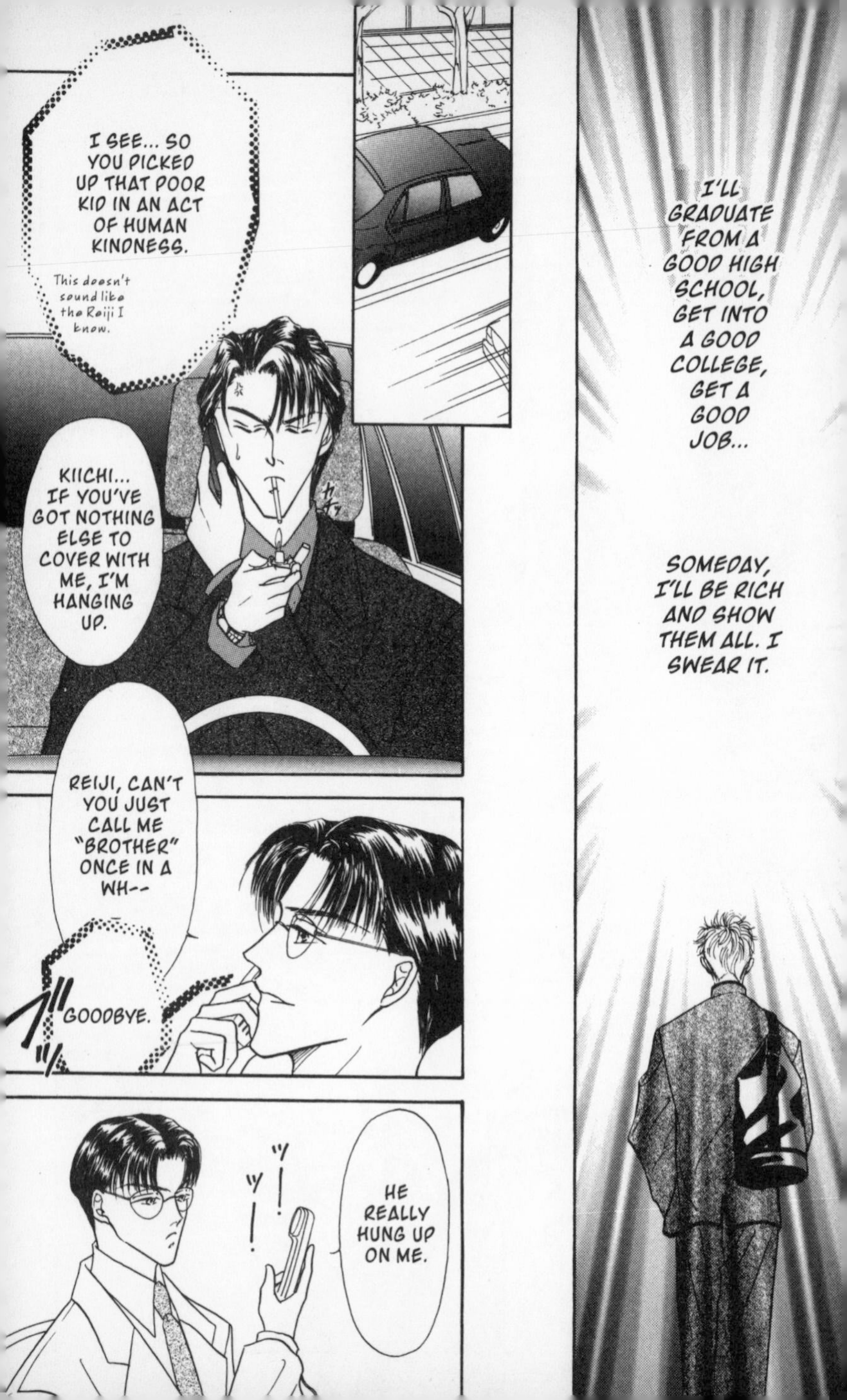
I'LL GRADUATE FROM A GOOD HIGH SCHOOL, GET INTO A GOOD COLLEGE, GET A GOOD JOB...
SOMEDAY, I'LL BE RICH AND SHOW THEM ALL. I SWEAR IT.
I SEE... SO YOU PICKED UP THAT POOR KID IN AN ACT OF HUMAN KINDNESS.
This doesn't sound like the Reiji I know.
KIICHI... IF YOU'VE GOT NOTHING ELSE TO COVER WITH ME, I'M HANGING UP.
REIJI, CAN'T YOU JUST CALL ME "BROTHER" ONCE IN A WH--
GOODBYE.
ツー!
ツー!
HE REALLY HUNG UP ON ME.

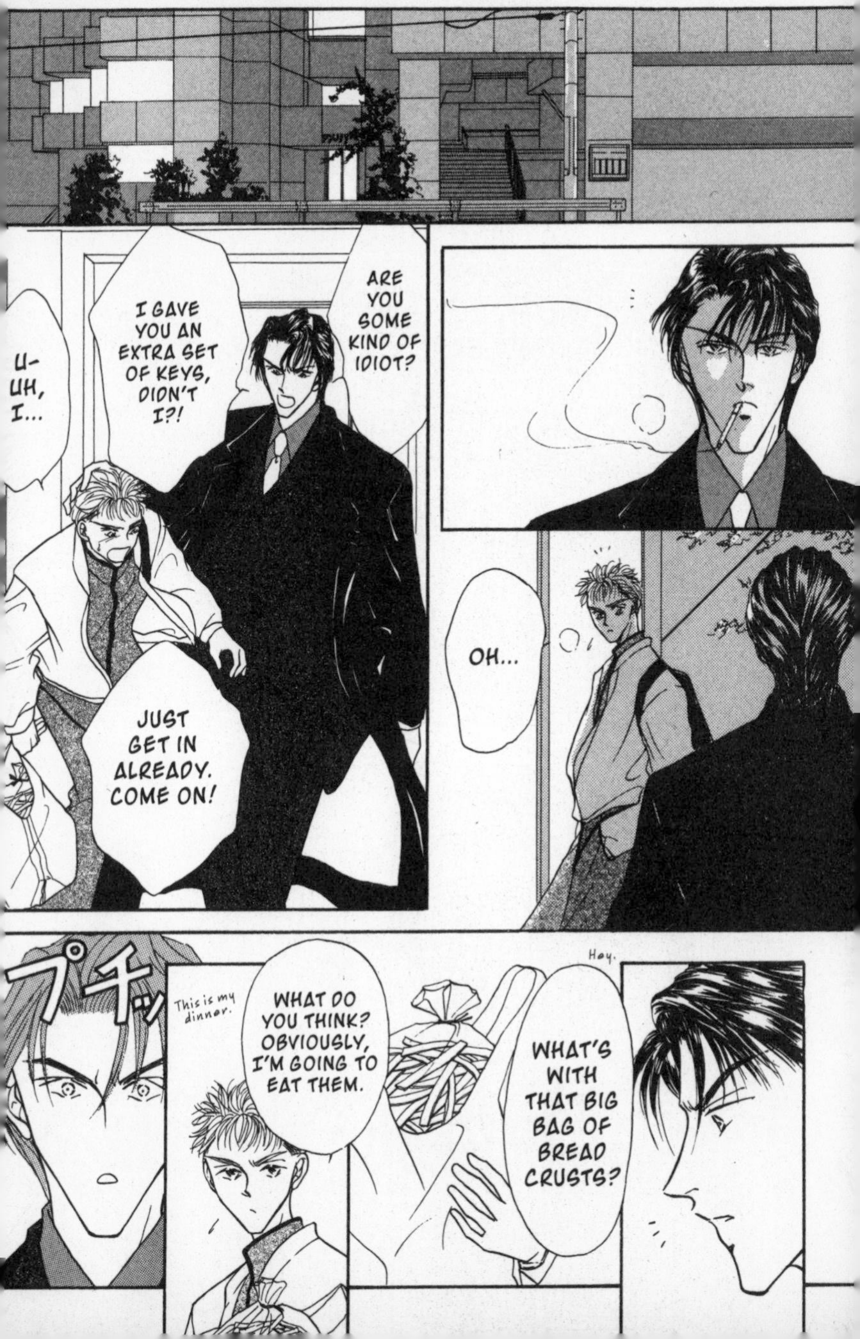
OH...
ARE YOU SOME KIND OF IDIOT?
I GAVE YOU AN EXTRA SET OF KEYS, DIDN'T I?!
U-UH, I...
JUST GET IN ALREADY. COME ON!
Hey.
WHAT'S WITH THAT BIG BAG OF BREAD CRUSTS?
WHAT DO YOU THINK? OBVIOUSLY, I'M GOING TO EAT THEM.
This is my dinner.
プチッ

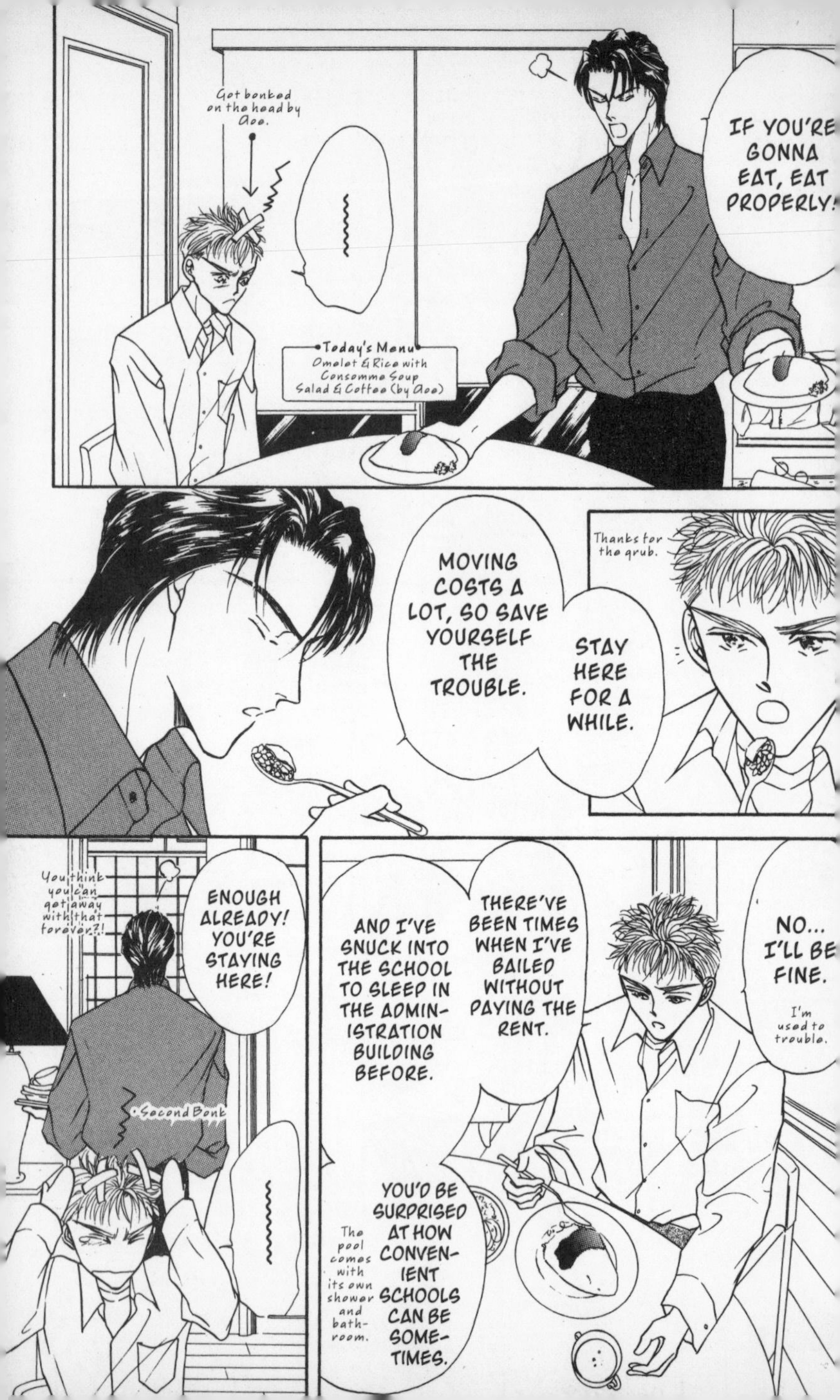
IF YOU'RE GONNA EAT, EAT PROPERLY!
Got bonked on the head by Aoe.
Today's Menu
Omelet & Rice with Consomme Soup Salad & Coffee (by Aoe)
Thanks for the grub.
STAY HERE FOR A WHILE.
MOVING COSTS A LOT, SO SAVE YOURSELF THE TROUBLE.
NO... I'LL BE FINE.
I'm used to trouble.
THERE'VE BEEN TIMES WHEN I'VE BAILED WITHOUT PAYING THE RENT.
AND I'VE SNUCK INTO THE SCHOOL TO SLEEP IN THE ADMINISTRATION BUILDING BEFORE.
YOU'D BE SURPRISED AT HOW CONVENIENT SCHOOLS CAN BE SOMETIMES.
The pool comes with its own shower and bathroom.
ENOUGH ALREADY! YOU'RE STAYING HERE!
You think you can get away with that forever?!
Second Bonk

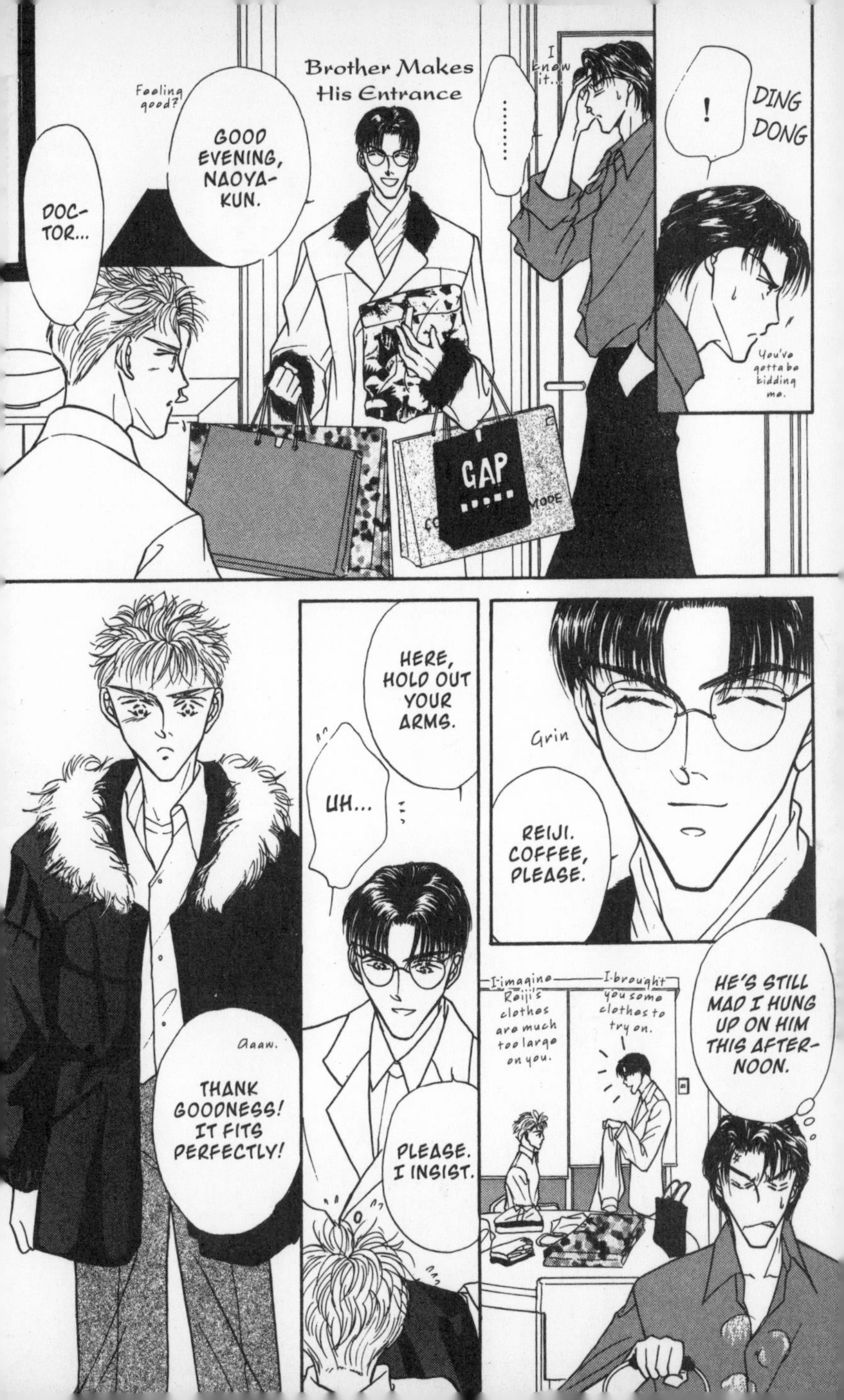

DING DONG
!
You've gotta be kidding me.
Brother Makes His Entrance
I knew it...
......
GOOD EVENING, NAOYA-KUN.
Feeling good?
DOCTOR...
GAP
Grin
REIJI. COFFEE, PLEASE.
HE'S STILL MAD I HUNG UP ON HIM THIS AFTERNOON.
I brought you some clothes to try on.
I imagine Reiji's clothes are much too large on you.
HERE, HOLD OUT YOUR ARMS.
UH...
PLEASE. I INSIST.
Aaaw.
THANK GOODNESS! IT FITS PERFECTLY!

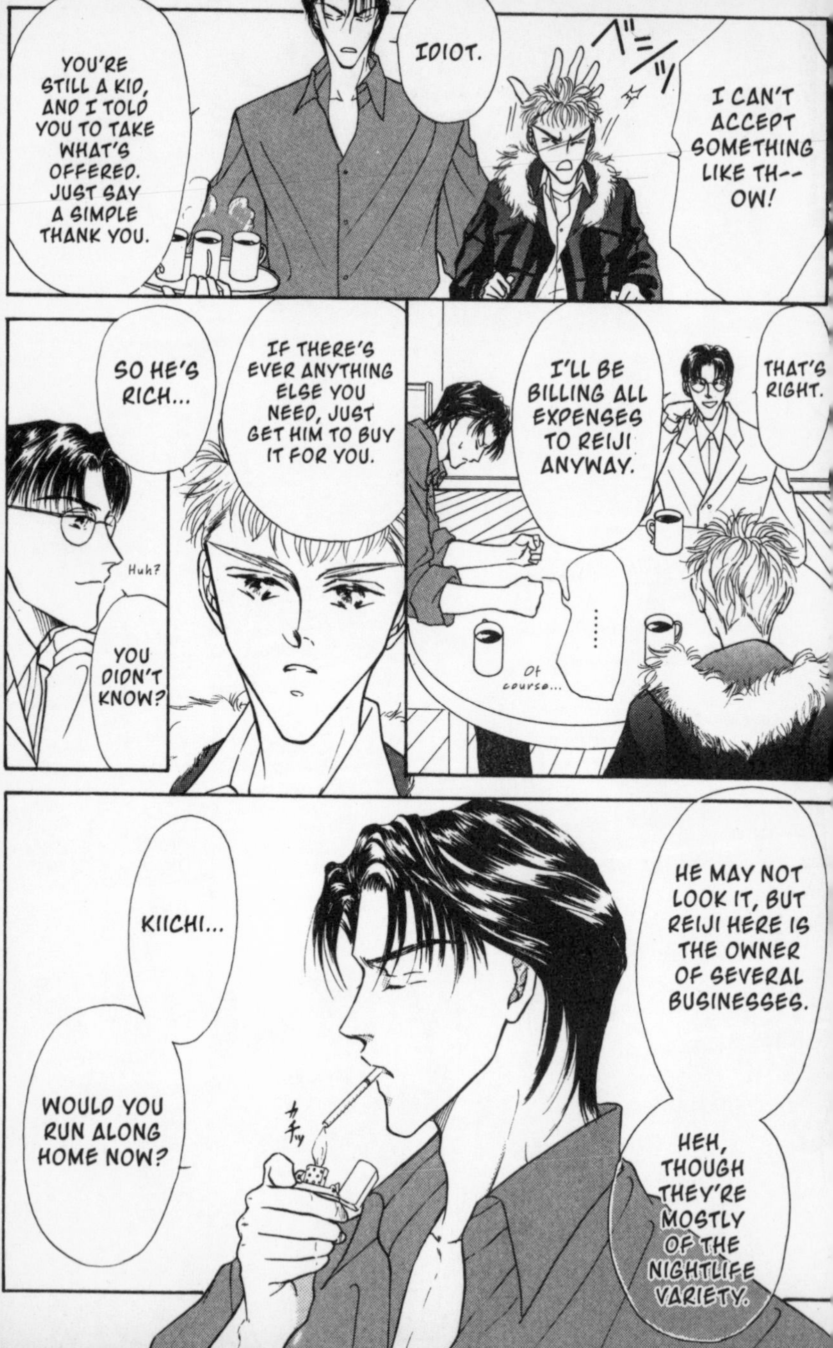
I CAN'T ACCEPT SOMETHING LIKE TH-- OW!
IDIOT.
YOU'RE STILL A KID, AND I TOLD YOU TO TAKE WHAT'S OFFERED. JUST SAY A SIMPLE THANK YOU.
THAT'S RIGHT.
I'LL BE BILLING ALL EXPENSES TO REIJI ANYWAY.
......
Of course...
IF THERE'S EVER ANYTHING ELSE YOU NEED, JUST GET HIM TO BUY IT FOR YOU.
SO HE'S RICH...
Huh?
YOU DIDN'T KNOW?
HE MAY NOT LOOK IT, BUT REIJI HERE IS THE OWNER OF SEVERAL BUSINESSES.
HEH, THOUGH THEY'RE MOSTLY OF THE NIGHTLIFE VARIETY.
カチッ
KIICHI...
WOULD YOU RUN ALONG HOME NOW?

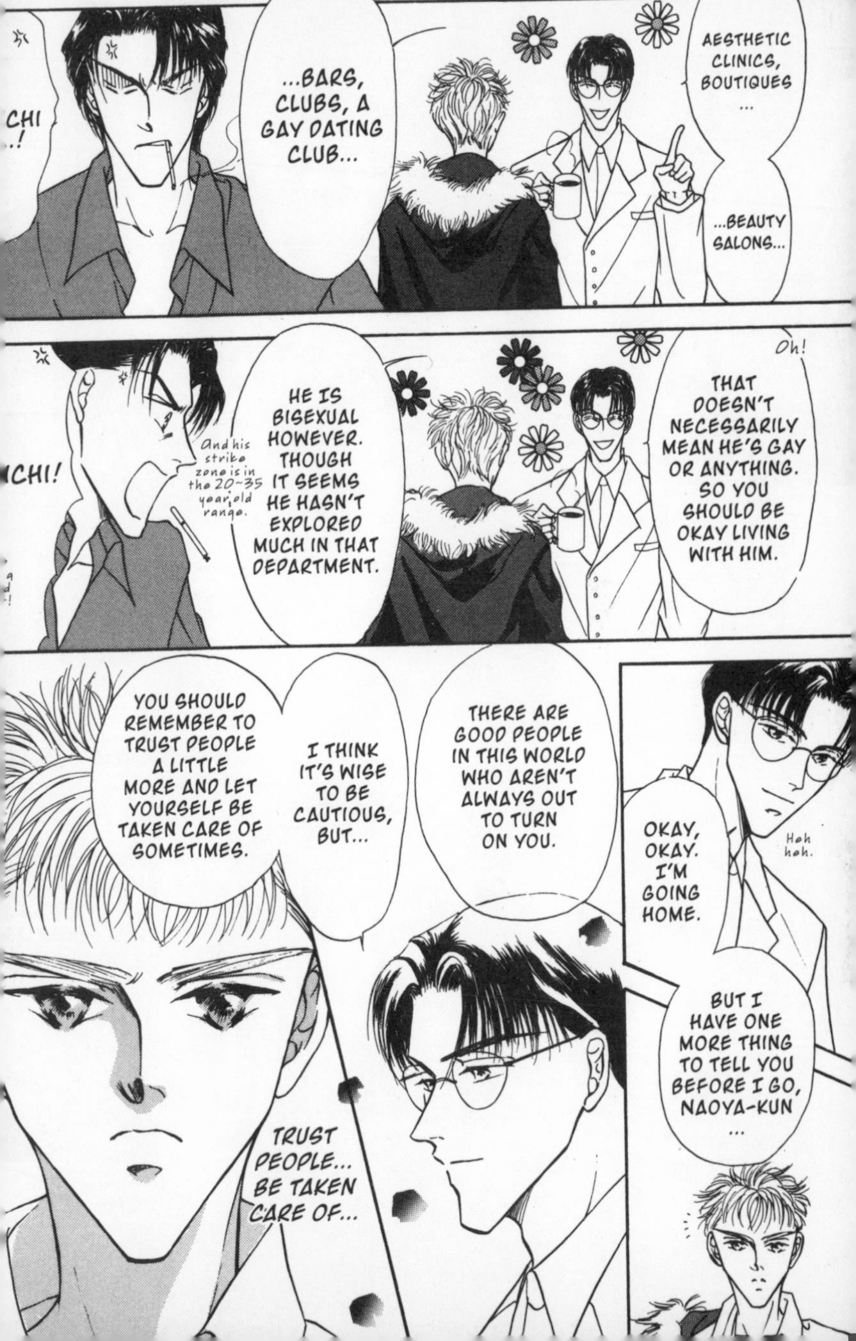
AESTHETIC CLINICS, BOUTIQUES ...
...BEAUTY SALONS...
...BARS, CLUBS, A GAY DATING CLUB...
CHI ..!
Oh!
THAT DOESN'T NECESSARILY MEAN HE'S GAY OR ANYTHING. SO YOU SHOULD BE OKAY LIVING WITH HIM.
HE IS BISEXUAL HOWEVER. THOUGH IT SEEMS HE HASN'T EXPLORED MUCH IN THAT DEPARTMENT.
And his strike zone is in the 20~35 year old range.
CHI!
OKAY, OKAY. I'M GOING HOME.
Heh heh.
BUT I HAVE ONE MORE THING TO TELL YOU BEFORE I GO, NAOYA-KUN ...
THERE ARE GOOD PEOPLE IN THIS WORLD WHO AREN'T ALWAYS OUT TO TURN ON YOU.
I THINK IT'S WISE TO BE CAUTIOUS, BUT...
YOU SHOULD REMEMBER TO TRUST PEOPLE A LITTLE MORE AND LET YOURSELF BE TAKEN CARE OF SOMETIMES.
TRUST PEOPLE... BE TAKEN CARE OF...

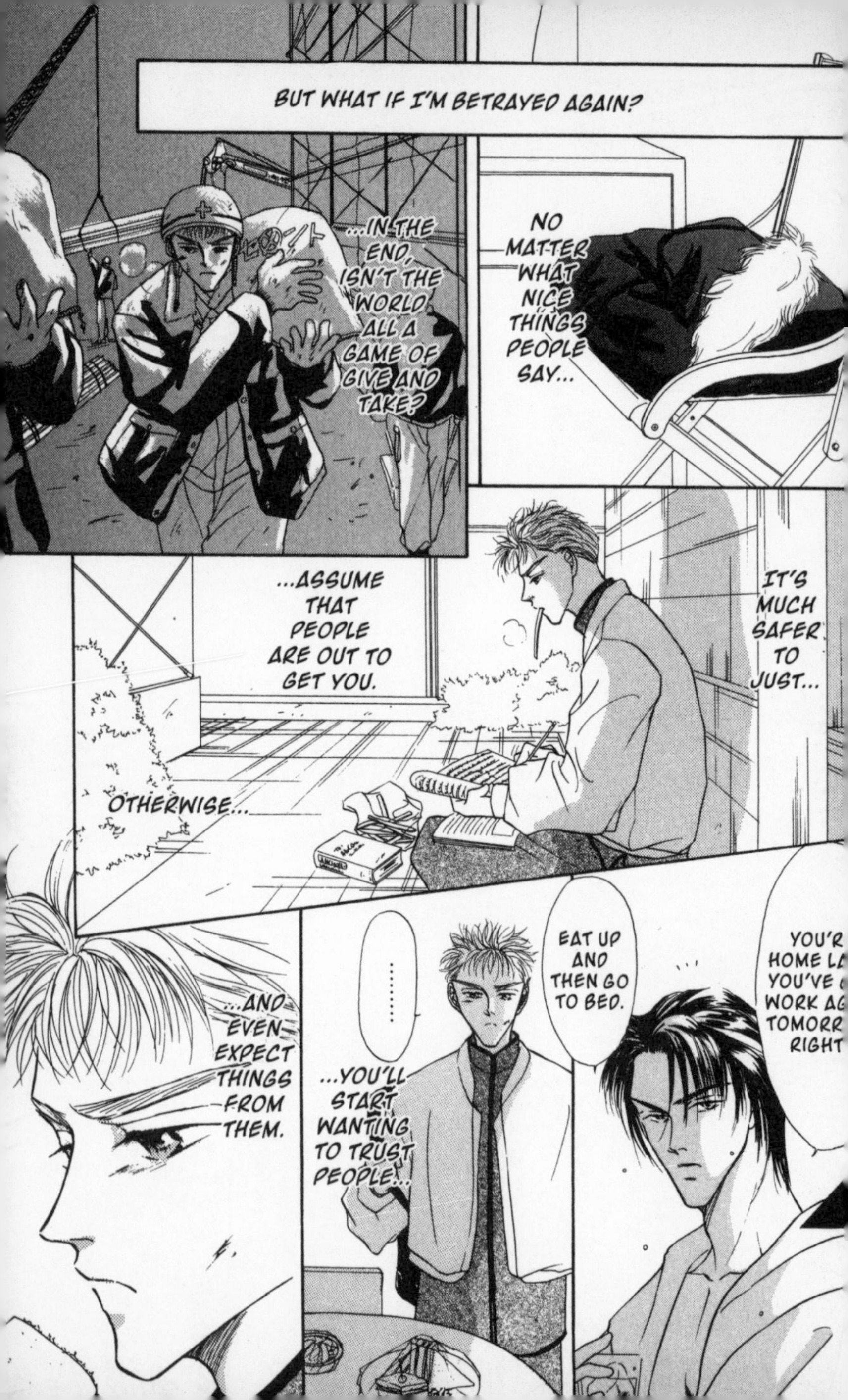
BUT WHAT IF I'M BETRAYED AGAIN?
NO MATTER WHAT NICE THINGS PEOPLE SAY...
...IN THE END, ISN'T THE WORLD ALL A GAME OF GIVE AND TAKE?
IT'S MUCH SAFER TO JUST...
...ASSUME THAT PEOPLE ARE OUT TO GET YOU.
OTHERWISE...
YOU'R HOME LA YOU'VE WORK AG TOMORR RIGHT
...
EAT UP AND THEN GO TO BED.
......
...YOU'LL START WANTING TO TRUST PEOPLE...
...AND EVEN EXPECT THINGS FROM THEM.

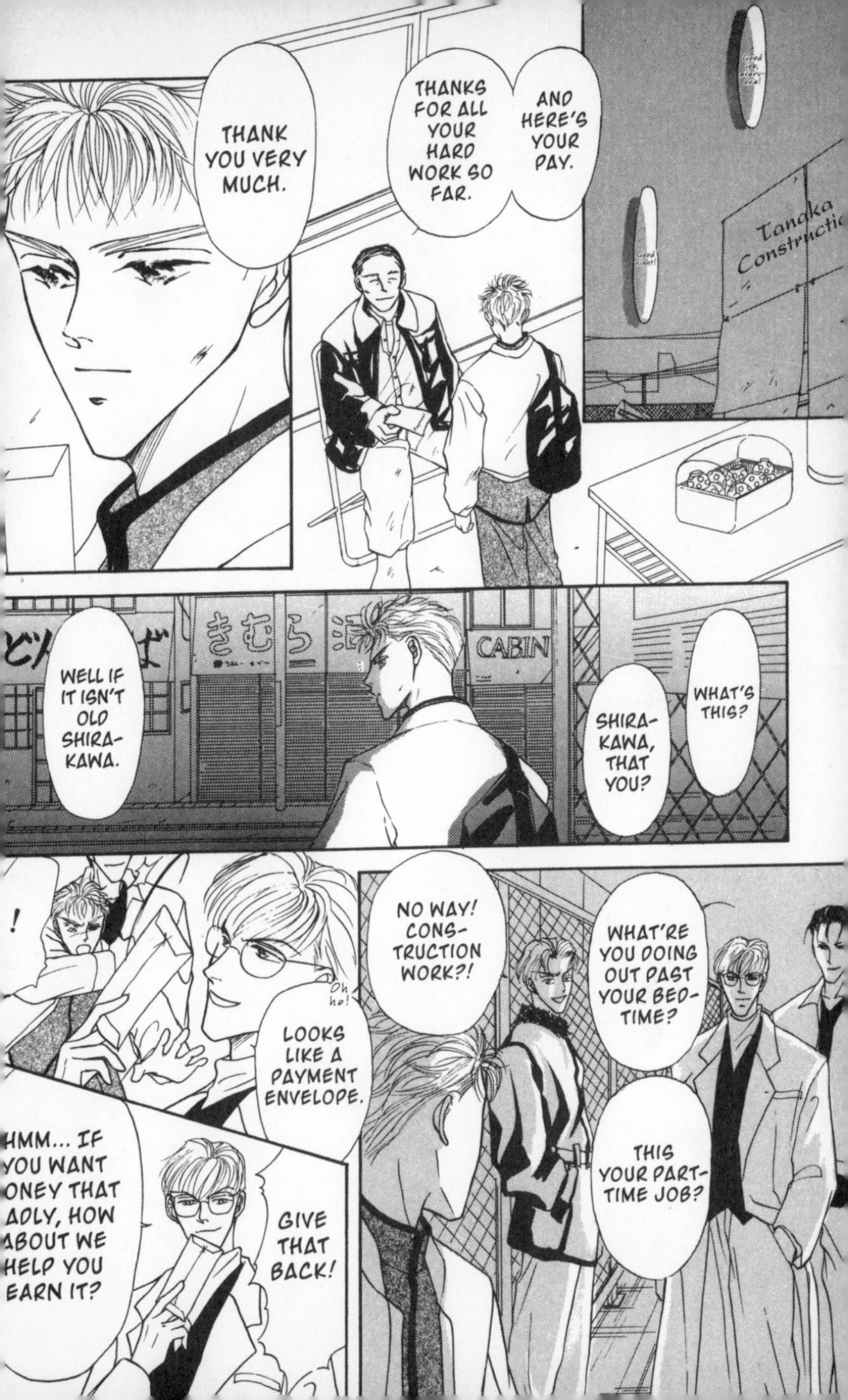
Good job, everyone!
Tanaka Construction
Good night!
AND HERE'S YOUR PAY.
THANKS FOR ALL YOUR HARD WORK SO FAR.
THANK YOU VERY MUCH.
WHAT'S THIS?
SHIRA-KAWA, THAT YOU?
CABIN
きむら
WELL IF IT ISN'T OLD SHIRA-KAWA.
WHAT'RE YOU DOING OUT PAST YOUR BED-TIME?
NO WAY! CONSTRUCTION WORK?!
THIS YOUR PART-TIME JOB?
Oh ho!
LOOKS LIKE A PAYMENT ENVELOPE.
!
GIVE THAT BACK!
HMM... IF YOU WANT ONEY THAT ADLY, HOW ABOUT WE HELP YOU EARN IT?

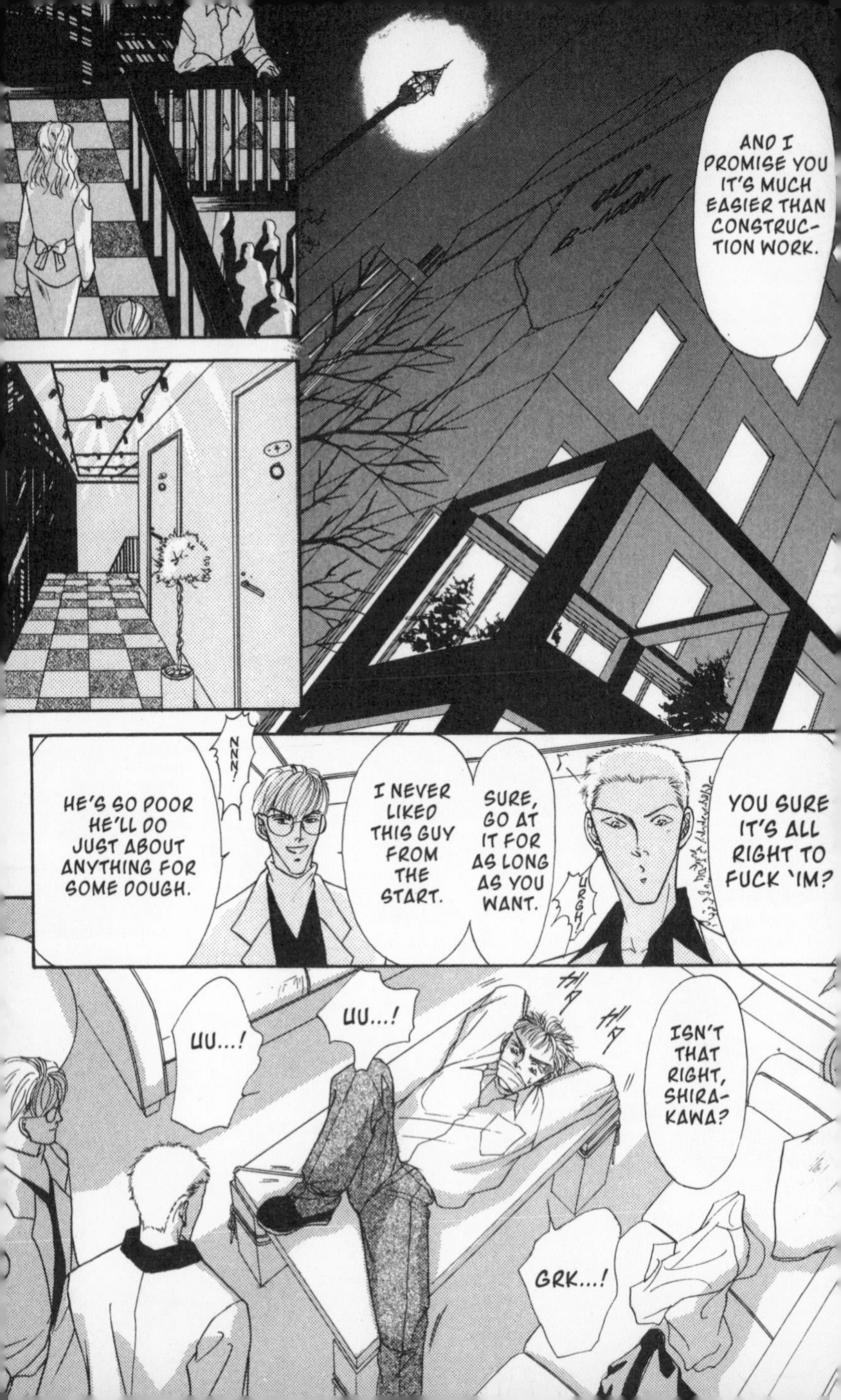
AND I PROMISE YOU IT'S MUCH EASIER THAN CONSTRUC-TION WORK.
YOU SURE IT'S ALL RIGHT TO FUCK 'IM?
URGH!
SURE, GO AT IT FOR AS LONG AS YOU WANT.
I NEVER LIKED THIS GUY FROM THE START.
NNN!
HE'S SO POOR HE'LL DO JUST ABOUT ANYTHING FOR SOME DOUGH.
ISN'T THAT RIGHT, SHIRA-KAWA?
UU...!
UU...!
GRK...!

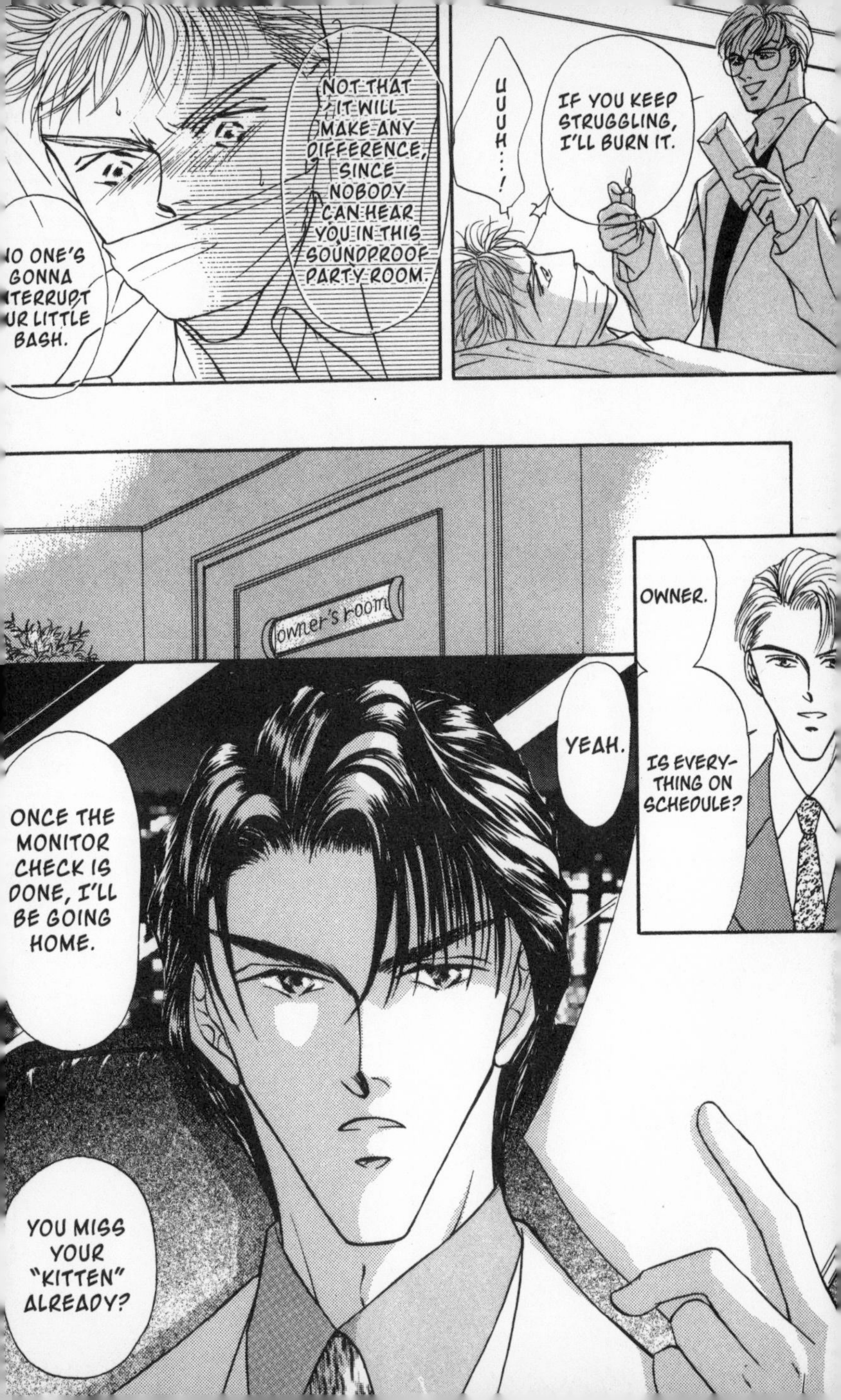
IF YOU KEEP STRUGGLING, I'LL BURN IT.
UUUH...!
NOT THAT IT WILL MAKE ANY DIFFERENCE, SINCE NOBODY CAN HEAR YOU IN THIS SOUNDPROOF PARTY ROOM.
O ONE'S GONNA ITERRUPT UR LITTLE BASH.
OWNER.
IS EVERY-THING ON SCHEDULE?
owner's room
YEAH.
ONCE THE MONITOR CHECK IS DONE, I'LL BE GOING HOME.
YOU MISS YOUR "KITTEN" ALREADY?

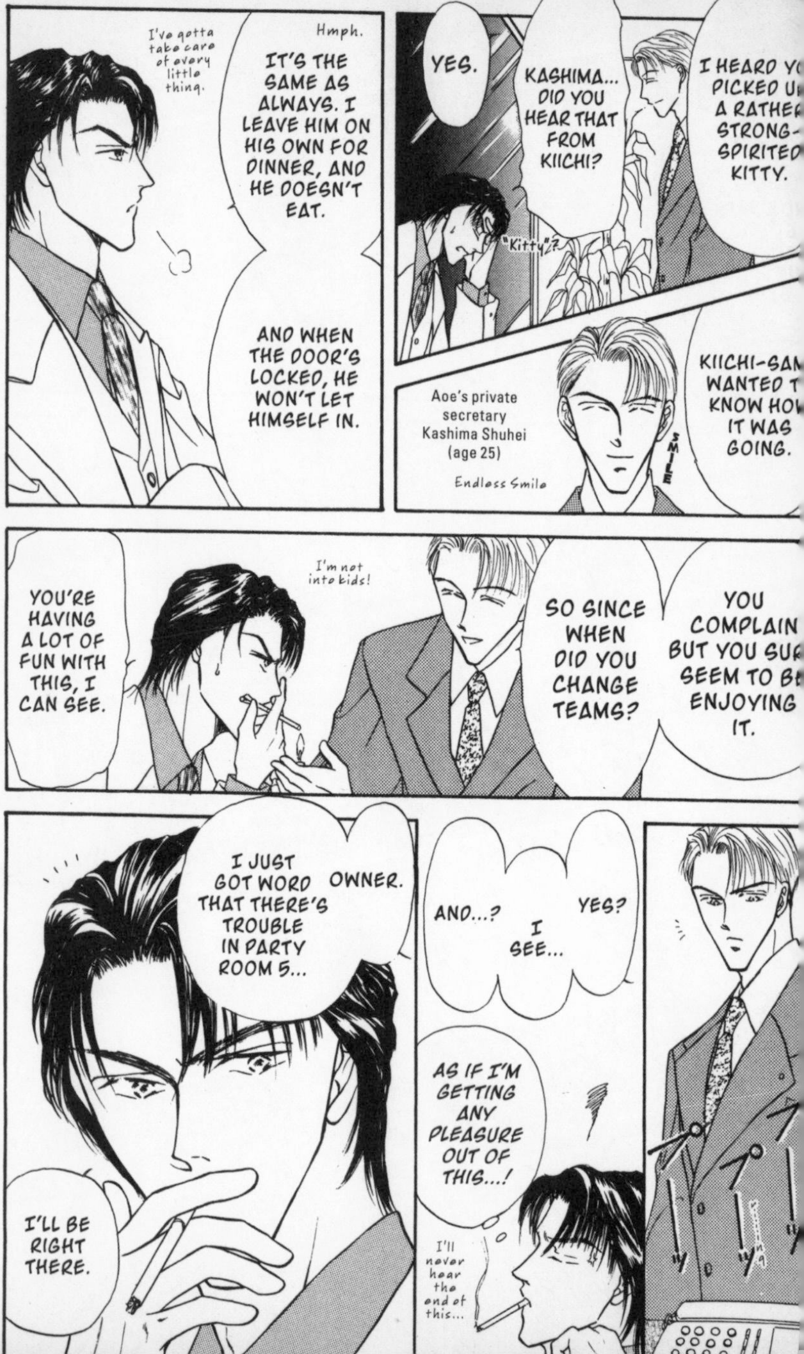
I HEARD YO PICKED U A RATHER STRONG- SPIRITED KITTY.
KASHIMA... DID YOU HEAR THAT FROM KIICHI?
YES.
"Kitty"?
KIICHI-SAM WANTED T KNOW HOW IT WAS GOING.
SMILE
Aoe's private secretary Kashima Shuhei (age 25)
Endless Smile
Hmph.
IT'S THE SAME AS ALWAYS. I LEAVE HIM ON HIS OWN FOR DINNER, AND HE DOESN'T EAT.
I've gotta take care of every little thing.
AND WHEN THE DOOR'S LOCKED, HE WON'T LET HIMSELF IN.
YOU COMPLAIN BUT YOU SUR SEEM TO BE ENJOYING IT.
SO SINCE WHEN DID YOU CHANGE TEAMS?
I'm not into kids!
YOU'RE HAVING A LOT OF FUN WITH THIS, I CAN SEE.
YES?
I SEE...
AND...?
AS IF I'M GETTING ANY PLEASURE OUT OF THIS...!
I'll never hear the end of this...
OWNER.
I JUST GOT WORD THAT THERE'S TROUBLE IN PARTY ROOM 5...
I'LL BE RIGHT THERE.

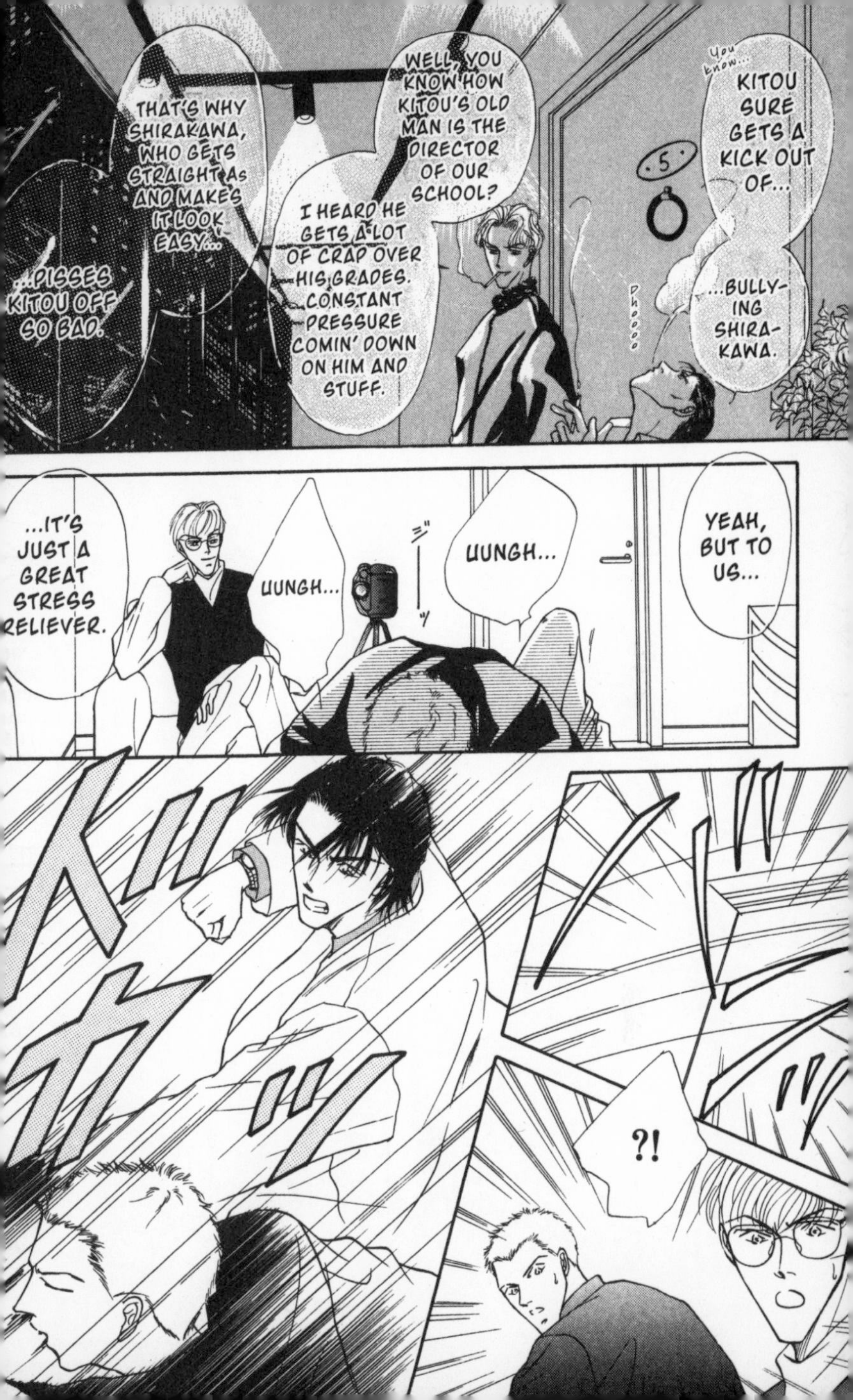
You know...
KITOU SURE GETS A KICK OUT OF...
...BULLYING SHIRAKAWA.
Phooooo
WELL, YOU KNOW HOW KITOU'S OLD MAN IS THE DIRECTOR OF OUR SCHOOL?
I HEARD HE GETS A LOT OF CRAP OVER HIS GRADES. CONSTANT PRESSURE COMIN' DOWN ON HIM AND STUFF.
THAT'S WHY SHIRAKAWA, WHO GETS STRAIGHT As AND MAKES IT LOOK EASY...
...PISSES KITOU OFF SO BAD.
YEAH, BUT TO US...
UUNGH...
UUNGH...
...IT'S JUST A GREAT STRESS RELIEVER.
?!

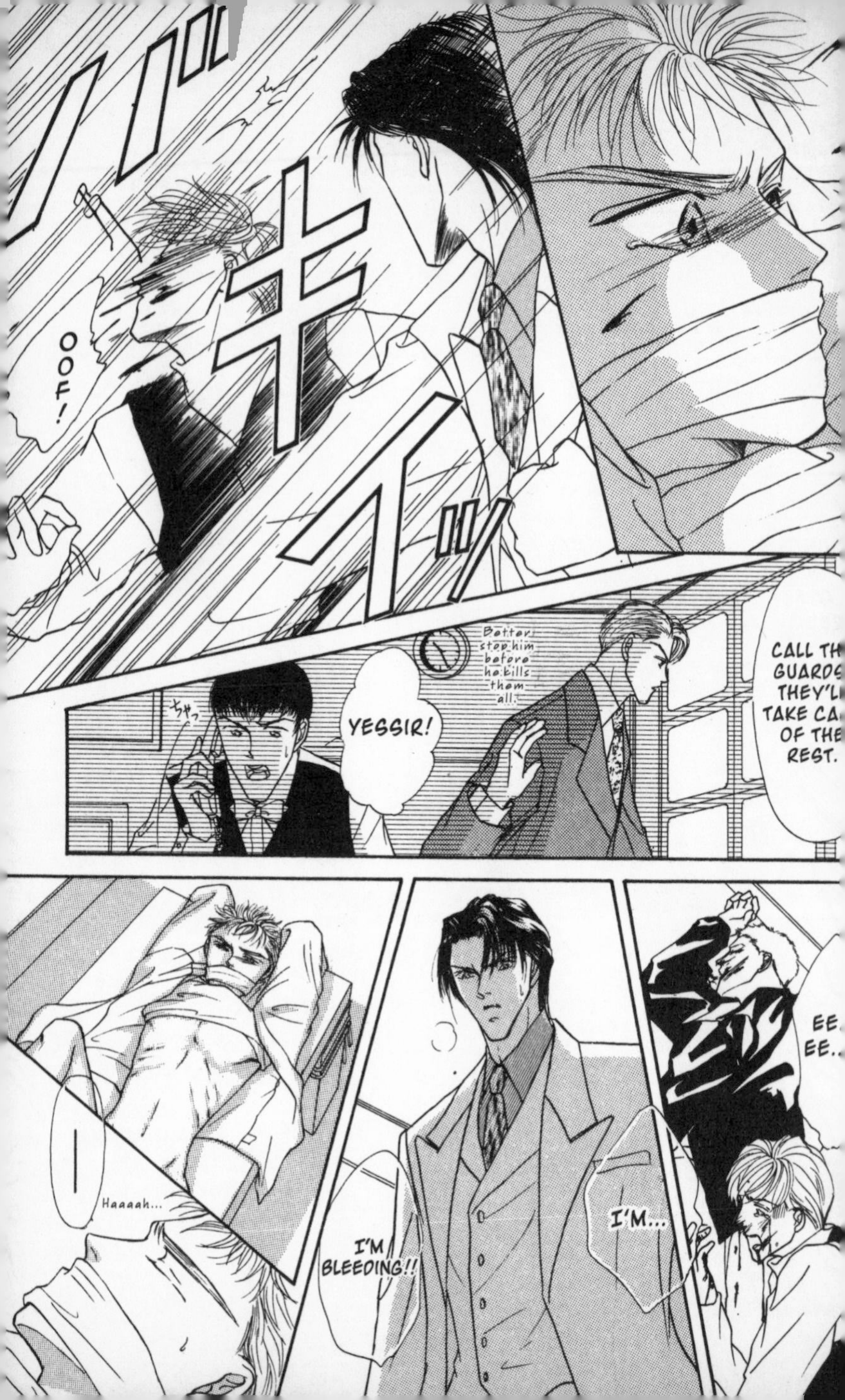
OOF!
CALL TH
GUARDS
THEY'L
TAKE CA
OF THE
REST.
Better stop him before he kills them all.
YESSIR!
EE..
EE..
I'M...
I'M BLEEDING!!
Haaaah...

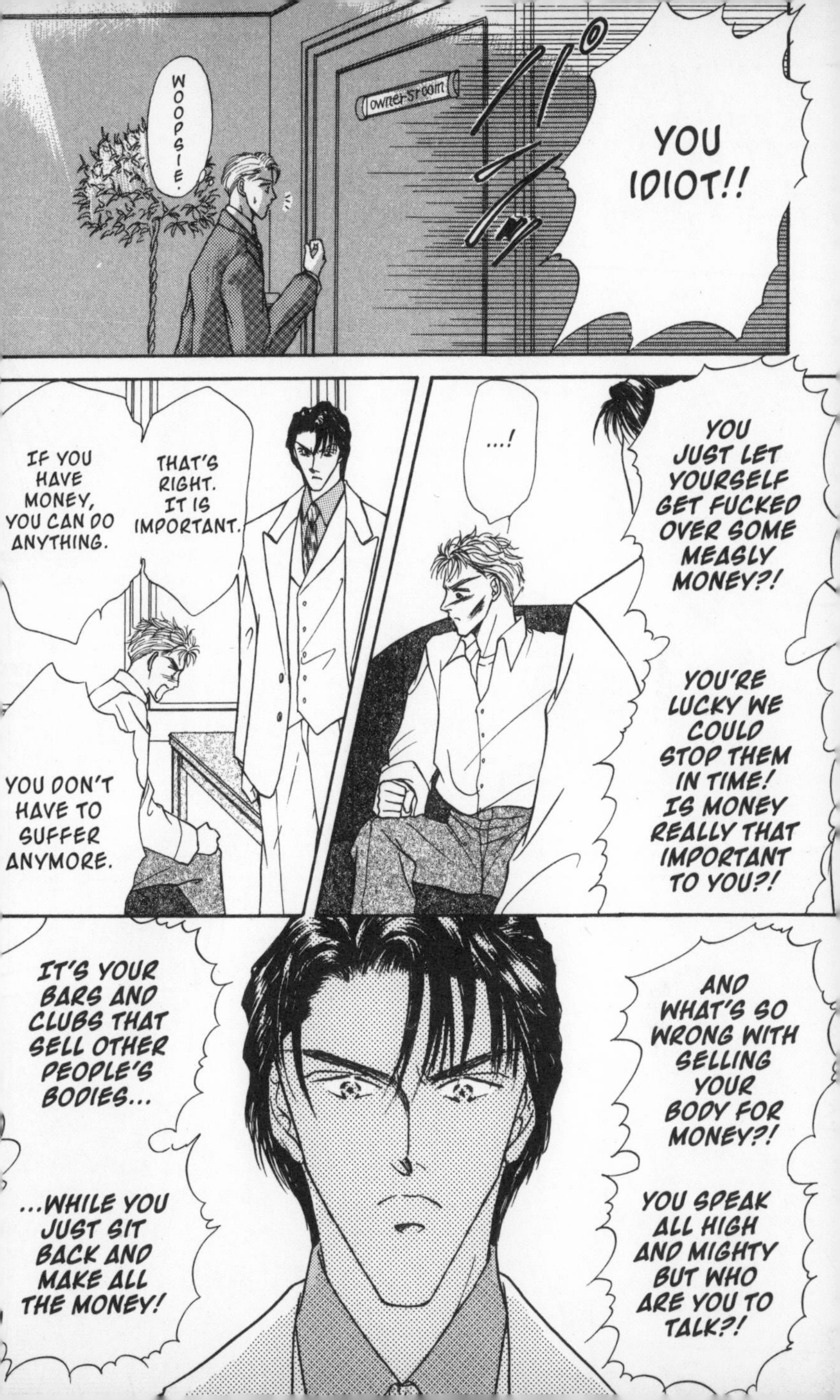
YOU IDIOT!!
WOOPSIE.
YOU JUST LET YOURSELF GET FUCKED OVER SOME MEASLY MONEY?!
YOU'RE LUCKY WE COULD STOP THEM IN TIME! IS MONEY REALLY THAT IMPORTANT TO YOU?!
...!
THAT'S RIGHT. IT IS IMPORTANT.
IF YOU HAVE MONEY, YOU CAN DO ANYTHING.
YOU DON'T HAVE TO SUFFER ANYMORE.
AND WHAT'S SO WRONG WITH SELLING YOUR BODY FOR MONEY?!
YOU SPEAK ALL HIGH AND MIGHTY BUT WHO ARE YOU TO TALK?!
IT'S YOUR BARS AND CLUBS THAT SELL OTHER PEOPLE'S BODIES...
...WHILE YOU JUST SIT BACK AND MAKE ALL THE MONEY!

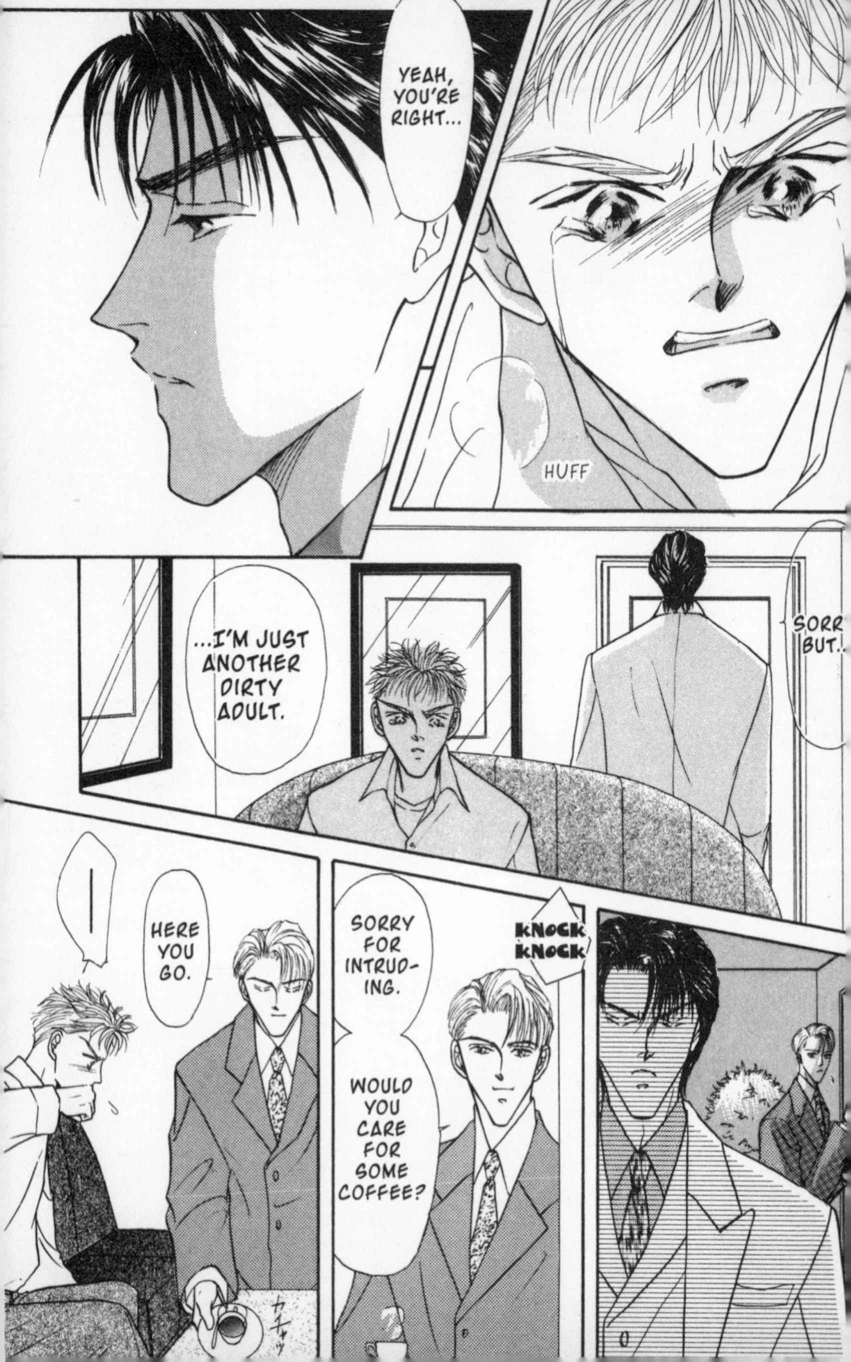
HUFF
YEAH, YOU'RE RIGHT...
SORR BUT..
...I'M JUST ANOTHER DIRTY ADULT.
KNOCK KNOCK
SORRY FOR INTRUD-ING.
WOULD YOU CARE FOR SOME COFFEE?
HERE YOU GO.
!

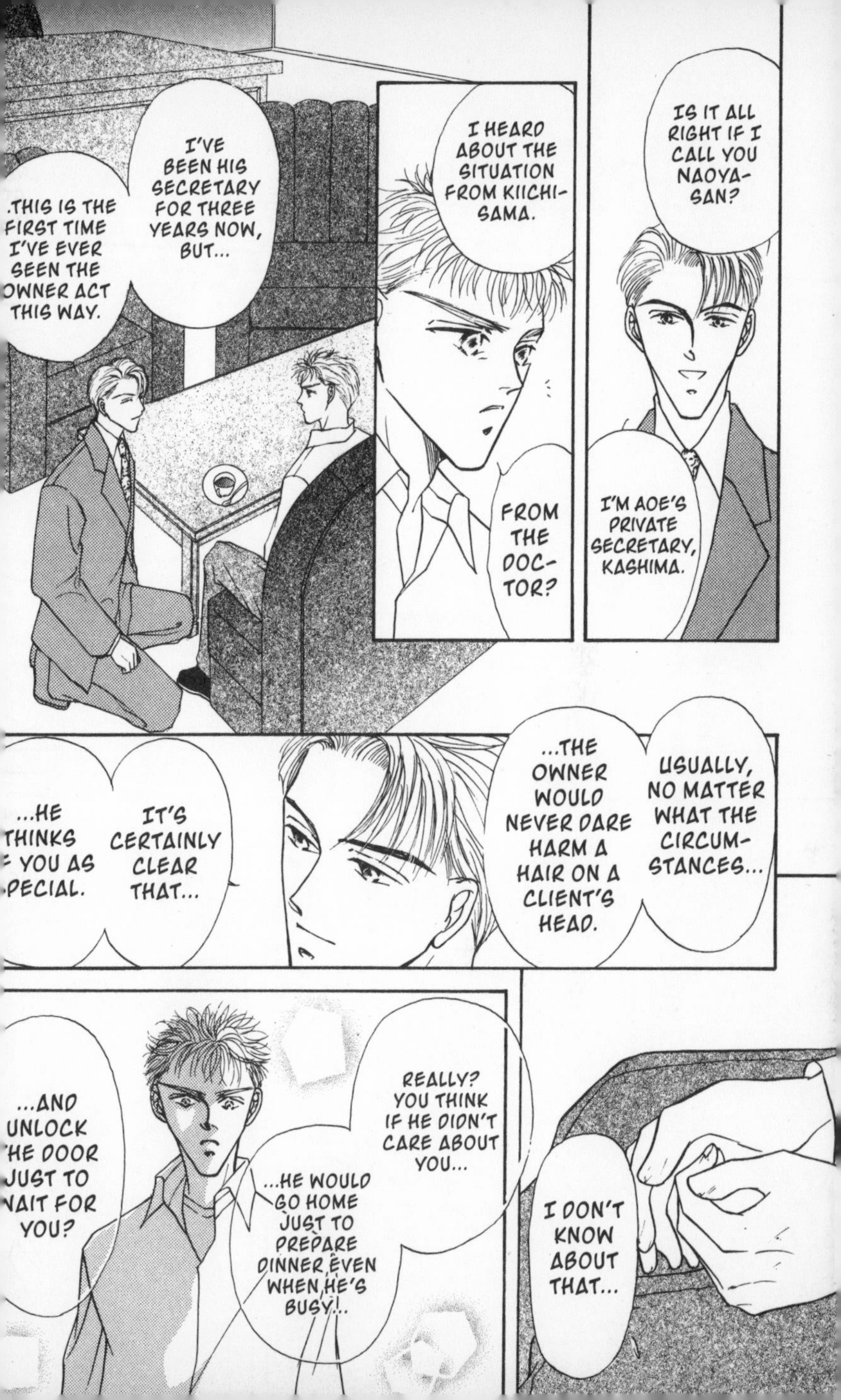
IS IT ALL RIGHT IF I CALL YOU NAOYA-SAN?
I'M AOE'S PRIVATE SECRETARY, KASHIMA.
I HEARD ABOUT THE SITUATION FROM KIICHI-SAMA.
FROM THE DOC-TOR?
I'VE BEEN HIS SECRETARY FOR THREE YEARS NOW, BUT...
.THIS IS THE FIRST TIME I'VE EVER SEEN THE OWNER ACT THIS WAY.
USUALLY, NO MATTER WHAT THE CIRCUM-STANCES...
...THE OWNER WOULD NEVER DARE HARM A HAIR ON A CLIENT'S HEAD.
IT'S CERTAINLY CLEAR THAT...
...HE THINKS YOU AS PECIAL.
I DON'T KNOW ABOUT THAT...
REALLY? YOU THINK IF HE DIDN'T CARE ABOUT YOU...
...HE WOULD GO HOME JUST TO PREPARE DINNER EVEN WHEN HE'S BUSY...
...AND UNLOCK HE DOOR JUST TO AIT FOR YOU?

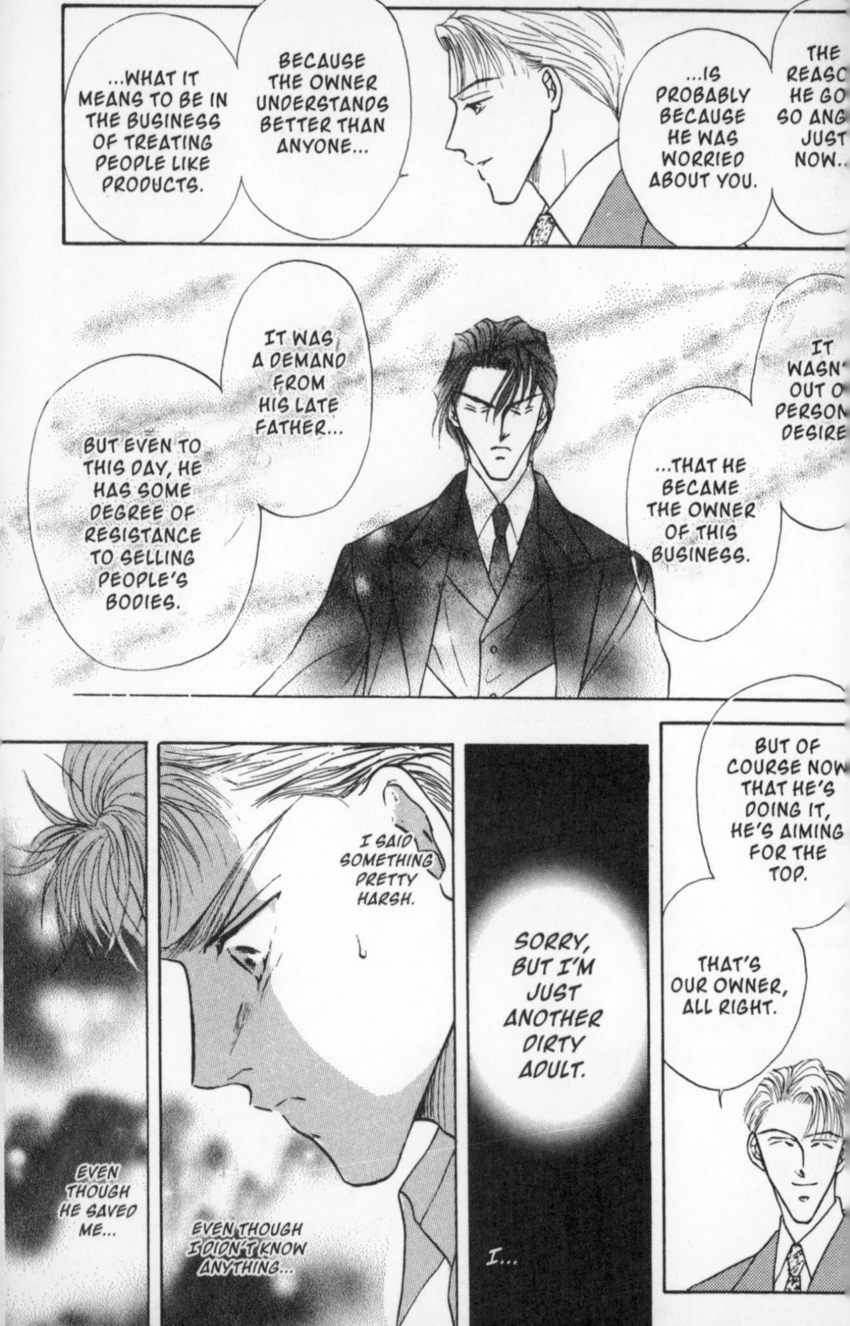
THE REASO HE GO SO ANG JUST NOW..
...IS PROBABLY BECAUSE HE WAS WORRIED ABOUT YOU.
BECAUSE THE OWNER UNDERSTANDS BETTER THAN ANYONE...
...WHAT IT MEANS TO BE IN THE BUSINESS OF TREATING PEOPLE LIKE PRODUCTS.
IT WASN' OUT O PERSON DESIRE
...THAT HE BECAME THE OWNER OF THIS BUSINESS.
IT WAS A DEMAND FROM HIS LATE FATHER...
BUT EVEN TO THIS DAY, HE HAS SOME DEGREE OF RESISTANCE TO SELLING PEOPLE'S BODIES.
BUT OF COURSE NOW THAT HE'S DOING IT, HE'S AIMING FOR THE TOP.
THAT'S OUR OWNER, ALL RIGHT.
SORRY, BUT I'M JUST ANOTHER DIRTY ADULT.
I...
I SAID SOMETHING PRETTY HARSH.
EVEN THOUGH I DIDN'T KNOW ANYTHING...
EVEN THOUGH HE SAVED ME...

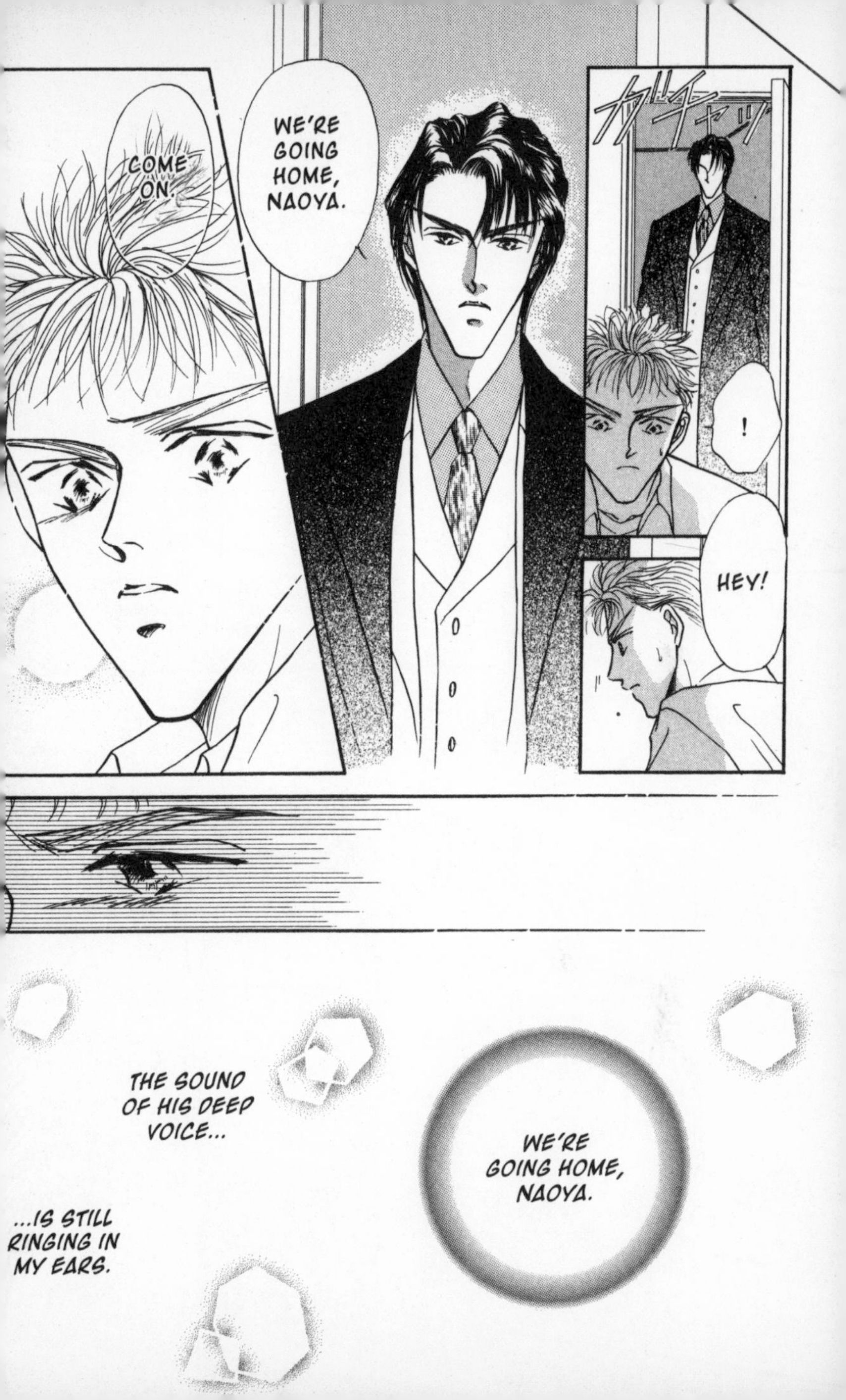
ガチャッ
!
HEY!
WE'RE GOING HOME, NAOYA.
COME ON.
WE'RE GOING HOME, NAOYA.
THE SOUND OF HIS DEEP VOICE...
...IS STILL RINGING IN MY EARS.

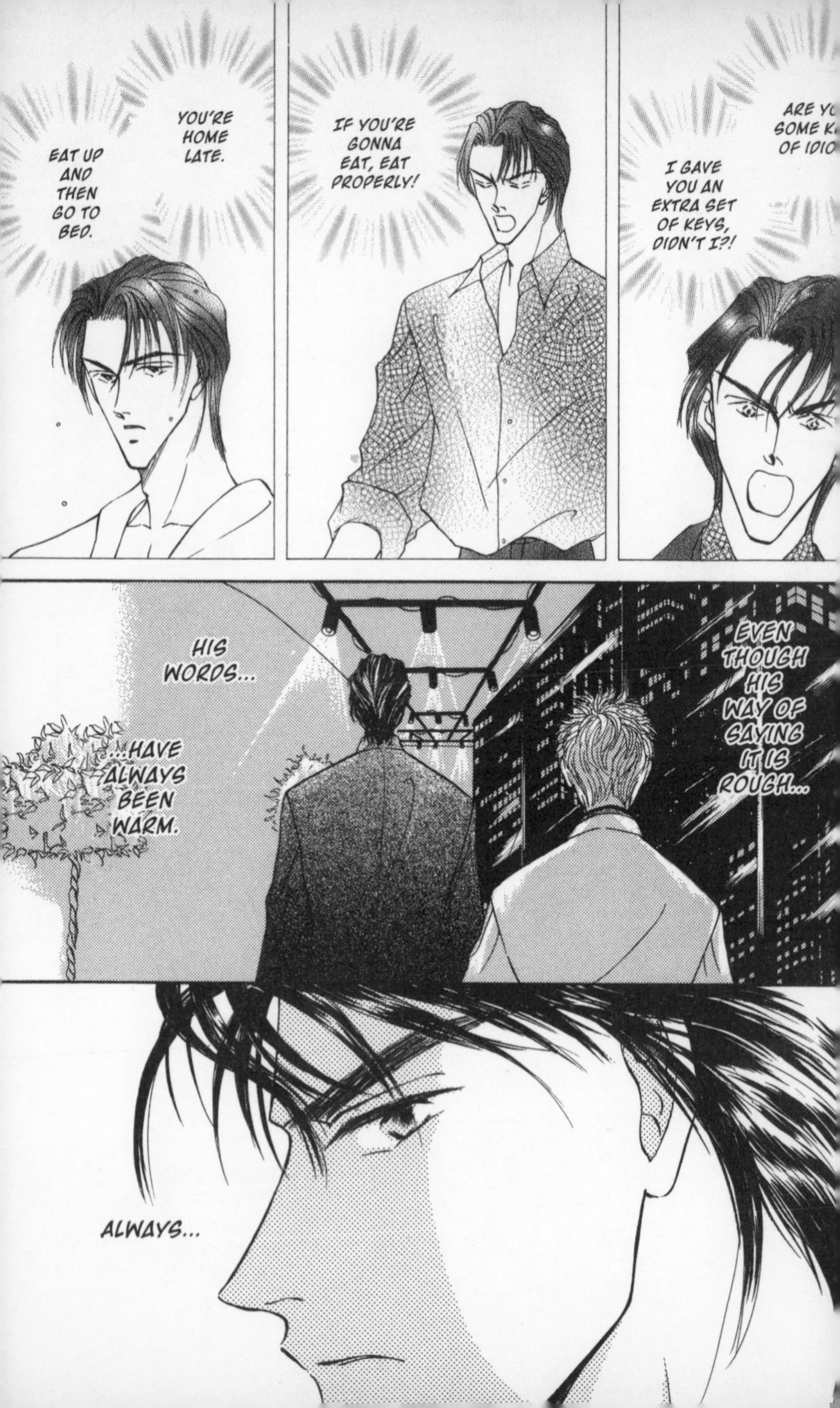
ARE YO SOME K OF IDIO
I GAVE YOU AN EXTRA SET OF KEYS, DIDN'T I?!
IF YOU'RE GONNA EAT, EAT PROPERLY!
YOU'RE HOME LATE.
EAT UP AND THEN GO TO BED.
EVEN THOUGH HIS WAY OF SAYING IT IS ROUGH...
HIS WORDS...
...HAVE ALWAYS BEEN WARM.
ALWAYS...

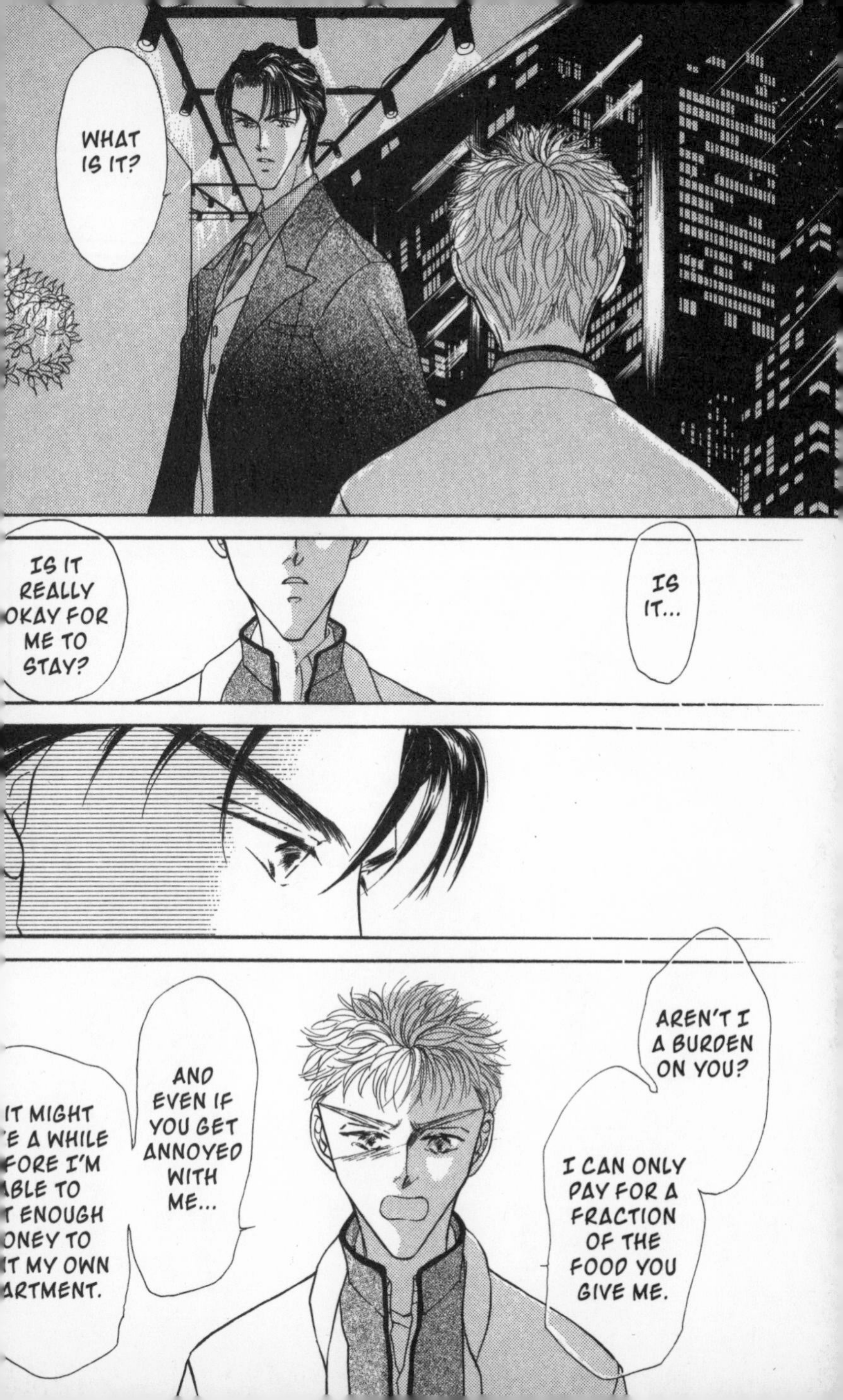
WHAT IS IT?
IS IT...
IS IT REALLY OKAY FOR ME TO STAY?
AREN'T I A BURDEN ON YOU?
I CAN ONLY PAY FOR A FRACTION OF THE FOOD YOU GIVE ME.
AND EVEN IF YOU GET ANNOYED WITH ME...
IT MIGHT 'E A WHILE FORE I'M ABLE TO T ENOUGH ONEY TO IT MY OWN ARTMENT.

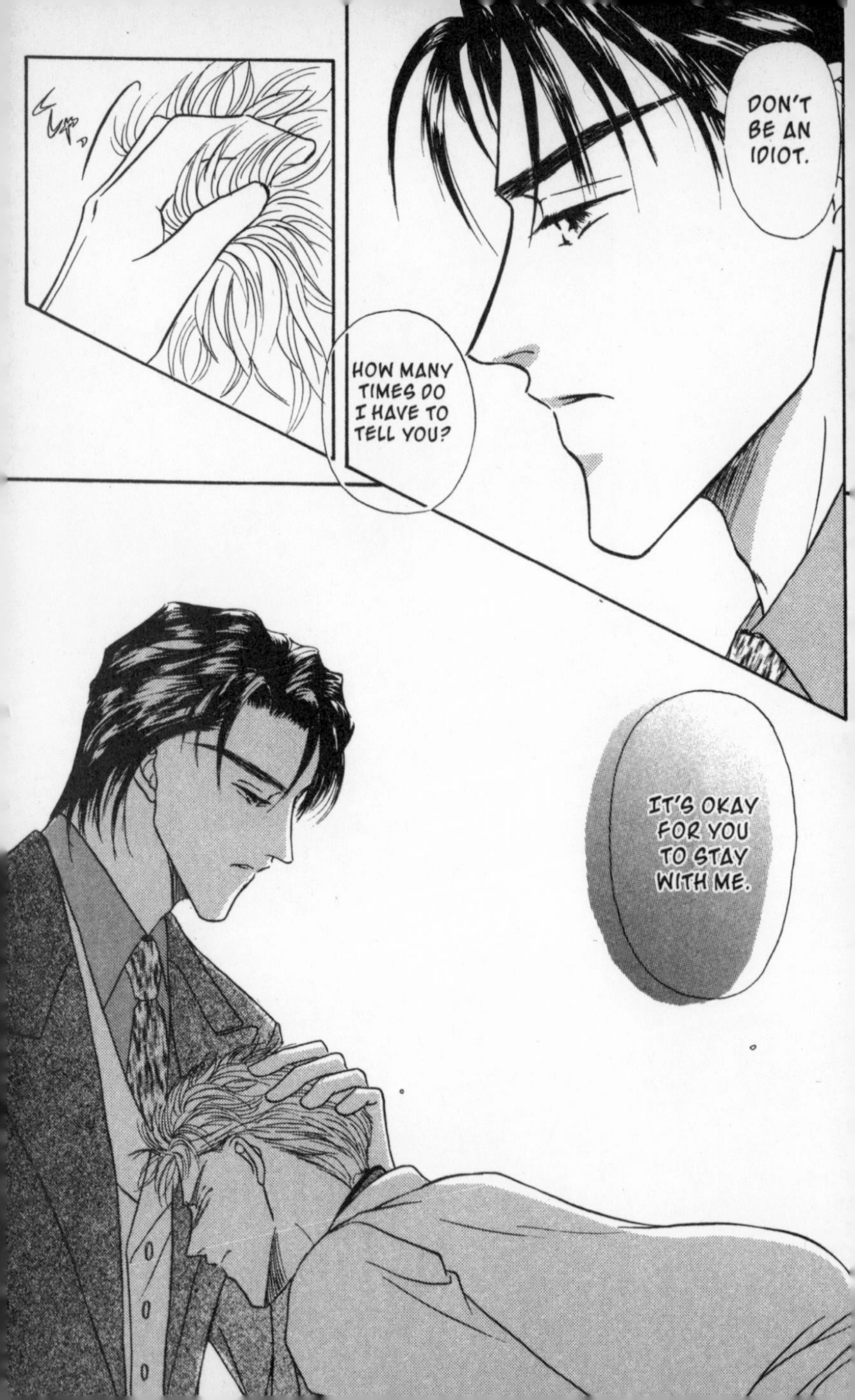
DON'T BE AN IDIOT.
HOW MANY TIMES DO I HAVE TO TELL YOU?
IT'S OKAY FOR YOU TO STAY WITH ME.

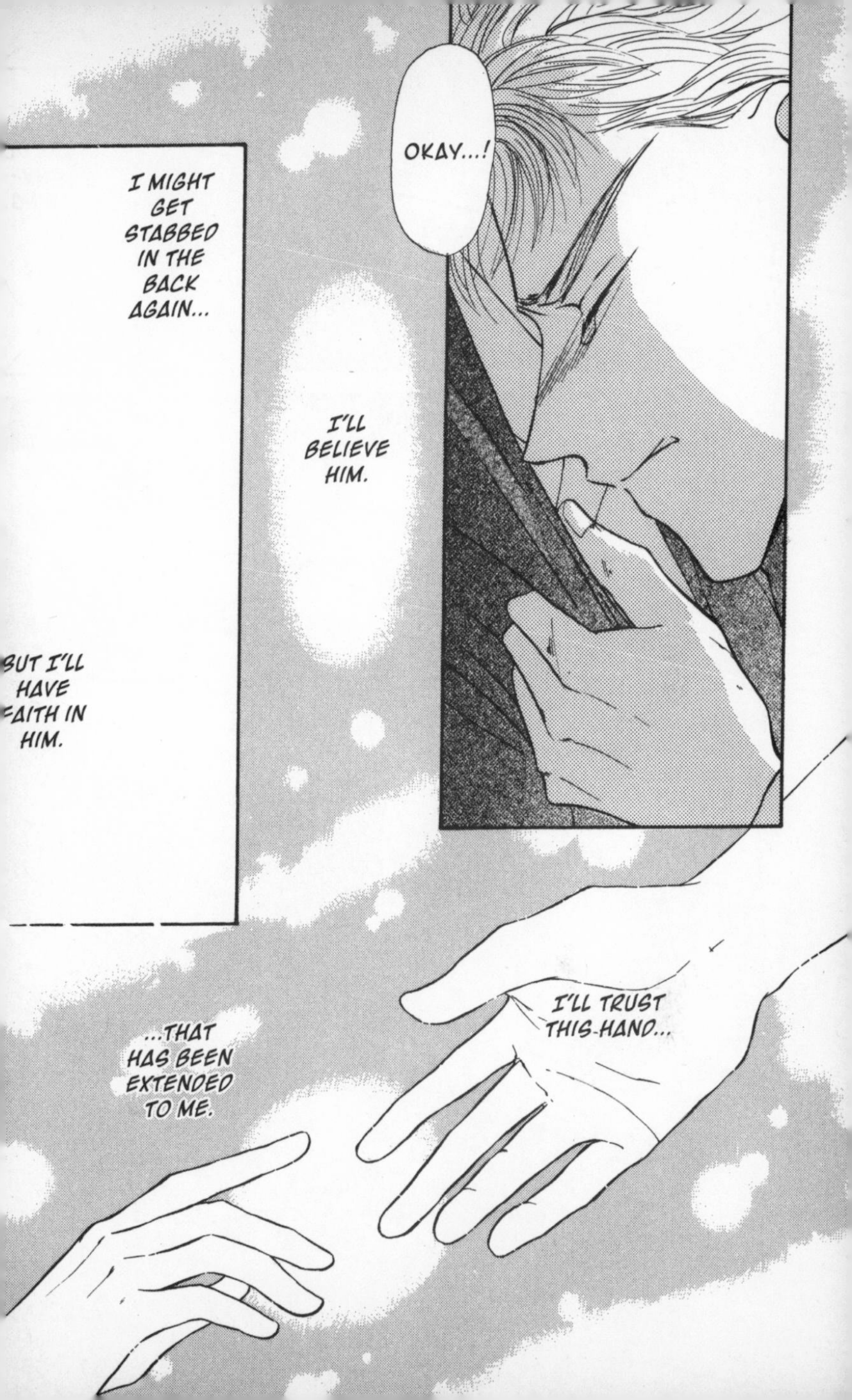
OKAY...!
I'LL BELIEVE HIM.
I MIGHT GET STABBED IN THE BACK AGAIN...
BUT I'LL HAVE FAITH IN HIM.
I'LL TRUST THIS HAND...
...THAT HAS BEEN EXTENDED TO ME.

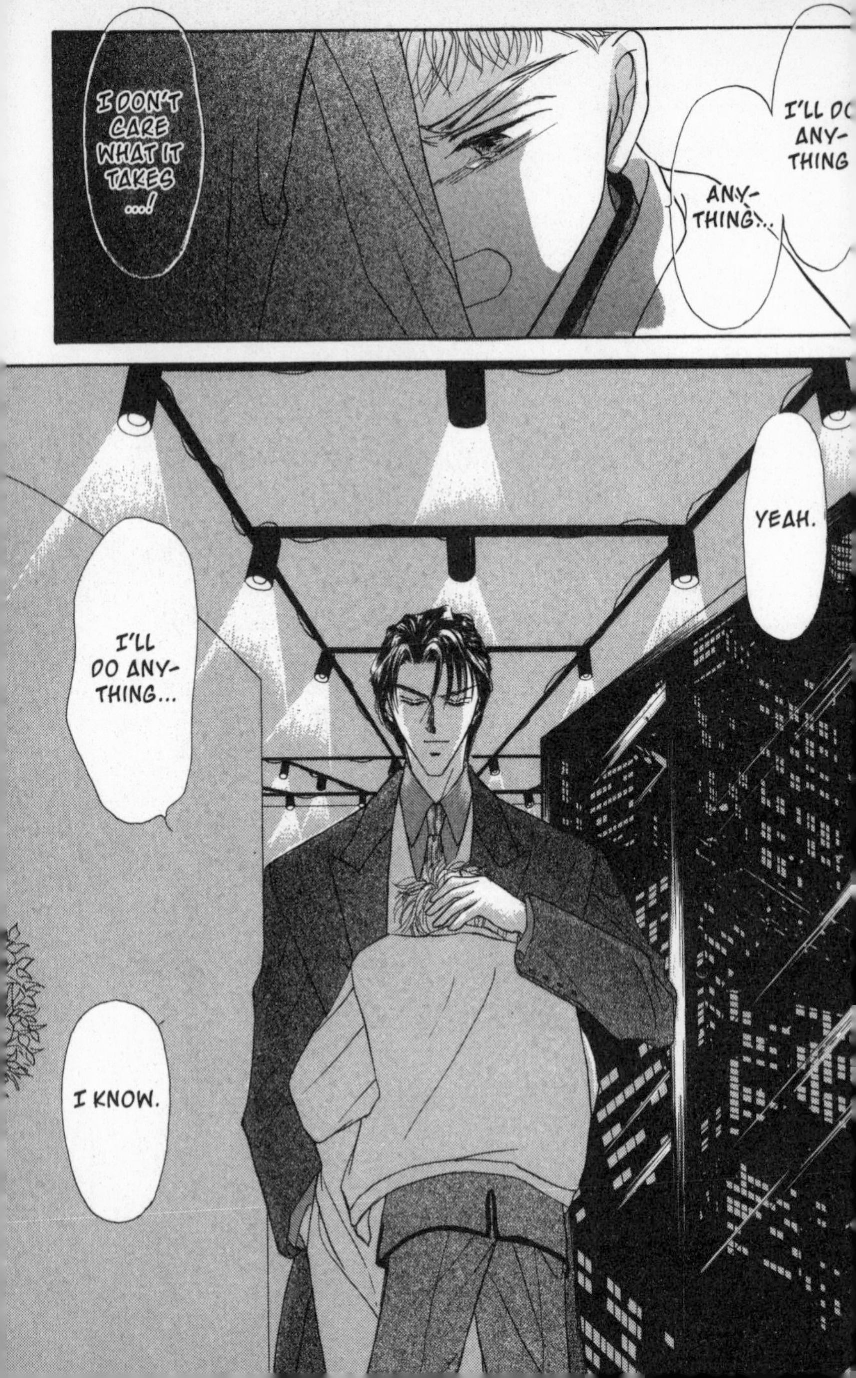
I'LL DO ANYTHING
ANY-THING...
I DON'T CARE WHAT IT TAKES ...!
YEAH.
I'LL DO ANY-THING...
I KNOW.

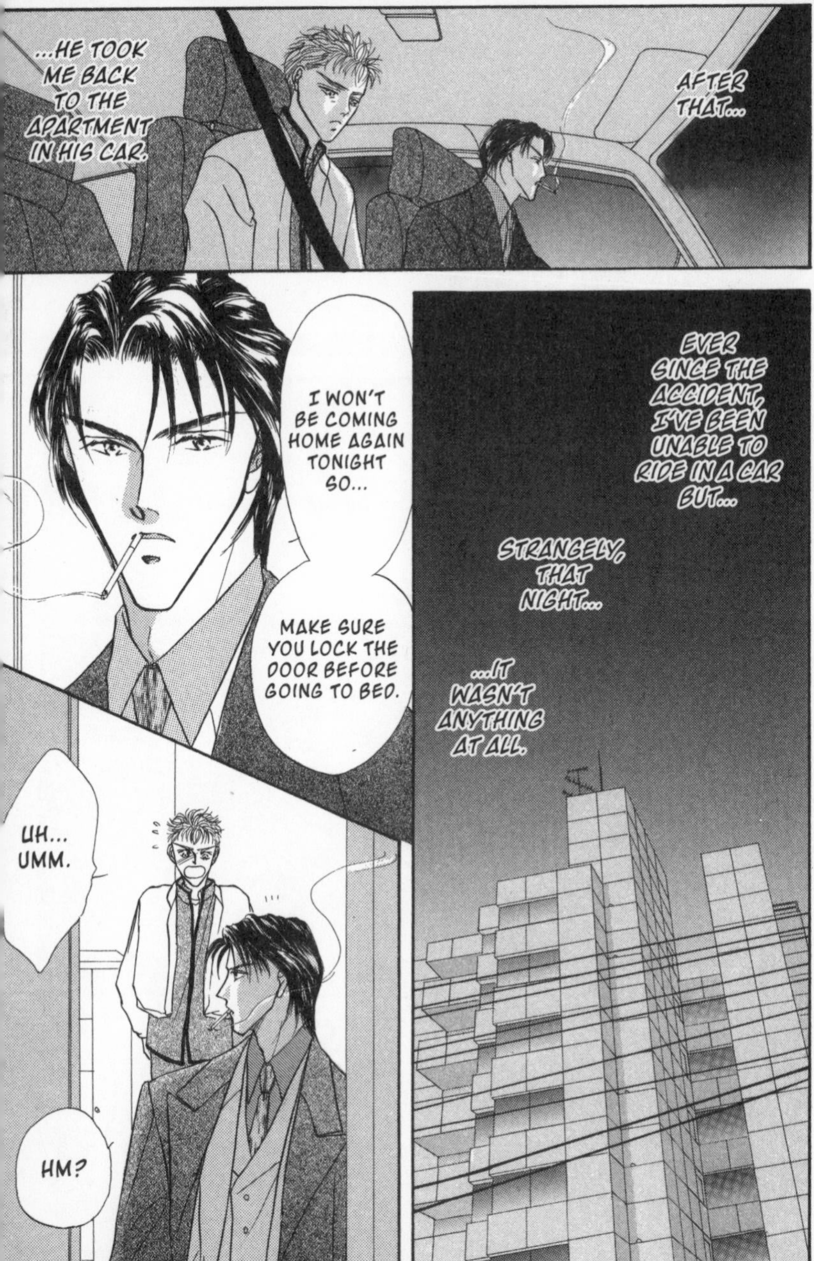
AFTER THAT...
...HE TOOK ME BACK TO THE APARTMENT IN HIS CAR.
EVER SINCE THE ACCIDENT, I'VE BEEN UNABLE TO RIDE IN A CAR BUT...
STRANGELY, THAT NIGHT...
...IT WASN'T ANYTHING AT ALL.
I WON'T BE COMING HOME AGAIN TONIGHT SO...
MAKE SURE YOU LOCK THE DOOR BEFORE GOING TO BED.
UH... UMM.
HM?

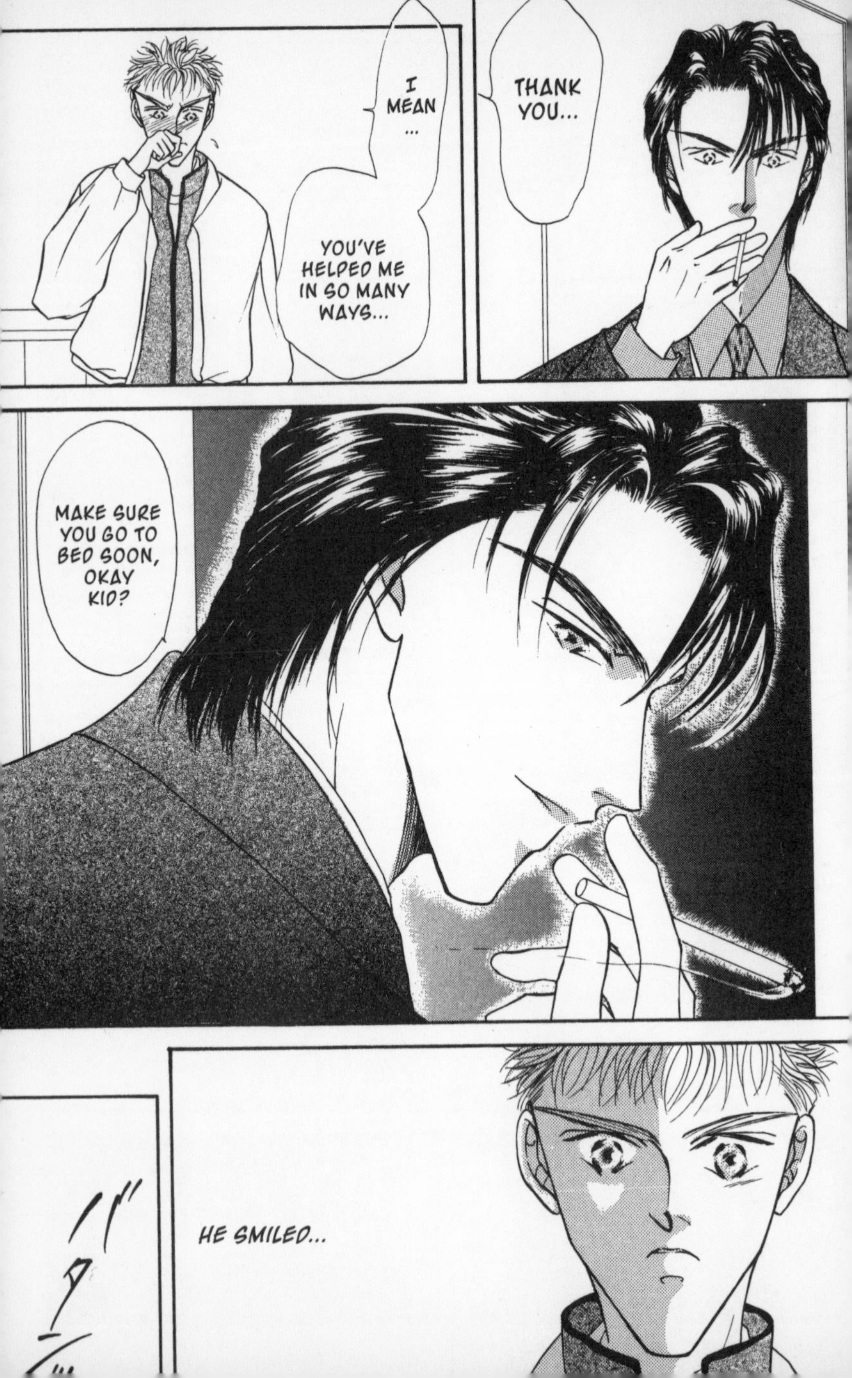
THANK YOU...
I MEAN ...
YOU'VE HELPED ME IN SO MANY WAYS...
MAKE SURE YOU GO TO BED SOON, OKAY KID?
HE SMILED...

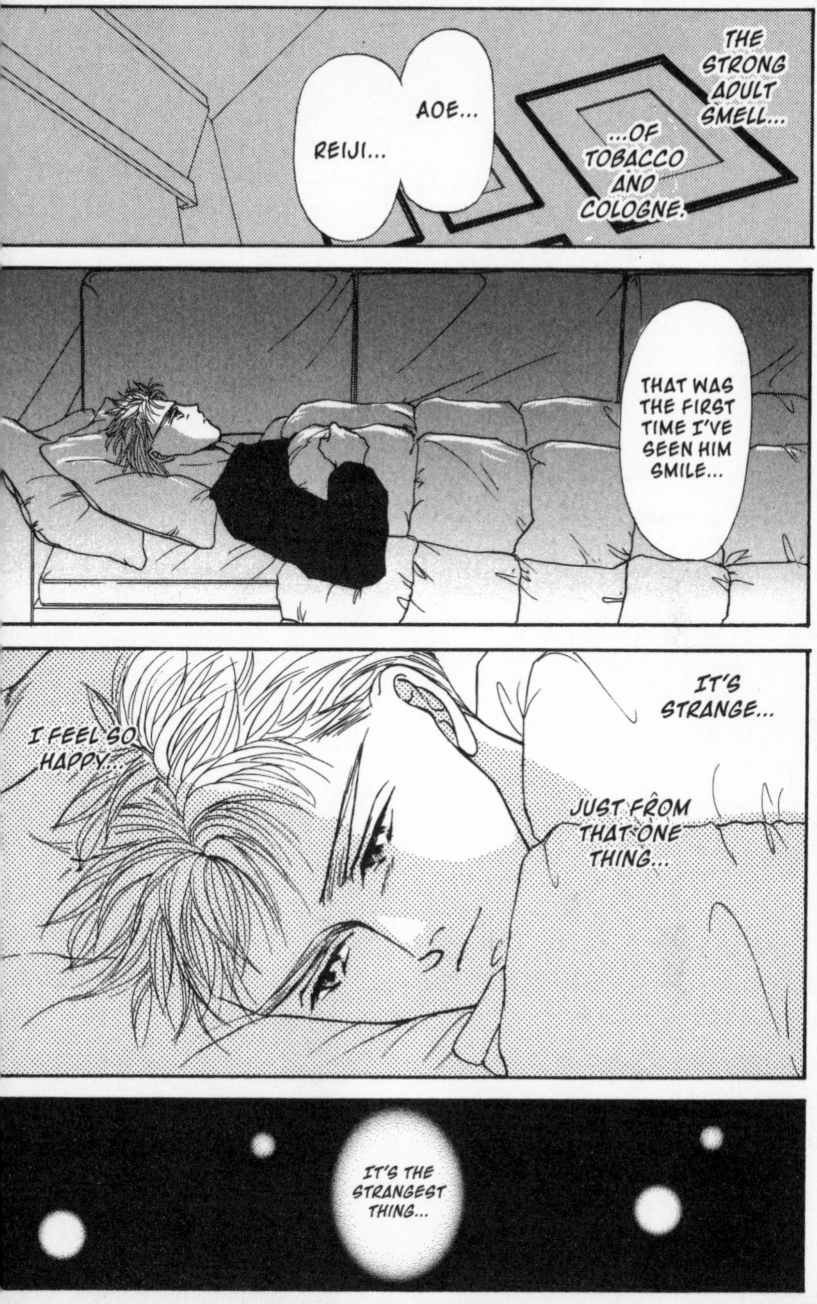
THE STRONG ADULT SMELL...
...OF TOBACCO AND COLOGNE.
AOE...
REIJI...
THAT WAS THE FIRST TIME I'VE SEEN HIM SMILE...
IT'S STRANGE...
JUST FROM THAT ONE THING...
I FEEL SO HAPPY...
IT'S THE STRANGEST THING...

Christmas Children

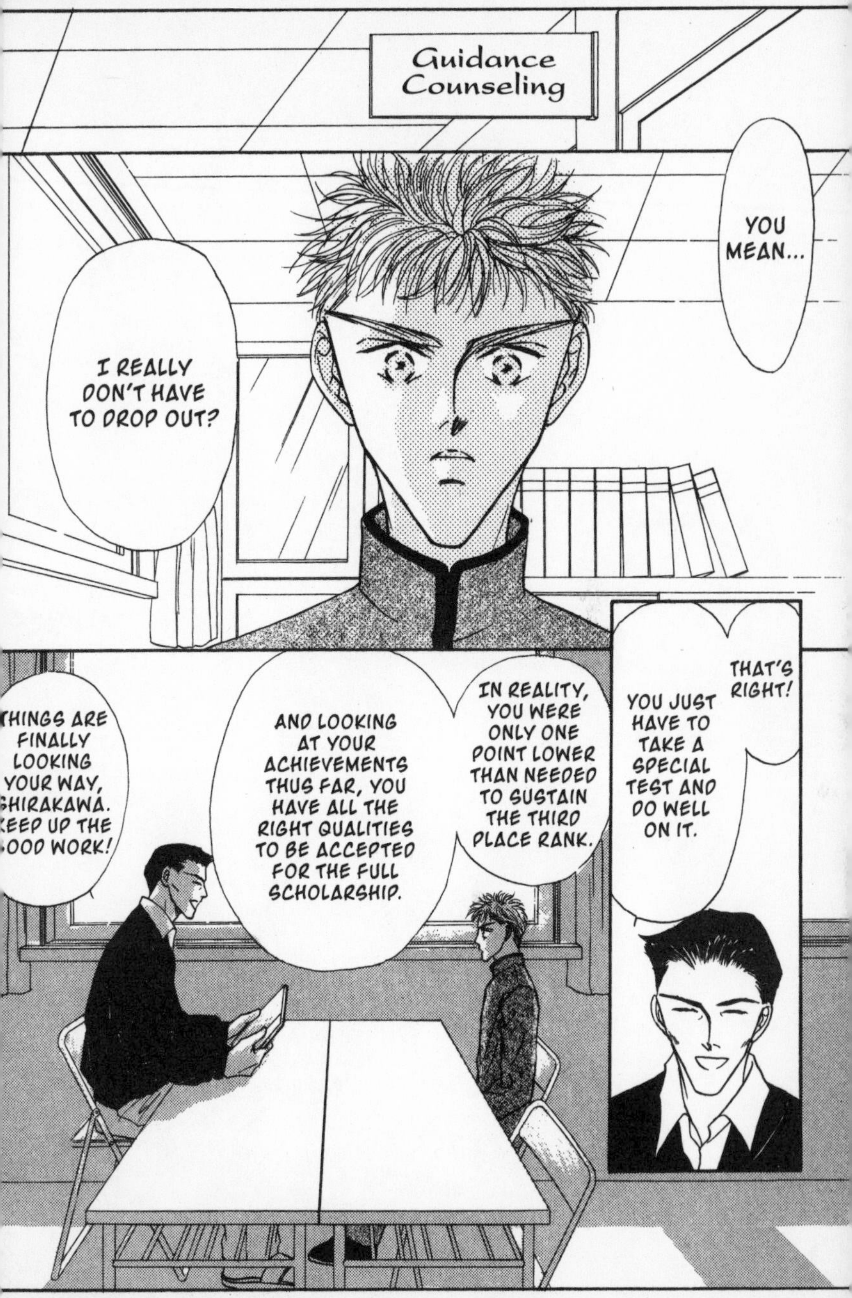
Guidance Counseling
YOU MEAN...
I REALLY DON'T HAVE TO DROP OUT?
THAT'S RIGHT!
YOU JUST HAVE TO TAKE A SPECIAL TEST AND DO WELL ON IT.
IN REALITY, YOU WERE ONLY ONE POINT LOWER THAN NEEDED TO SUSTAIN THE THIRD PLACE RANK.
AND LOOKING AT YOUR ACHIEVEMENTS THUS FAR, YOU HAVE ALL THE RIGHT QUALITIES TO BE ACCEPTED FOR THE FULL SCHOLARSHIP.
THINGS ARE FINALLY LOOKING YOUR WAY, SHIRAKAWA. KEEP UP THE GOOD WORK!

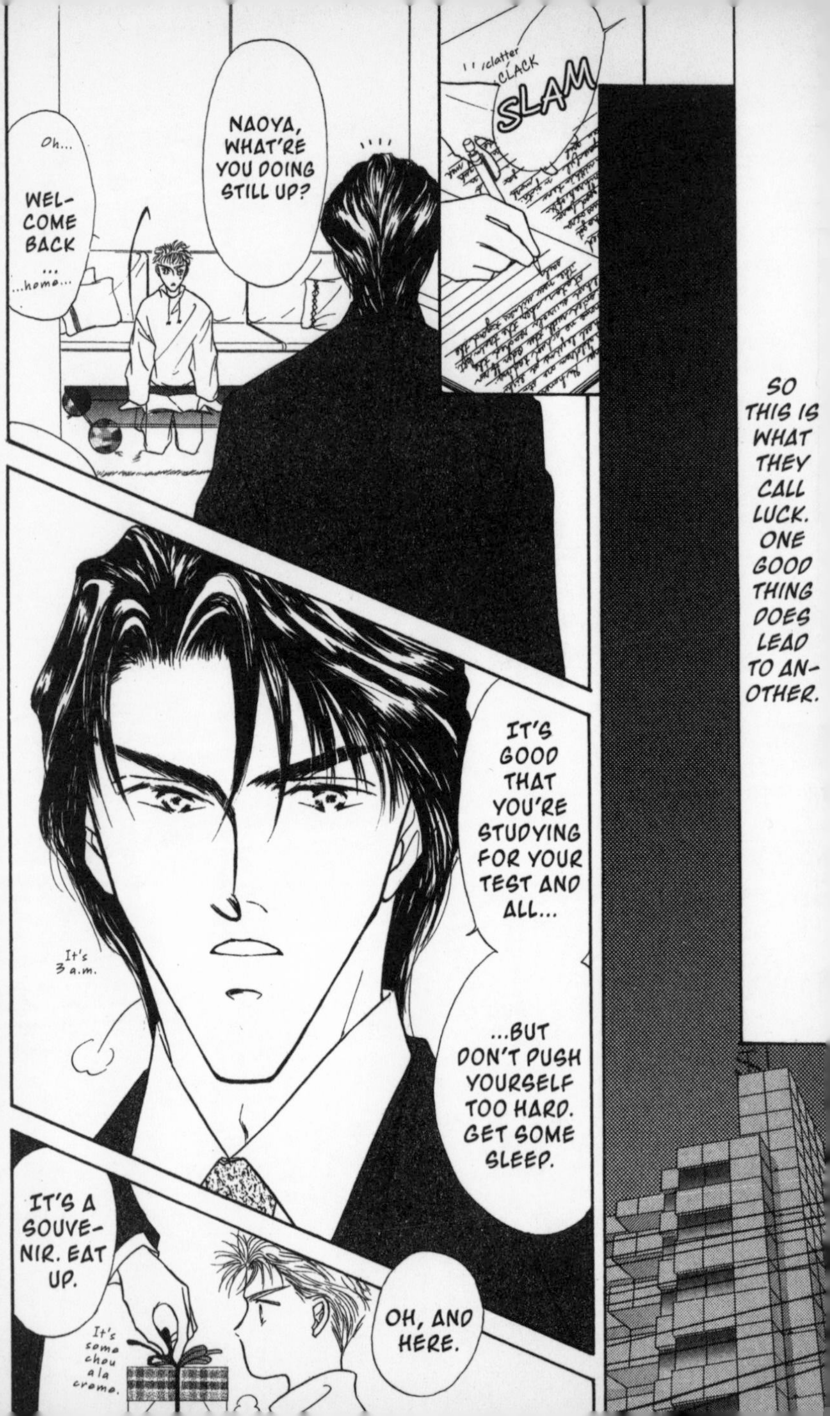
SO THIS IS WHAT THEY CALL LUCK. ONE GOOD THING DOES LEAD TO ANOTHER.
clatter CLACK
SLAM
NAOYA, WHAT'RE YOU DOING STILL UP?
Oh... WEL-COME BACK ... ...home...
IT'S GOOD THAT YOU'RE STUDYING FOR YOUR TEST AND ALL...
...BUT DON'T PUSH YOURSELF TOO HARD. GET SOME SLEEP.
It's 3 a.m.
OH, AND HERE.
IT'S A SOUVE-NIR. EAT UP.
It's some chou a la creme.

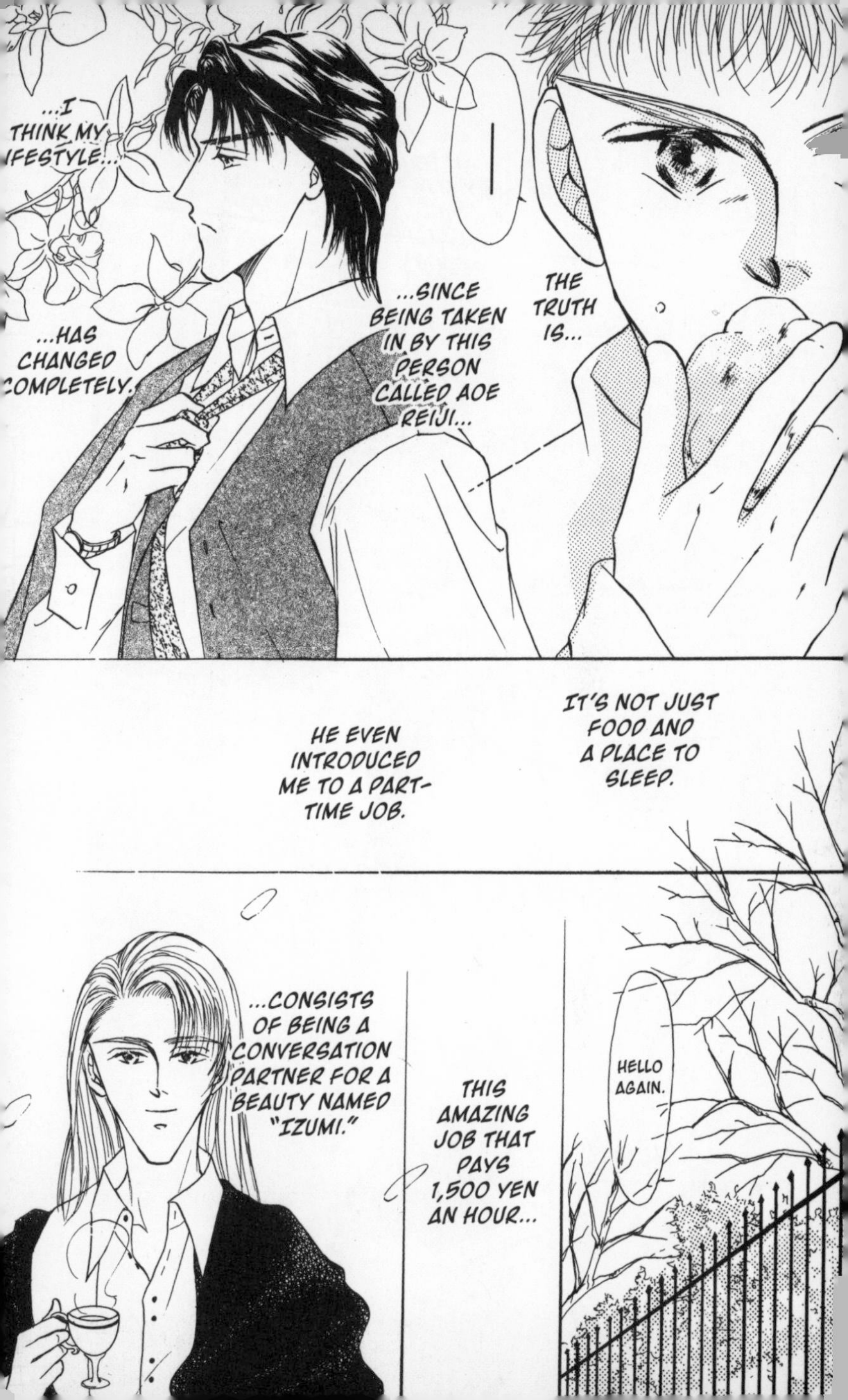
THE TRUTH IS...
...SINCE BEING TAKEN IN BY THIS PERSON CALLED AOE REIJI...
...I THINK MY IFESTYLE...
...HAS CHANGED OMPLETELY.
IT'S NOT JUST FOOD AND A PLACE TO SLEEP.
HE EVEN INTRODUCED ME TO A PART-TIME JOB.
HELLO AGAIN.
THIS AMAZING JOB THAT PAYS 1,500 YEN AN HOUR...
...CONSISTS OF BEING A CONVERSATION PARTNER FOR A BEAUTY NAMED "IZUMI."

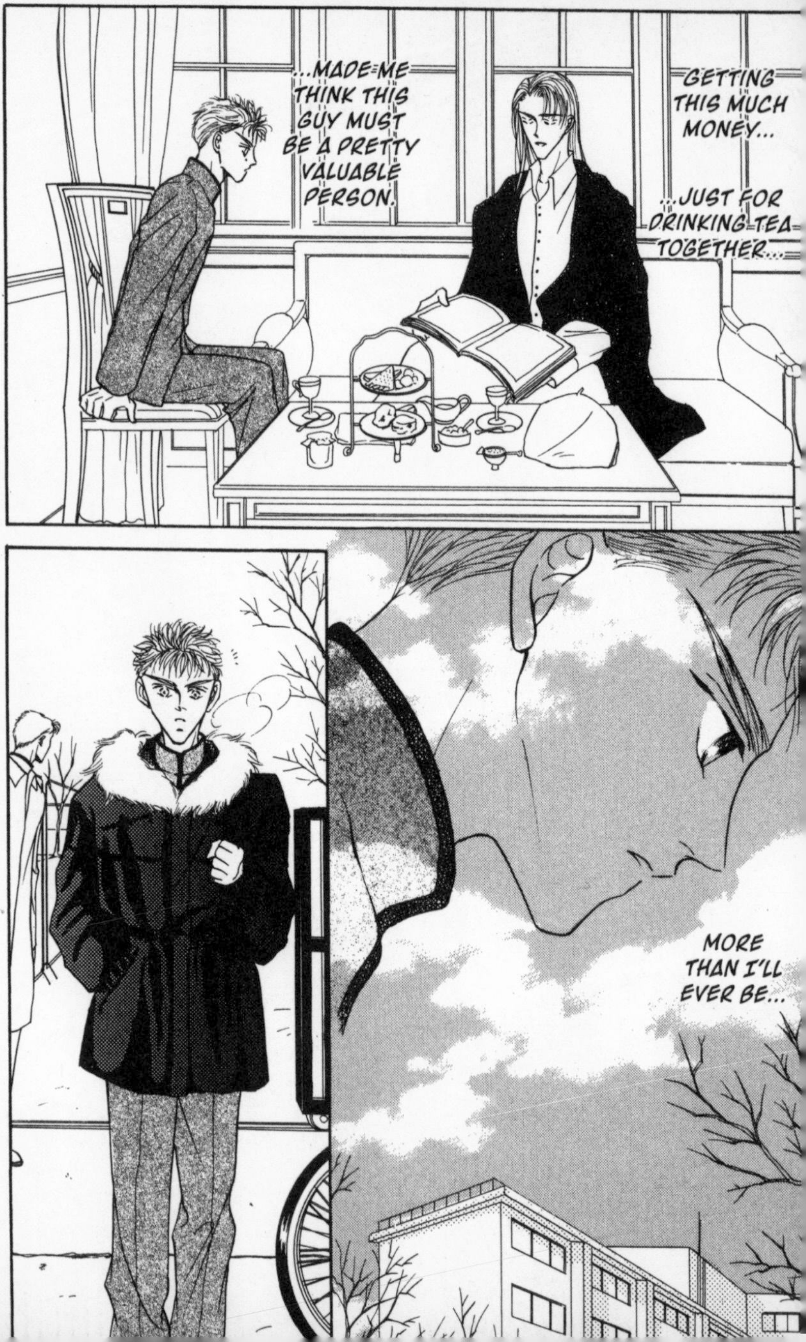
GETTING THIS MUCH MONEY...
...JUST FOR DRINKING TEA TOGETHER...
...MADE ME THINK THIS GUY MUST BE A PRETTY VALUABLE PERSON.
MORE THAN I'LL EVER BE...

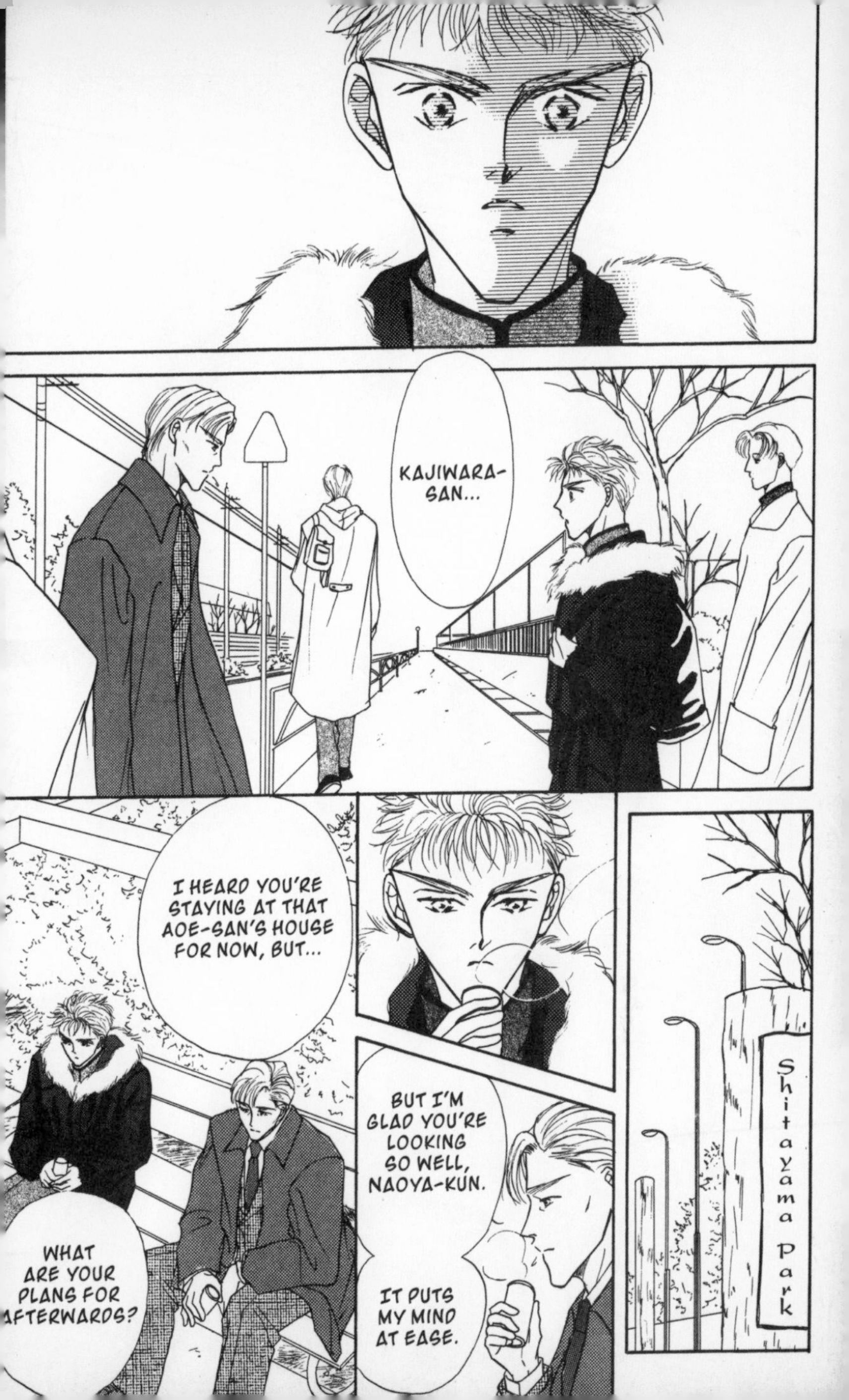
KAJIWARA-SAN...
Shitayama Park
BUT I'M GLAD YOU'RE LOOKING SO WELL, NAOYA-KUN.
IT PUTS MY MIND AT EASE.
I HEARD YOU'RE STAYING AT THAT AOE-SAN'S HOUSE FOR NOW, BUT...
WHAT ARE YOUR PLANS FOR AFTERWARDS?

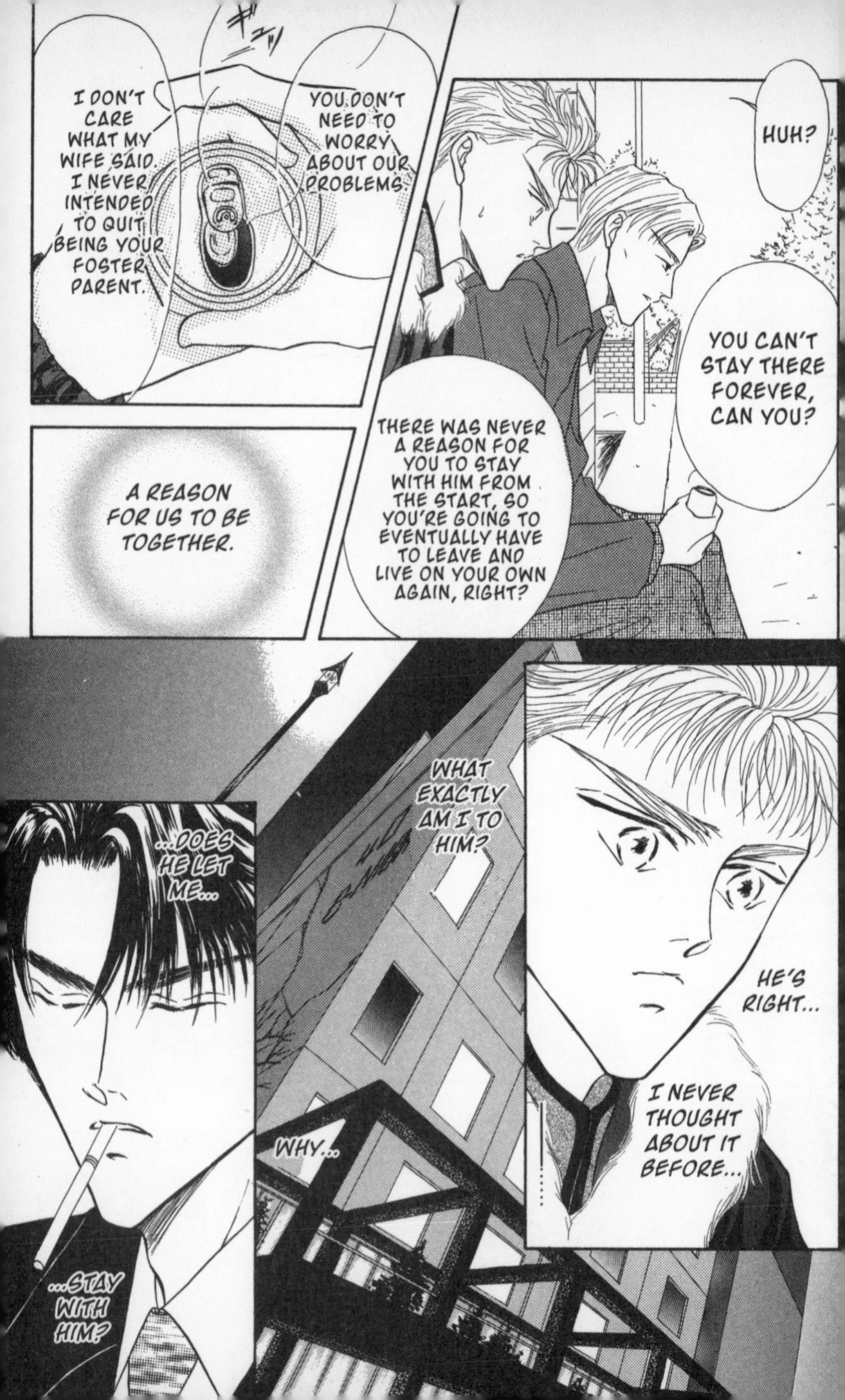
HUH?
YOU CAN'T STAY THERE FOREVER, CAN YOU?
THERE WAS NEVER A REASON FOR YOU TO STAY WITH HIM FROM THE START, SO YOU'RE GOING TO EVENTUALLY HAVE TO LEAVE AND LIVE ON YOUR OWN AGAIN, RIGHT?
YOU DON'T NEED TO WORRY ABOUT OUR PROBLEMS.
I DON'T CARE WHAT MY WIFE SAID. I NEVER INTENDED TO QUIT BEING YOUR FOSTER PARENT.
A REASON FOR US TO BE TOGETHER.
HE'S RIGHT...
I NEVER THOUGHT ABOUT IT BEFORE...
WHAT EXACTLY AM I TO HIM?
WHY...
...DOES HE LET ME...
...STAY WITH HIM?

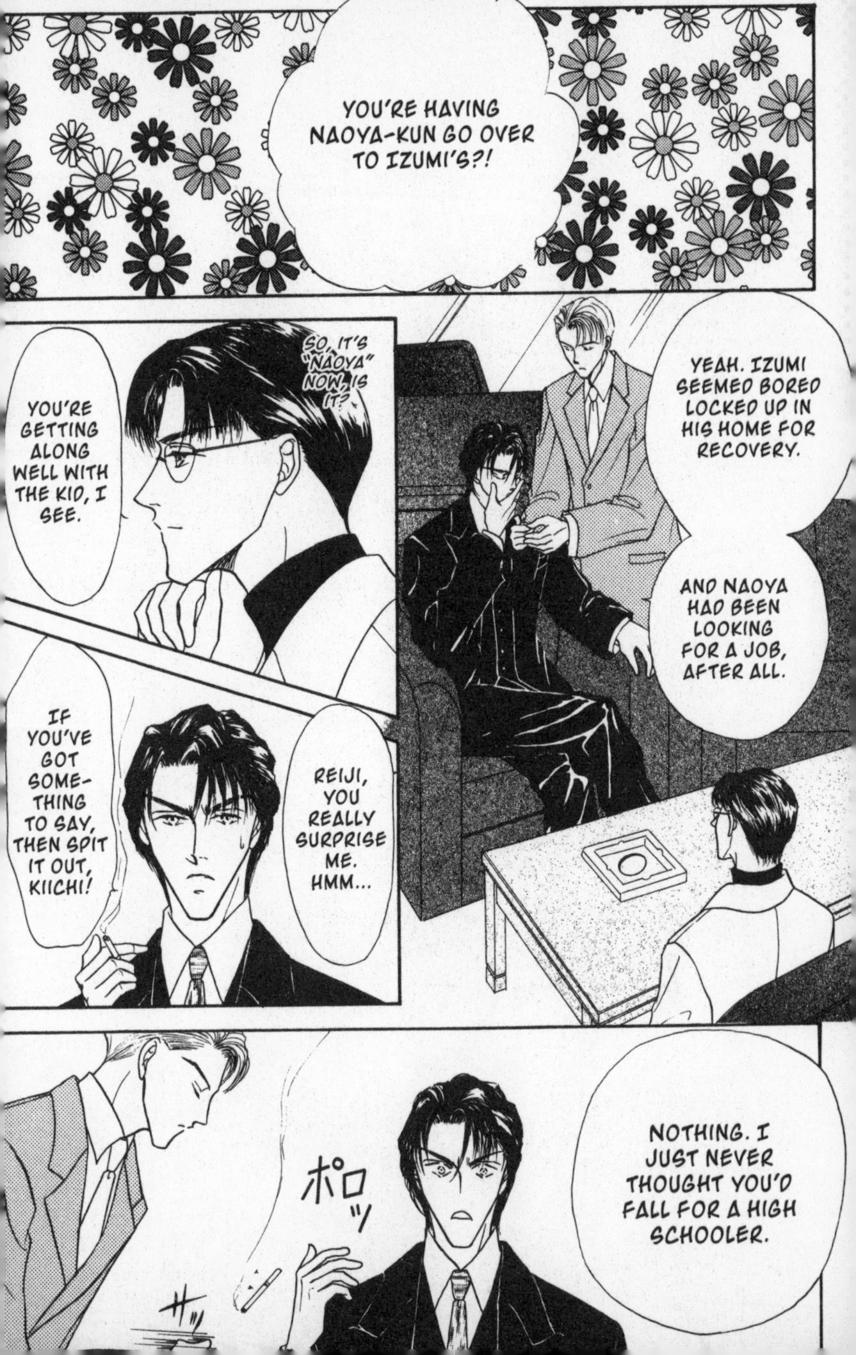
YOU'RE HAVING NAOYA-KUN GO OVER TO IZUMI'S?!
YEAH. IZUMI SEEMED BORED LOCKED UP IN HIS HOME FOR RECOVERY.
AND NAOYA HAD BEEN LOOKING FOR A JOB, AFTER ALL.
SO, IT'S "NAOYA" NOW, IS IT?
YOU'RE GETTING ALONG WELL WITH THE KID, I SEE.
REIJI, YOU REALLY SURPRISE ME. HMM...
IF YOU'VE GOT SOME-THING TO SAY, THEN SPIT IT OUT, KIICHI!
NOTHING. I JUST NEVER THOUGHT YOU'D FALL FOR A HIGH SCHOOLER.
ポロッ
サッ

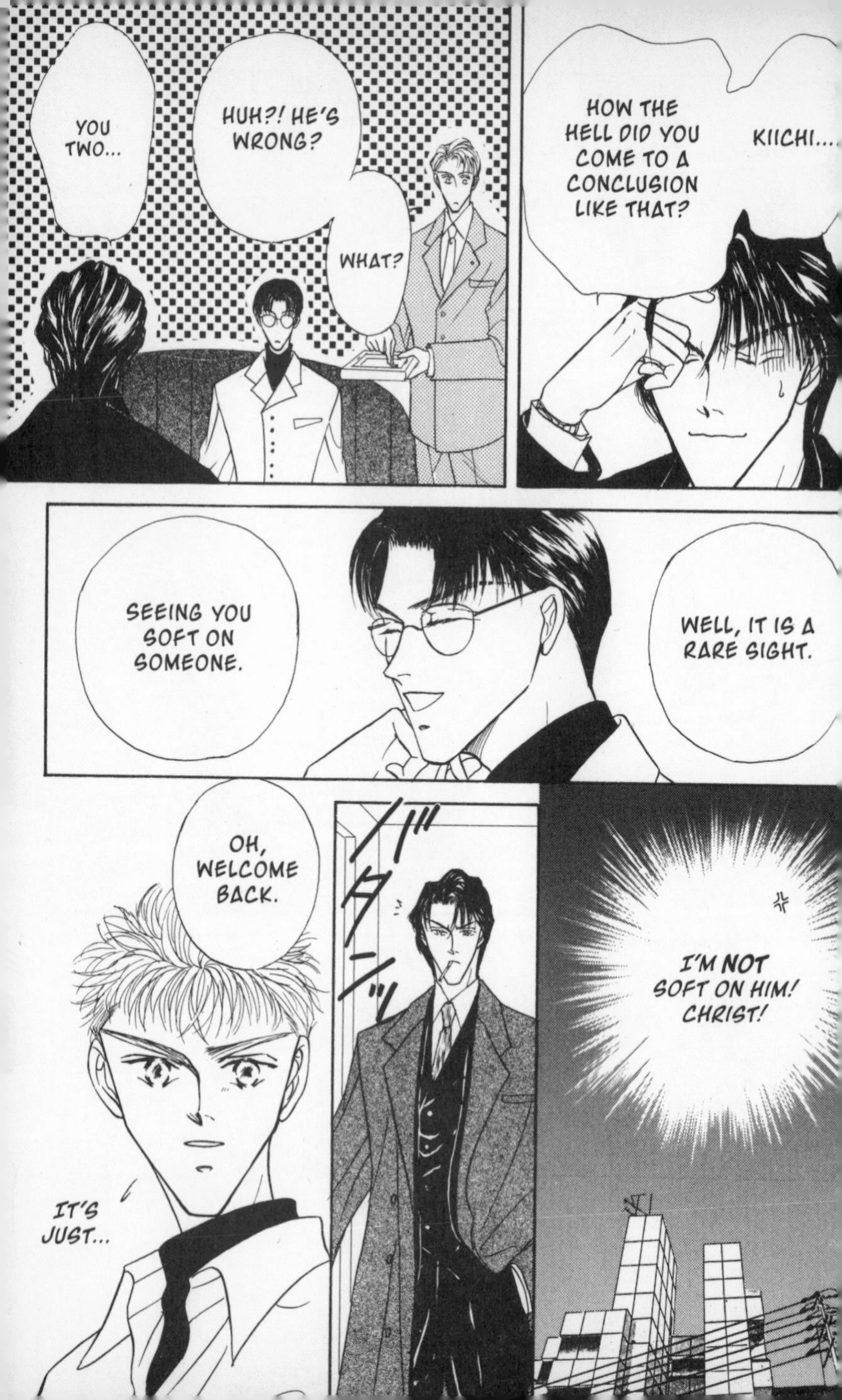
KIICHI....
HOW THE HELL DID YOU COME TO A CONCLUSION LIKE THAT?
HUH?! HE'S WRONG?
WHAT?
YOU TWO...
WELL, IT IS A RARE SIGHT.
SEEING YOU SOFT ON SOMEONE.
I'M **NOT** SOFT ON HIM! CHRIST!
バタンッ
OH, WELCOME BACK.
IT'S JUST...

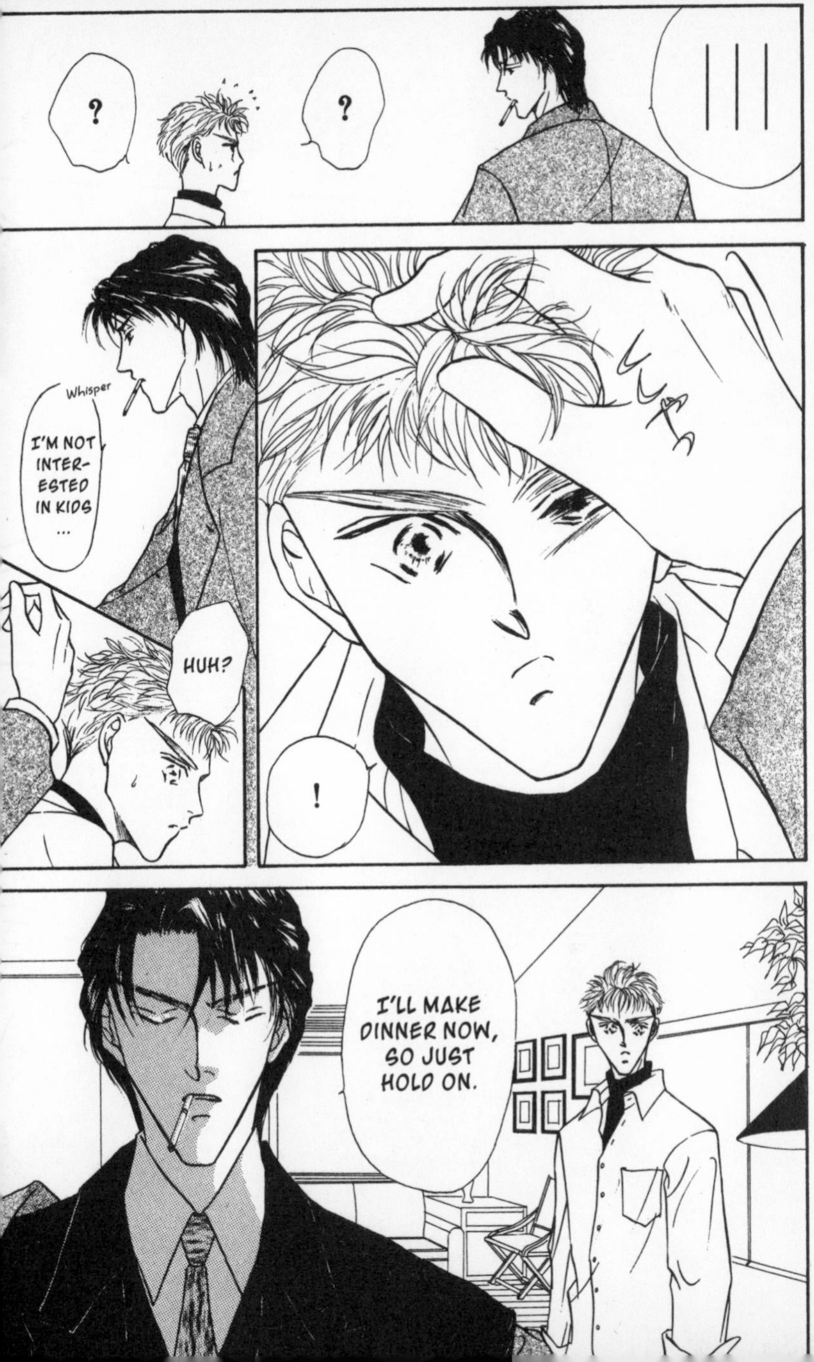
?
?
!
Whisper
I'M NOT INTERESTED IN KIDS ...
HUH?
I'LL MAKE DINNER NOW, SO JUST HOLD ON.

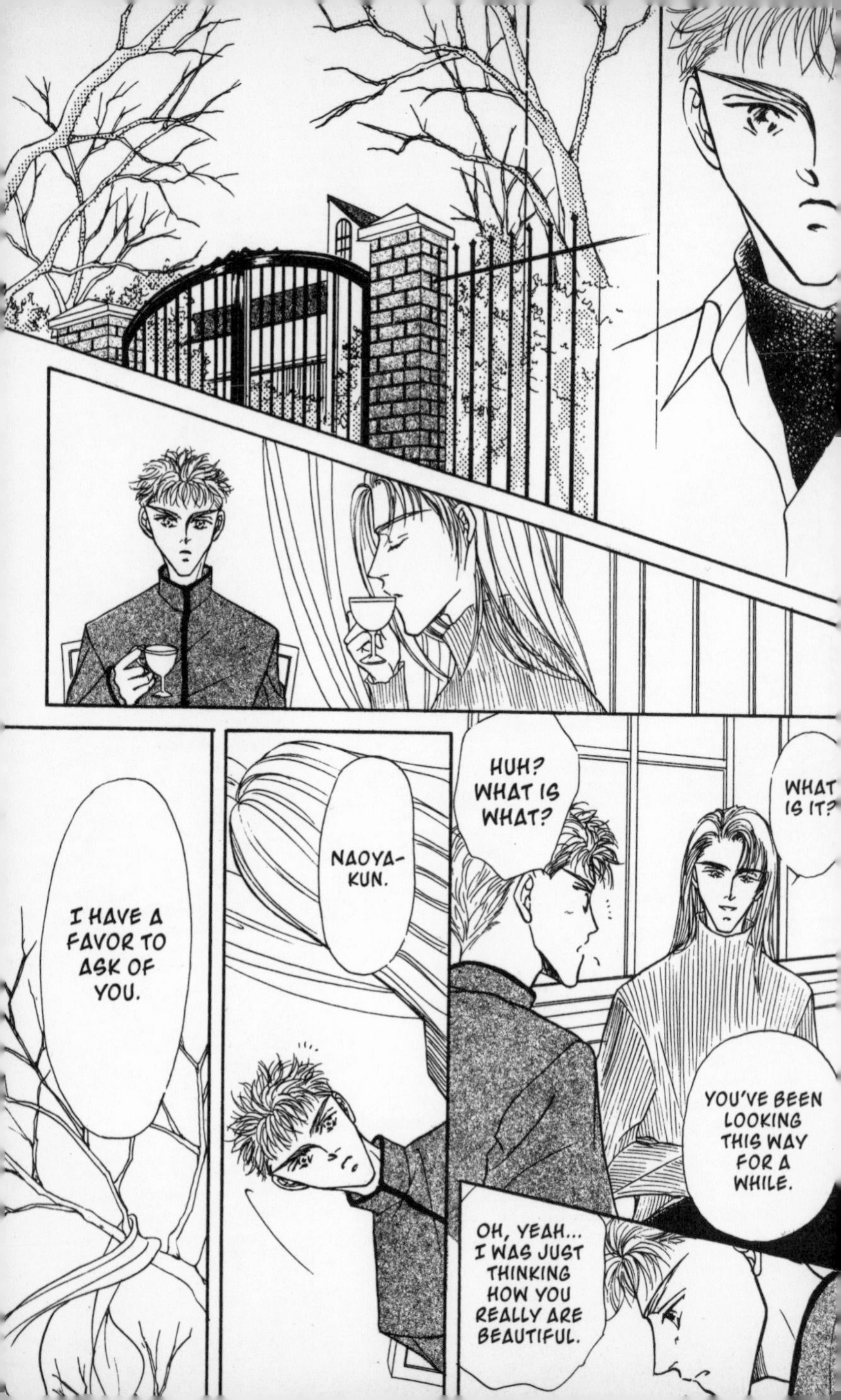
WHAT IS IT?
HUH? WHAT IS WHAT?
YOU'VE BEEN LOOKING THIS WAY FOR A WHILE.
OH, YEAH... I WAS JUST THINKING HOW YOU REALLY ARE BEAUTIFUL.
NAOYA-KUN.
I HAVE A FAVOR TO ASK OF YOU.

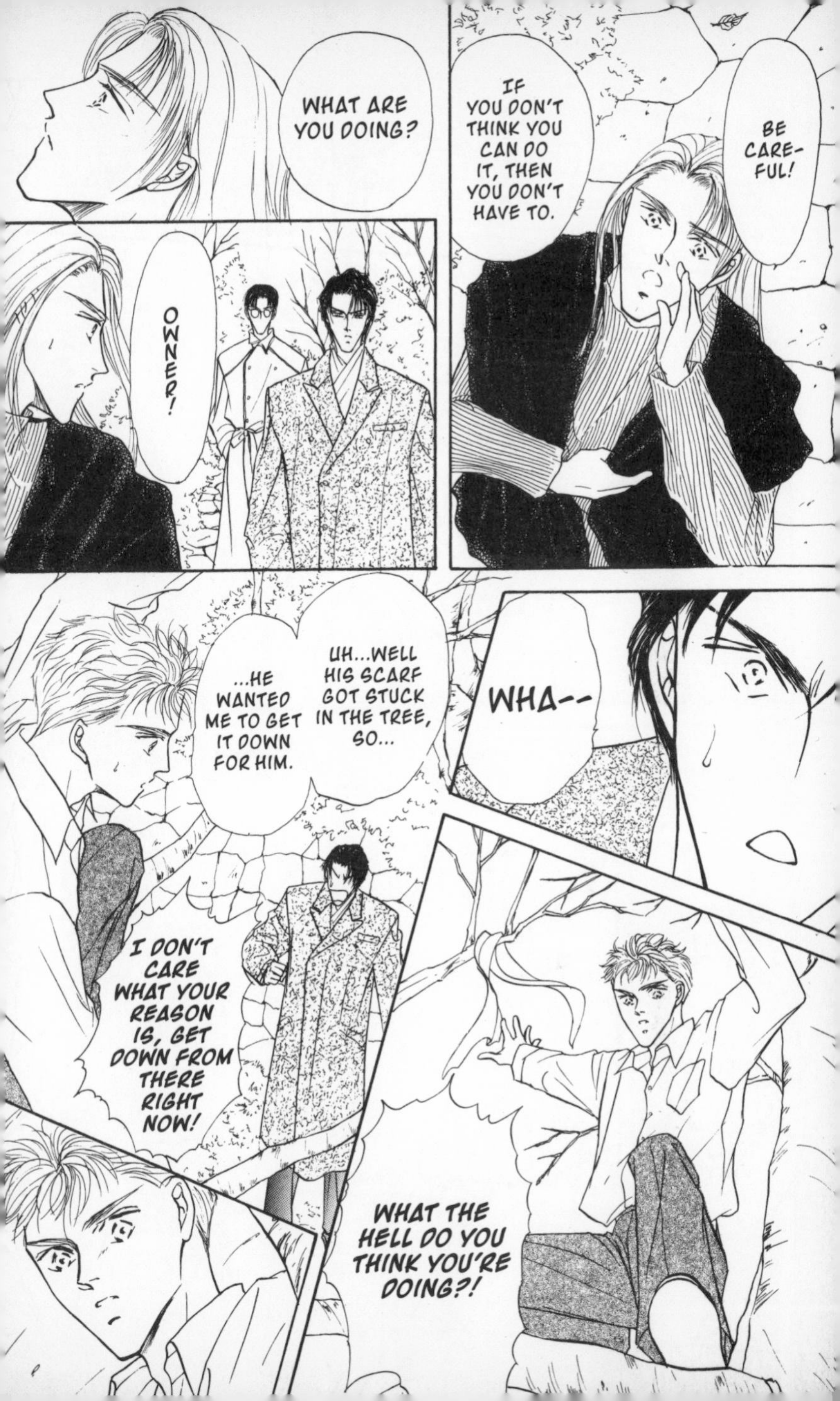
BE CARE-FUL!
IF YOU DON'T THINK YOU CAN DO IT, THEN YOU DON'T HAVE TO.
WHAT ARE YOU DOING?
OWNER!
WHA--
WHAT THE HELL DO YOU THINK YOU'RE DOING?!
UH...WELL HIS SCARF GOT STUCK IN THE TREE, SO...
...HE WANTED ME TO GET IT DOWN FOR HIM.
I DON'T CARE WHAT YOUR REASON IS, GET DOWN FROM THERE RIGHT NOW!

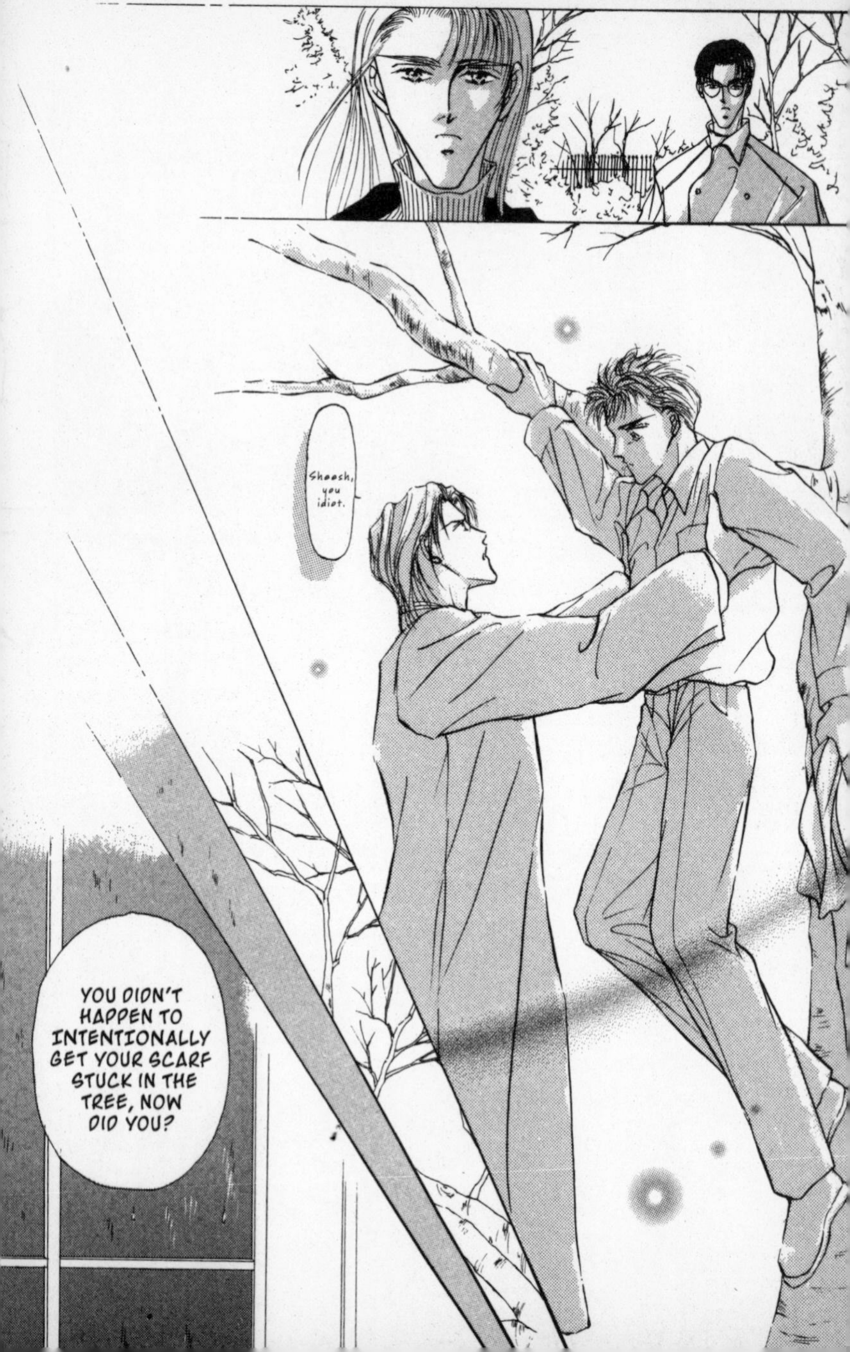
Sheesh, you idiot.
YOU DIDN'T HAPPEN TO INTENTIONALLY GET YOUR SCARF STUCK IN THE TREE, NOW DID YOU?

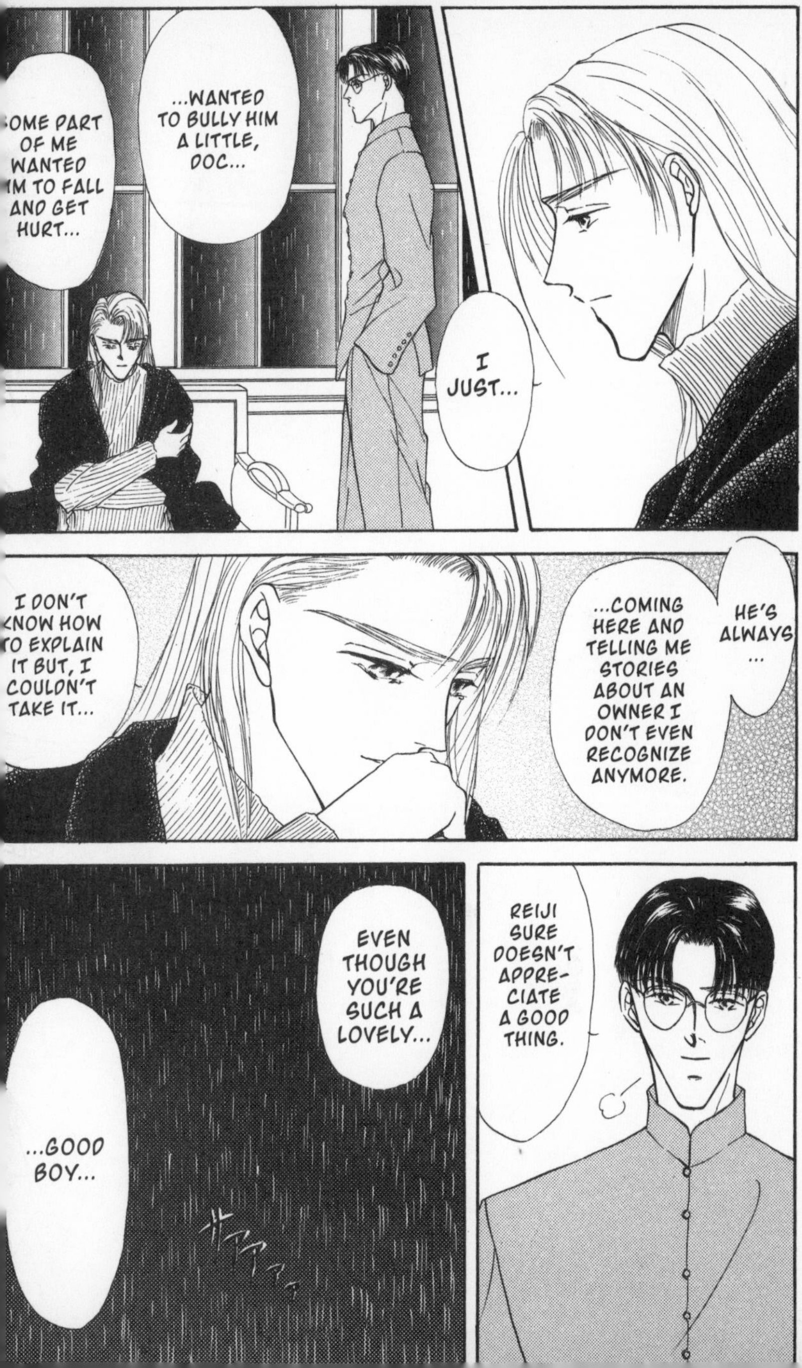
I JUST...
...WANTED TO BULLY HIM A LITTLE, DOC...
OME PART OF ME WANTED IM TO FALL AND GET HURT...
HE'S ALWAYS ...
...COMING HERE AND TELLING ME STORIES ABOUT AN OWNER I DON'T EVEN RECOGNIZE ANYMORE.
I DON'T KNOW HOW O EXPLAIN IT BUT, I COULDN'T TAKE IT...
REIJI SURE DOESN'T APPRE-CIATE A GOOD THING.
EVEN THOUGH YOU'RE SUCH A LOVELY...
...GOOD BOY...

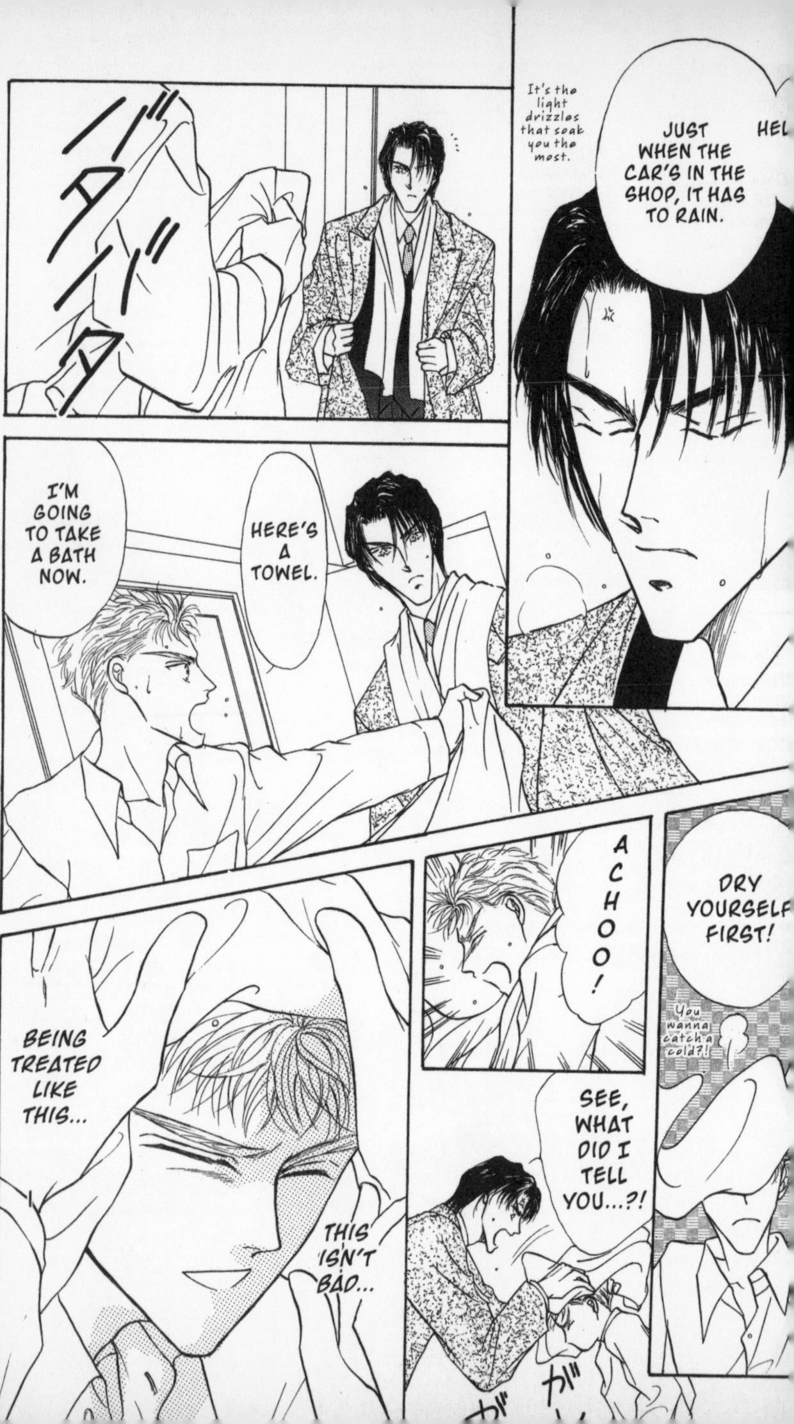
It's the light drizzles that soak you the most.
JUST WHEN THE CAR'S IN THE SHOP, IT HAS TO RAIN.
バタバタ
HERE'S A TOWEL.
I'M GOING TO TAKE A BATH NOW.
DRY YOURSELF FIRST!
You wanna catch a cold?!
ACHOO!
SEE, WHAT DID I TELL YOU...?!
ガ ガ
BEING TREATED LIKE THIS...
THIS ISN'T BAD...

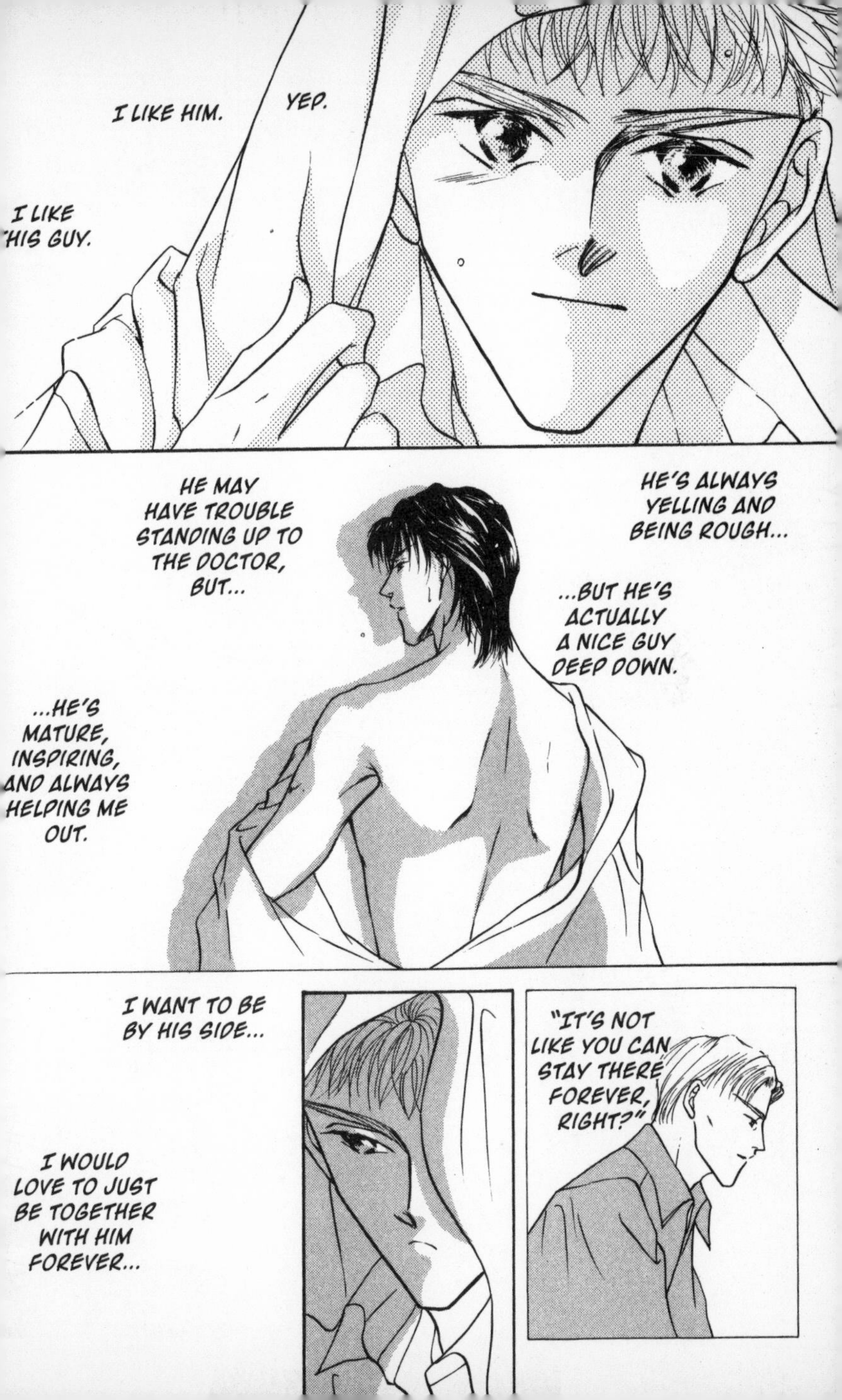
YEP.
I LIKE HIM.
I LIKE HIS GUY.
HE'S ALWAYS YELLING AND BEING ROUGH...
...BUT HE'S ACTUALLY A NICE GUY DEEP DOWN.
HE MAY HAVE TROUBLE STANDING UP TO THE DOCTOR, BUT...
...HE'S MATURE, INSPIRING, ND ALWAYS HELPING ME OUT.
"IT'S NOT LIKE YOU CAN STAY THERE FOREVER, RIGHT?"
I WANT TO BE BY HIS SIDE...
I WOULD LOVE TO JUST BE TOGETHER WITH HIM FOREVER...

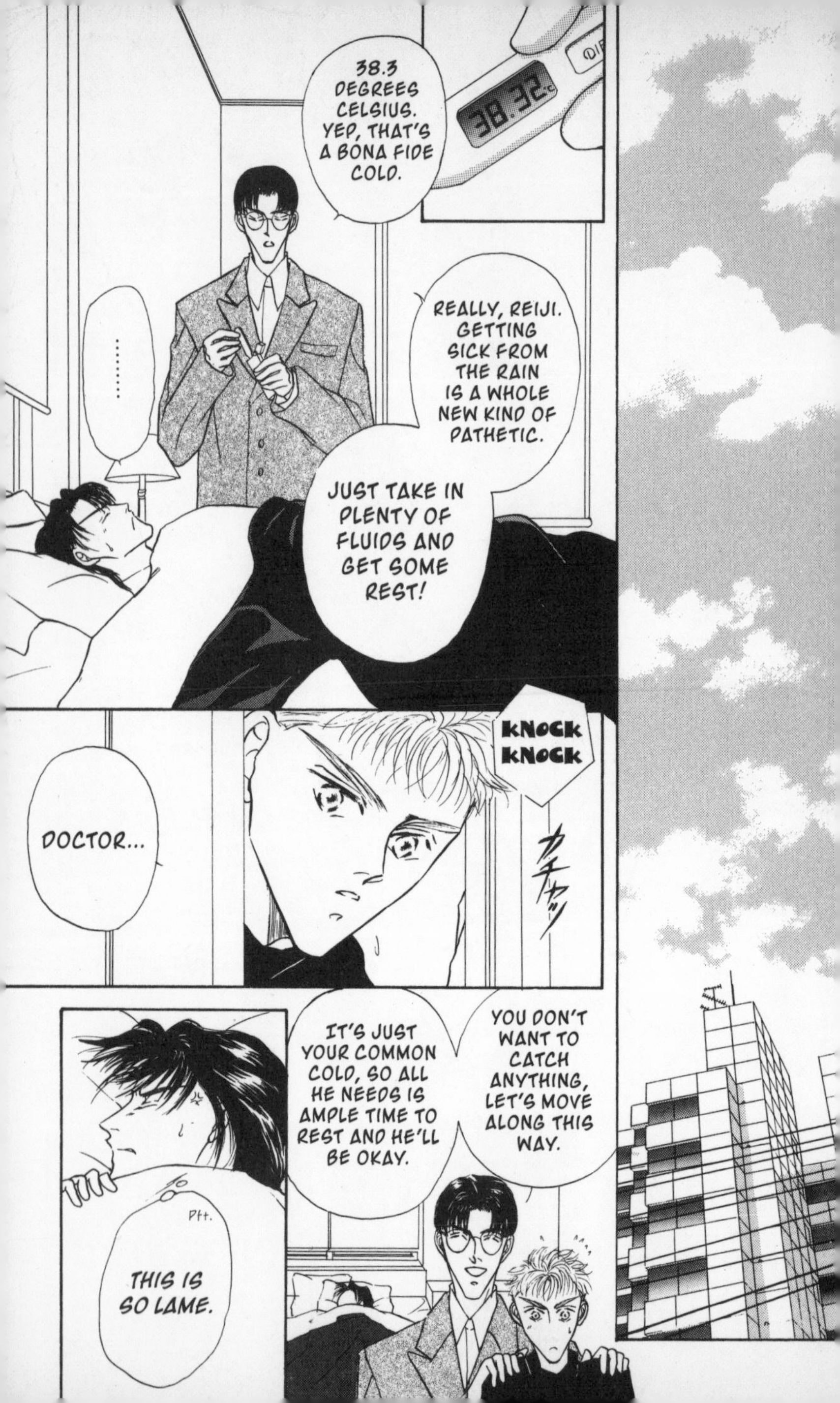
38.3 DEGREES CELSIUS. YEP, THAT'S A BONA FIDE COLD.
REALLY, REIJI. GETTING SICK FROM THE RAIN IS A WHOLE NEW KIND OF PATHETIC.
......
JUST TAKE IN PLENTY OF FLUIDS AND GET SOME REST!
KNOCK KNOCK
カチャッ
DOCTOR...
YOU DON'T WANT TO CATCH ANYTHING, LET'S MOVE ALONG THIS WAY.
IT'S JUST YOUR COMMON COLD, SO ALL HE NEEDS IS AMPLE TIME TO REST AND HE'LL BE OKAY.
Pft.
THIS IS SO LAME.

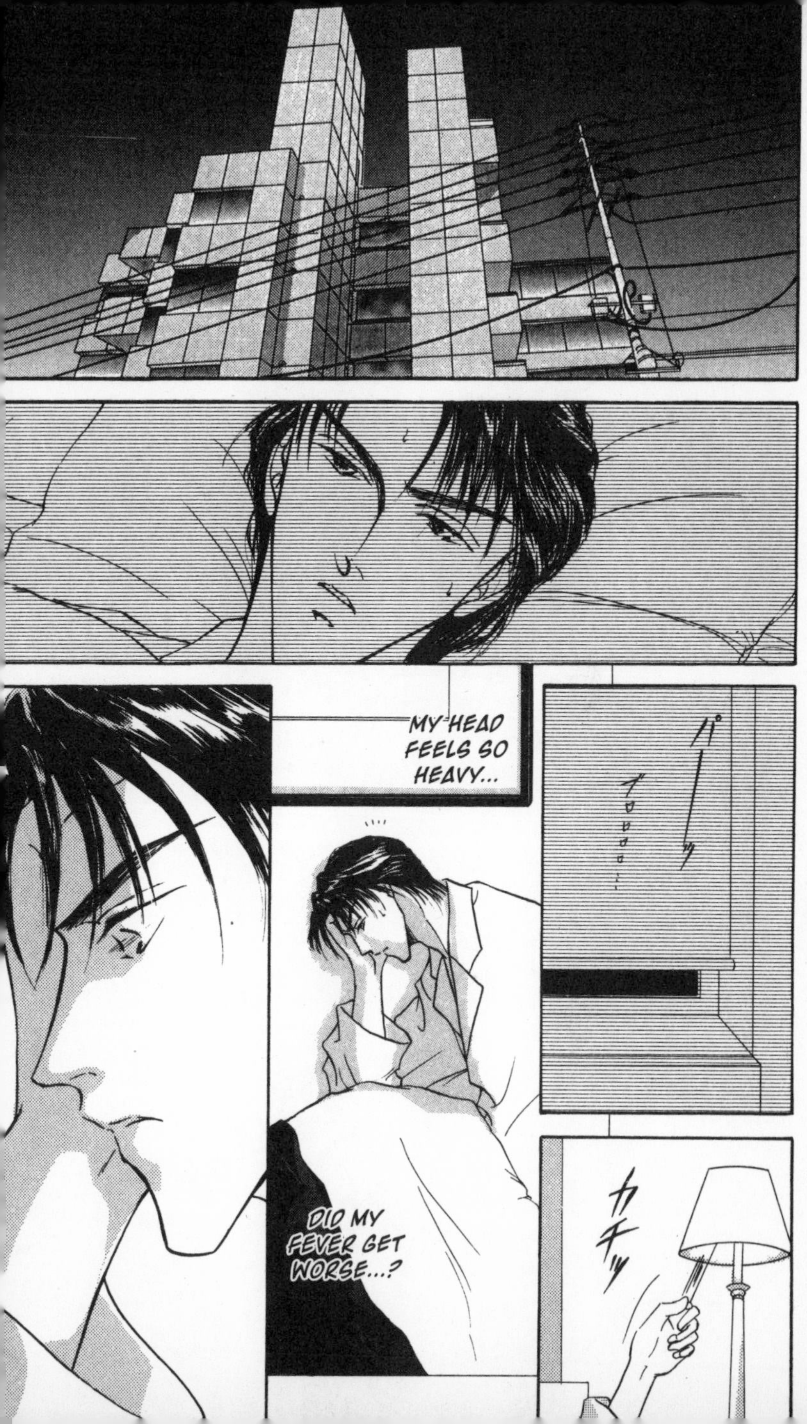

パーーッ
ブロロロロ…
カチッ
MY HEAD FEELS SO HEAVY...
DID MY FEVER GET WORSE...?

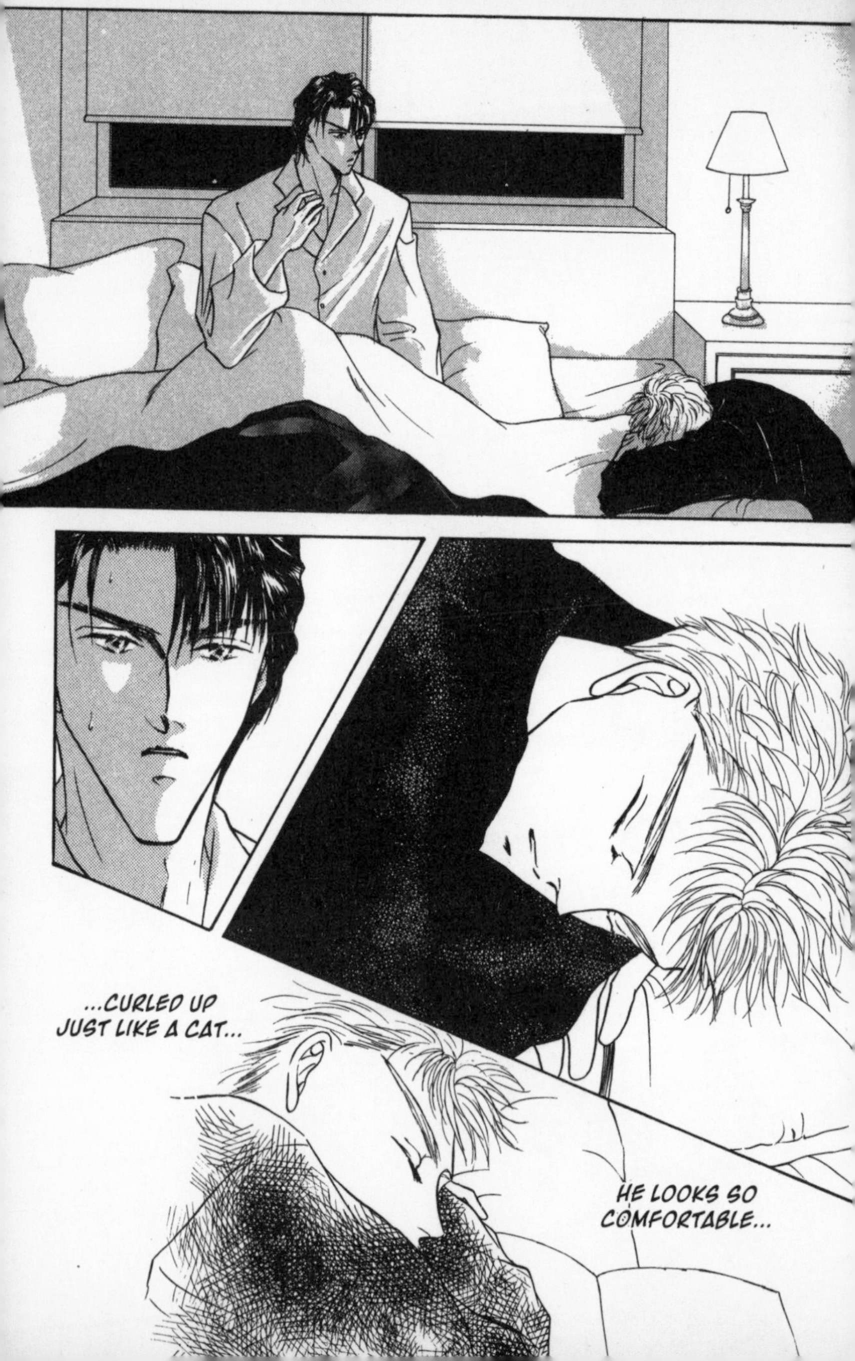
HE LOOKS SO COMFORTABLE...
...CURLED UP JUST LIKE A CAT...

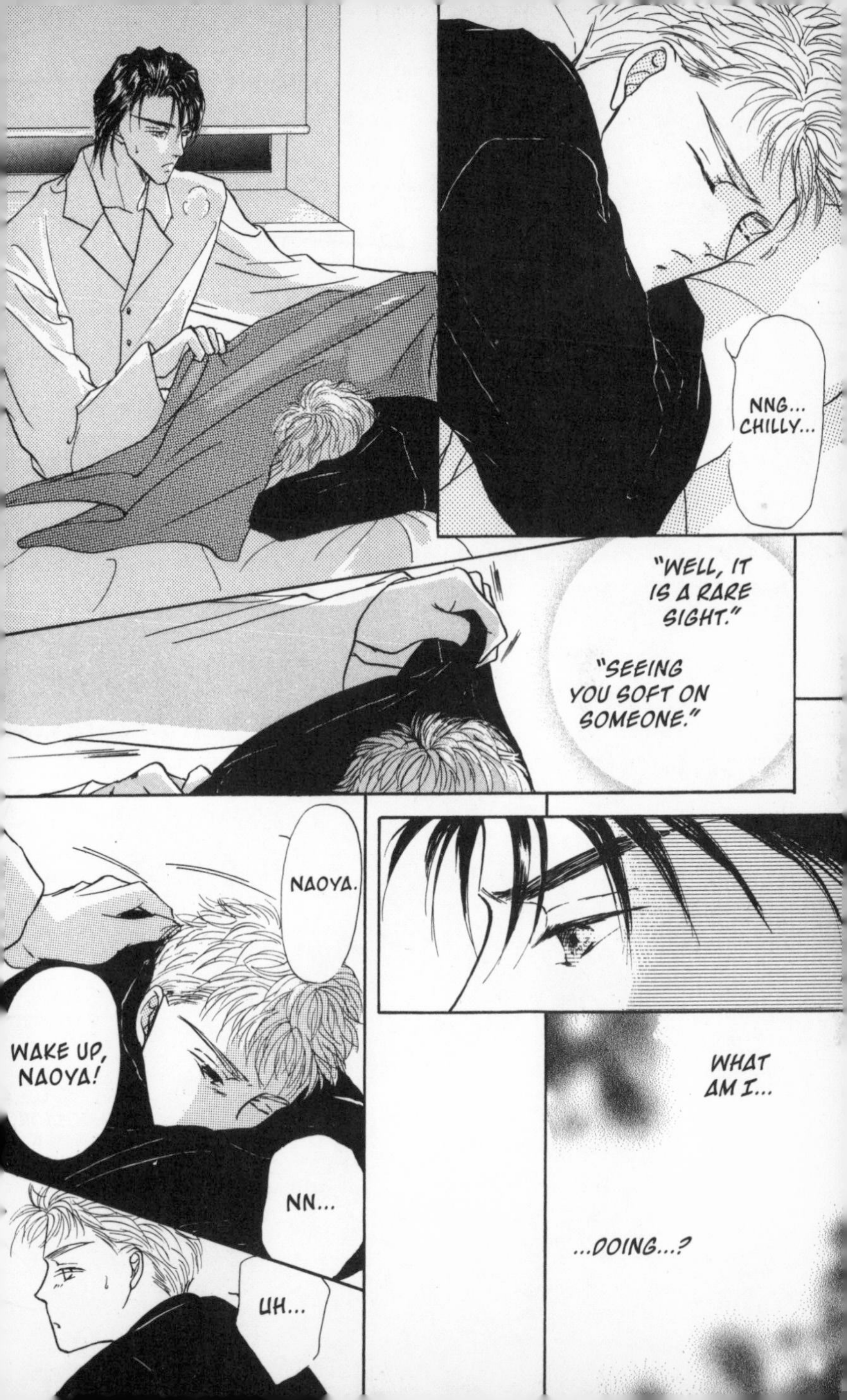
NNG... CHILLY...
"WELL, IT IS A RARE SIGHT."
"SEEING YOU SOFT ON SOMEONE."
WHAT AM I...
...DOING...?
NAOYA.
WAKE UP, NAOYA!
NN...
UH...

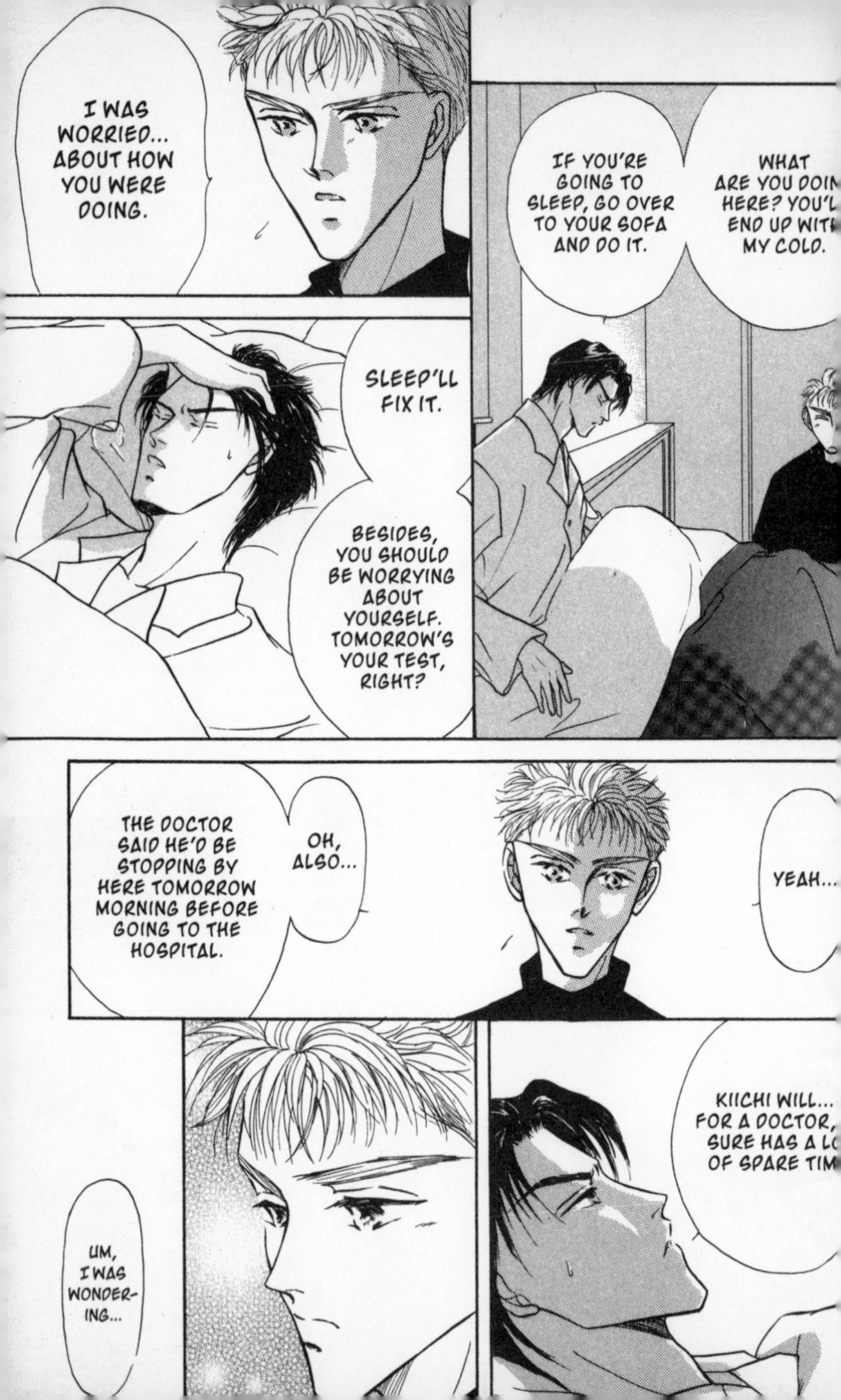

WHAT ARE YOU DOIN HERE? YOU'L END UP WIT MY COLD.
IF YOU'RE GOING TO SLEEP, GO OVER TO YOUR SOFA AND DO IT.
I WAS WORRIED... ABOUT HOW YOU WERE DOING.
SLEEP'LL FIX IT.
BESIDES, YOU SHOULD BE WORRYING ABOUT YOURSELF. TOMORROW'S YOUR TEST, RIGHT?
YEAH...
OH, ALSO...
THE DOCTOR SAID HE'D BE STOPPING BY HERE TOMORROW MORNING BEFORE GOING TO THE HOSPITAL.
KIICHI WILL... FOR A DOCTOR, SURE HAS A L OF SPARE TIM
UM, I WAS WONDER-ING...

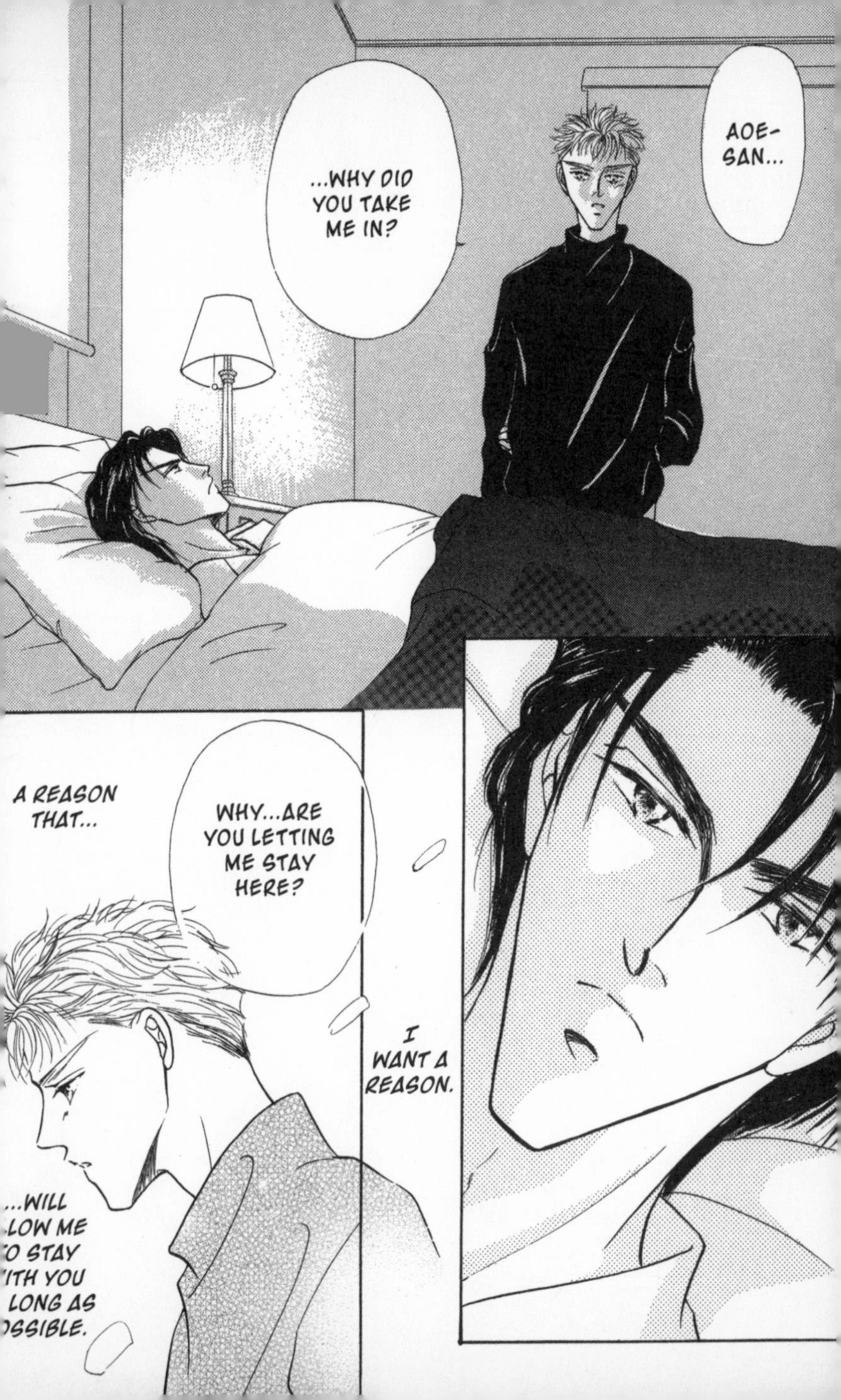
AOE-SAN...
...WHY DID YOU TAKE ME IN?
WHY...ARE YOU LETTING ME STAY HERE?
I WANT A REASON.
A REASON THAT...
...WILL
LOW ME
O STAY
ITH YOU
LONG AS
OSSIBLE.

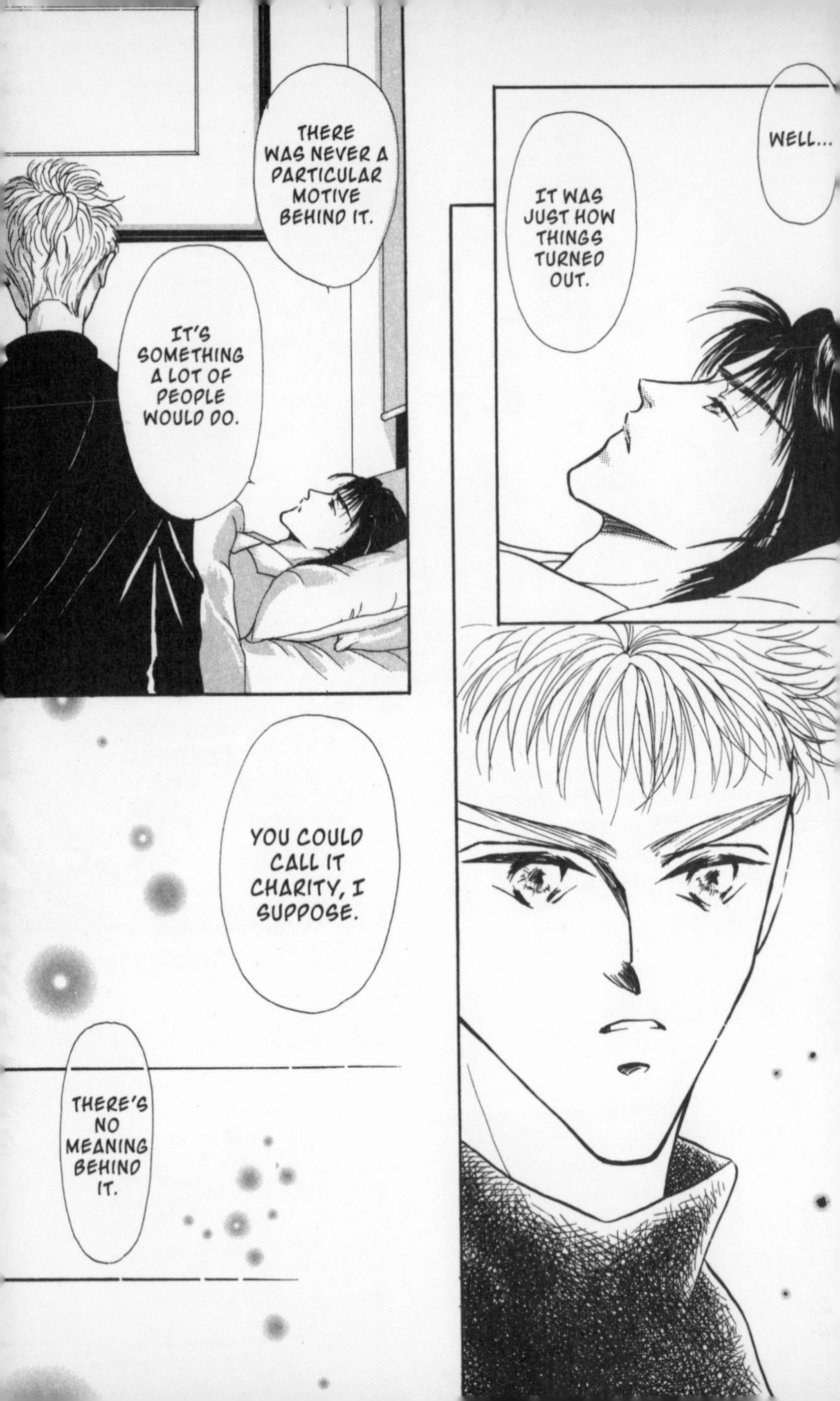
WELL...
IT WAS JUST HOW THINGS TURNED OUT.
THERE WAS NEVER A PARTICULAR MOTIVE BEHIND IT.
IT'S SOMETHING A LOT OF PEOPLE WOULD DO.
YOU COULD CALL IT CHARITY, I SUPPOSE.
THERE'S NO MEANING BEHIND IT.

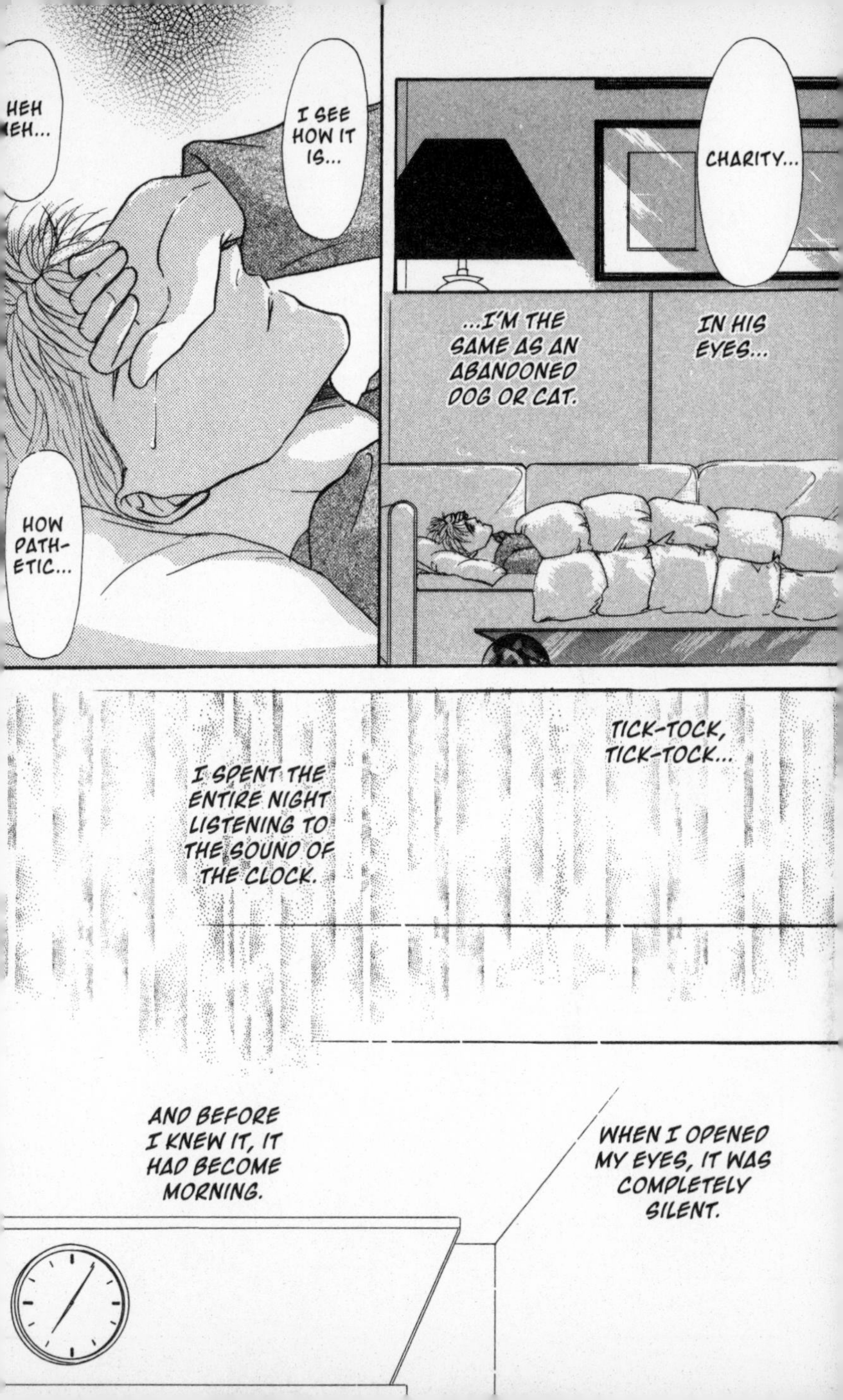
CHARITY...
IN HIS EYES...
...I'M THE SAME AS AN ABANDONED DOG OR CAT.
I SEE HOW IT IS...
HEH EH...
HOW PATH-ETIC...
TICK-TOCK, TICK-TOCK...
I SPENT THE ENTIRE NIGHT LISTENING TO THE SOUND OF THE CLOCK.
WHEN I OPENED MY EYES, IT WAS COMPLETELY SILENT.
AND BEFORE I KNEW IT, IT HAD BECOME MORNING.

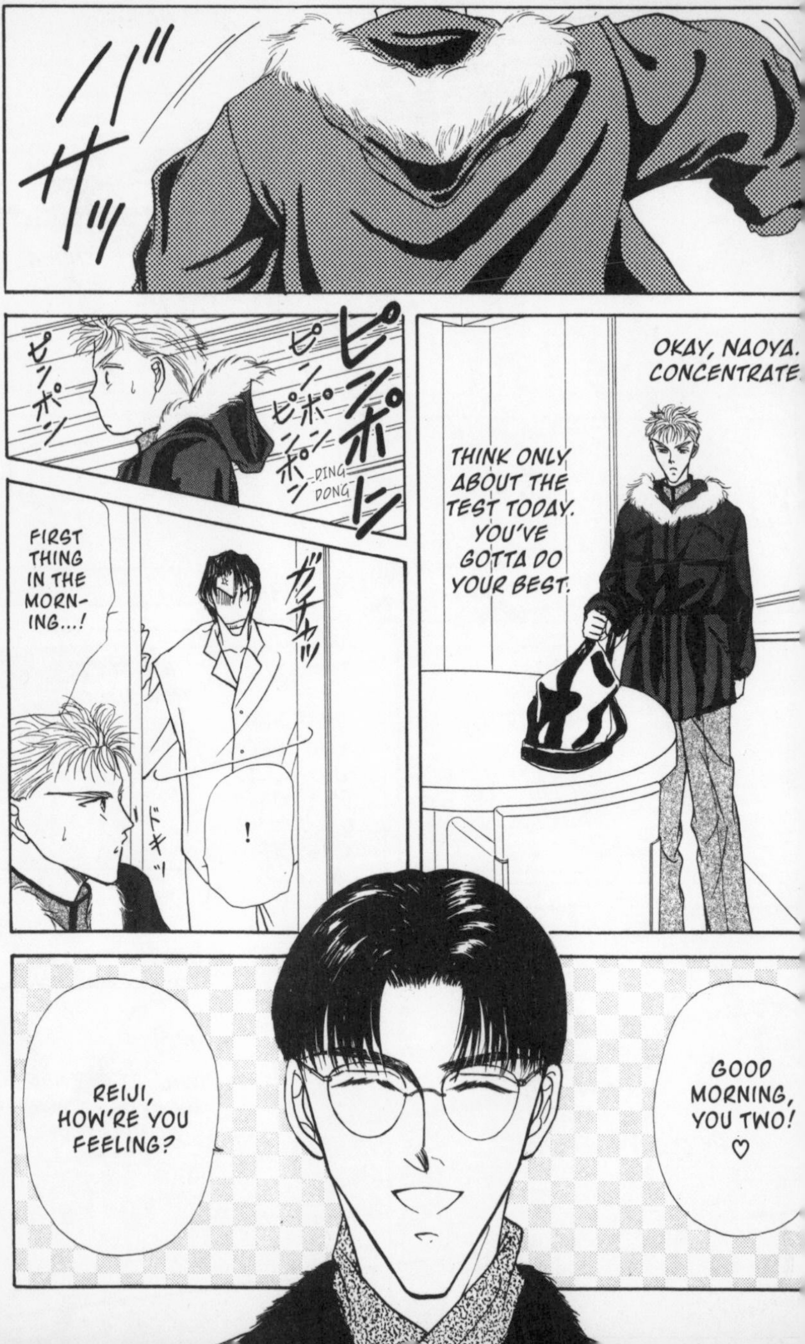
バサッ
OKAY, NAOYA. CONCENTRATE.
THINK ONLY ABOUT THE TEST TODAY. YOU'VE GOTTA DO YOUR BEST.
ピンポン
ピンポンピンポンポン
DING DONG
ピンポン
ガチャッ
FIRST THING IN THE MORN-ING...!
!
ドキッ
GOOD MORNING, YOU TWO! ♡
REIJI, HOW'RE YOU FEELING?

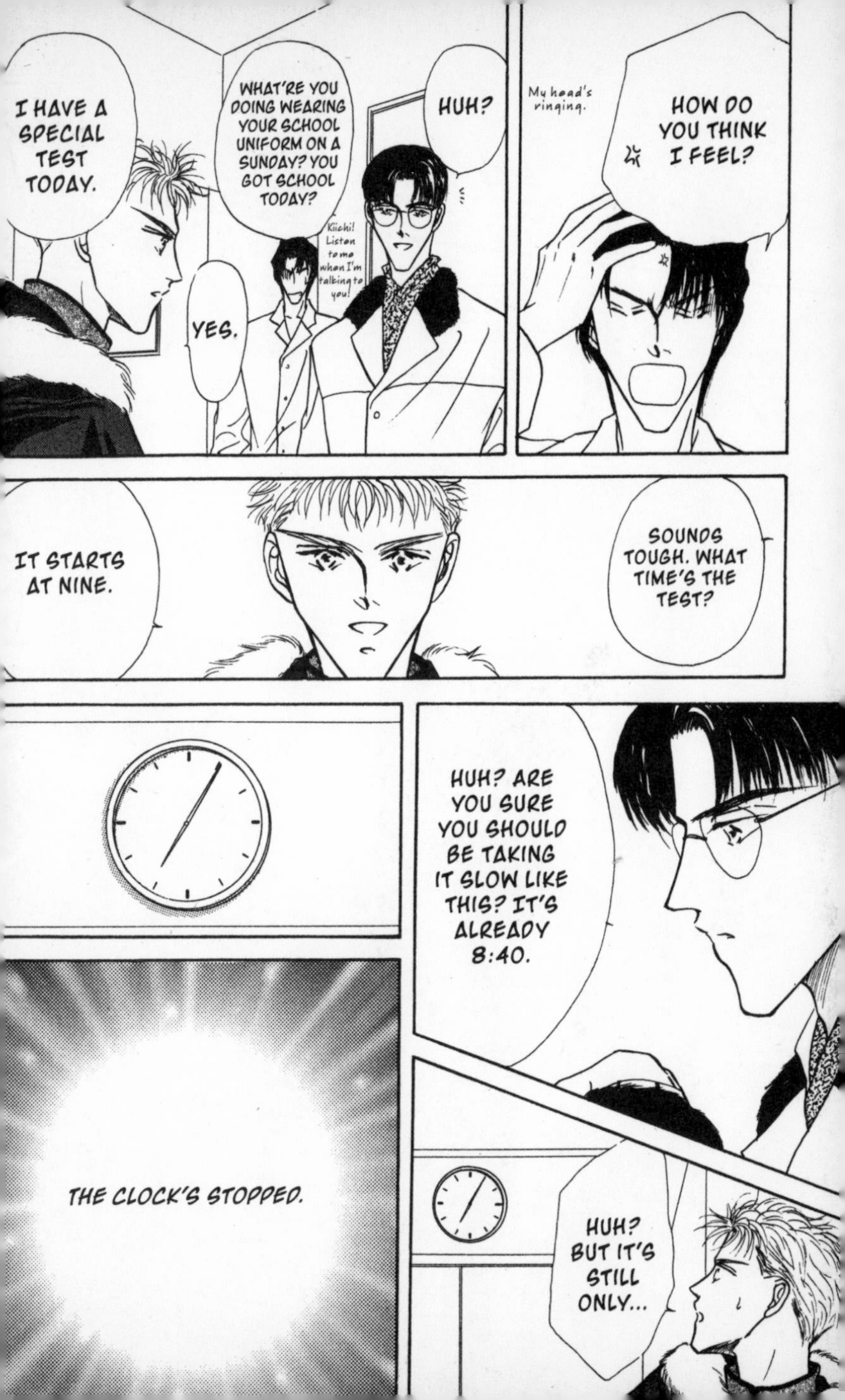
My head's ringing.
HOW DO YOU THINK I FEEL?
HUH?
Kiichi! Listen to me when I'm talking to you!
WHAT'RE YOU DOING WEARING YOUR SCHOOL UNIFORM ON A SUNDAY? YOU GOT SCHOOL TODAY?
YES.
I HAVE A SPECIAL TEST TODAY.
SOUNDS TOUGH. WHAT TIME'S THE TEST?
IT STARTS AT NINE.
HUH? ARE YOU SURE YOU SHOULD BE TAKING IT SLOW LIKE THIS? IT'S ALREADY 8:40.
HUH? BUT IT'S STILL ONLY...
THE CLOCK'S STOPPED.

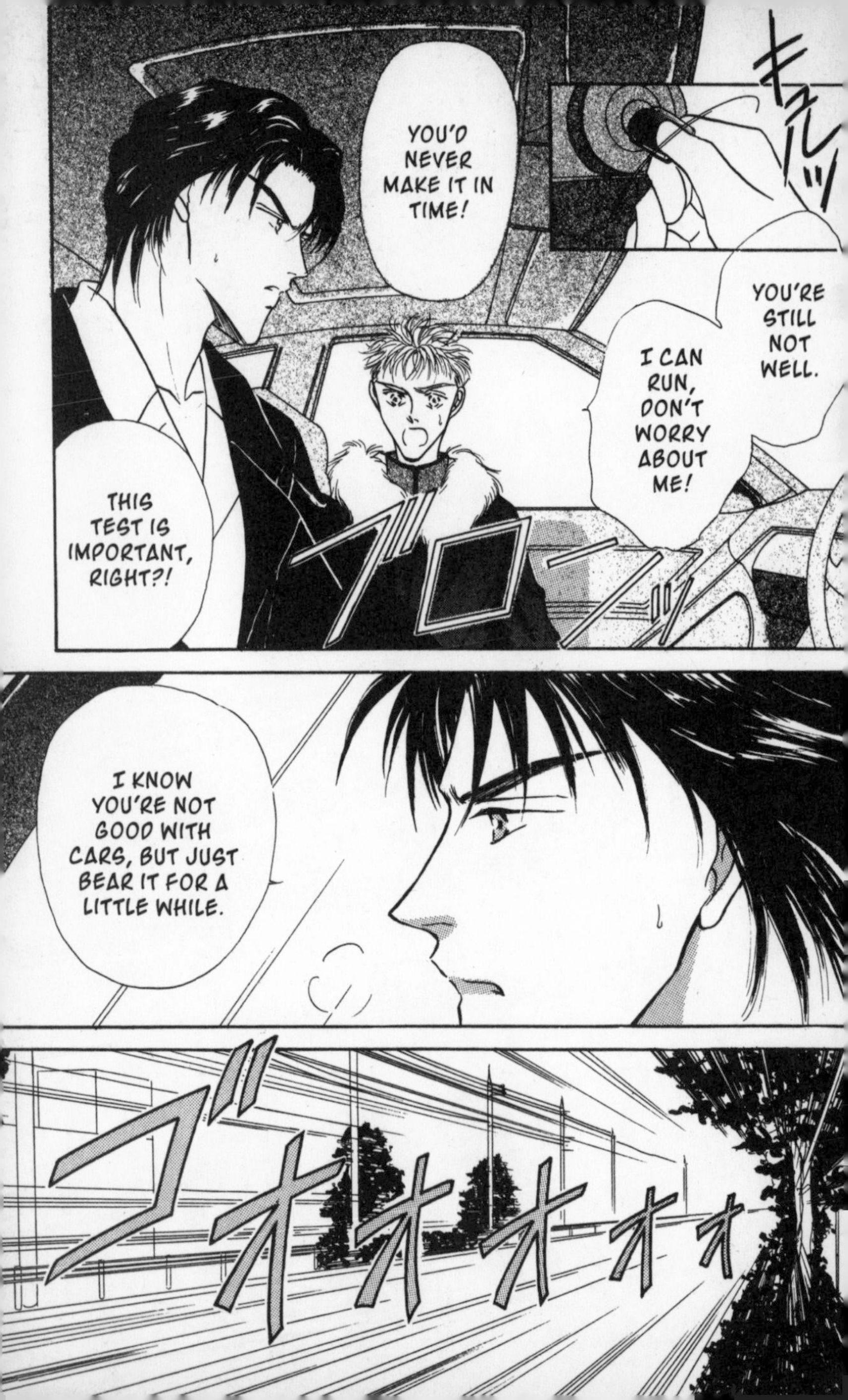
キュルッ
YOU'RE STILL NOT WELL.
I CAN RUN, DON'T WORRY ABOUT ME!
YOU'D NEVER MAKE IT IN TIME!
THIS TEST IS IMPORTANT, RIGHT?!
I KNOW YOU'RE NOT GOOD WITH CARS, BUT JUST BEAR IT FOR A LITTLE WHILE.
ゴオオオォォ

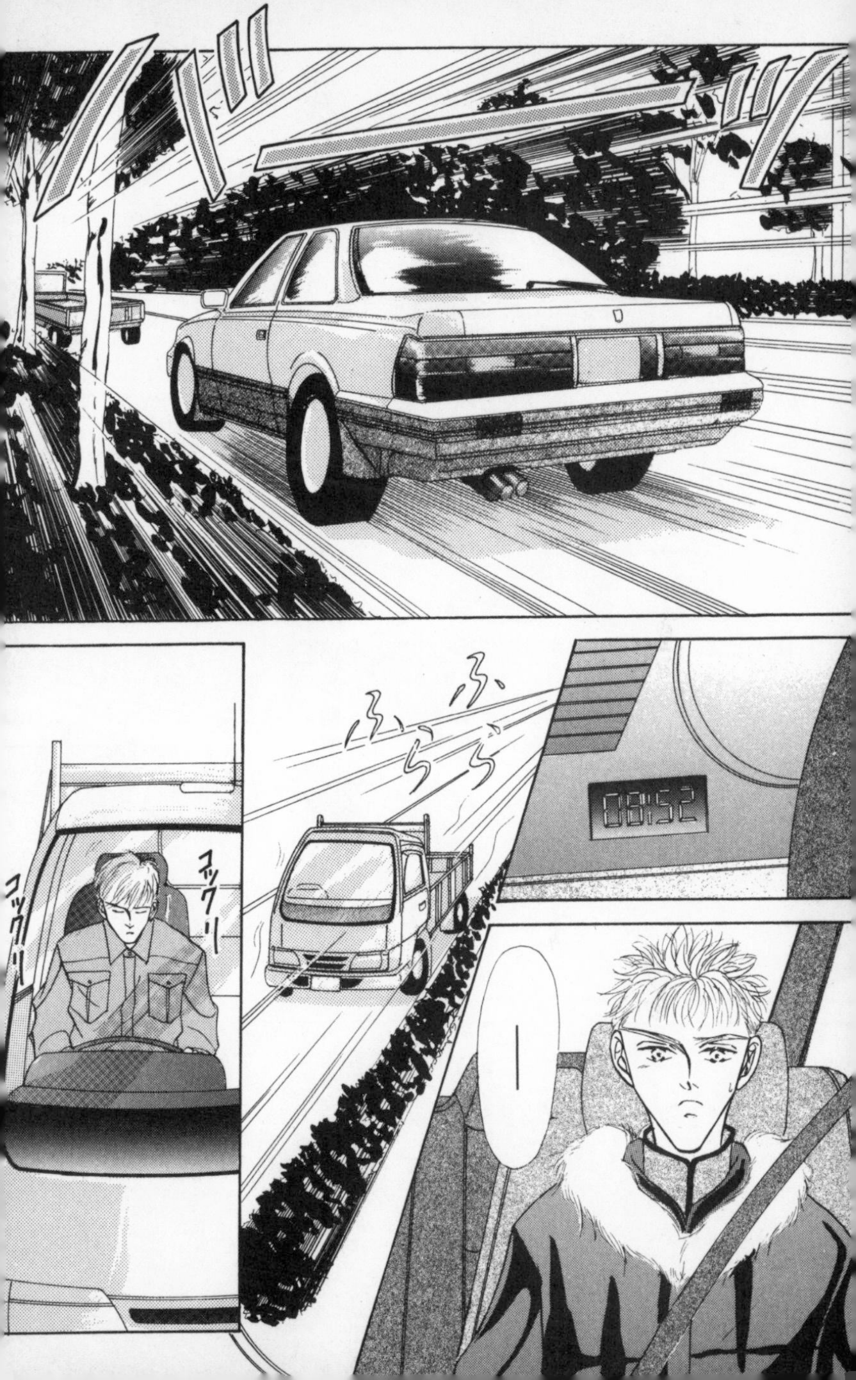
08:52
—
ふらふら
ふらふら
コックリー
コックリー

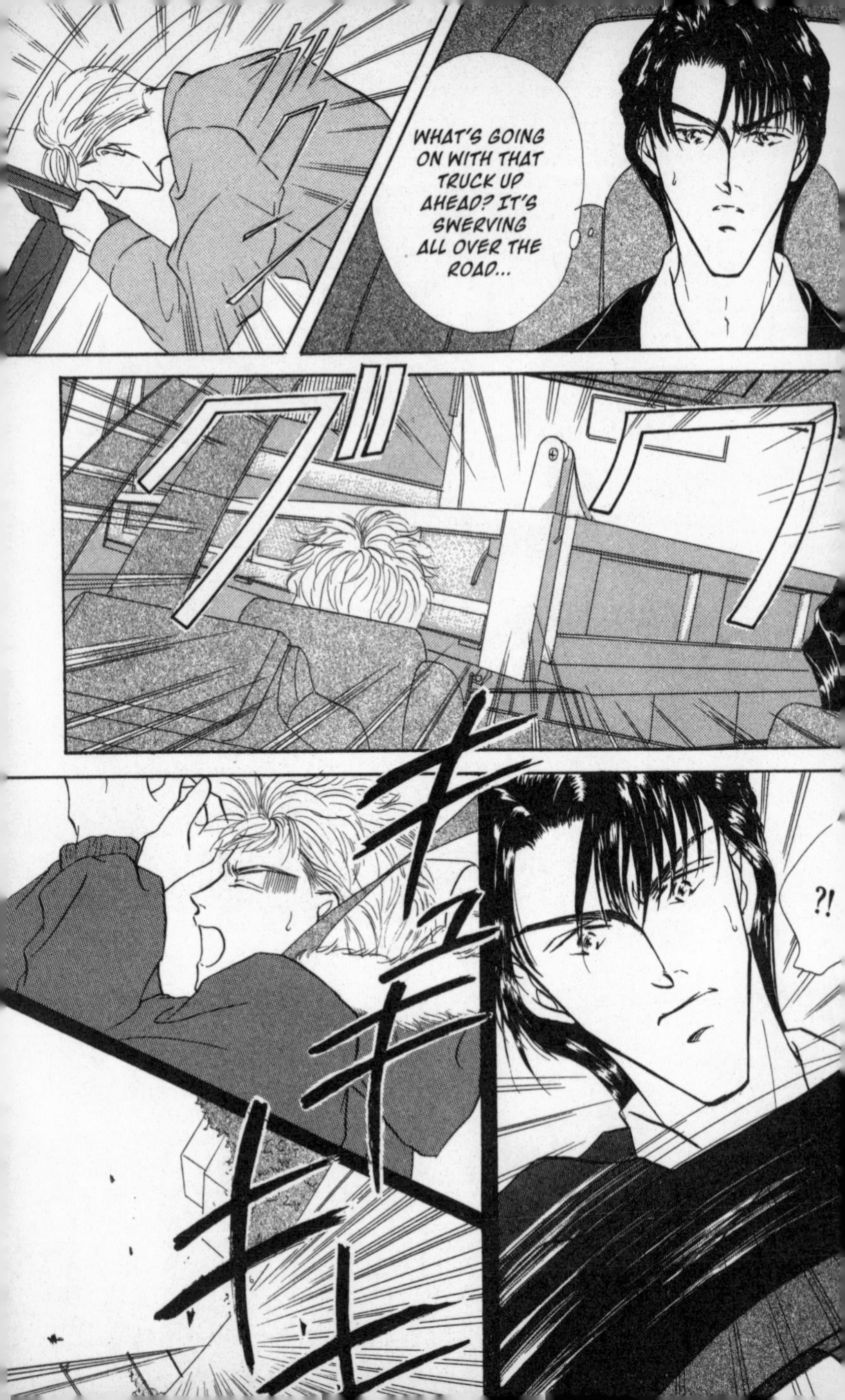
WHAT'S GOING ON WITH THAT TRUCK UP AHEAD? IT'S SWERVING ALL OVER THE ROAD...
?!

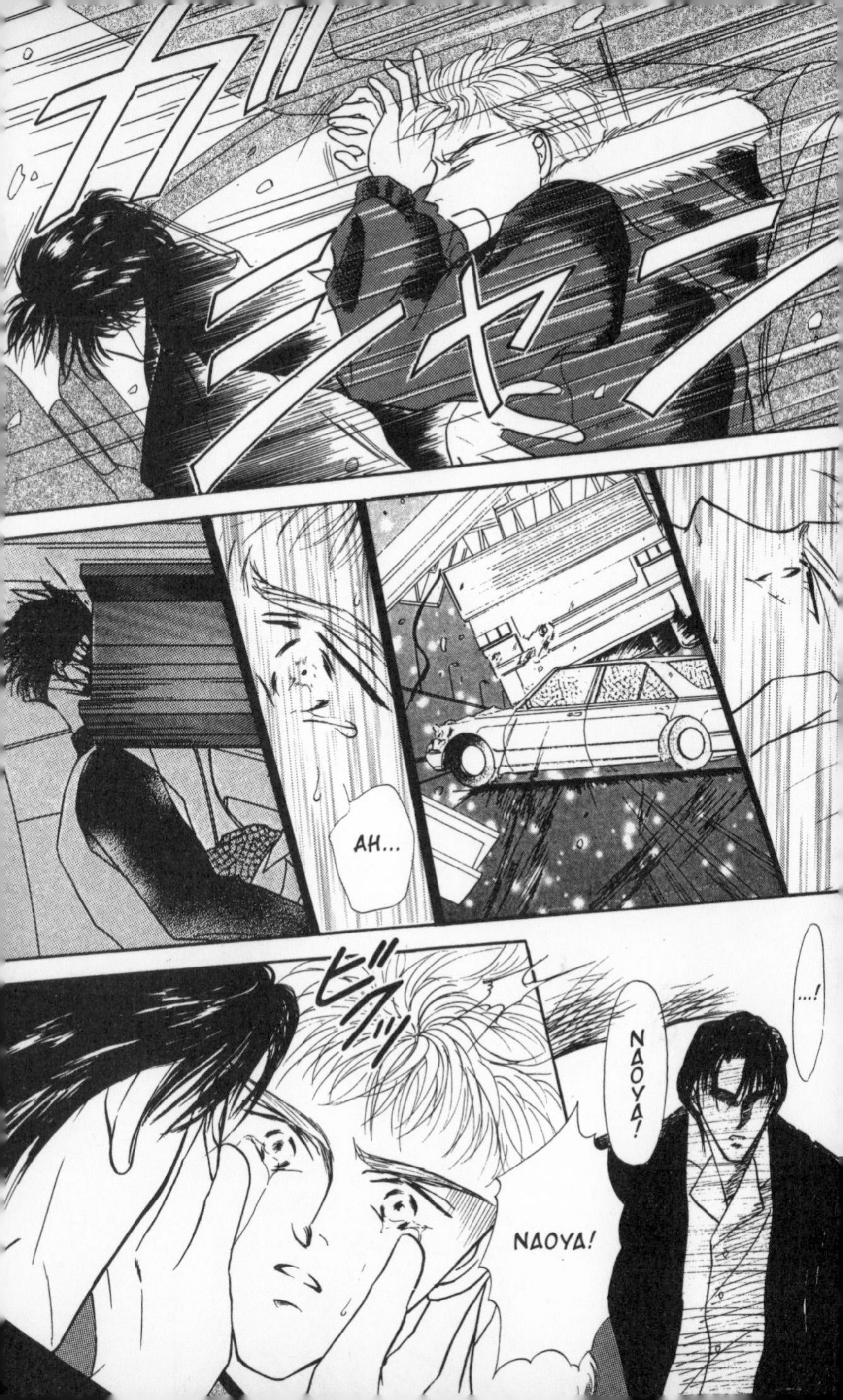
AH...
...!
NAOYA!
NAOYA!

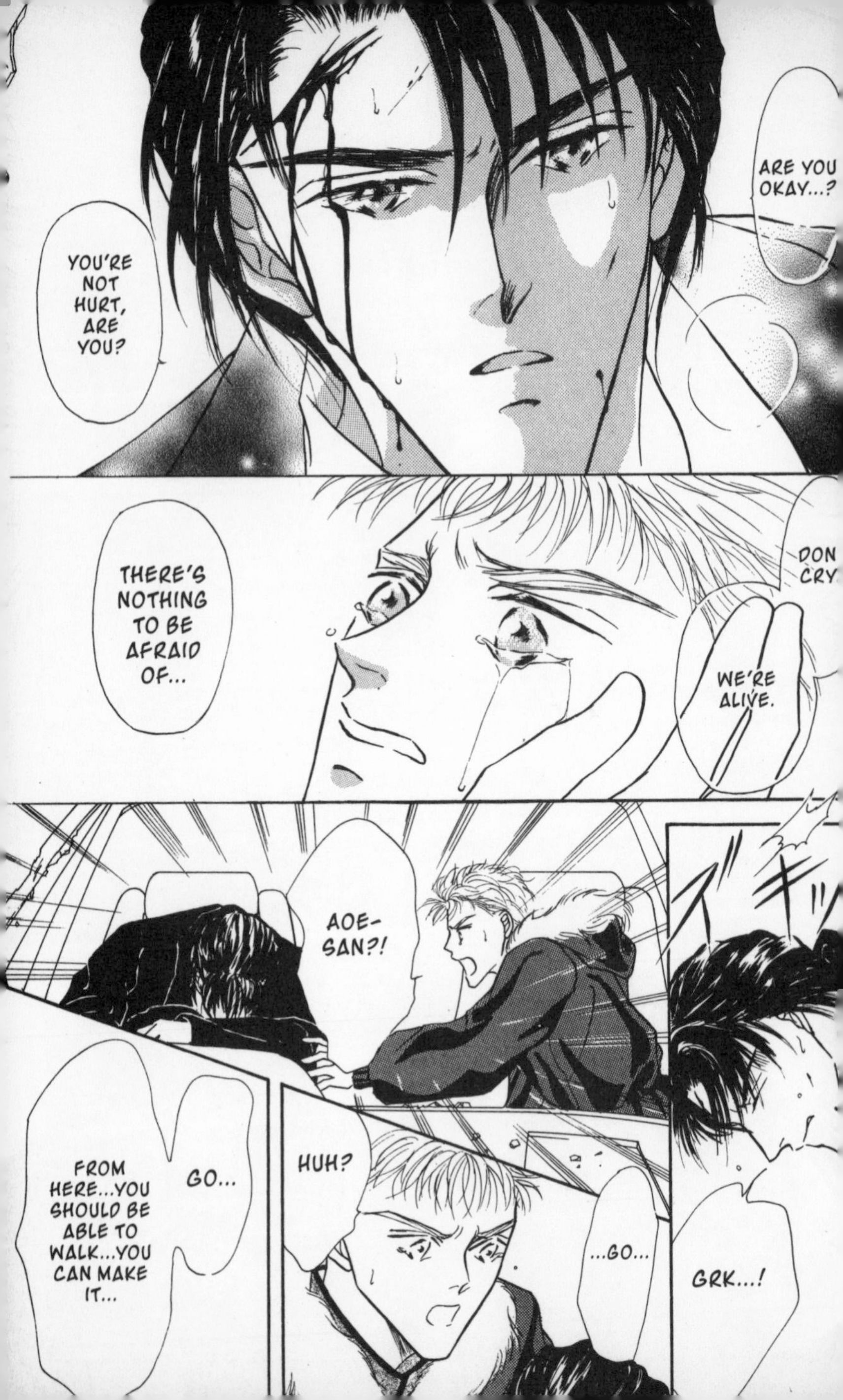
ARE YOU OKAY...?
YOU'RE NOT HURT, ARE YOU?
DON CRY
WE'RE ALIVE.
THERE'S NOTHING TO BE AFRAID OF...
ズキッ
GRK...!
AOE-SAN?!
...GO...
HUH?
GO...
FROM HERE...YOU SHOULD BE ABLE TO WALK...YOU CAN MAKE IT...

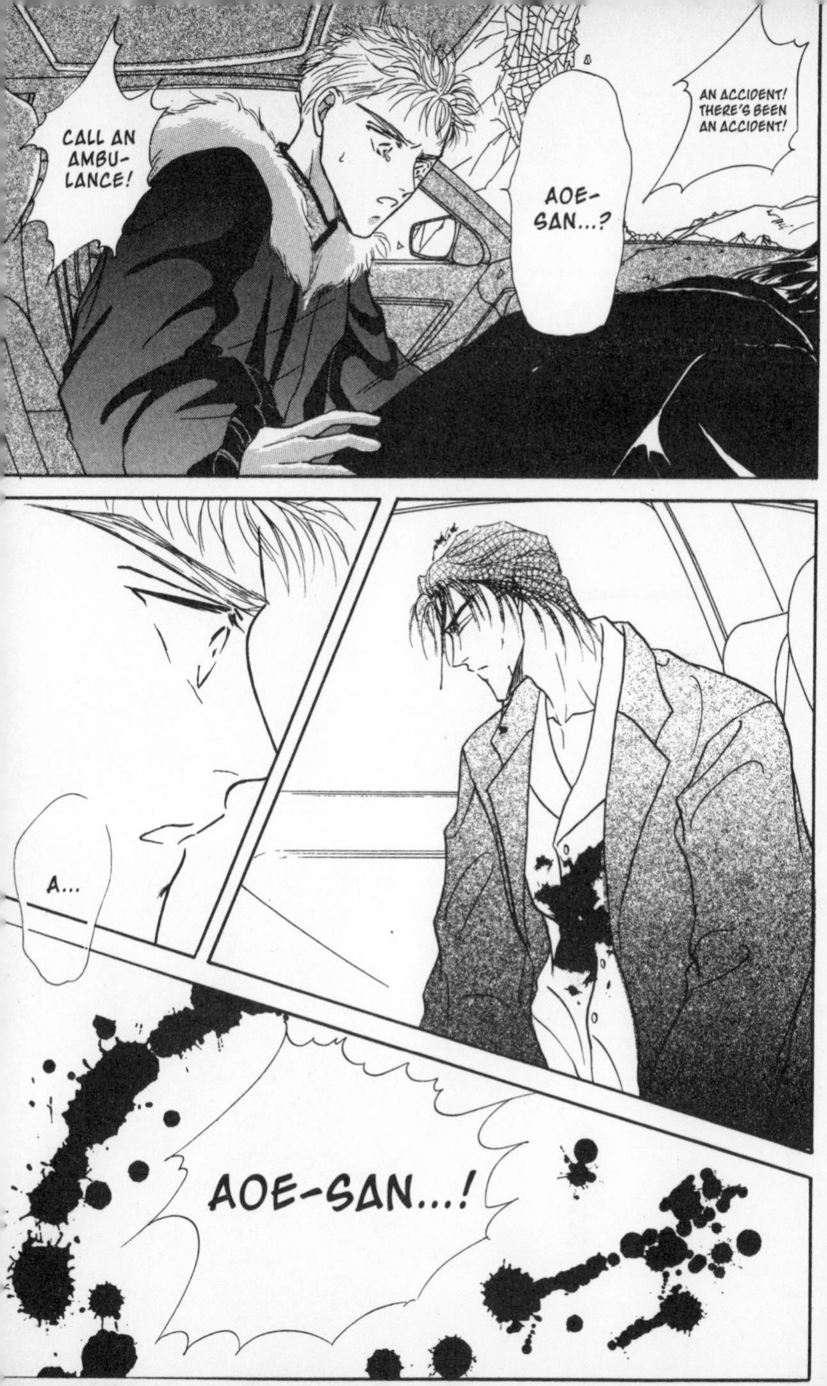
AN ACCIDENT! THERE'S BEEN AN ACCIDENT!
AOE-SAN...?
CALL AN AMBULANCE!
A...
AOE-SAN...!

Christmas Children

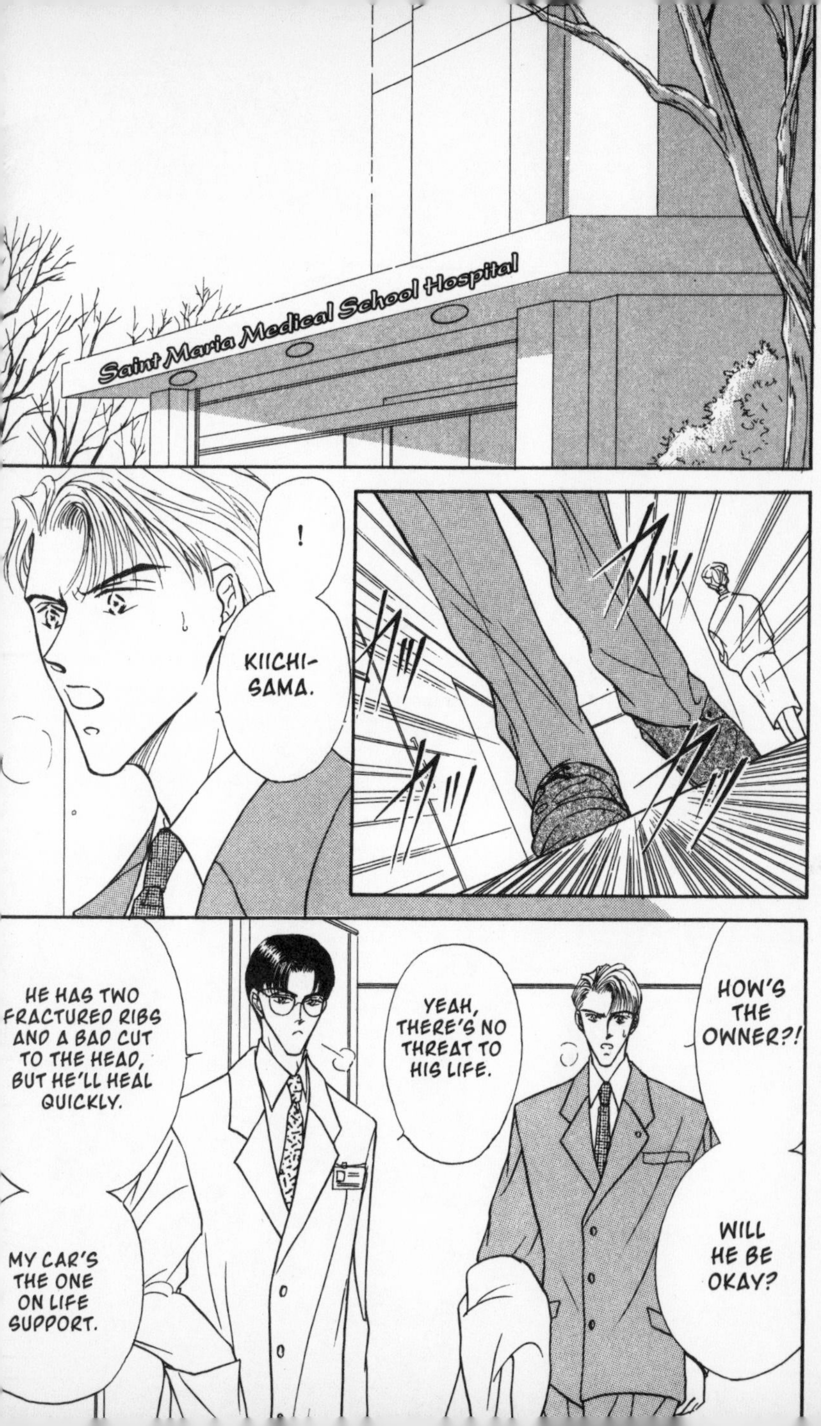
Saint Maria Medical School Hospital
!
KIICHI-SAMA.
HOW'S THE OWNER?!
WILL HE BE OKAY?
YEAH, THERE'S NO THREAT TO HIS LIFE.
HE HAS TWO FRACTURED RIBS AND A BAD CUT TO THE HEAD, BUT HE'LL HEAL QUICKLY.
MY CAR'S THE ONE ON LIFE SUPPORT.

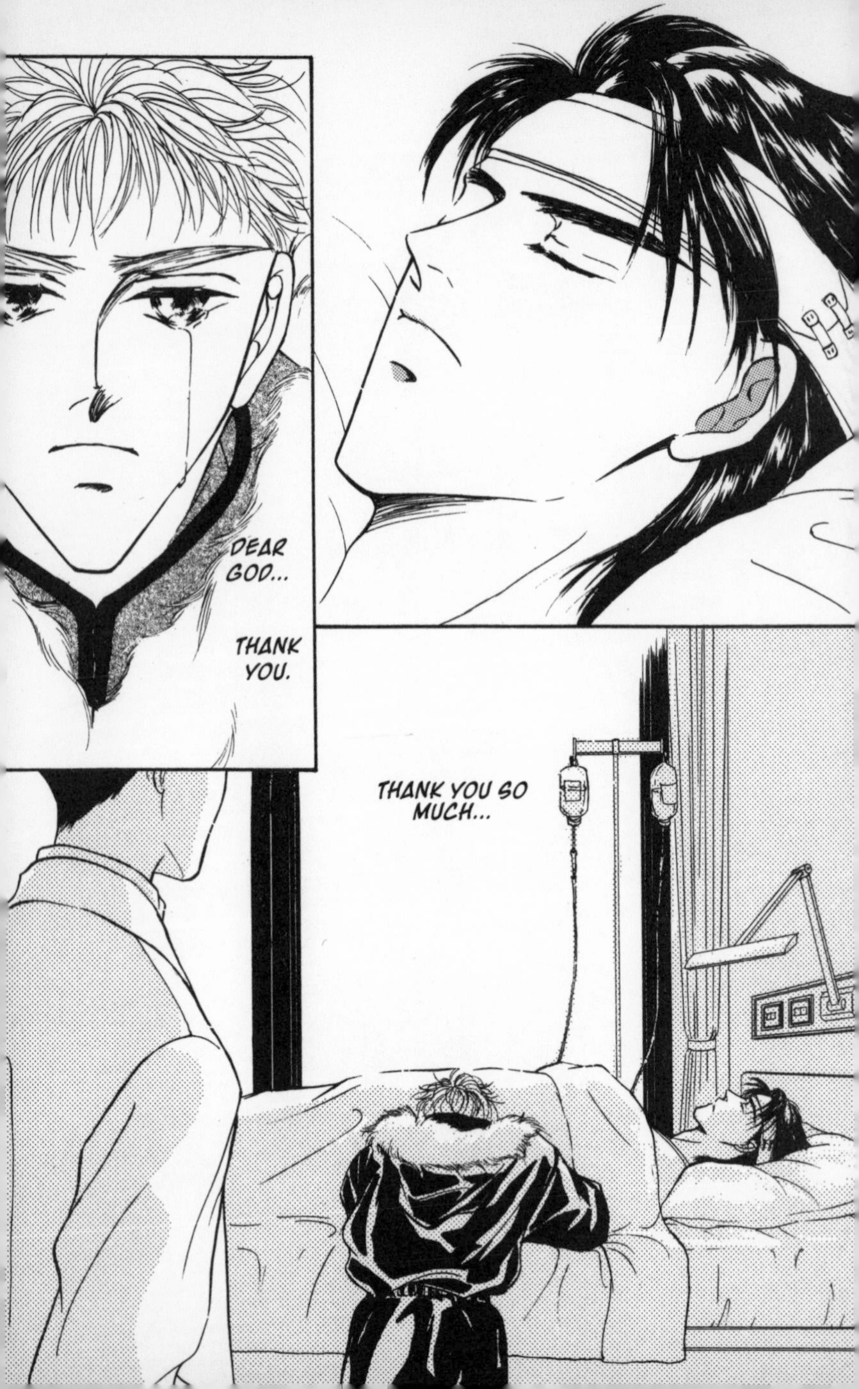
DEAR GOD...
THANK YOU.
THANK YOU SO MUCH...

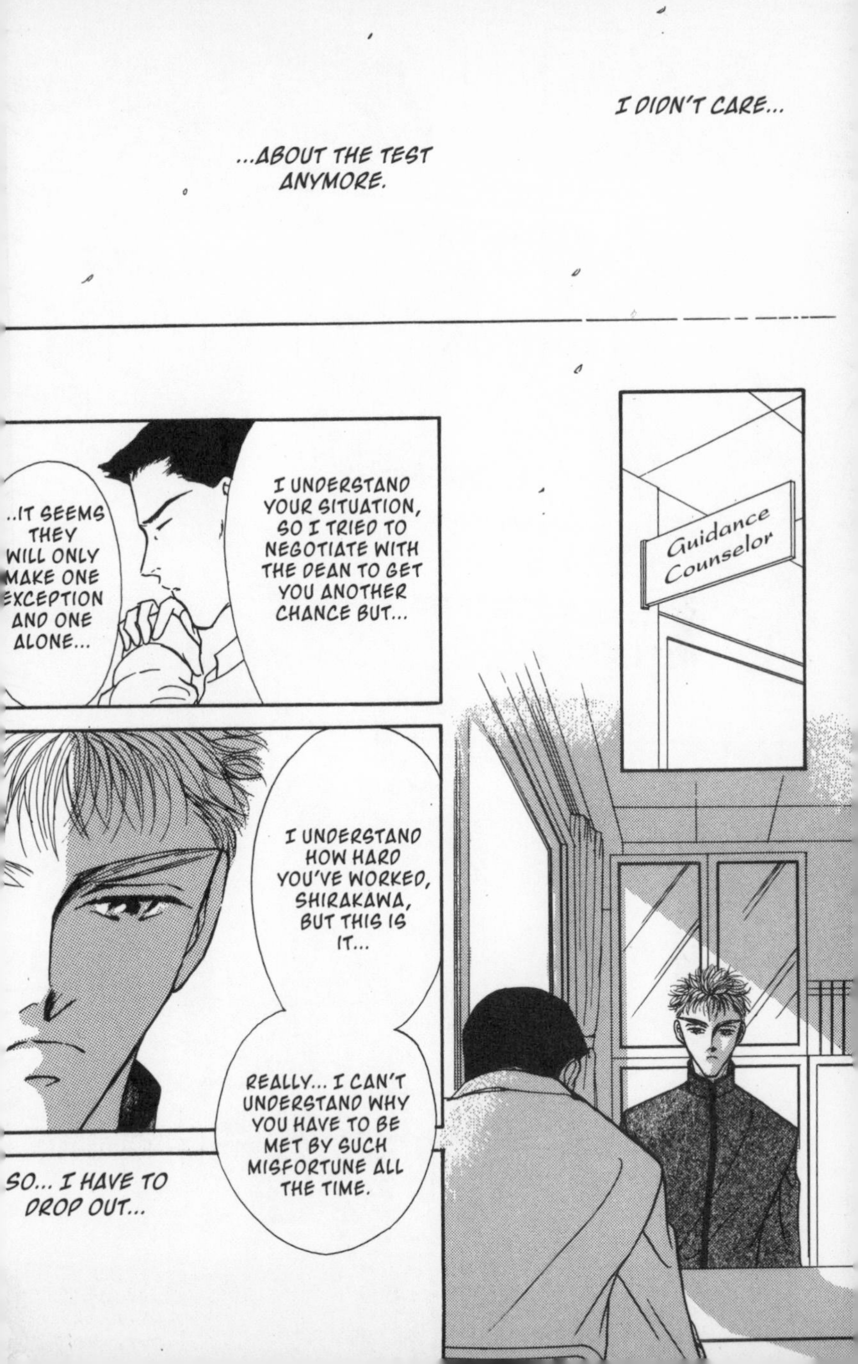
I DIDN'T CARE...
...ABOUT THE TEST ANYMORE.
Guidance Counselor
I UNDERSTAND YOUR SITUATION, SO I TRIED TO NEGOTIATE WITH THE DEAN TO GET YOU ANOTHER CHANCE BUT...
...IT SEEMS THEY WILL ONLY MAKE ONE EXCEPTION AND ONE ALONE...
I UNDERSTAND HOW HARD YOU'VE WORKED, SHIRAKAWA, BUT THIS IS IT...
REALLY... I CAN'T UNDERSTAND WHY YOU HAVE TO BE MET BY SUCH MISFORTUNE ALL THE TIME.
SO... I HAVE TO DROP OUT...

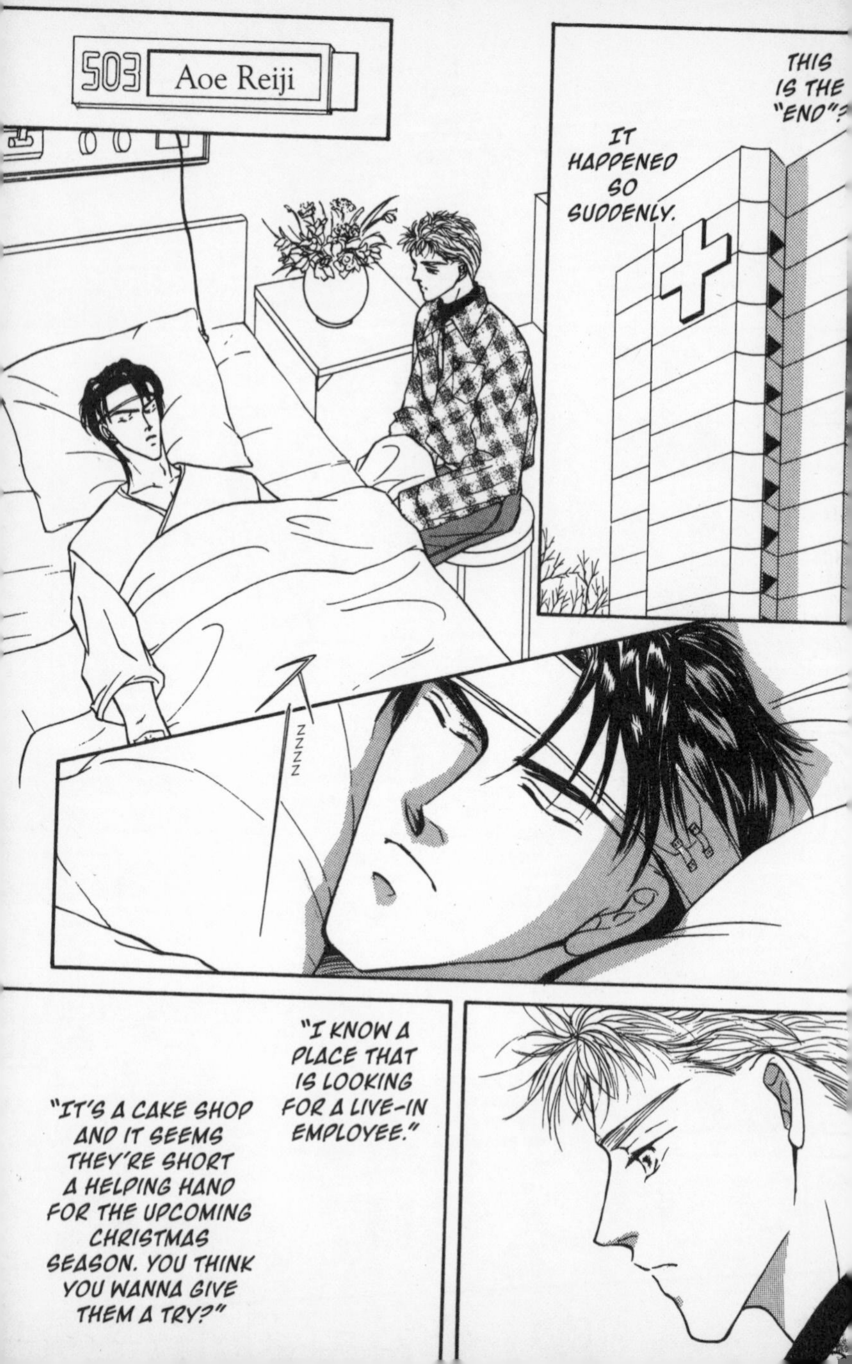
THIS IS THE "END"?
IT HAPPENED SO SUDDENLY.
503 Aoe Reiji
ZZZZ
"I KNOW A PLACE THAT IS LOOKING FOR A LIVE-IN EMPLOYEE."
"IT'S A CAKE SHOP AND IT SEEMS THEY'RE SHORT A HELPING HAND FOR THE UPCOMING CHRISTMAS SEASON. YOU THINK YOU WANNA GIVE THEM A TRY?"

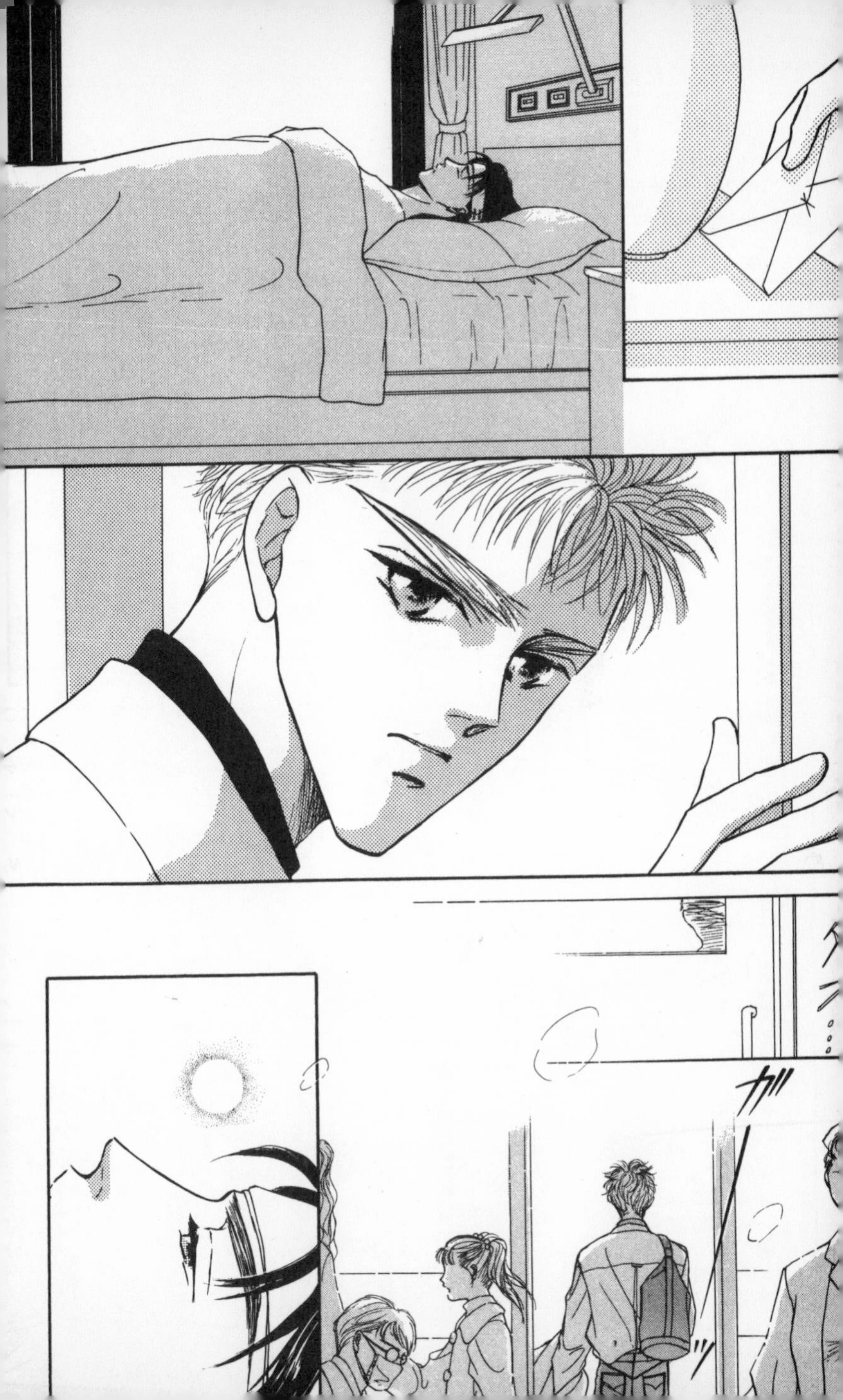
スー…
ガッ

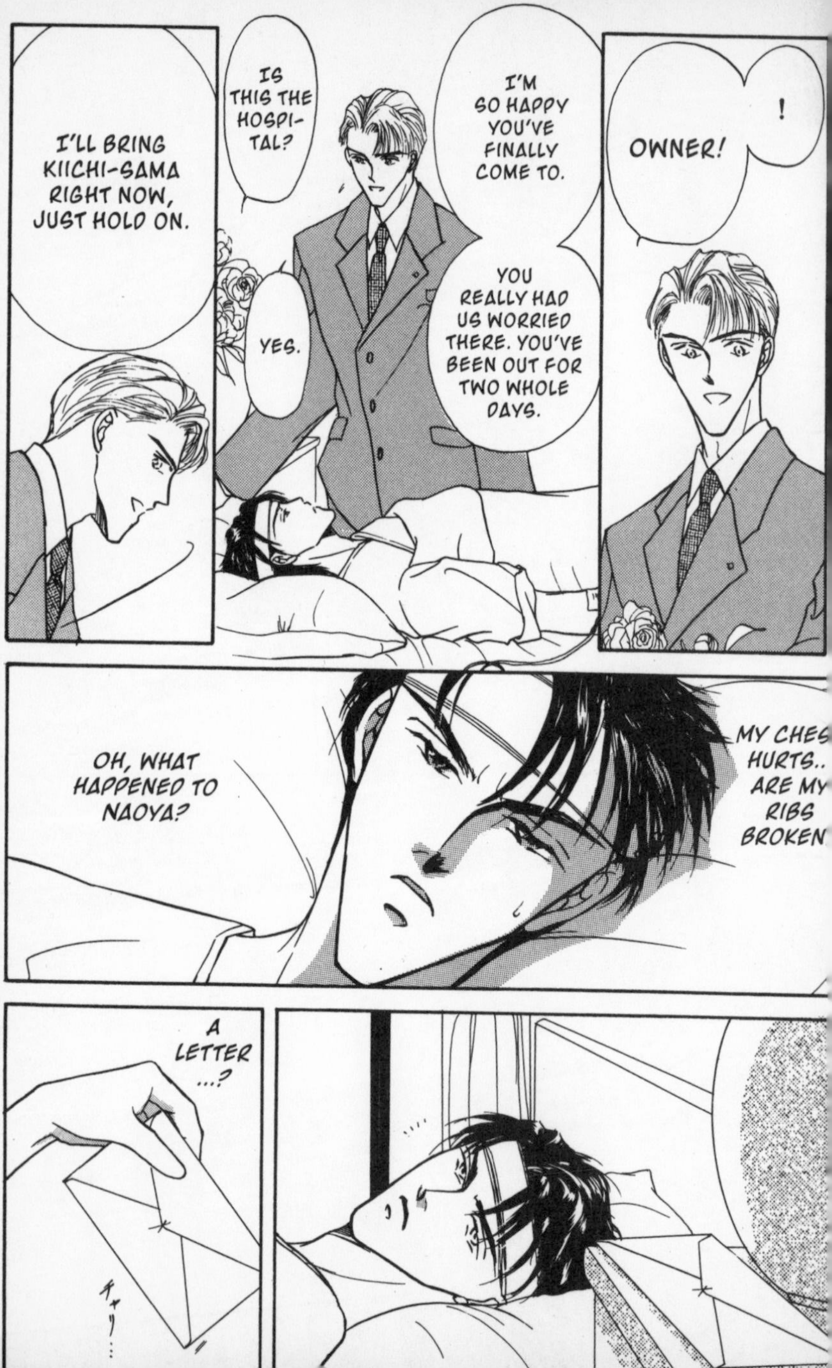
!
OWNER!
I'M SO HAPPY YOU'VE FINALLY COME TO.
YOU REALLY HAD US WORRIED THERE. YOU'VE BEEN OUT FOR TWO WHOLE DAYS.
IS THIS THE HOSPI-TAL?
YES.
I'LL BRING KIICHI-SAMA RIGHT NOW, JUST HOLD ON.
MY CHES HURTS.. ARE MY RIBS BROKEN
OH, WHAT HAPPENED TO NAOYA?
...
A LETTER ...?
チャリ…

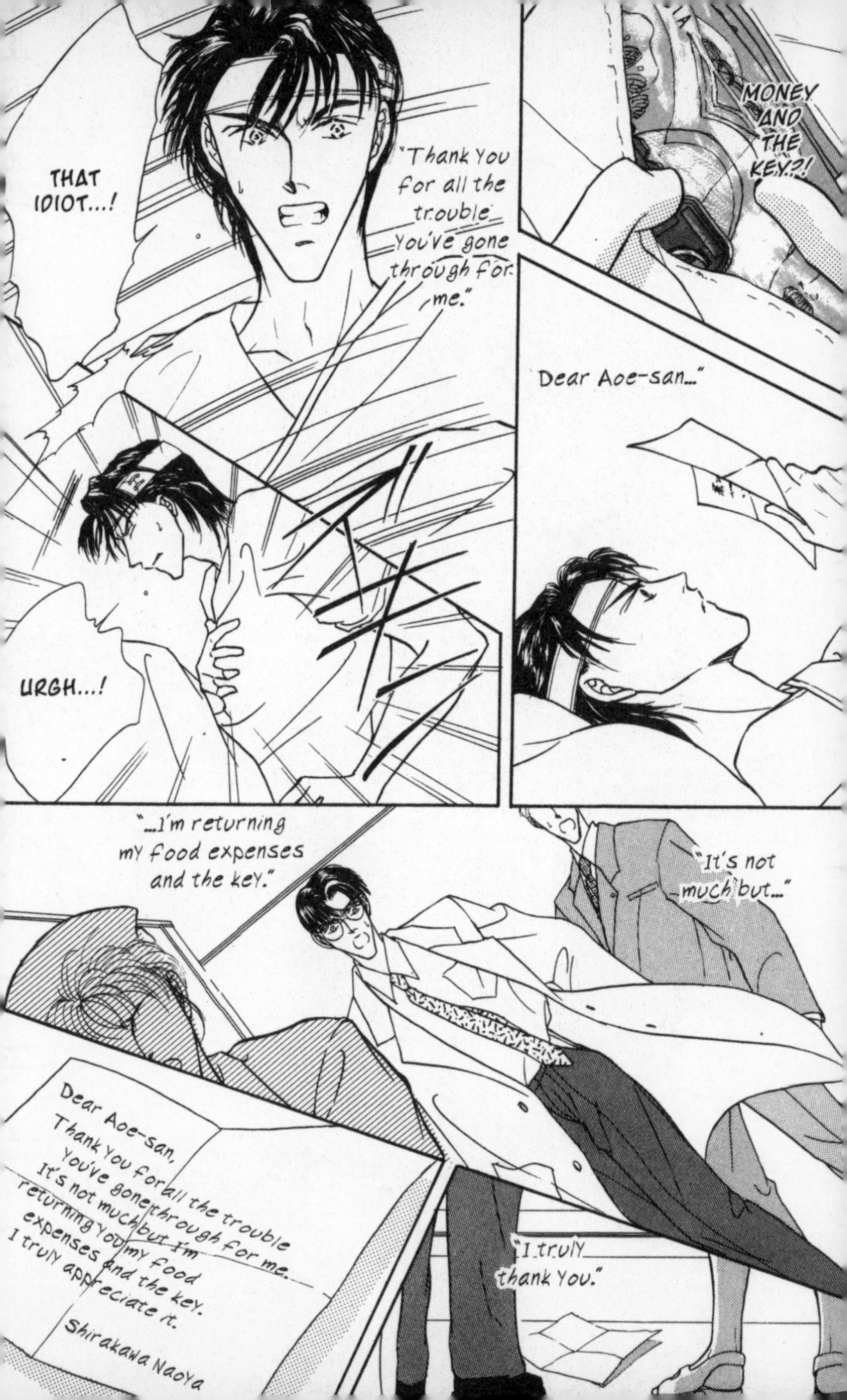
MONEY AND THE KEY?!
Dear Aoe-san..."
"Thank you for all the trouble you've gone through for me."
THAT IDIOT...!
URGH...!
"It's not much but..."
"...I'm returning my food expenses and the key."
"I truly thank you."
Dear Aoe-san,
Thank you for all the trouble you've gone through for me.
It's not much but I'm returning you my food expenses and the key.
I truly appreciate it.
Shirakawa Naoya

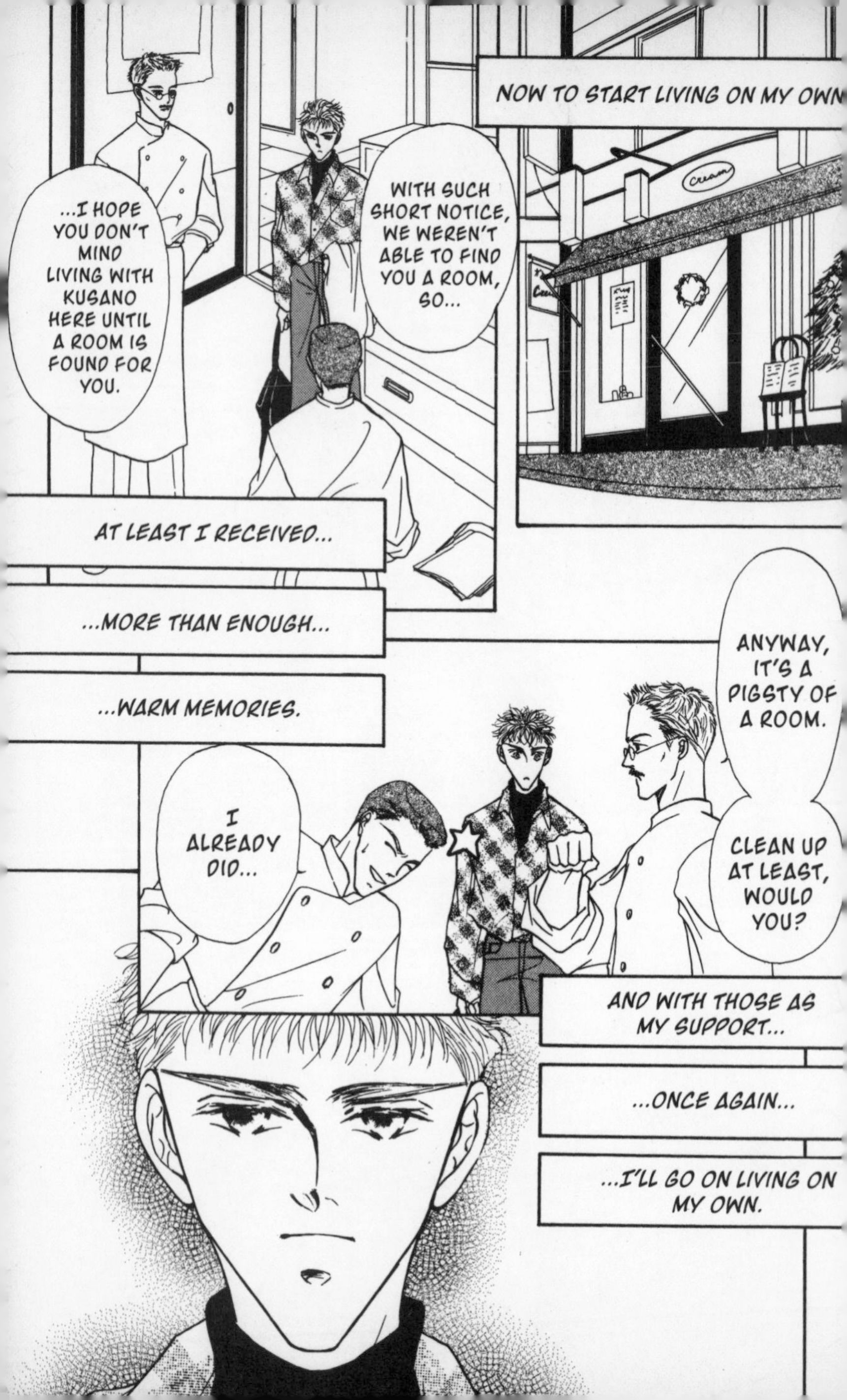
NOW TO START LIVING ON MY OWN
WITH SUCH SHORT NOTICE, WE WEREN'T ABLE TO FIND YOU A ROOM, SO...
...I HOPE YOU DON'T MIND LIVING WITH KUSANO HERE UNTIL A ROOM IS FOUND FOR YOU.
AT LEAST I RECEIVED...
...MORE THAN ENOUGH...
...WARM MEMORIES.
ANYWAY, IT'S A PIGSTY OF A ROOM.
CLEAN UP AT LEAST, WOULD YOU?
I ALREADY DID...
AND WITH THOSE AS MY SUPPORT...
...ONCE AGAIN...
...I'LL GO ON LIVING ON MY OWN.

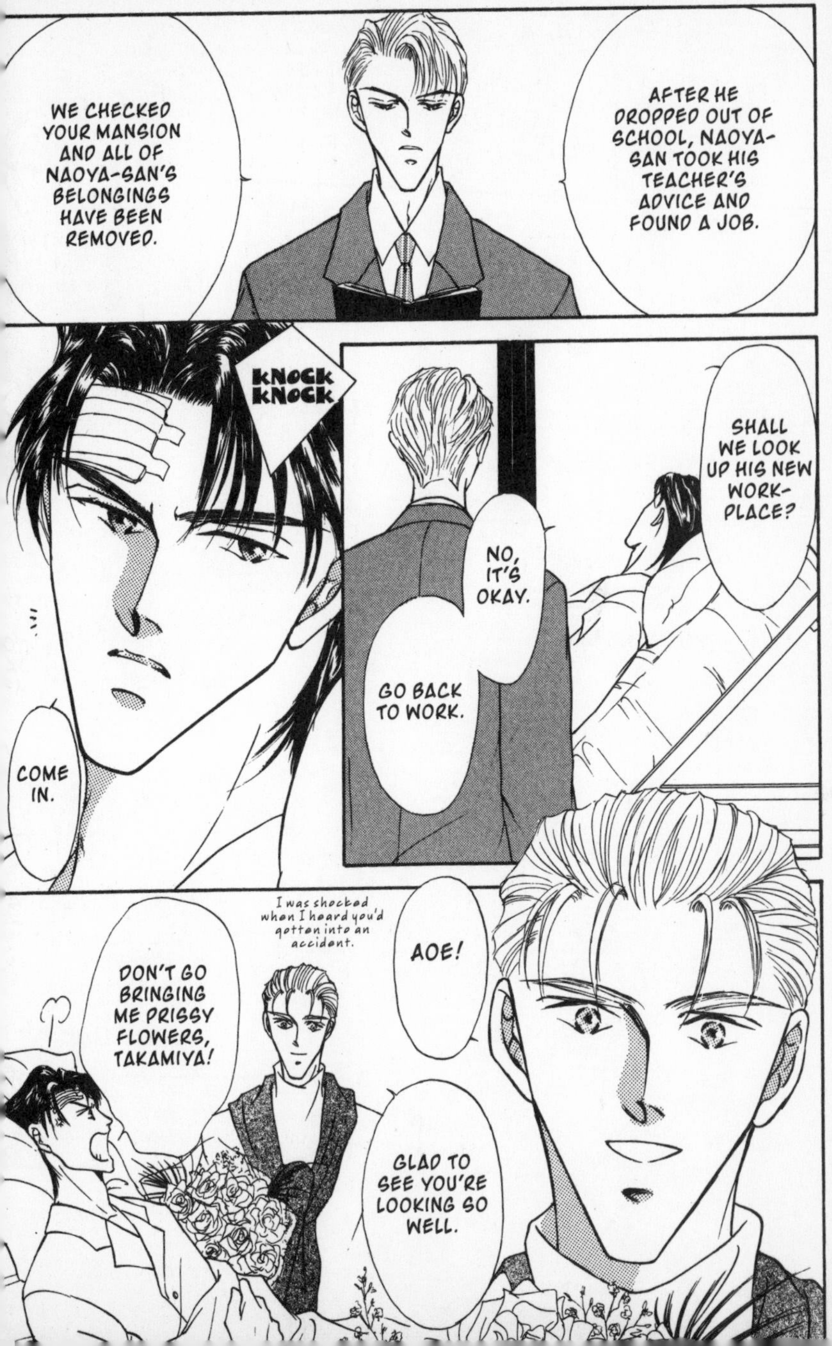
AFTER HE DROPPED OUT OF SCHOOL, NAOYA-SAN TOOK HIS TEACHER'S ADVICE AND FOUND A JOB.
WE CHECKED YOUR MANSION AND ALL OF NAOYA-SAN'S BELONGINGS HAVE BEEN REMOVED.
SHALL WE LOOK UP HIS NEW WORK-PLACE?
NO, IT'S OKAY.
GO BACK TO WORK.
KNOCK KNOCK
COME IN.
AOE!
GLAD TO SEE YOU'RE LOOKING SO WELL.
I was shocked when I heard you'd gotten into an accident.
DON'T GO BRINGING ME PRISSY FLOWERS, TAKAMIYA!

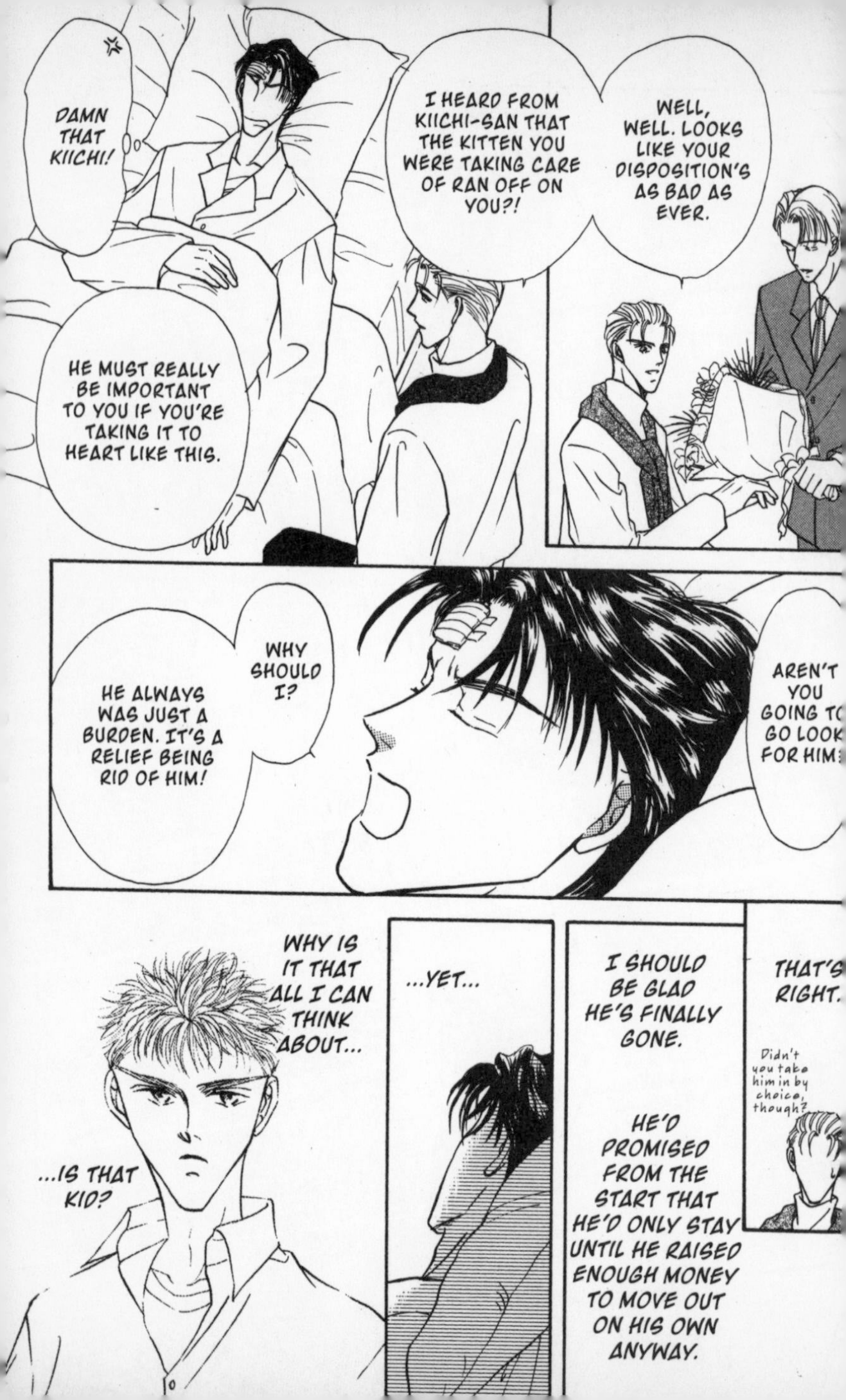
WELL, WELL. LOOKS LIKE YOUR DISPOSITION'S AS BAD AS EVER.
I HEARD FROM KIICHI-SAN THAT THE KITTEN YOU WERE TAKING CARE OF RAN OFF ON YOU?!
DAMN THAT KIICHI!
HE MUST REALLY BE IMPORTANT TO YOU IF YOU'RE TAKING IT TO HEART LIKE THIS.
AREN'T YOU GOING TO GO LOOK FOR HIM?
WHY SHOULD I?
HE ALWAYS WAS JUST A BURDEN. IT'S A RELIEF BEING RID OF HIM!
THAT'S RIGHT.
Didn't you take him in by choice, though?
I SHOULD BE GLAD HE'S FINALLY GONE.
HE'D PROMISED FROM THE START THAT HE'D ONLY STAY UNTIL HE RAISED ENOUGH MONEY TO MOVE OUT ON HIS OWN ANYWAY.
...YET...
WHY IS IT THAT ALL I CAN THINK ABOUT...
...IS THAT KID?

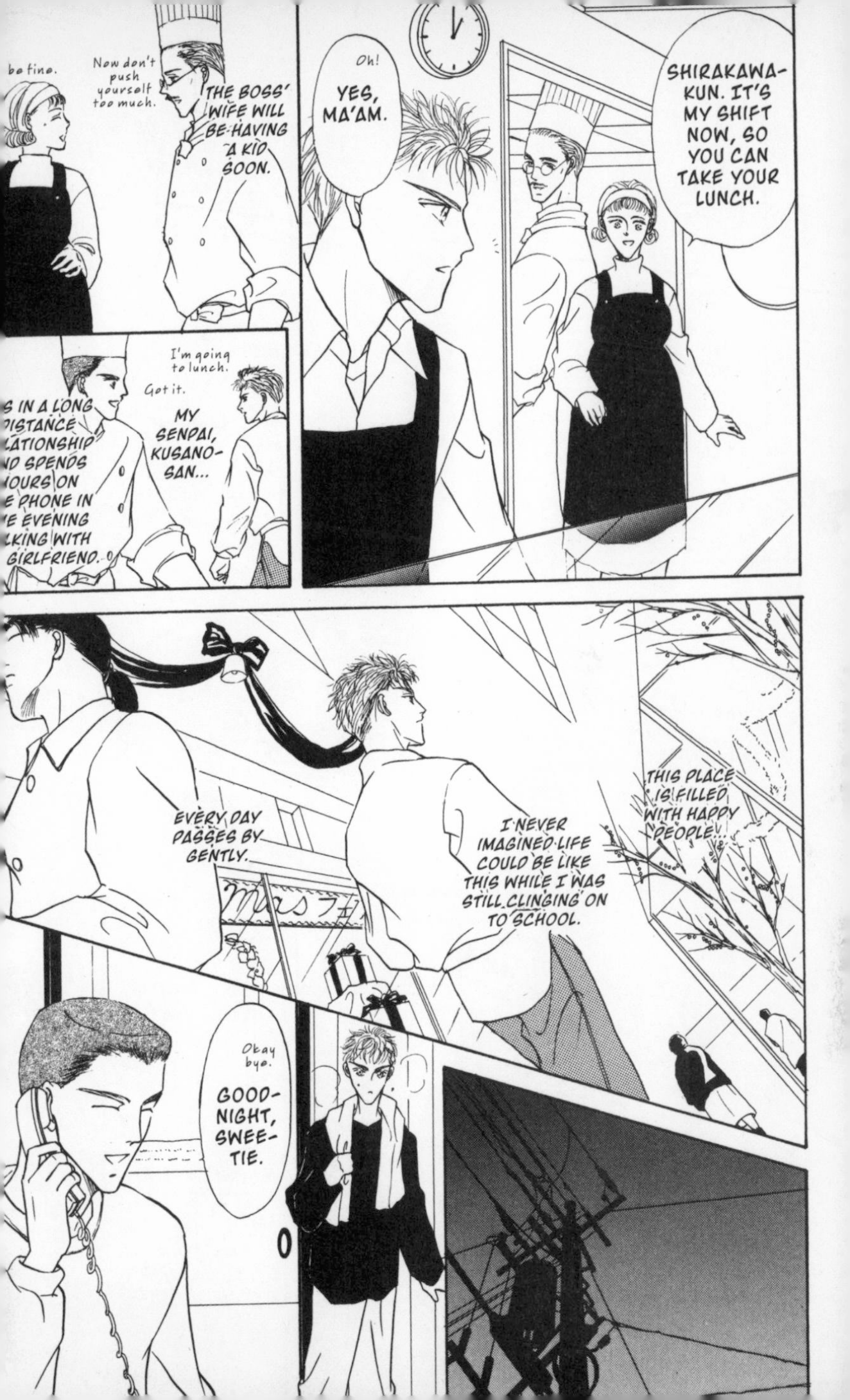
SHIRAKAWA-KUN. IT'S MY SHIFT NOW, SO YOU CAN TAKE YOUR LUNCH.
Oh!
YES, MA'AM.
THE BOSS' WIFE WILL BE HAVING A KID SOON.
Now don't push yourself too much.
be fine.
I'm going to lunch.
Got it.
MY SENPAI, KUSANO-SAN...
S IN A LONG DISTANCE LATIONSHIP ND SPENDS HOURS ON E PHONE IN E EVENING LKING WITH GIRLFRIEND.
THIS PLACE IS FILLED WITH HAPPY PEOPLE...
I NEVER IMAGINED LIFE COULD BE LIKE THIS WHILE I WAS STILL CLINGING ON TO SCHOOL.
EVERY DAY PASSES BY GENTLY.
Okay bye.
GOOD-NIGHT, SWEE-TIE.

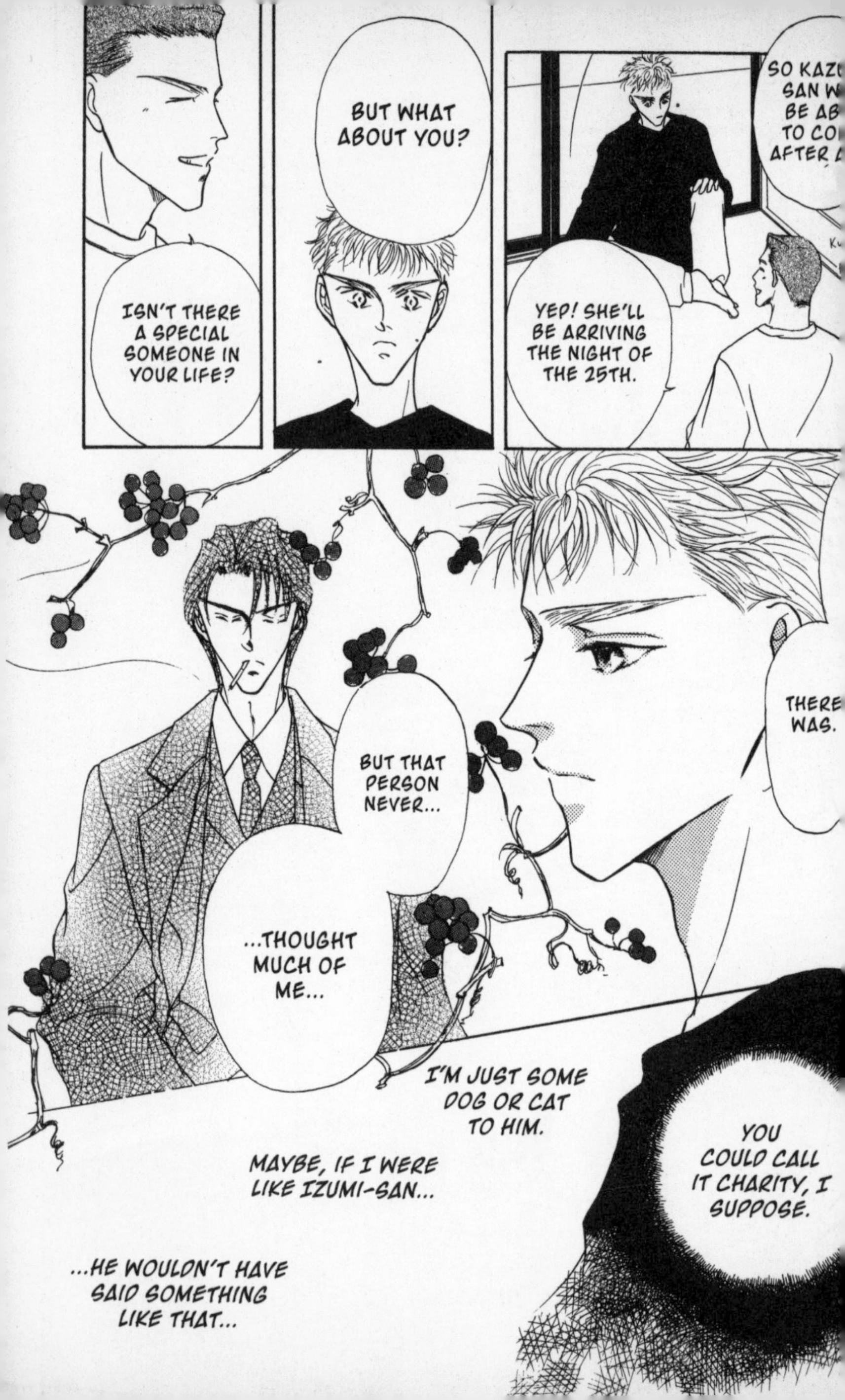
SO KAZ SAN W BE AB TO CO AFTER
YEP! SHE'LL BE ARRIVING THE NIGHT OF THE 25TH.
BUT WHAT ABOUT YOU?
ISN'T THERE A SPECIAL SOMEONE IN YOUR LIFE?
THERE WAS.
BUT THAT PERSON NEVER...
...THOUGHT MUCH OF ME...
YOU COULD CALL IT CHARITY, I SUPPOSE.
I'M JUST SOME DOG OR CAT TO HIM.
MAYBE, IF I WERE LIKE IZUMI-SAN...
...HE WOULDN'T HAVE SAID SOMETHING LIKE THAT...

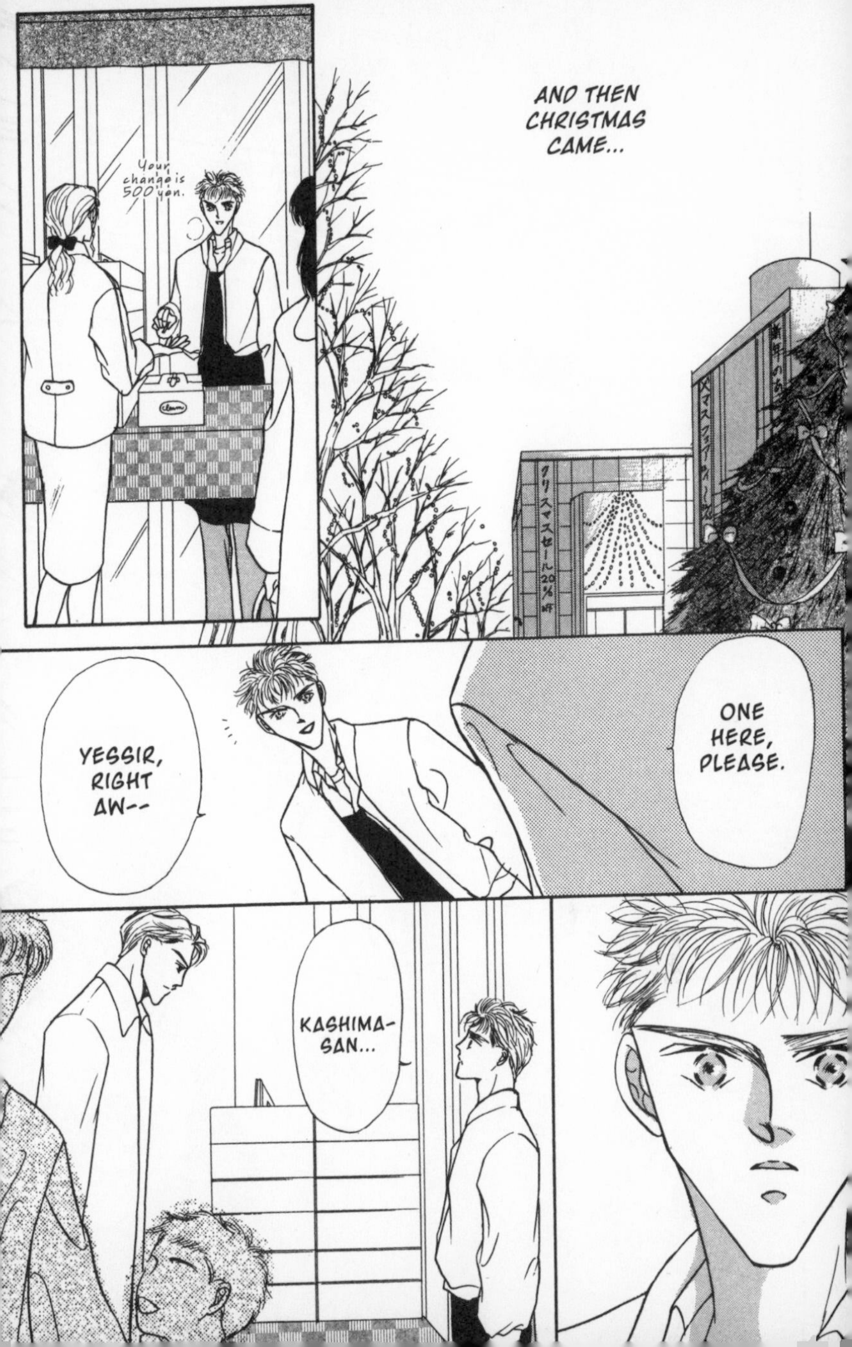
AND THEN CHRISTMAS CAME...
Your change is 500 yen.
ONE HERE, PLEASE.
YESSIR, RIGHT AW--
KASHIMA-SAN...

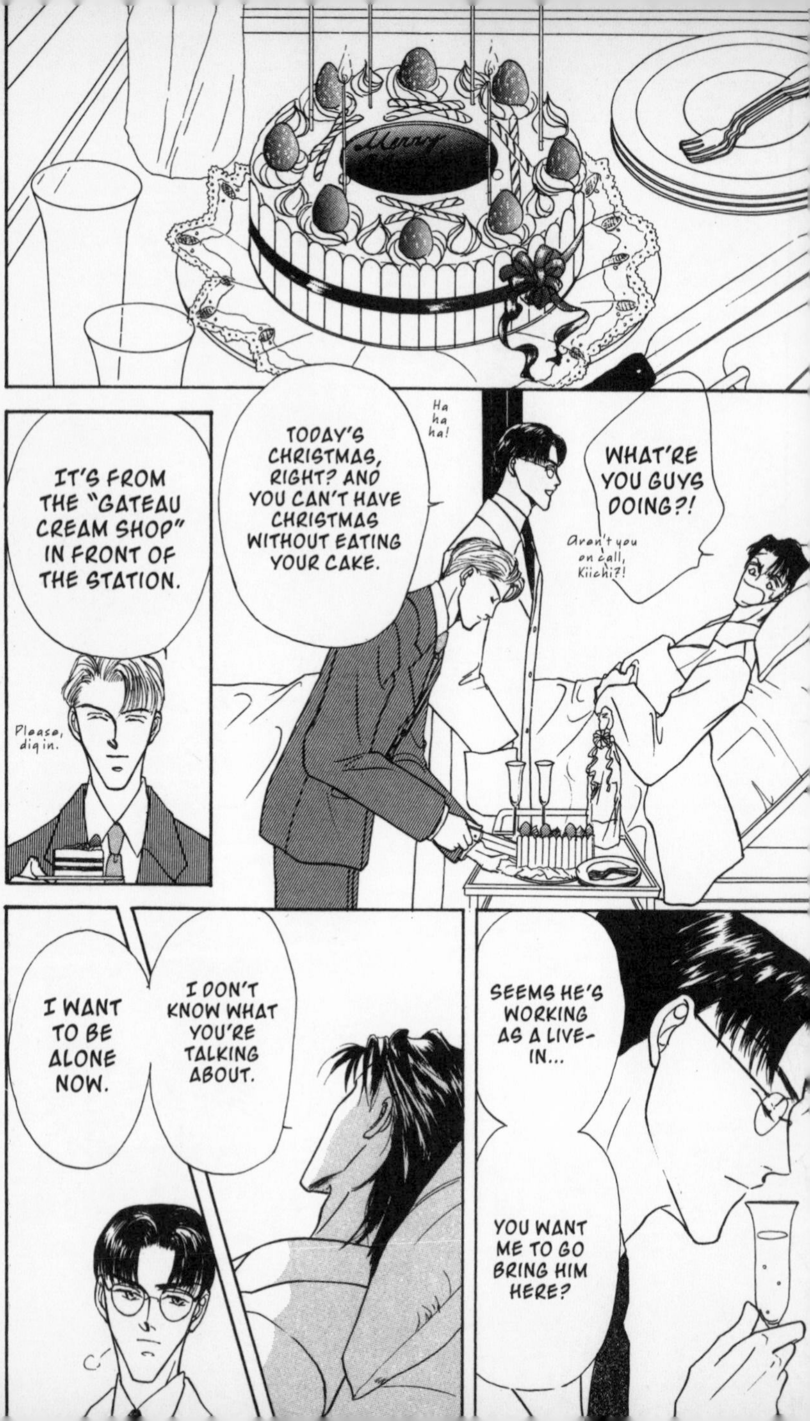
Merry
WHAT'RE YOU GUYS DOING?!
Aren't you on call, Kiichi?!
Ha ha ha!
TODAY'S CHRISTMAS, RIGHT? AND YOU CAN'T HAVE CHRISTMAS WITHOUT EATING YOUR CAKE.
IT'S FROM THE "GATEAU CREAM SHOP" IN FRONT OF THE STATION.
Please, dig in.
SEEMS HE'S WORKING AS A LIVE-IN...
YOU WANT ME TO GO BRING HIM HERE?
I DON'T KNOW WHAT YOU'RE TALKING ABOUT.
I WANT TO BE ALONE NOW.

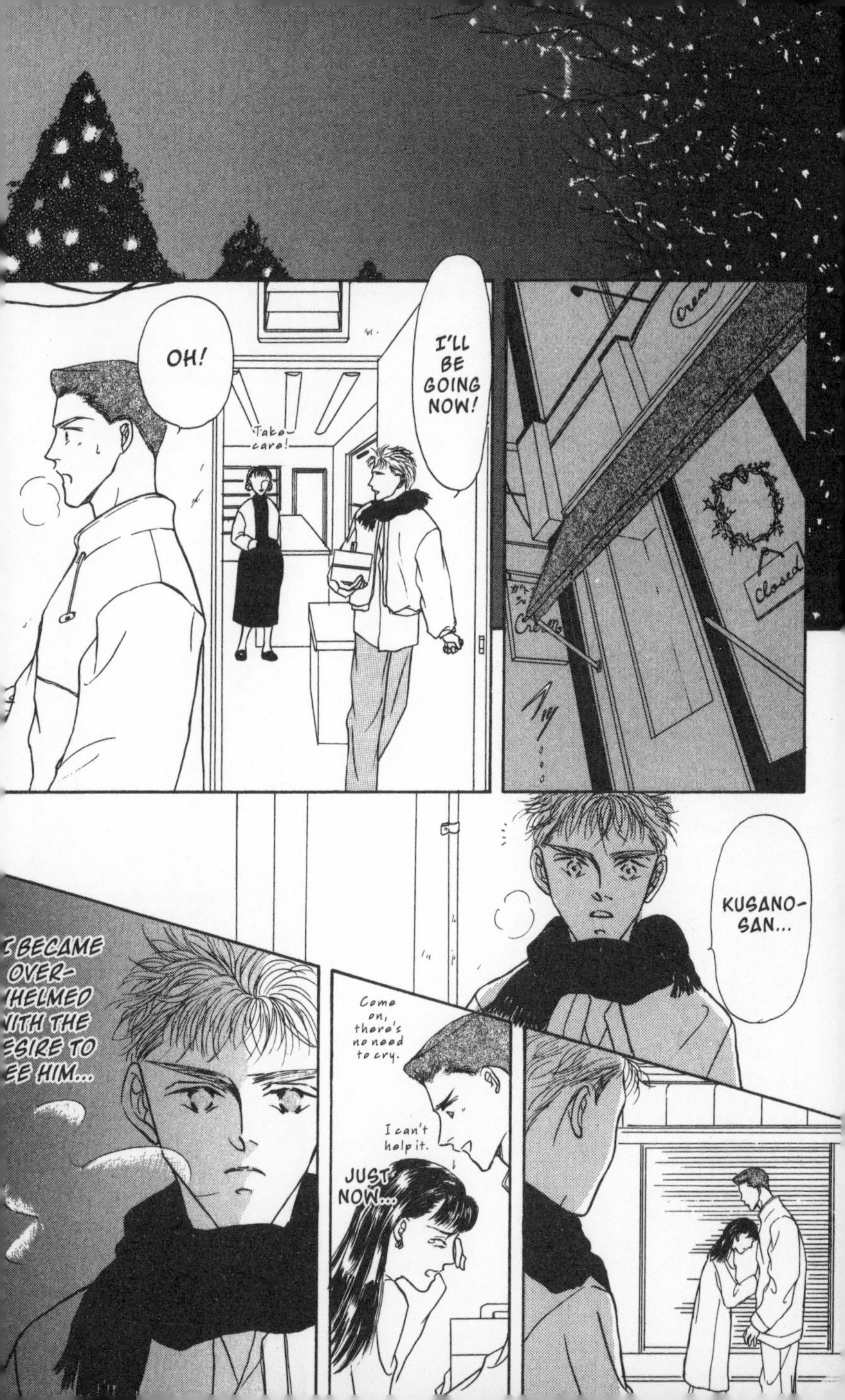
Closed
I'LL BE GOING NOW!
Take care!
OH!
KUSANO-SAN...
Come on, there's no need to cry.
I can't help it.
JUST NOW...
I BECAME OVER-WHELMED WITH THE ESIRE TO EE HIM...

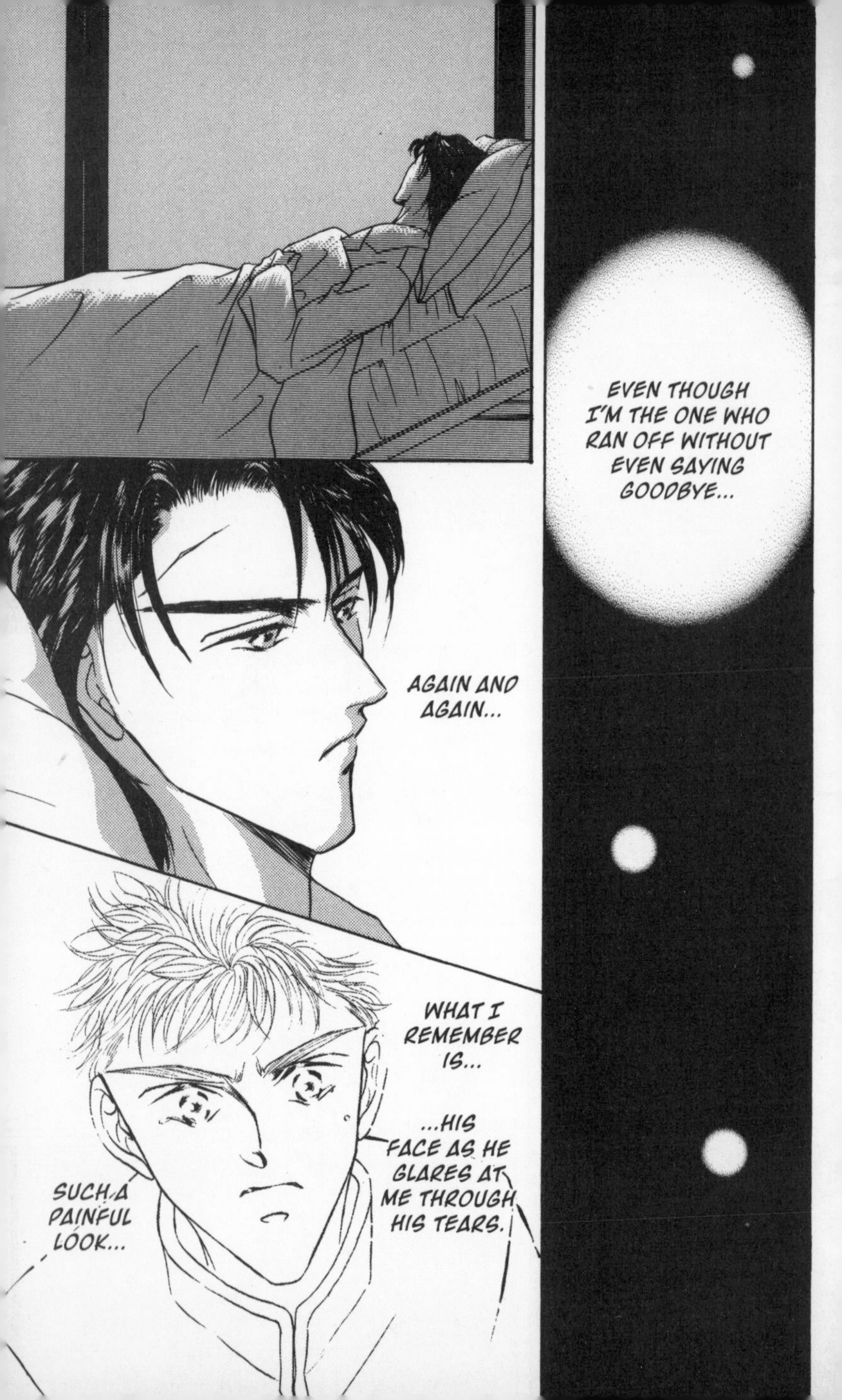
EVEN THOUGH I'M THE ONE WHO RAN OFF WITHOUT EVEN SAYING GOODBYE...
AGAIN AND AGAIN...
WHAT I REMEMBER IS...
...HIS FACE AS HE GLARES AT ME THROUGH HIS TEARS.
SUCH A PAINFUL LOOK...

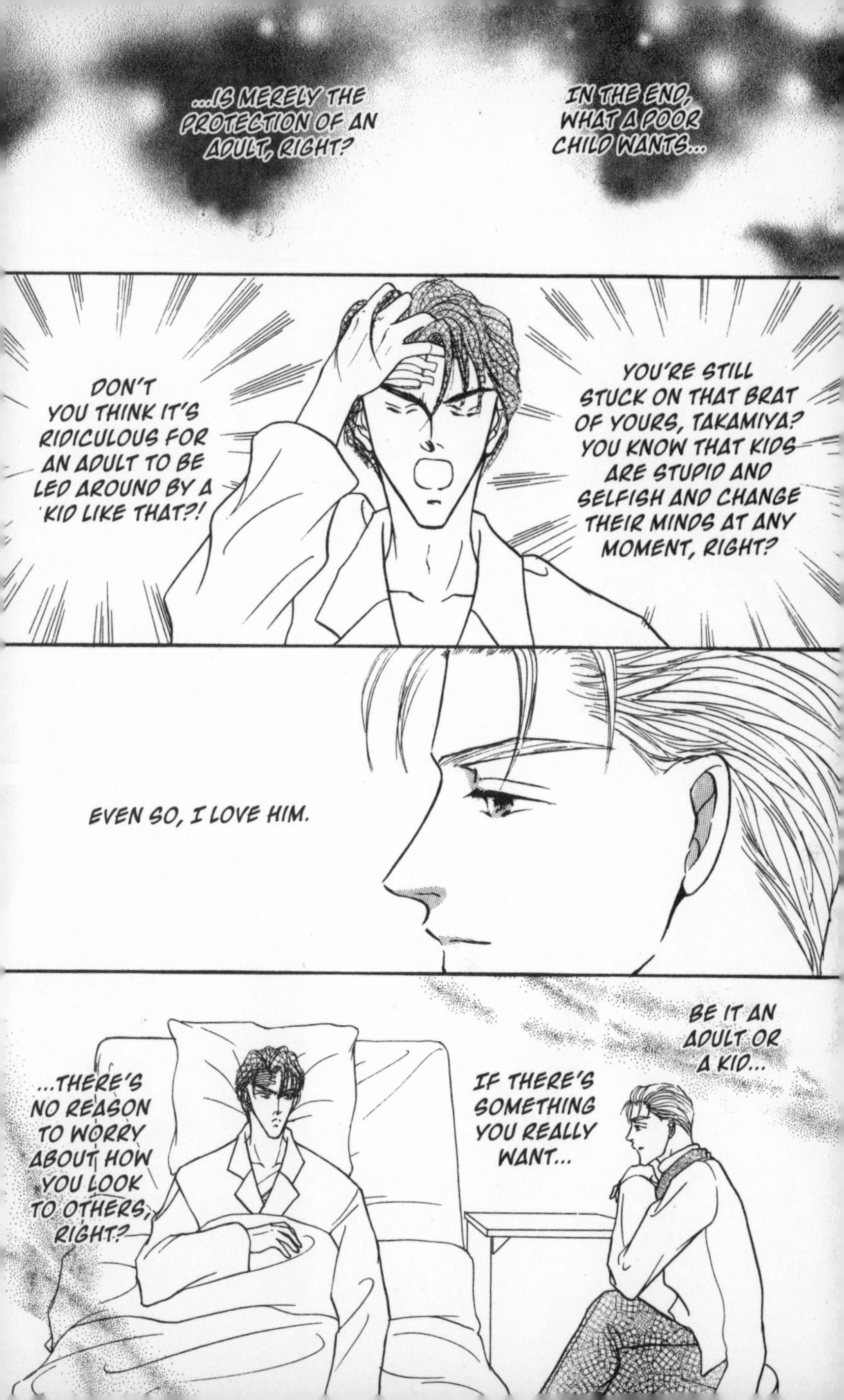
IN THE END, WHAT A POOR CHILD WANTS...
...IS MERELY THE PROTECTION OF AN ADULT, RIGHT?
YOU'RE STILL STUCK ON THAT BRAT OF YOURS, TAKAMIYA? YOU KNOW THAT KIDS ARE STUPID AND SELFISH AND CHANGE THEIR MINDS AT ANY MOMENT, RIGHT?
DON'T YOU THINK IT'S RIDICULOUS FOR AN ADULT TO BE LED AROUND BY A KID LIKE THAT?!
EVEN SO, I LOVE HIM.
BE IT AN ADULT OR A KID...
IF THERE'S SOMETHING YOU REALLY WANT...
...THERE'S NO REASON TO WORRY ABOUT HOW YOU LOOK TO OTHERS, RIGHT?

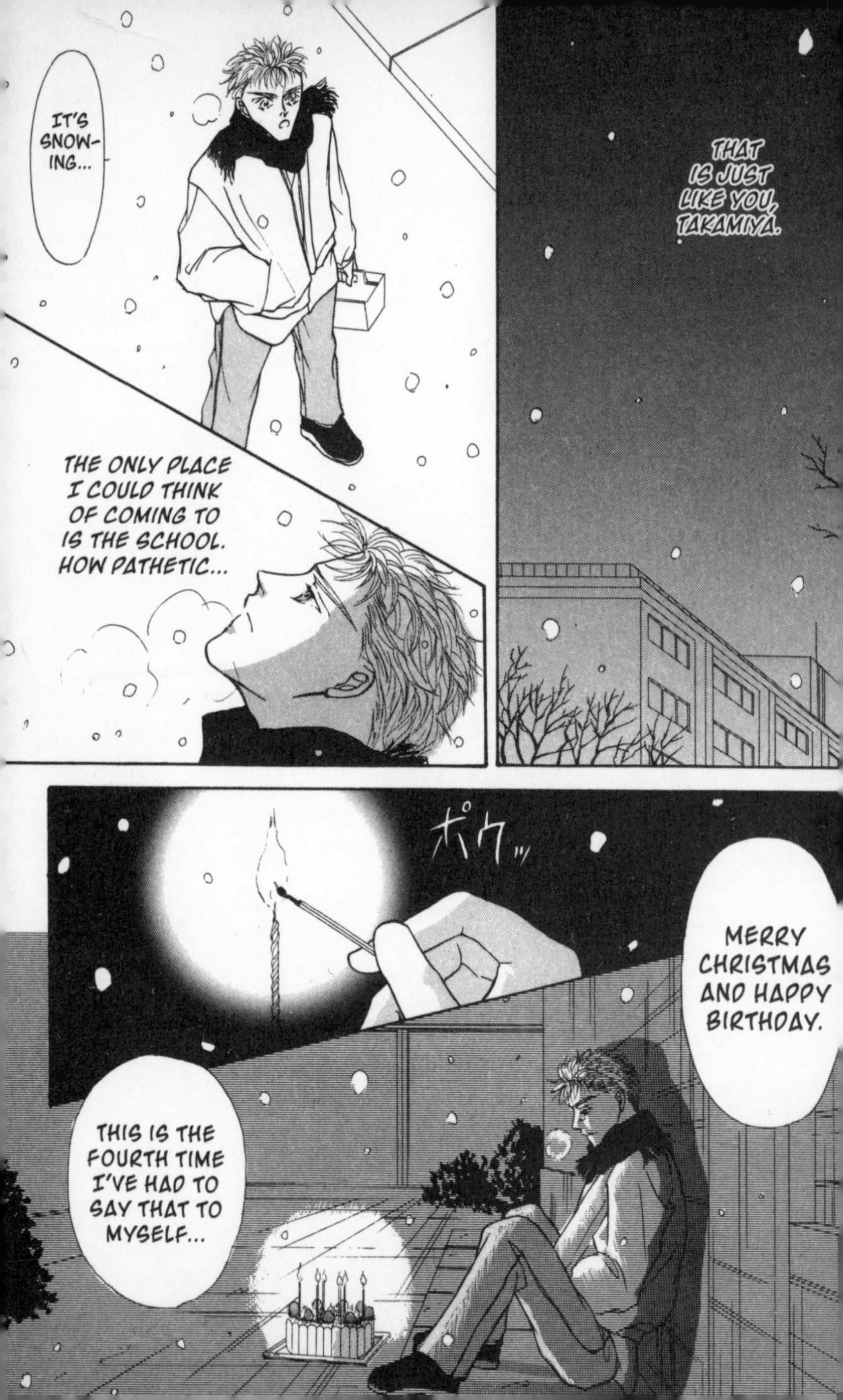
THAT IS JUST LIKE YOU, TAKAMIYA.
IT'S SNOWING...
THE ONLY PLACE I COULD THINK OF COMING TO IS THE SCHOOL. HOW PATHETIC...
ポウッ
MERRY CHRISTMAS AND HAPPY BIRTHDAY.
THIS IS THE FOURTH TIME I'VE HAD TO SAY THAT TO MYSELF...

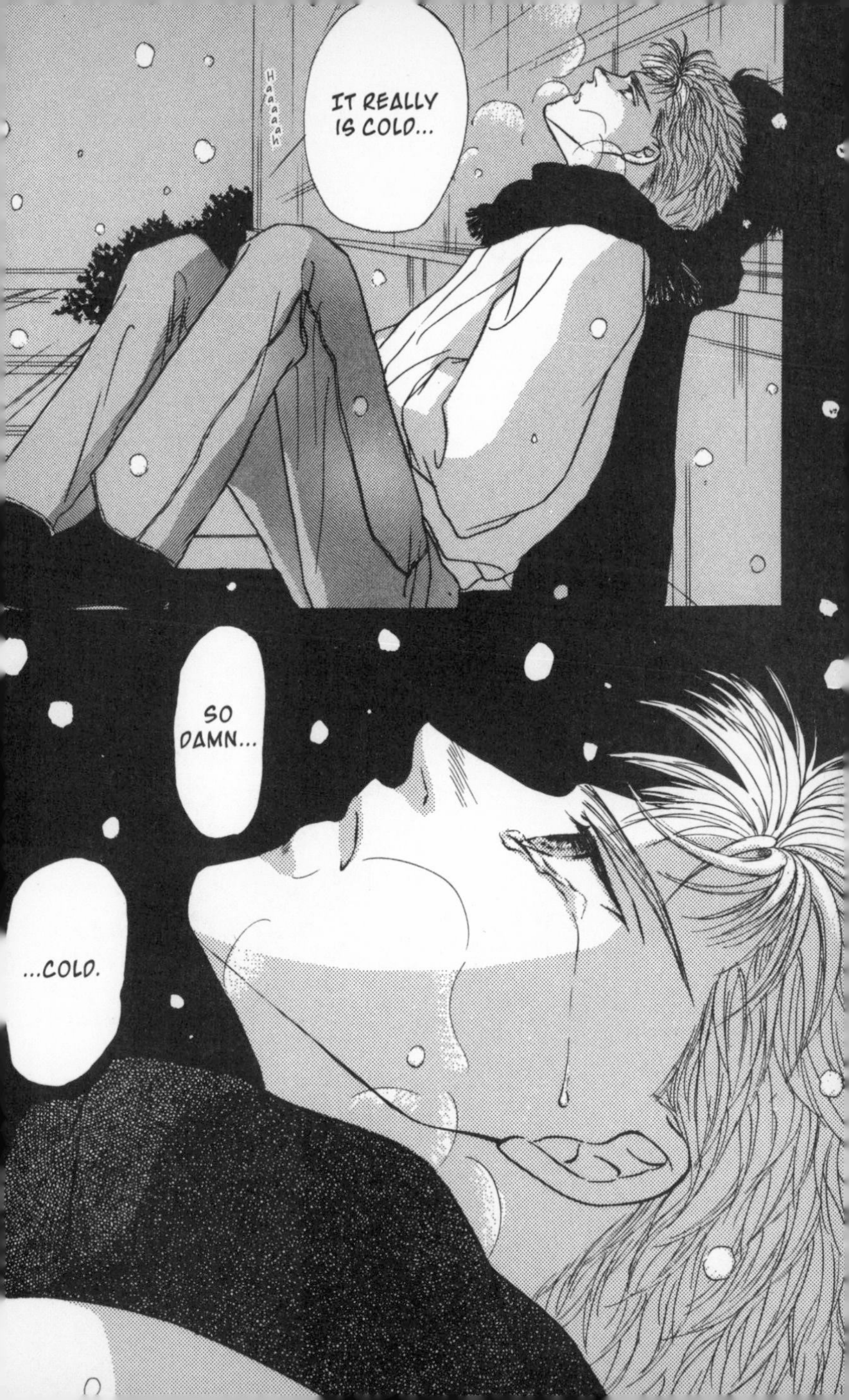
Haaaaah
IT REALLY IS COLD...
SO DAMN...
...COLD.

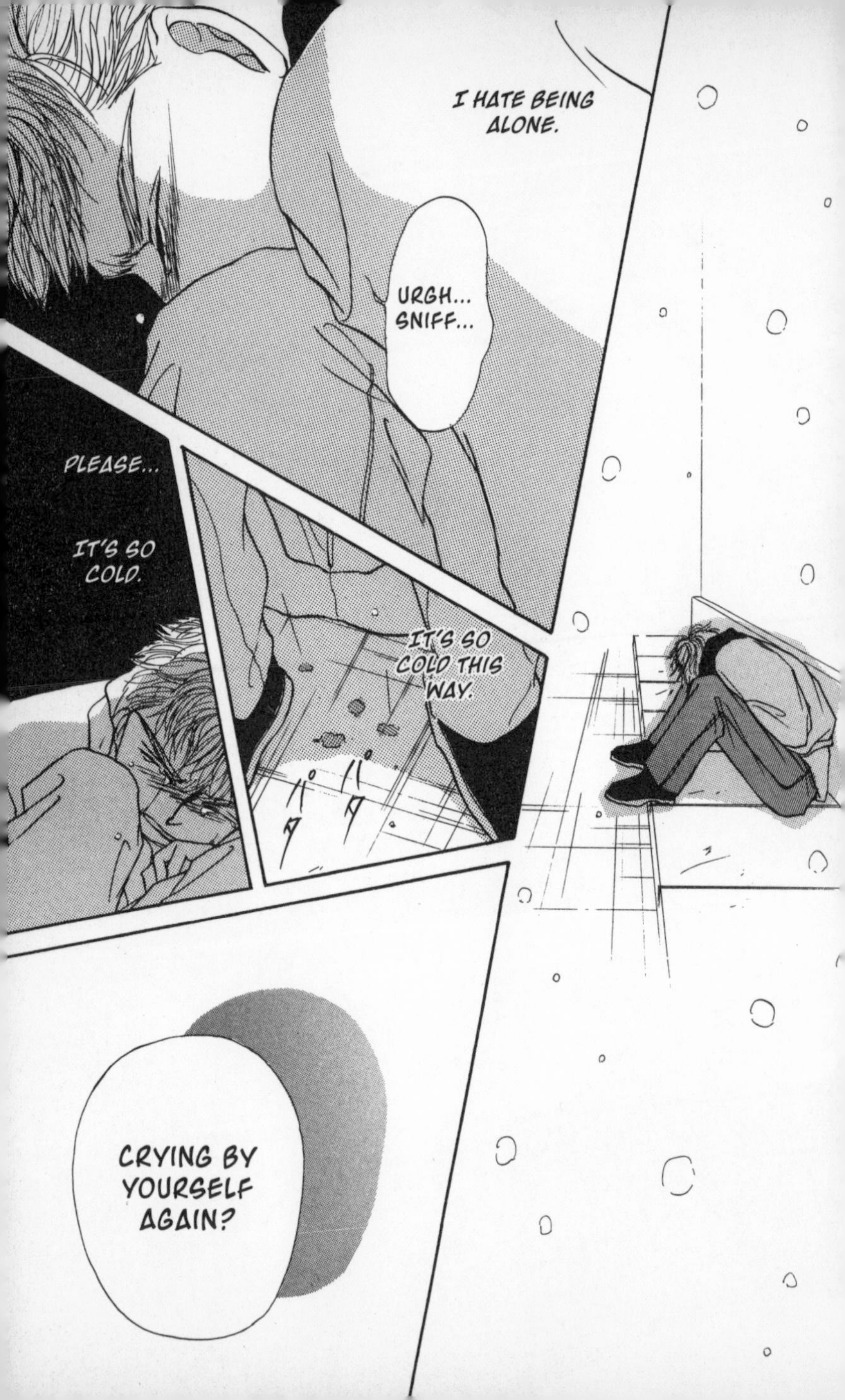
I HATE BEING ALONE.
URGH... SNIFF...
IT'S SO COLD THIS WAY.
PLEASE...
IT'S SO COLD.
CRYING BY YOURSELF AGAIN?

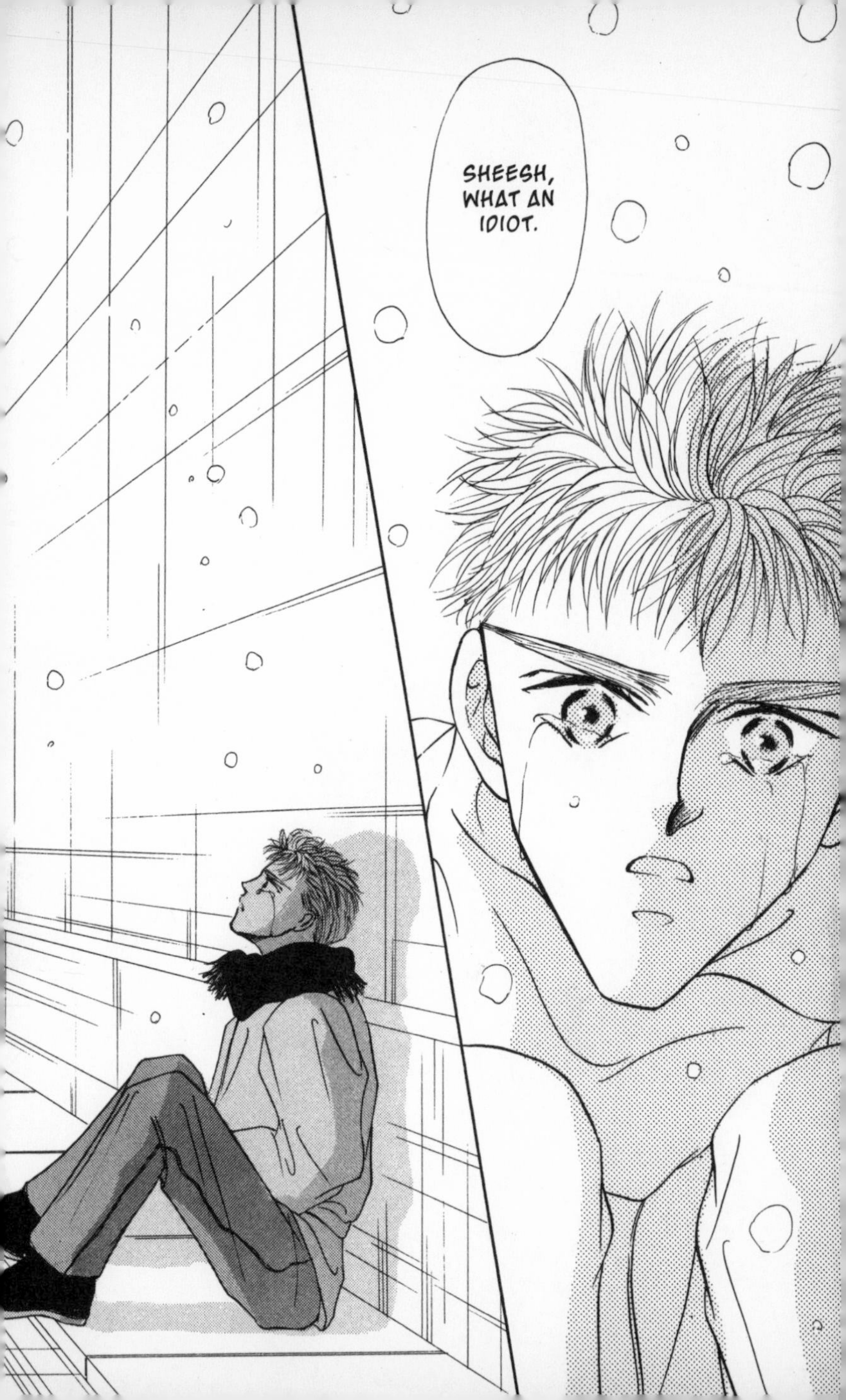
SHEESH, WHAT AN IDIOT.

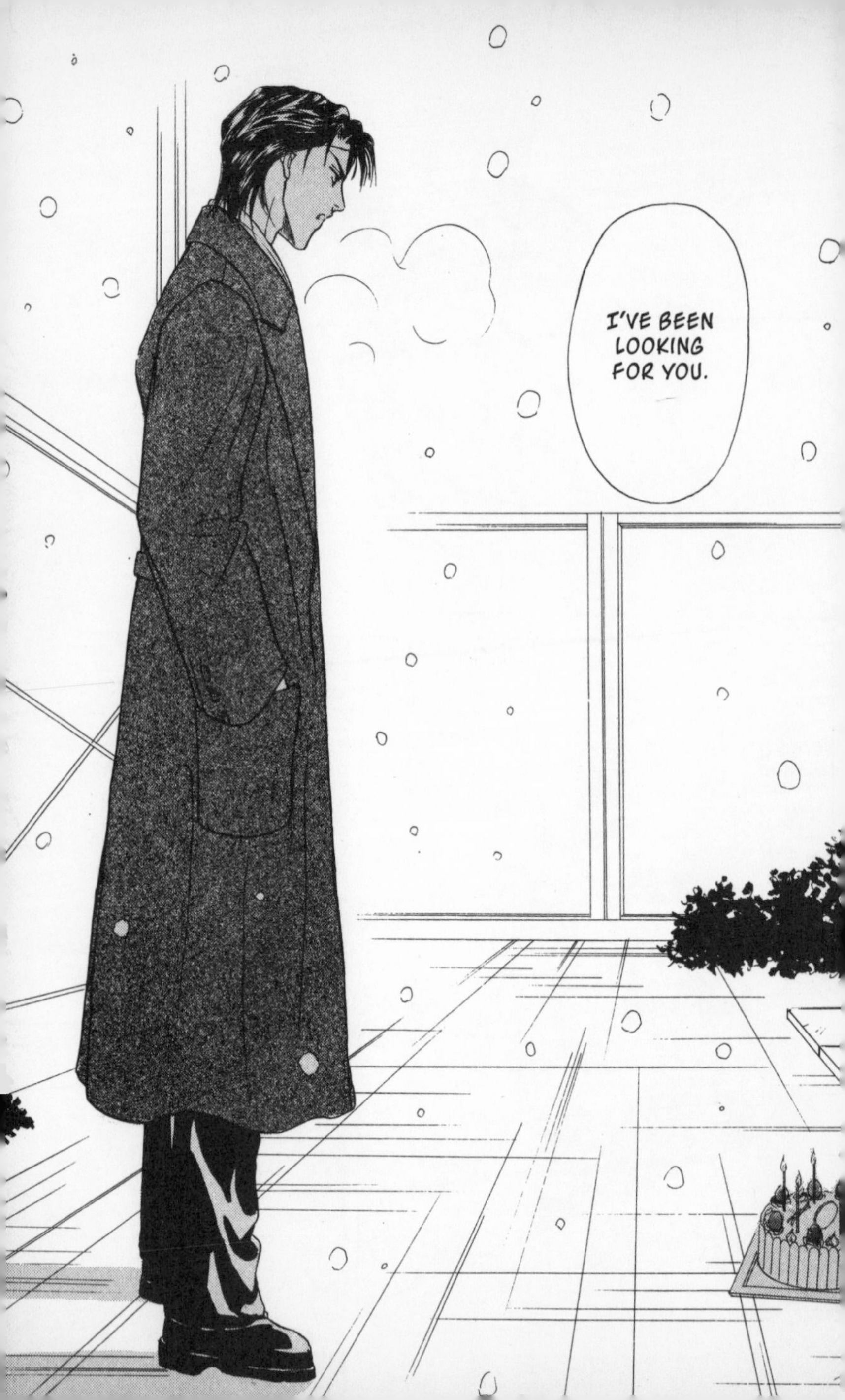
I'VE BEEN LOOKING FOR YOU.

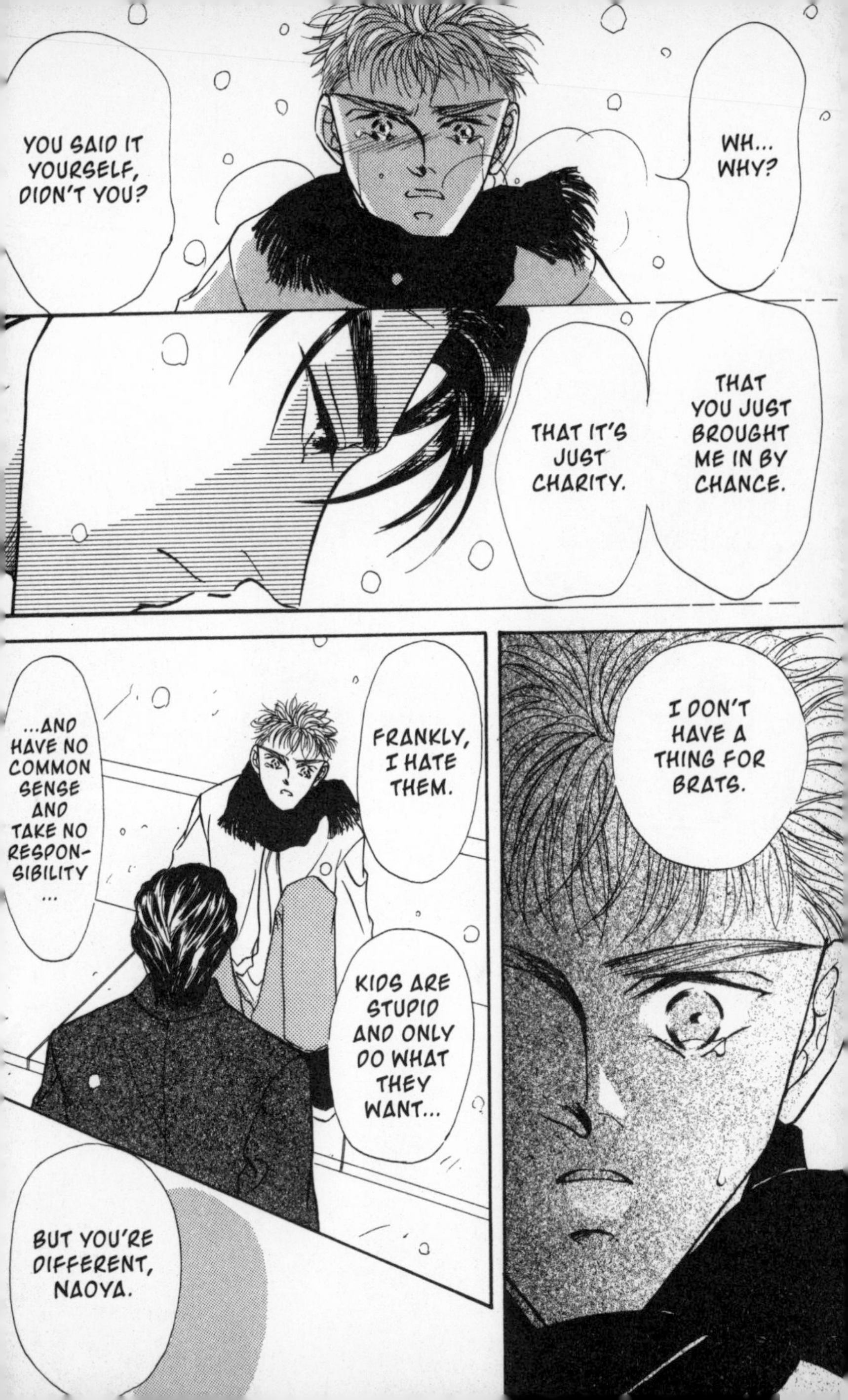
WH... WHY?
YOU SAID IT YOURSELF, DIDN'T YOU?
THAT YOU JUST BROUGHT ME IN BY CHANCE.
THAT IT'S JUST CHARITY.
I DON'T HAVE A THING FOR BRATS.
FRANKLY, I HATE THEM.
KIDS ARE STUPID AND ONLY DO WHAT THEY WANT...
...AND HAVE NO COMMON SENSE AND TAKE NO RESPON-SIBILITY...
BUT YOU'RE DIFFERENT, NAOYA.

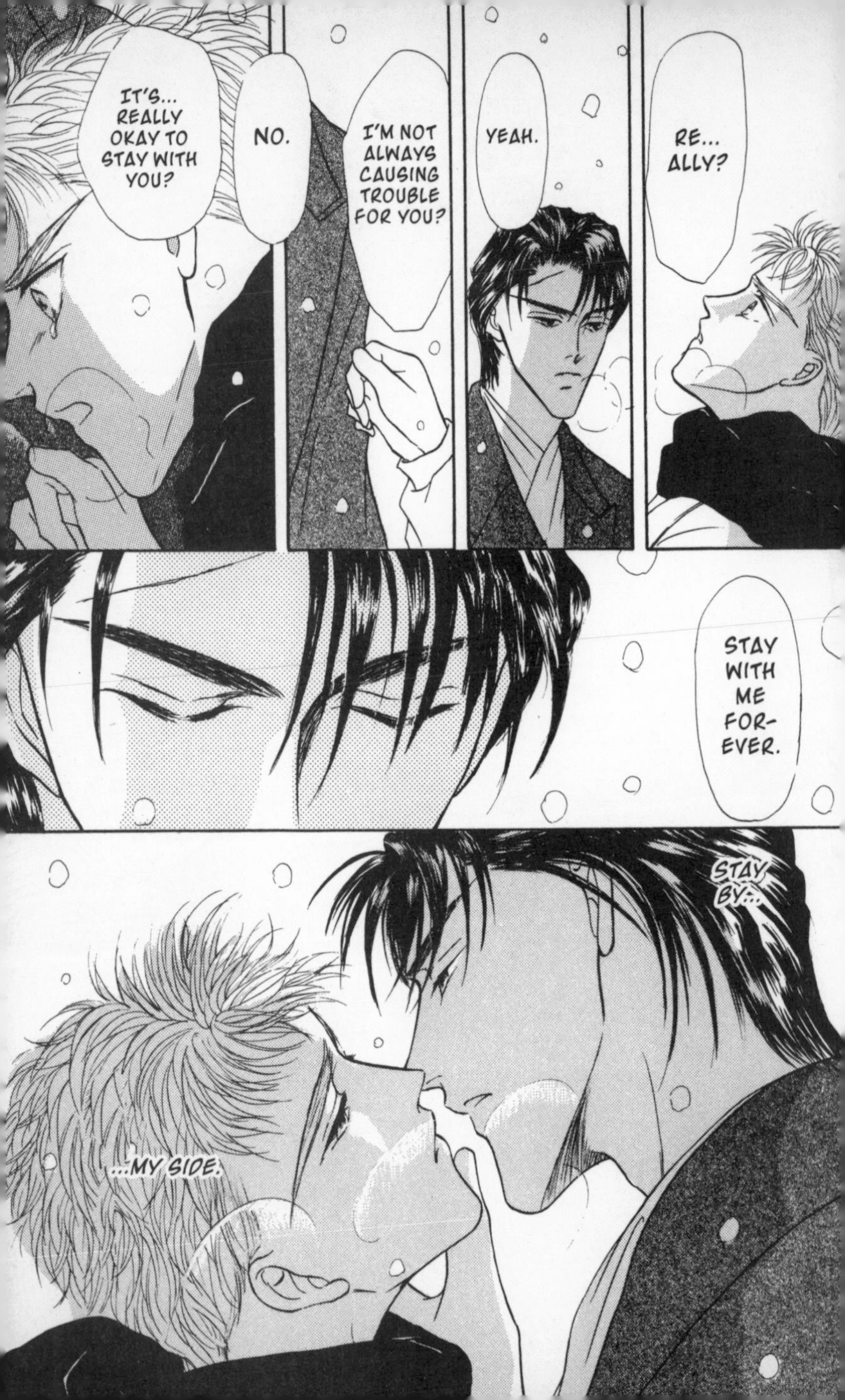
RE... ALLY?
YEAH.
I'M NOT ALWAYS CAUSING TROUBLE FOR YOU?
NO.
IT'S... REALLY OKAY TO STAY WITH YOU?
STAY WITH ME FOR-EVER.
STAY BY...
...MY SIDE.

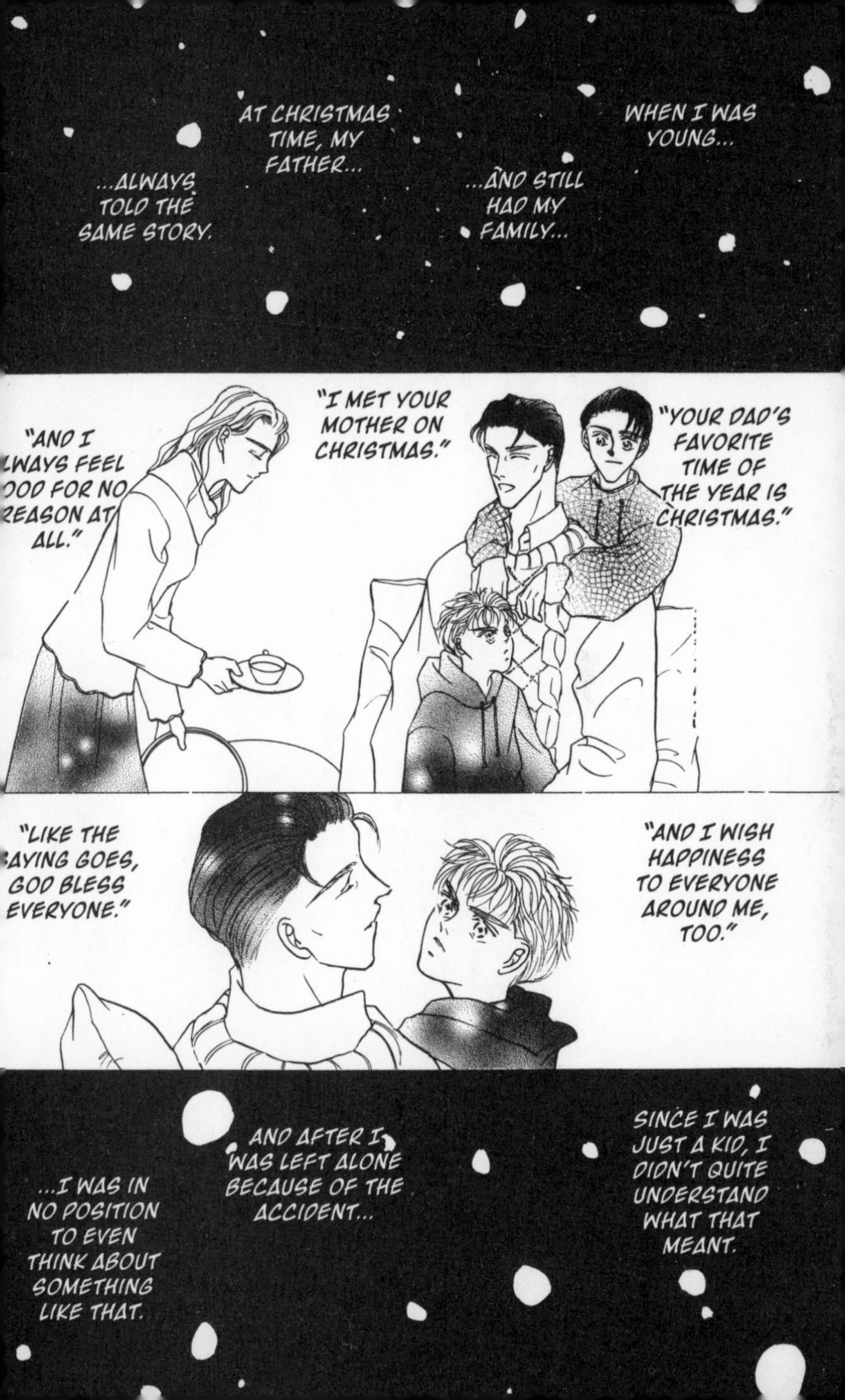
WHEN I WAS YOUNG...
...AND STILL HAD MY FAMILY...
AT CHRISTMAS TIME, MY FATHER...
...ALWAYS TOLD THE SAME STORY.
"YOUR DAD'S FAVORITE TIME OF THE YEAR IS CHRISTMAS."
"I MET YOUR MOTHER ON CHRISTMAS."
"AND I LWAYS FEEL OOD FOR NO REASON AT ALL."
"AND I WISH HAPPINESS TO EVERYONE AROUND ME, TOO."
"LIKE THE AYING GOES, GOD BLESS EVERYONE."
SINCE I WAS JUST A KID, I DIDN'T QUITE UNDERSTAND WHAT THAT MEANT.
AND AFTER I WAS LEFT ALONE BECAUSE OF THE ACCIDENT...
...I WAS IN NO POSITION TO EVEN THINK ABOUT SOMETHING LIKE THAT.

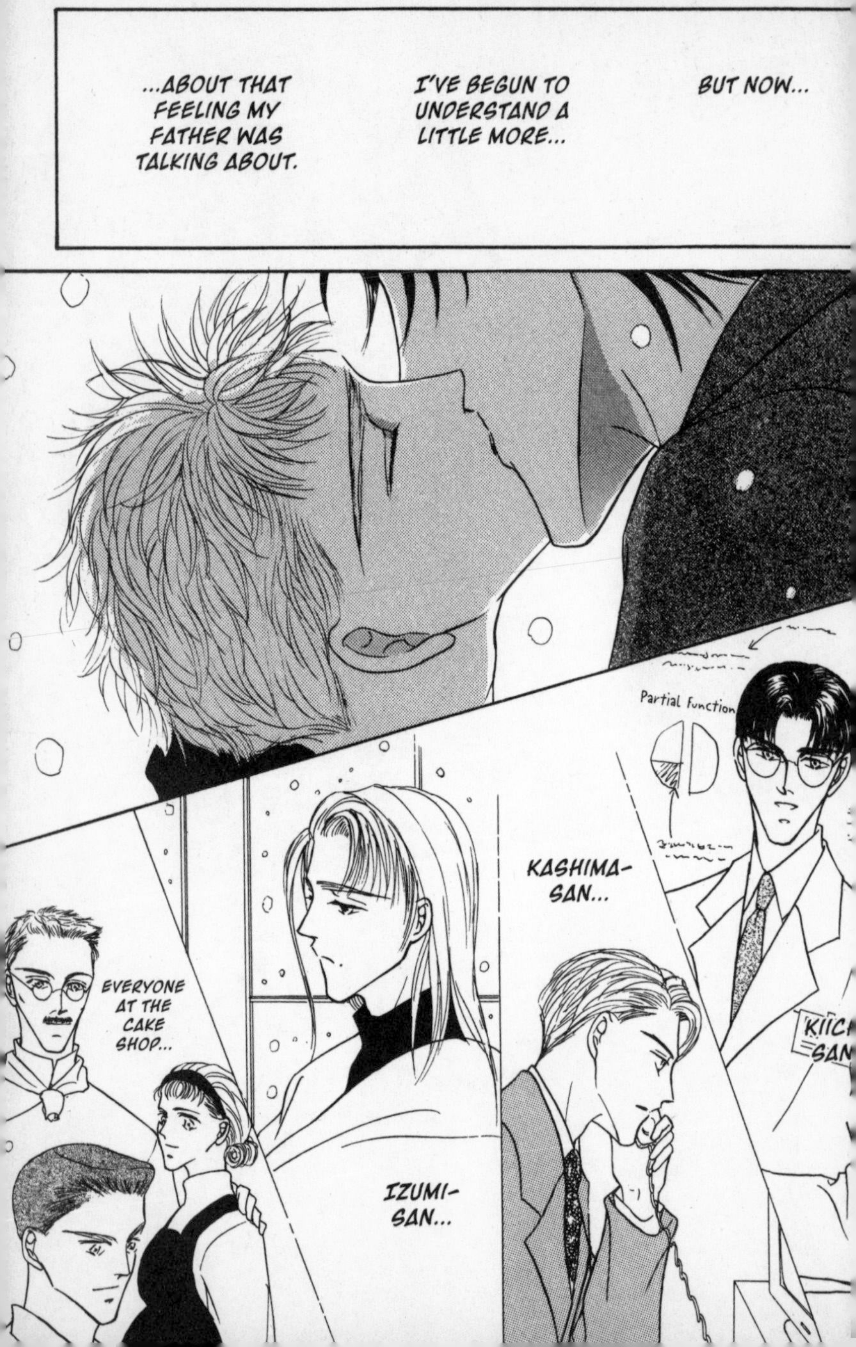
BUT NOW...
I'VE BEGUN TO UNDERSTAND A LITTLE MORE...
...ABOUT THAT FEELING MY FATHER WAS TALKING ABOUT.
Partial Function
KIICH SAN
KASHIMA-SAN...
IZUMI-SAN...
EVERYONE AT THE CAKE SHOP...

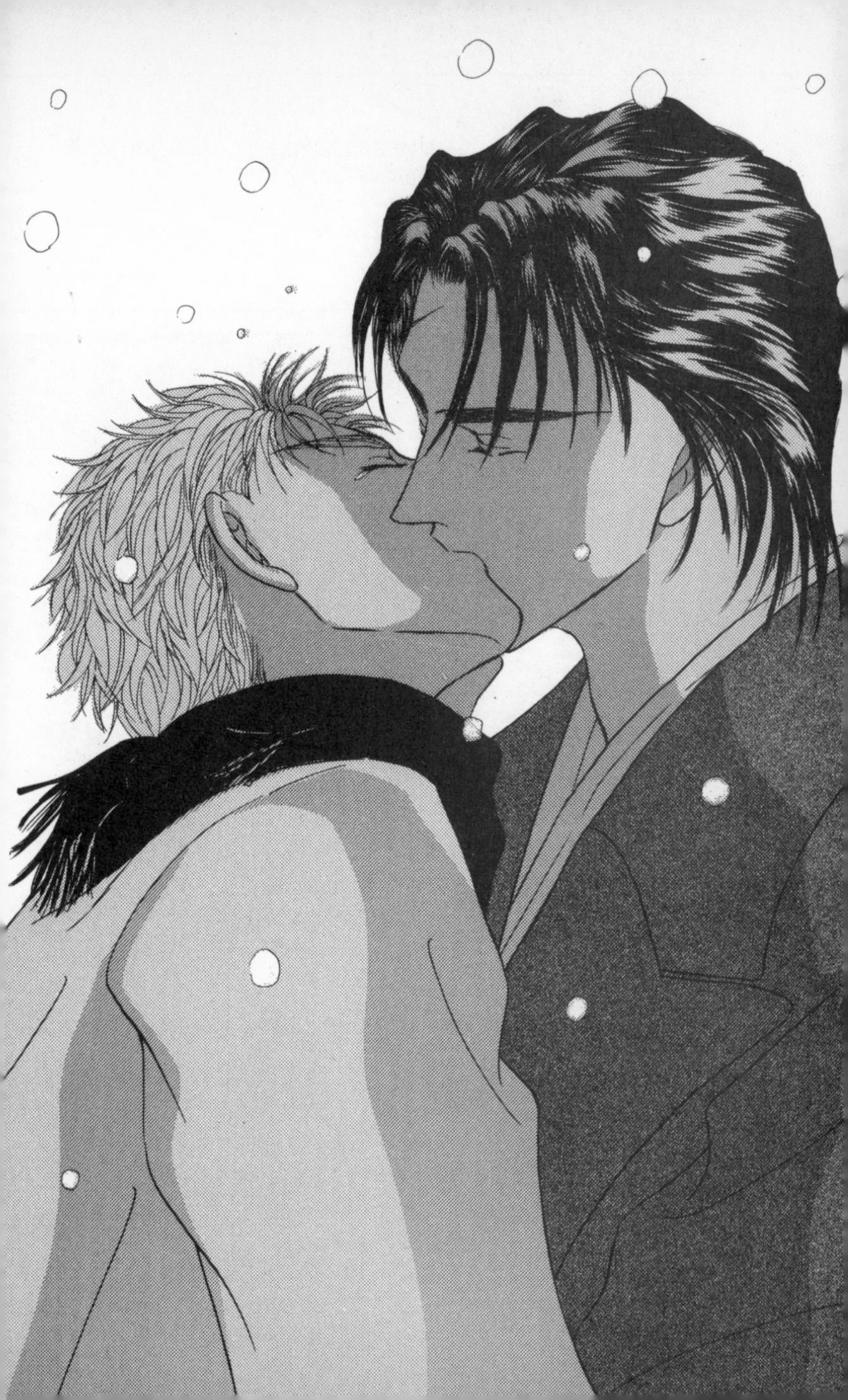

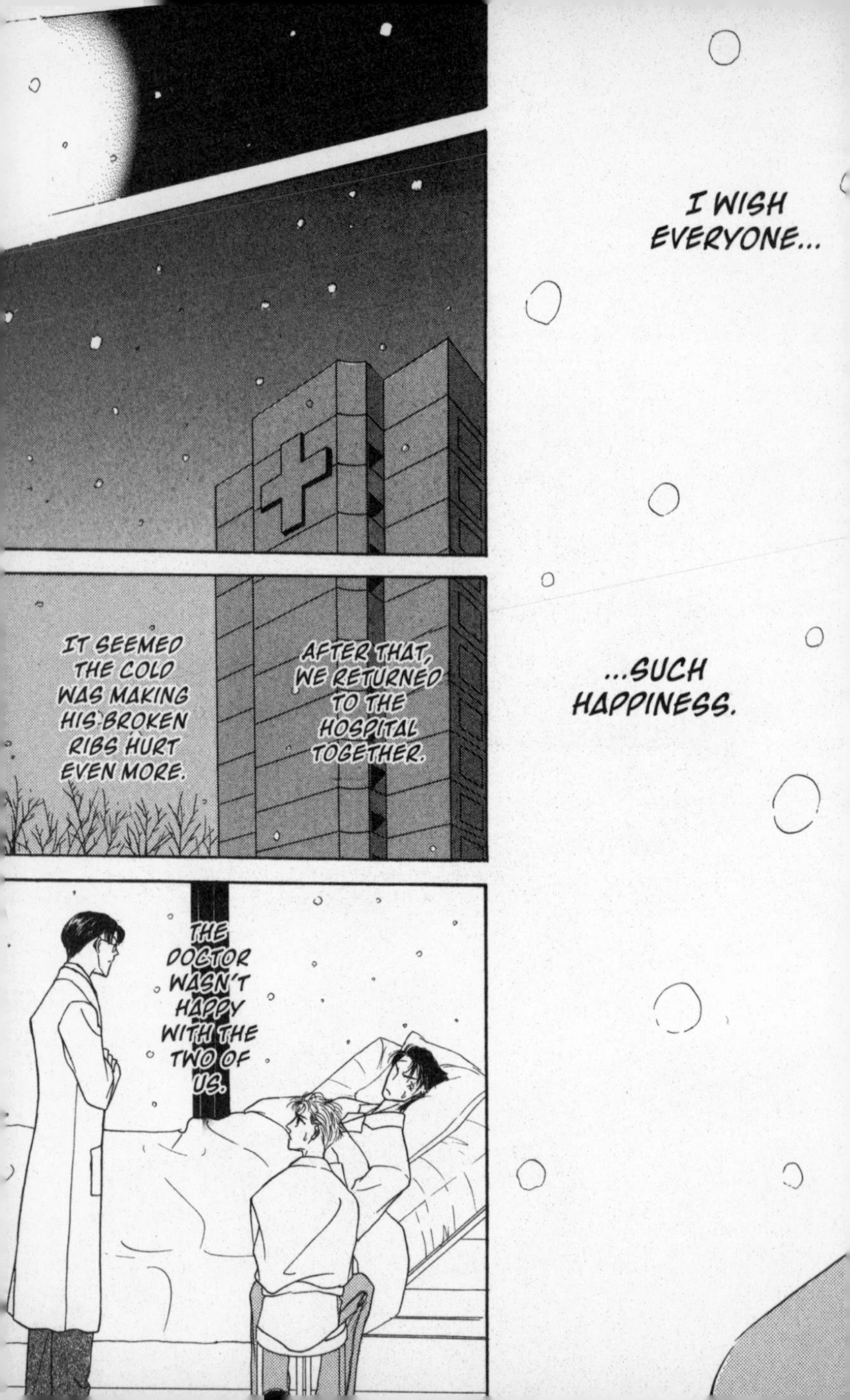
I WISH EVERYONE...
...SUCH HAPPINESS.
AFTER THAT, WE RETURNED TO THE HOSPITAL TOGETHER.
IT SEEMED THE COLD WAS MAKING HIS BROKEN RIBS HURT EVEN MORE.
THE DOCTOR WASN'T HAPPY WITH THE TWO OF US.

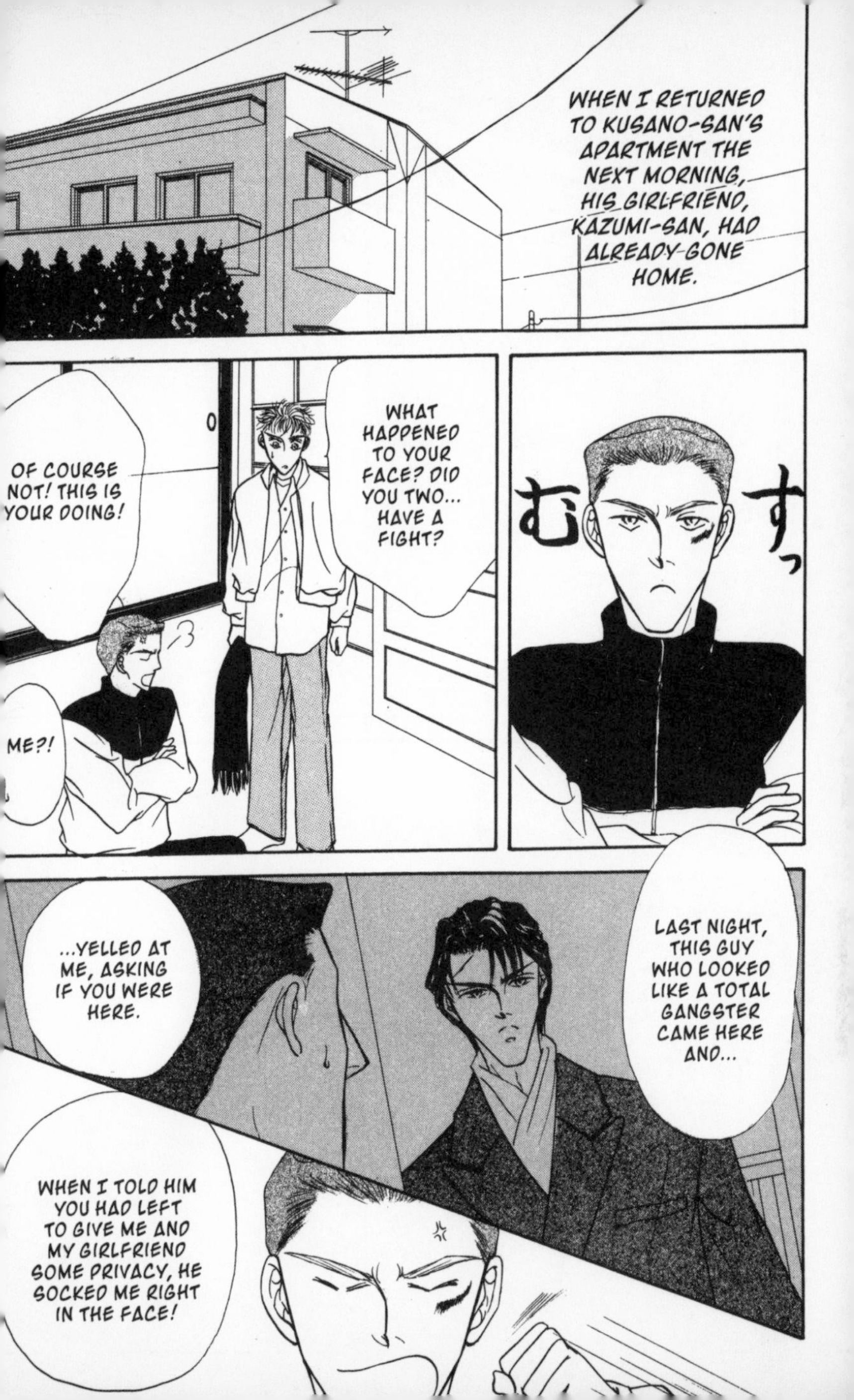
WHEN I RETURNED TO KUSANO-SAN'S APARTMENT THE NEXT MORNING, HIS GIRLFRIEND, KAZUMI-SAN, HAD ALREADY GONE HOME.
むすっ
WHAT HAPPENED TO YOUR FACE? DID YOU TWO... HAVE A FIGHT?
OF COURSE NOT! THIS IS YOUR DOING!
ME?!
LAST NIGHT, THIS GUY WHO LOOKED LIKE A TOTAL GANGSTER CAME HERE AND...
...YELLED AT ME, ASKING IF YOU WERE HERE.
WHEN I TOLD HIM YOU HAD LEFT TO GIVE ME AND MY GIRLFRIEND SOME PRIVACY, HE SOCKED ME RIGHT IN THE FACE!

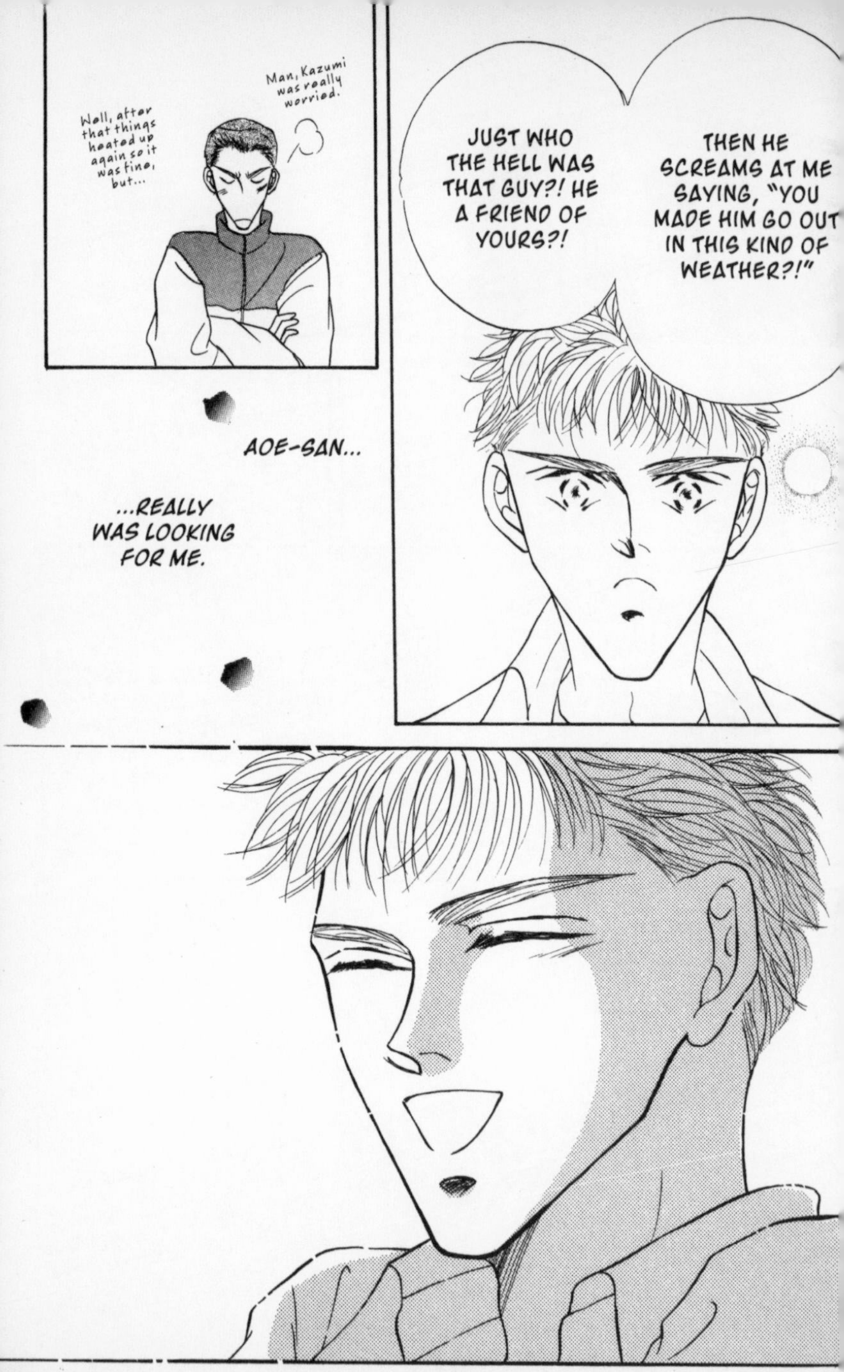
JUST WHO THE HELL WAS THAT GUY?! HE A FRIEND OF YOURS?!
THEN HE SCREAMS AT ME SAYING, "YOU MADE HIM GO OUT IN THIS KIND OF WEATHER?!"
Man, Kazumi was really worried.
Well, after that things heated up again so it was fine, but...
AOE-SAN...
...REALLY WAS LOOKING FOR ME.

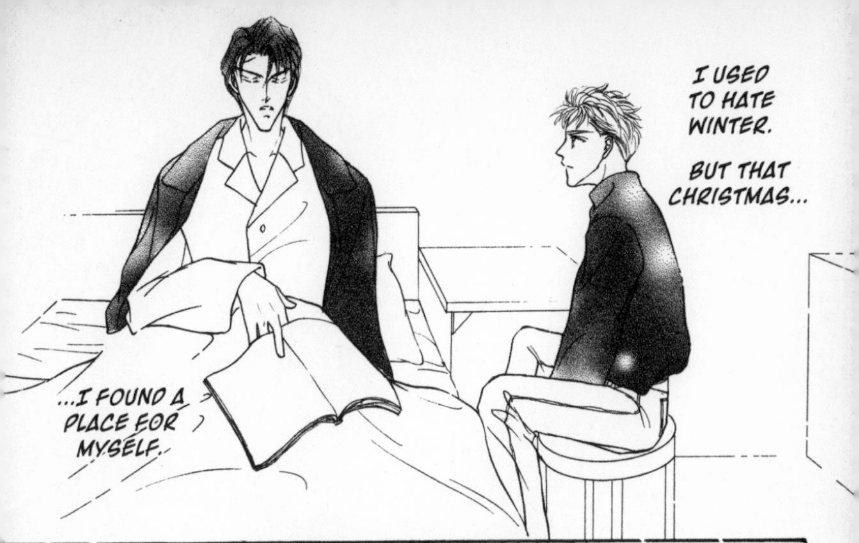
I USED TO HATE WINTER.
BUT THAT CHRISTMAS...
...I FOUND A PLACE FOR MYSELF.

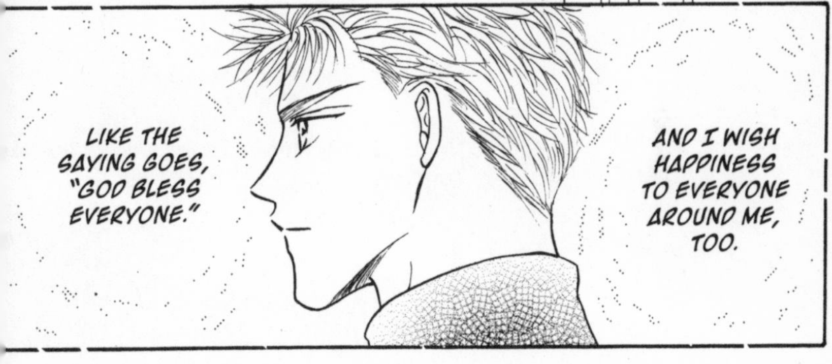
LIKE THE SAYING GOES, "GOD BLESS EVERYONE."
AND I WISH HAPPINESS TO EVERYONE AROUND ME, TOO.

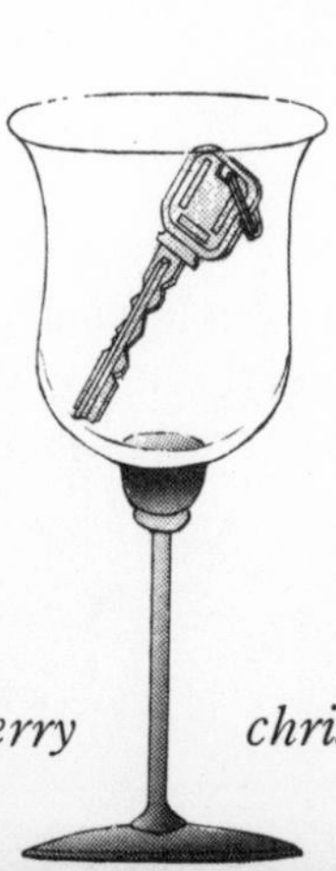

merry merry christmas childen.

• CHILDREN / END

Shirakawa Naoya
Born December 25th Capricorn (the reliable type?)
Blood Type A 168cm 47kg,
No living relatives, hates cars
Special Skill (?): He can live under any circumstances

Aoe Reiji
Born August 7th. Leo (Goes his own path)
Blood Type B 187cm 79kg,
Owner of B&B, hates kids
Cooking Specialty: Egg recipes (he can also make a mean pudding)

Thanks a million ♥

All righty! Thank you for picking up this second volume of *LOVE MODE*. Hey all, this is Shimizu Yuki. How did everyone like "Christmas Children"? While it was being serialized, I was always fretting about whether everyone was enjoying it or not. But since there were so many people who liked it, I was quite relieved (laugh). And to all those who sent me letters, tapes and other presents--thank you very much!! I hold each and every one of them dear to my heart. (Oh and the chocolate was DELICIOUS! ^_^) My replies are all going to be rather late but I swear they will get out eventually, so I hope you can all wait patiently. Anyway, so for this volume's bonus manga...

(NEXT ⇐

⇨

2

...I had hoped to cover Takamiya & Izumi's story and the Aoe household's New Year, but stupid me could only fit in Takamiya & Izumi. I had to choke back my tears and leave Aoe's story for volume 3. For having troubled so many people and received so much help, I must say this is really pathetic of me. So, to make up for it, though there's just one extra manga, I decided to have a little wicked mischief and feature three bonus pages of Aoe & Naoya Valentine fun! I hope you enjoy it! Of course it's sweet lovin' (laugh).
Once again, opinions are appreciated! I try really hard to fulfill everyone's requests and what'dya know, the most frequent request has been "Aoe and Naoya's first sex scene," but that'll be for another time (laugh). I do actually already have the outline for it though...
Well now, on with the show: Please enjoy Takamiya & Izumi's part of the book. And last but not least, to my editor, Ishimoto-sama, my comic editor Arakawa-sama, and to all those who told me they like my manga... I give you my deepest gratitude.
Really, thank you very much. Until next time...

Sachie, thank you for always helping me out.
Please stay that way, 'kay?
Thanks for the vodafone, too.

Let's go drinking again sometime.

Sincerely,
Shimizu Yuki

Oh! I'm always asked this but no, I do not participate in doujinshi (Though I do like to read them).
Also, I have no plans to draw for other publications so just keep an eye on Biblos publications (BExBOY, etc).

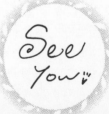

See you

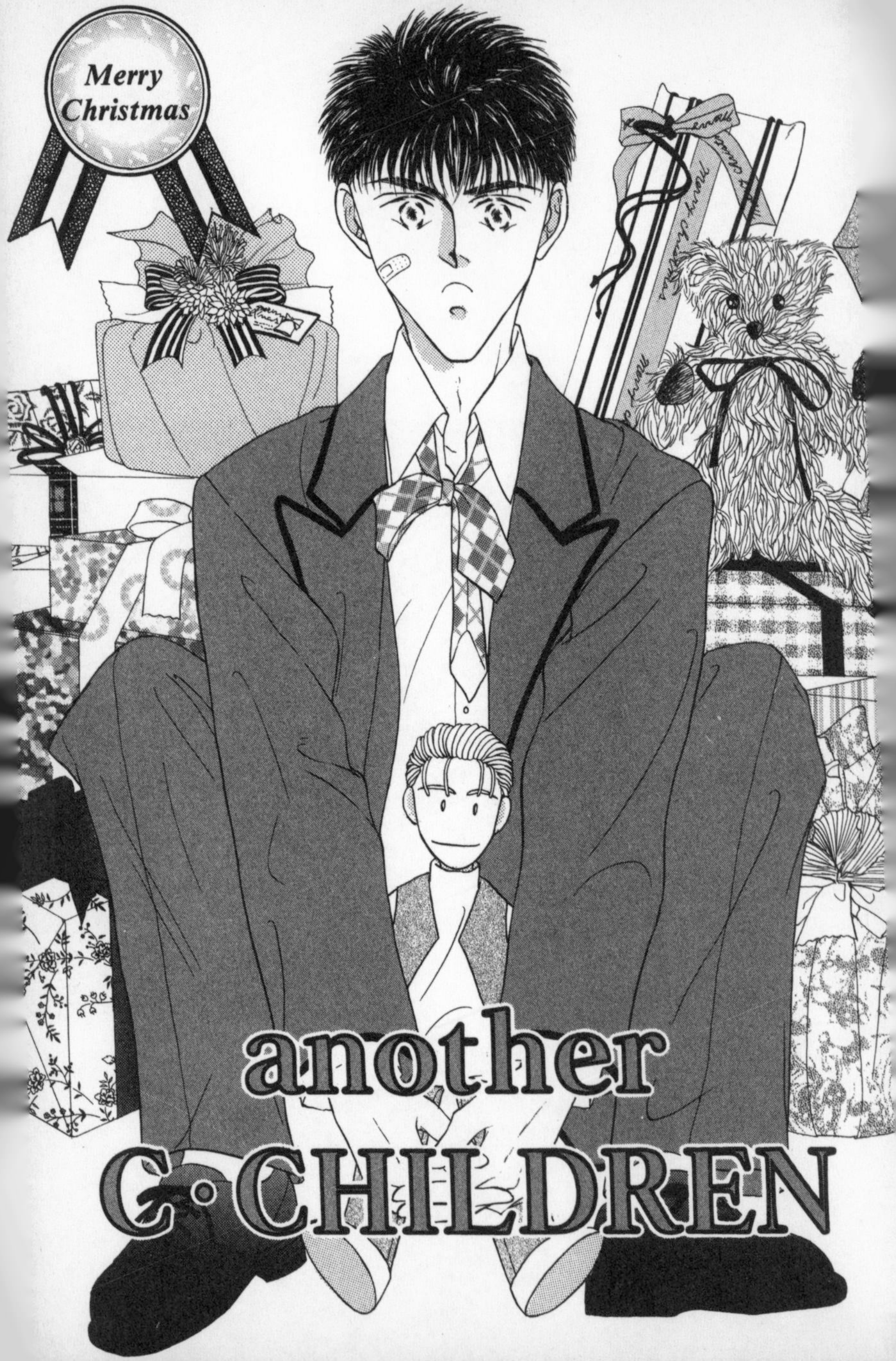
Merry Christmas
another
C·CHILDREN

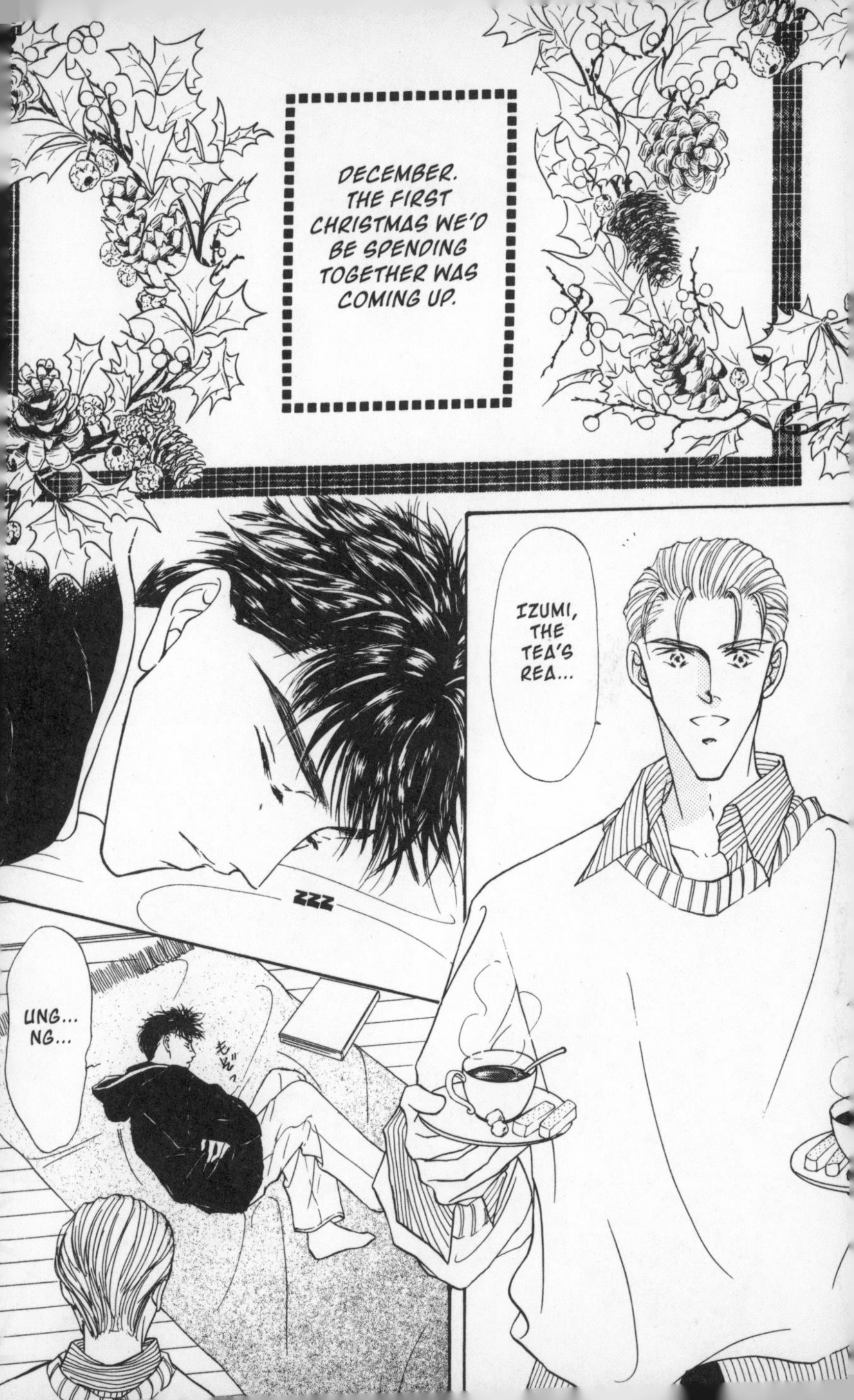
DECEMBER. THE FIRST CHRISTMAS WE'D BE SPENDING TOGETHER WAS COMING UP.
IZUMI, THE TEA'S REA...
ZZZ
UNG... NG...

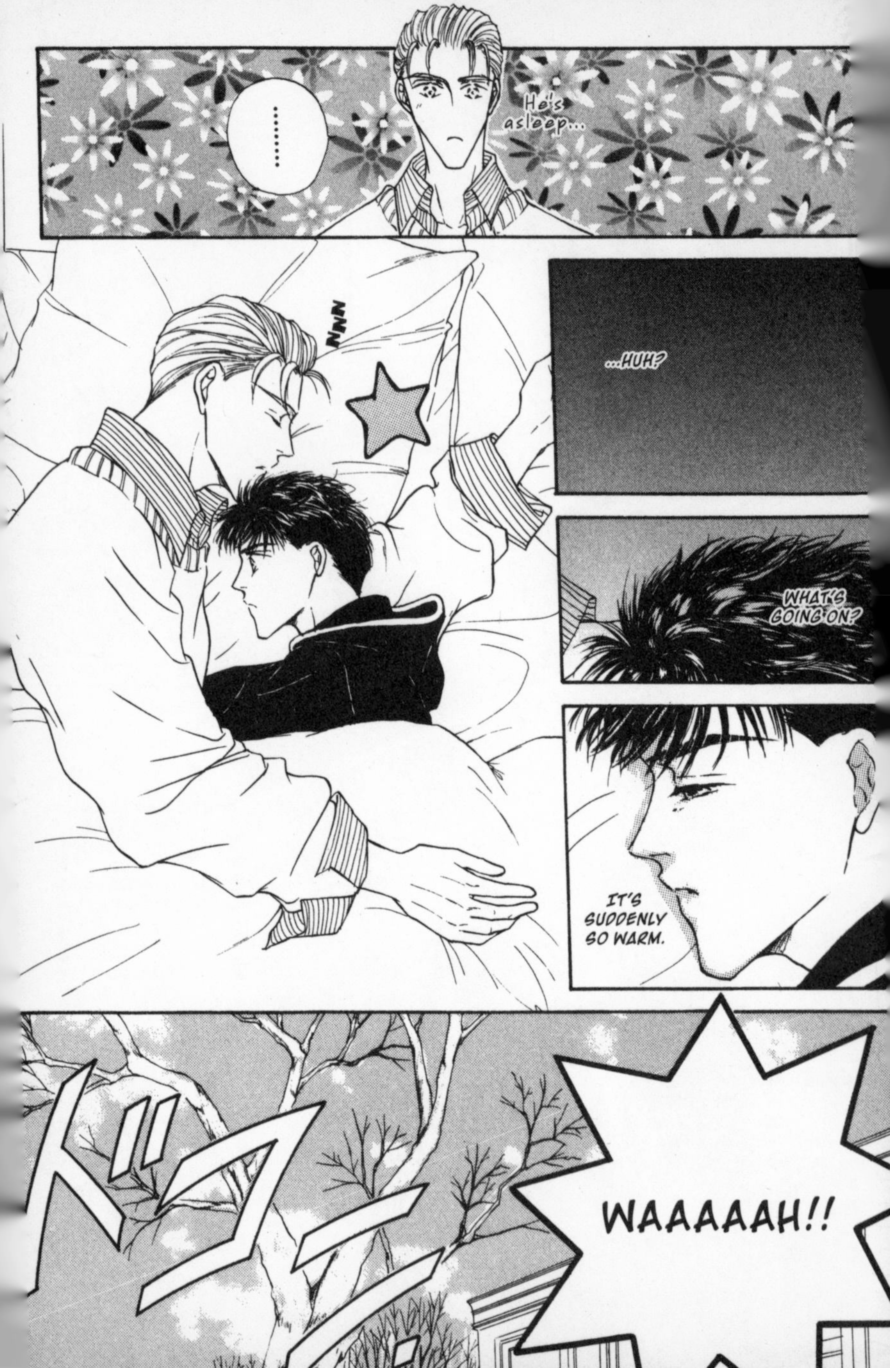
He's asleep...
......
...HUH?
WHAT'S GOING ON?
IT'S SUDDENLY SO WARM.
NNN
WAAAAAH!!

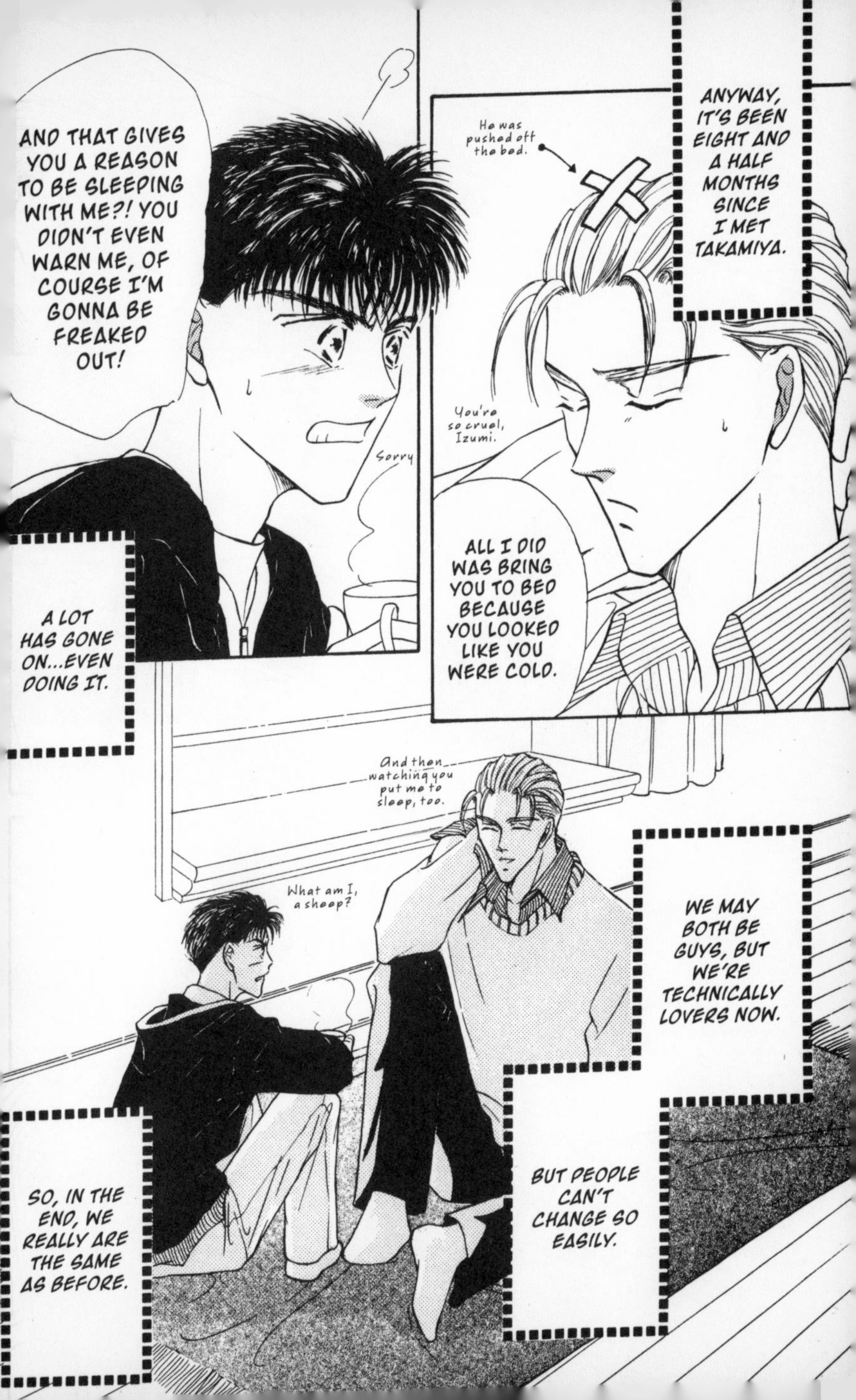
ANYWAY, IT'S BEEN EIGHT AND A HALF MONTHS SINCE I MET TAKAMIYA.
He was pushed off the bed.
You're so cruel, Izumi.
ALL I DID WAS BRING YOU TO BED BECAUSE YOU LOOKED LIKE YOU WERE COLD.
AND THAT GIVES YOU A REASON TO BE SLEEPING WITH ME?! YOU DIDN'T EVEN WARN ME, OF COURSE I'M GONNA BE FREAKED OUT!
Sorry
A LOT HAS GONE ON...EVEN DOING IT.
WE MAY BOTH BE GUYS, BUT WE'RE TECHNICALLY LOVERS NOW.
And then watching you put me to sleep, too.
What am I, a sheep?
BUT PEOPLE CAN'T CHANGE SO EASILY.
SO, IN THE END, WE REALLY ARE THE SAME AS BEFORE.

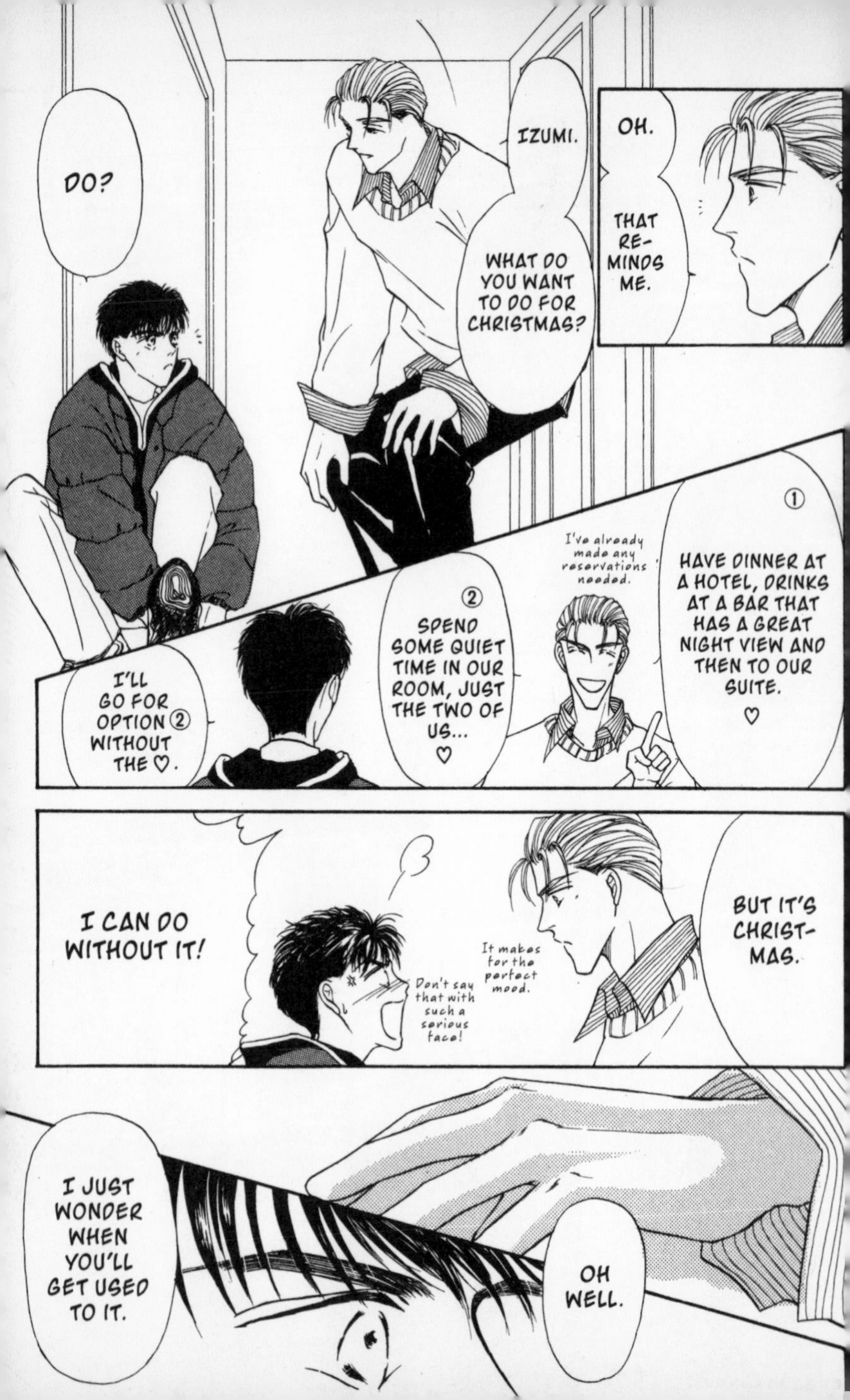
OH.
THAT REMINDS ME.
IZUMI.
WHAT DO YOU WANT TO DO FOR CHRISTMAS?
DO?
① HAVE DINNER AT A HOTEL, DRINKS AT A BAR THAT HAS A GREAT NIGHT VIEW AND THEN TO OUR SUITE. ♡
I've already made any reservations needed.
② SPEND SOME QUIET TIME IN OUR ROOM, JUST THE TWO OF US... ♡
I'LL GO FOR OPTION ② WITHOUT THE ♡.
BUT IT'S CHRISTMAS.
It makes for the perfect mood.
I CAN DO WITHOUT IT!
Don't say that with such a serious face!
OH WELL.
I JUST WONDER WHEN YOU'LL GET USED TO IT.

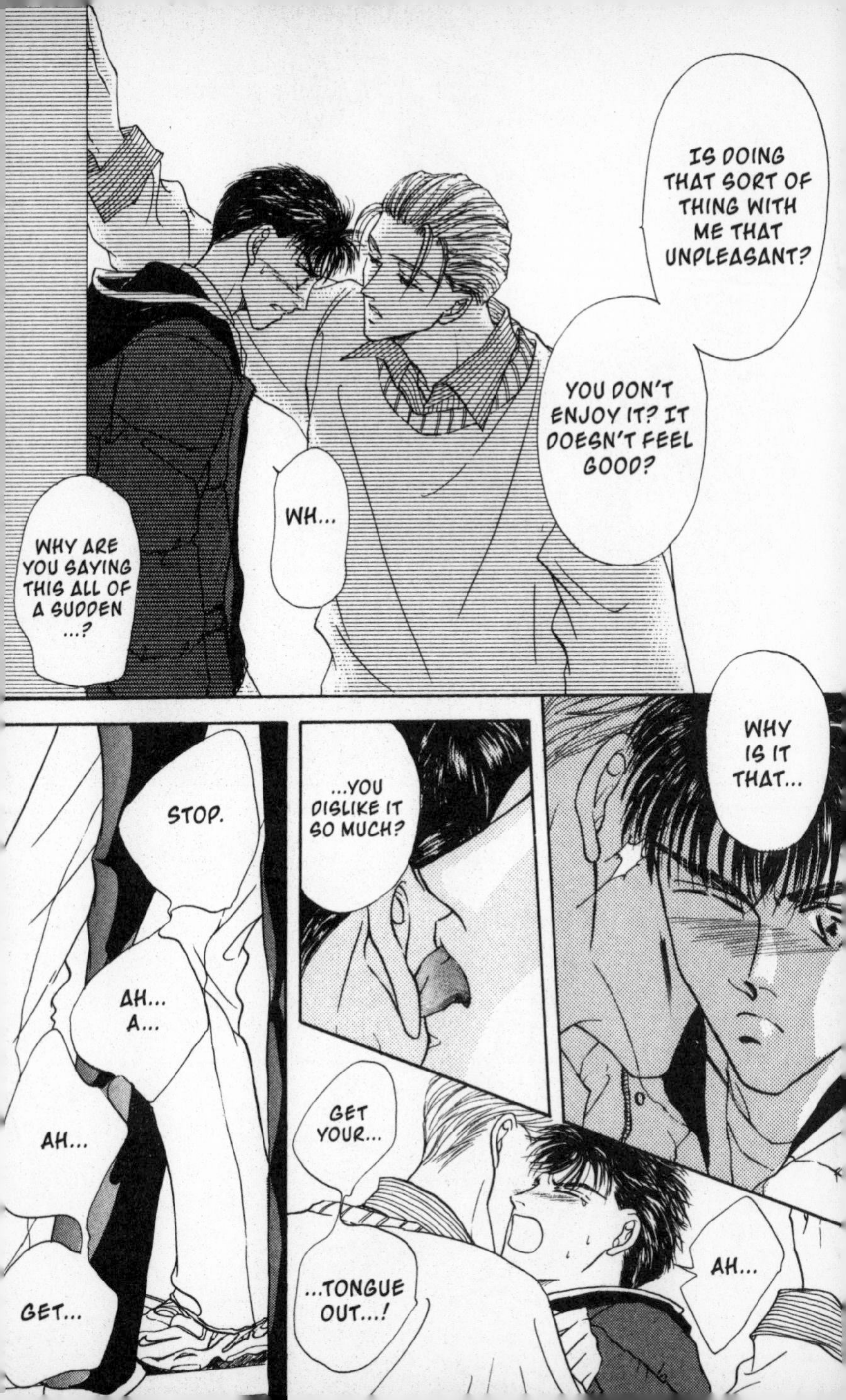
IS DOING THAT SORT OF THING WITH ME THAT UNPLEASANT?
YOU DON'T ENJOY IT? IT DOESN'T FEEL GOOD?
WH...
WHY ARE YOU SAYING THIS ALL OF A SUDDEN ...?
WHY IS IT THAT...
...YOU DISLIKE IT SO MUCH?
AH...
GET YOUR...
...TONGUE OUT...!
STOP.
AH... A...
AH...
GET...

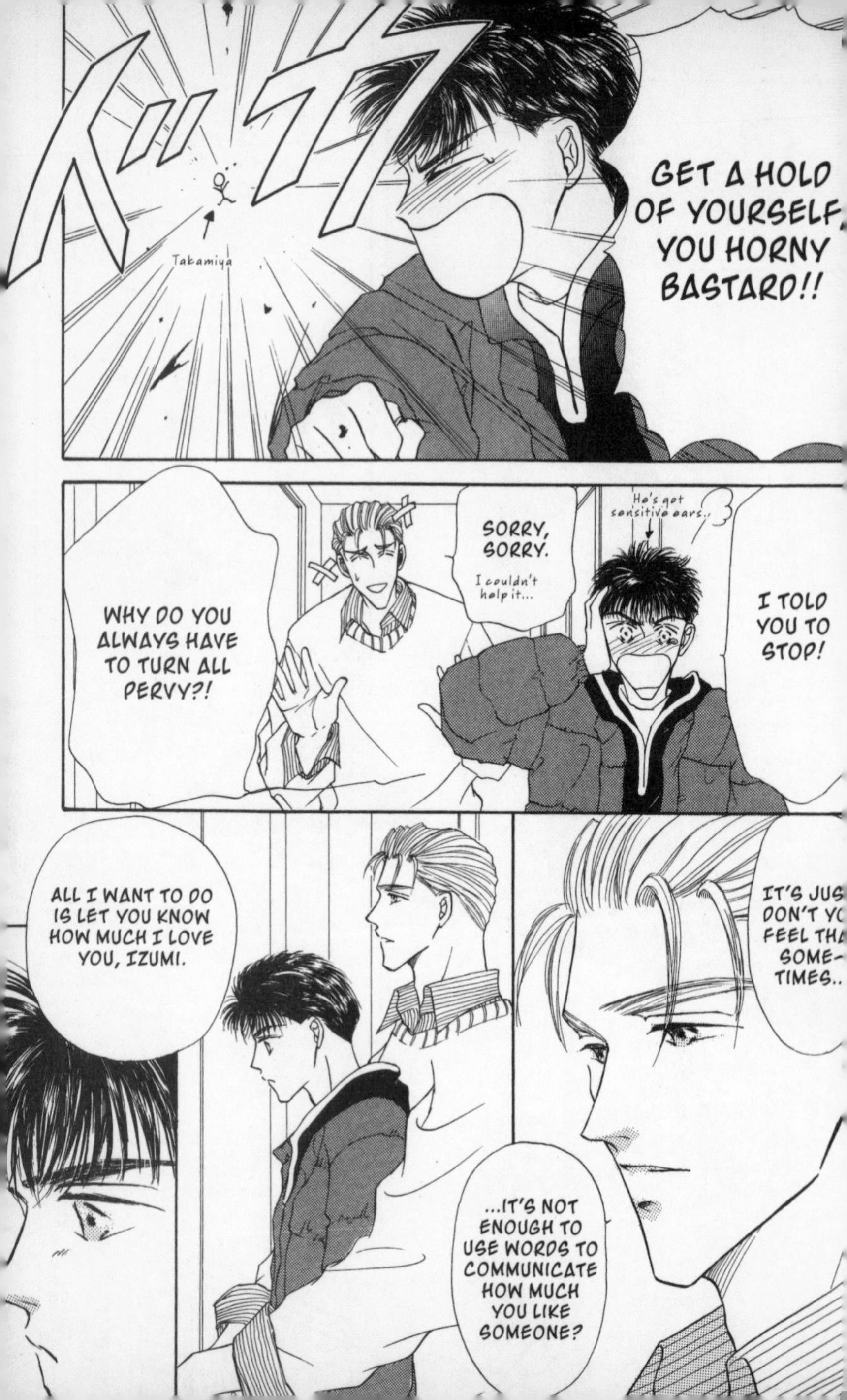
GET A HOLD OF YOURSELF, YOU HORNY BASTARD!!
Takamiya
I TOLD YOU TO STOP!
He's got sensitive ears..
SORRY, SORRY.
I couldn't help it...
WHY DO YOU ALWAYS HAVE TO TURN ALL PERVY?!
IT'S JUS DON'T YO FEEL THA SOME-TIMES..
...IT'S NOT ENOUGH TO USE WORDS TO COMMUNICATE HOW MUCH YOU LIKE SOMEONE?
ALL I WANT TO DO IS LET YOU KNOW HOW MUCH I LOVE YOU, IZUMI.

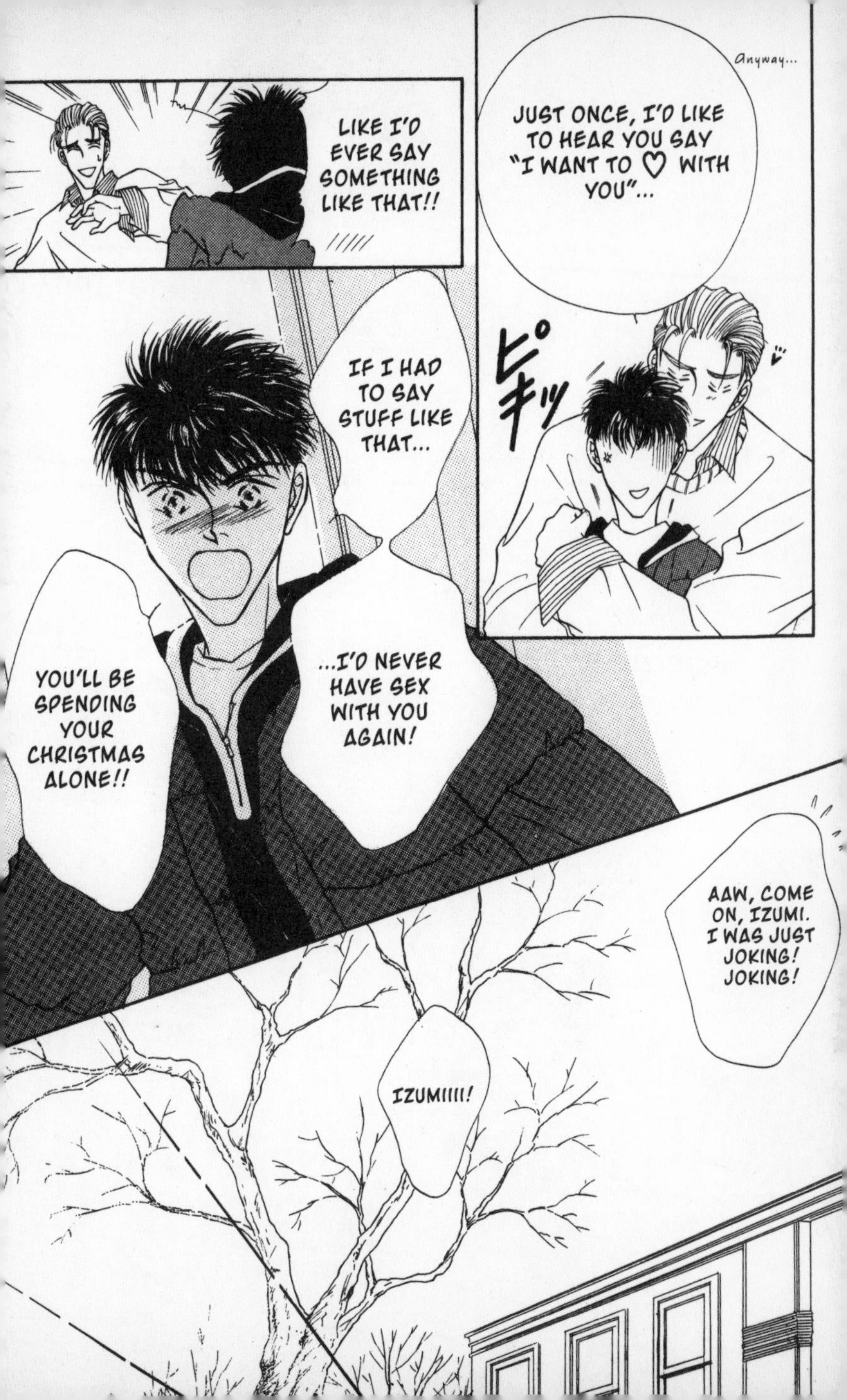

Anyway...
JUST ONCE, I'D LIKE TO HEAR YOU SAY "I WANT TO ♡ WITH YOU"...
ピキッ
LIKE I'D EVER SAY SOMETHING LIKE THAT!!
IF I HAD TO SAY STUFF LIKE THAT...
...I'D NEVER HAVE SEX WITH YOU AGAIN!
YOU'LL BE SPENDING YOUR CHRISTMAS ALONE!!
AAW, COME ON, IZUMI. I WAS JUST JOKING! JOKING!
IZUMIIIII!

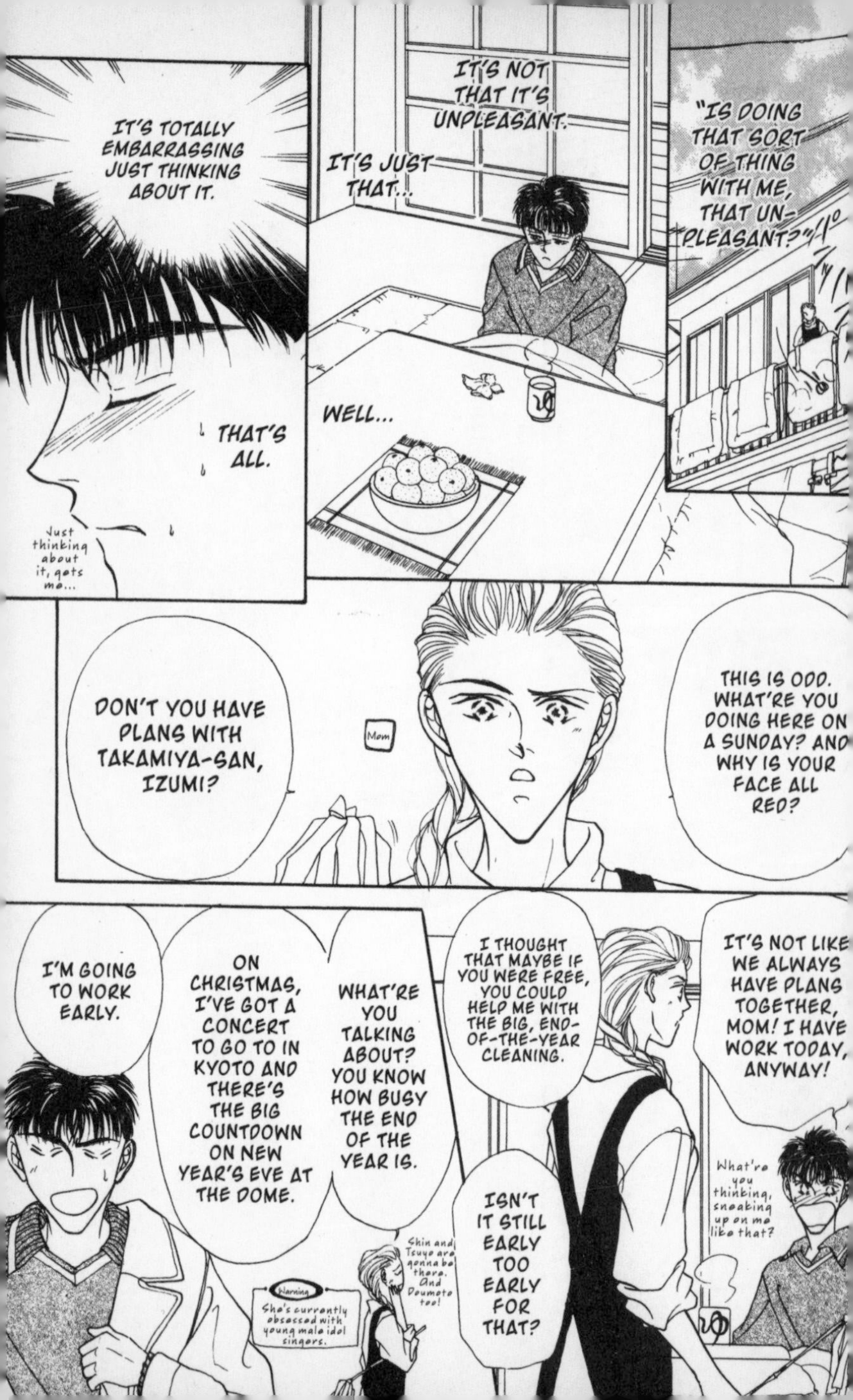
"IS DOING THAT SORT OF THING WITH ME, THAT UN-PLEASANT?"
IT'S NOT THAT IT'S UNPLEASANT.
IT'S JUST THAT...
WELL...
IT'S TOTALLY EMBARRASSING JUST THINKING ABOUT IT.
THAT'S ALL.
Just thinking about it, gets me...
THIS IS ODD. WHAT'RE YOU DOING HERE ON A SUNDAY? AND WHY IS YOUR FACE ALL RED?
Mom
DON'T YOU HAVE PLANS WITH TAKAMIYA-SAN, IZUMI?
IT'S NOT LIKE WE ALWAYS HAVE PLANS TOGETHER, MOM! I HAVE WORK TODAY, ANYWAY!
What're you thinking, sneaking up on me like that?
I THOUGHT THAT MAYBE IF YOU WERE FREE, YOU COULD HELP ME WITH THE BIG, END-OF-THE-YEAR CLEANING.
ISN'T IT STILL EARLY TOO EARLY FOR THAT?
WHAT'RE YOU TALKING ABOUT? YOU KNOW HOW BUSY THE END OF THE YEAR IS.
ON CHRISTMAS, I'VE GOT A CONCERT TO GO TO IN KYOTO AND THERE'S THE BIG COUNTDOWN ON NEW YEAR'S EVE AT THE DOME.
Shin and Tsuyo are gonna be there. And Doumoto too!
Warning
She's currently obsessed with young male idol singers.
I'M GOING TO WORK EARLY.

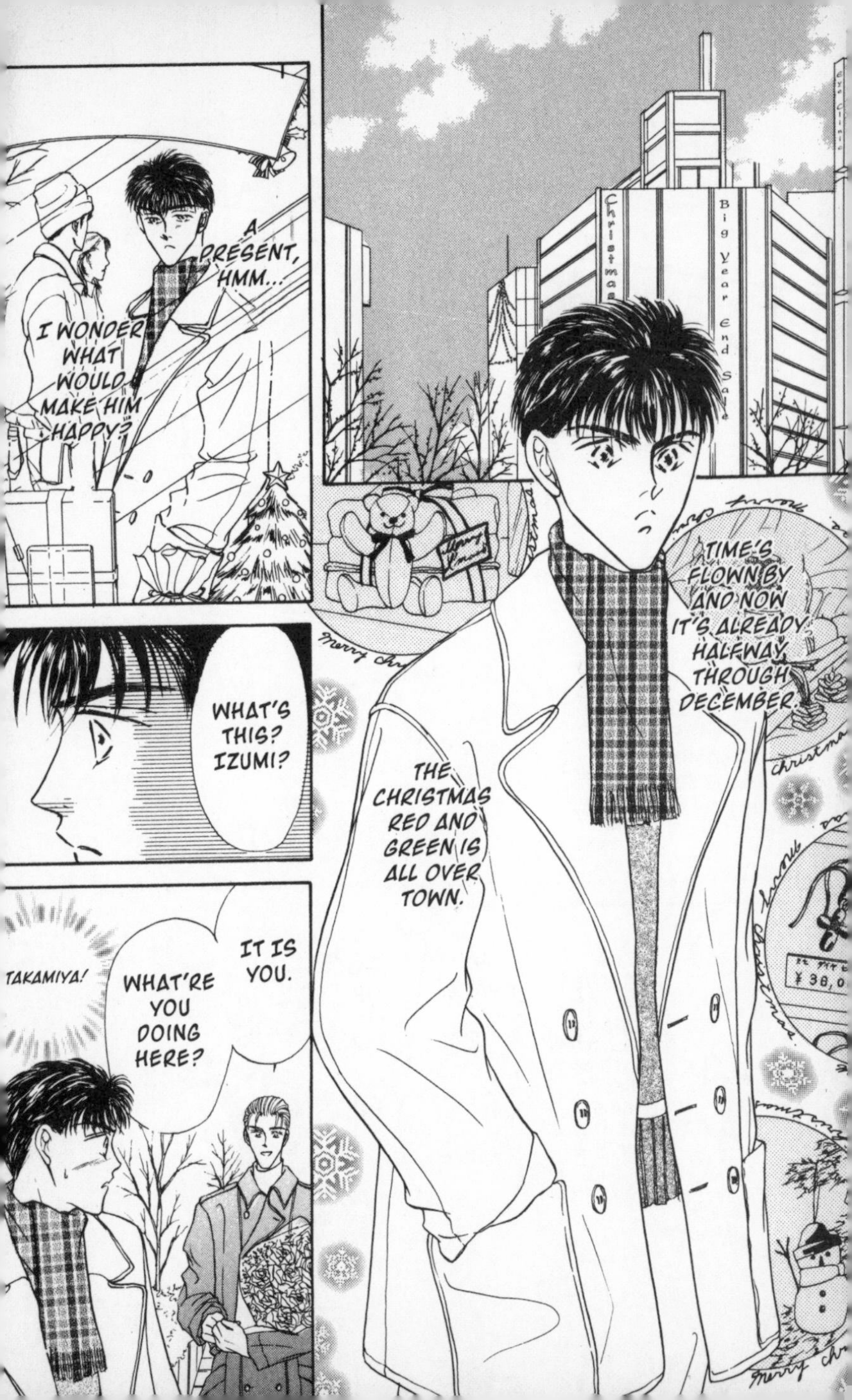
Eye Clinic
Big Year End Sale
Christmas
TIME'S FLOWN BY AND NOW IT'S ALREADY HALFWAY THROUGH DECEMBER.
THE CHRISTMAS RED AND GREEN IS ALL OVER TOWN.
A PRESENT, HMM...
I WONDER WHAT WOULD MAKE HIM HAPPY?
WHAT'S THIS? IZUMI?
IT IS YOU.
WHAT'RE YOU DOING HERE?
TAKAMIYA!

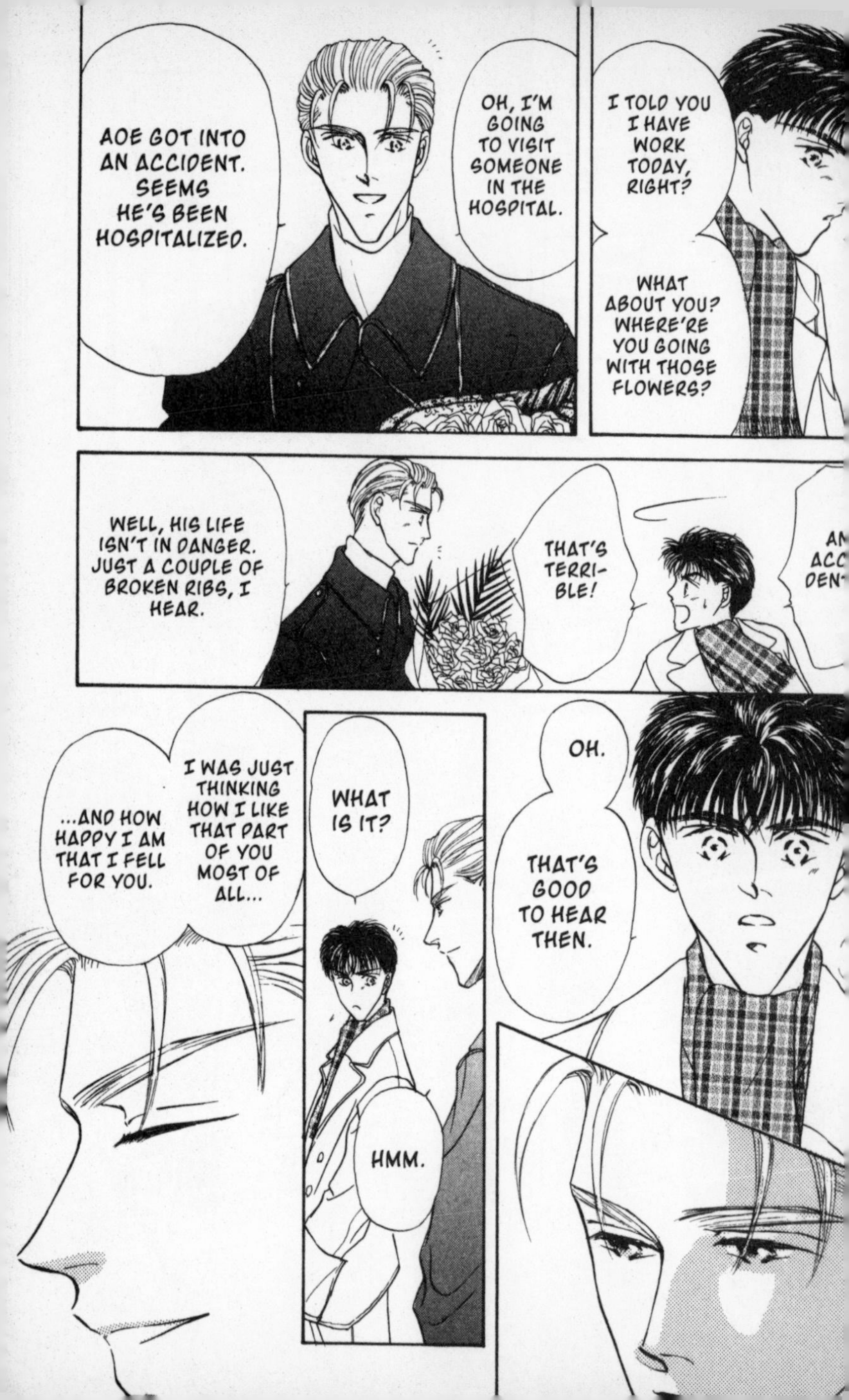
I TOLD YOU I HAVE WORK TODAY, RIGHT?
WHAT ABOUT YOU? WHERE'RE YOU GOING WITH THOSE FLOWERS?
OH, I'M GOING TO VISIT SOMEONE IN THE HOSPITAL.
AOE GOT INTO AN ACCIDENT. SEEMS HE'S BEEN HOSPITALIZED.
THAT'S TERRI- BLE!
WELL, HIS LIFE ISN'T IN DANGER. JUST A COUPLE OF BROKEN RIBS, I HEAR.
OH.
THAT'S GOOD TO HEAR THEN.
WHAT IS IT?
HMM.
I WAS JUST THINKING HOW I LIKE THAT PART OF YOU MOST OF ALL...
...AND HOW HAPPY I AM THAT I FELL FOR YOU.

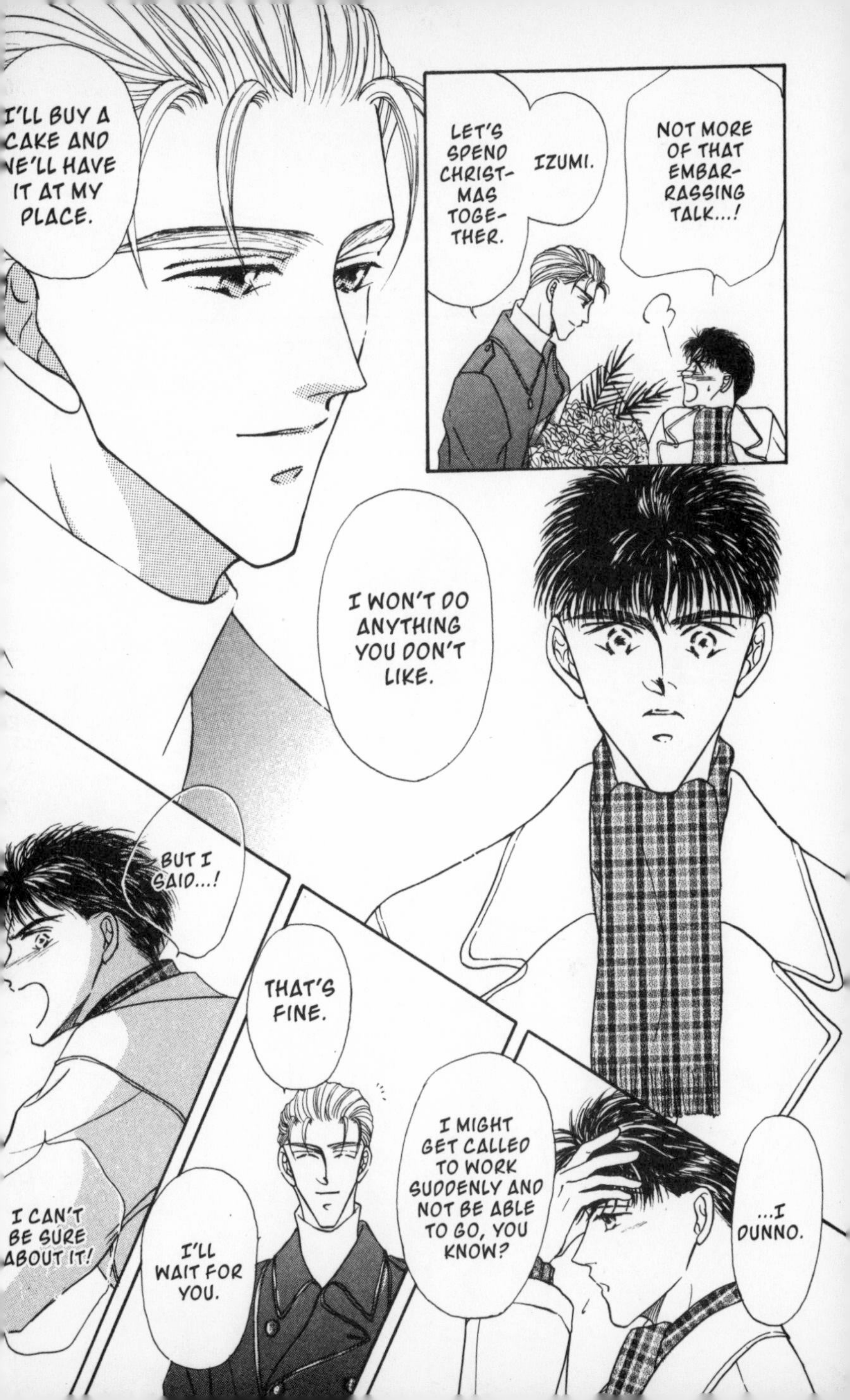
NOT MORE OF THAT EMBARRASSING TALK...!
IZUMI.
LET'S SPEND CHRISTMAS TOGETHER.
I'LL BUY A CAKE AND WE'LL HAVE IT AT MY PLACE.
I WON'T DO ANYTHING YOU DON'T LIKE.
...I DUNNO.
I MIGHT GET CALLED TO WORK SUDDENLY AND NOT BE ABLE TO GO, YOU KNOW?
THAT'S FINE.
I'LL WAIT FOR YOU.
BUT I SAID...!
I CAN'T BE SURE ABOUT IT!

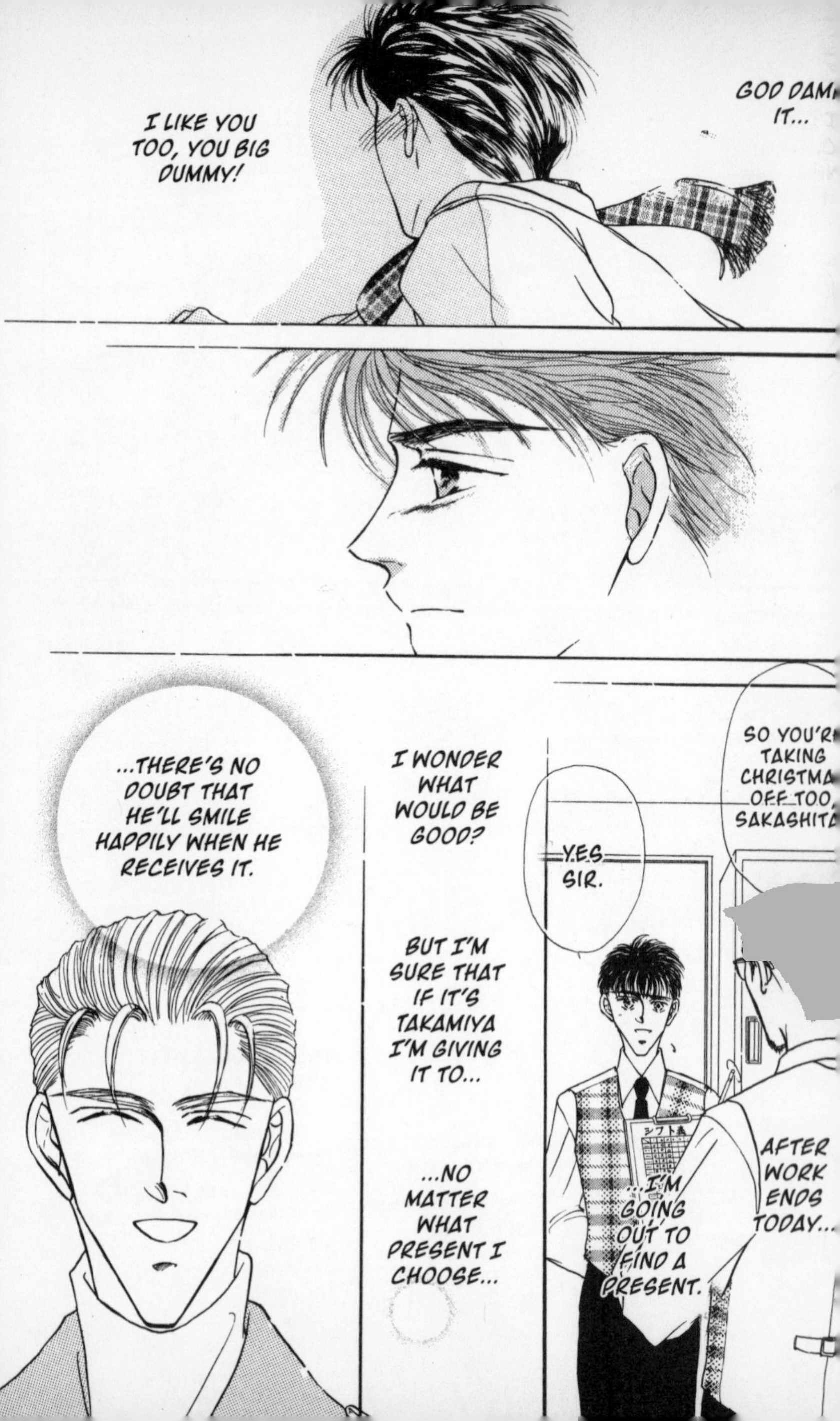
GOD DAM IT...
I LIKE YOU TOO, YOU BIG DUMMY!
SO YOU'R TAKING CHRISTMA OFF TOO, SAKASHITA
YES SIR.
AFTER WORK ENDS TODAY...
...I'M GOING OUT TO FIND A PRESENT.
I WONDER WHAT WOULD BE GOOD?
BUT I'M SURE THAT IF IT'S TAKAMIYA I'M GIVING IT TO...
...NO MATTER WHAT PRESENT I CHOOSE...
...THERE'S NO DOUBT THAT HE'LL SMILE HAPPILY WHEN HE RECEIVES IT.

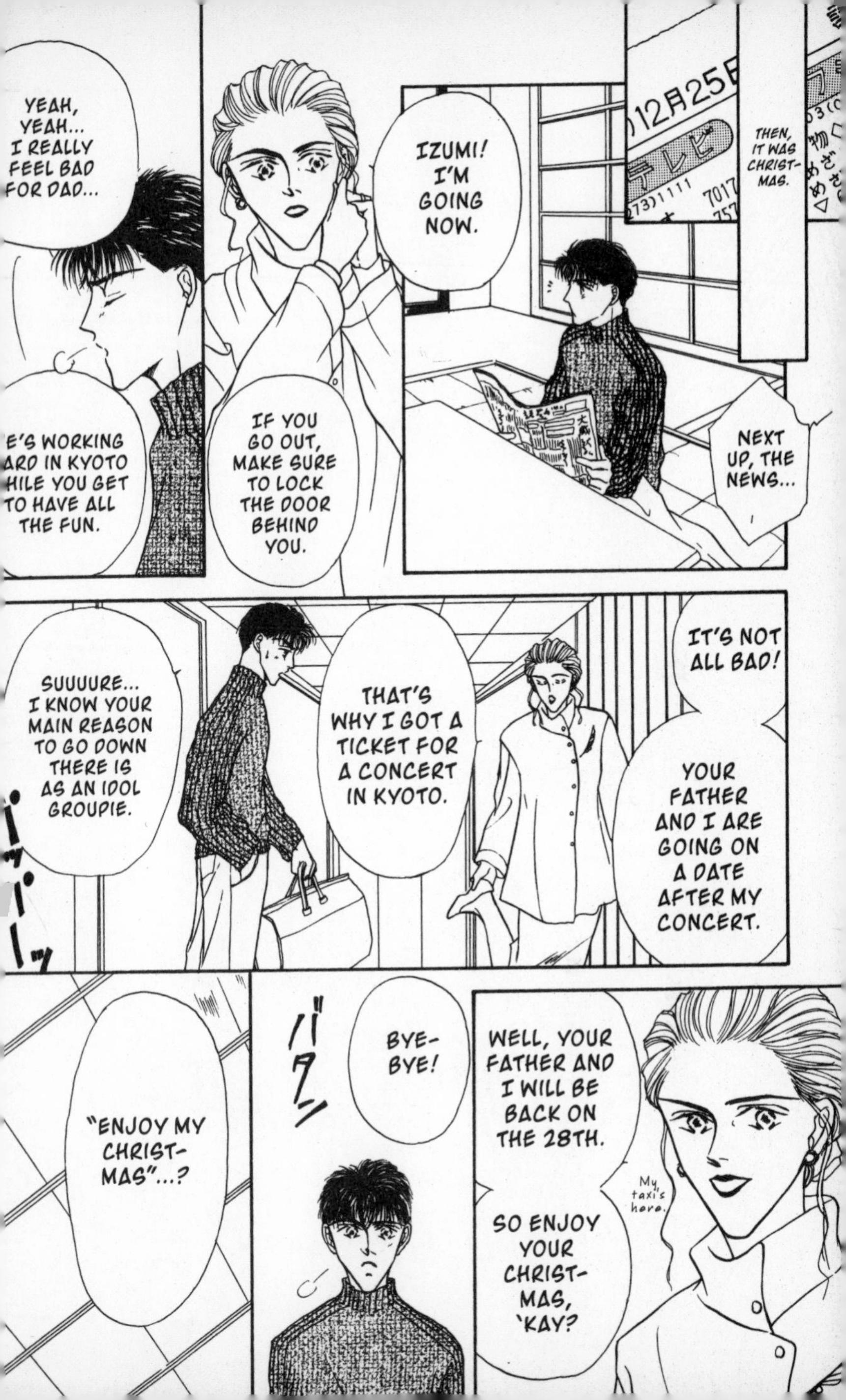
12月25日
テレビ
THEN, IT WAS CHRIST-MAS.
NEXT UP, THE NEWS...
IZUMI! I'M GOING NOW.
IF YOU GO OUT, MAKE SURE TO LOCK THE DOOR BEHIND YOU.
YEAH, YEAH... I REALLY FEEL BAD FOR DAD...
E'S WORKING ARD IN KYOTO HILE YOU GET TO HAVE ALL THE FUN.
IT'S NOT ALL BAD!
YOUR FATHER AND I ARE GOING ON A DATE AFTER MY CONCERT.
THAT'S WHY I GOT A TICKET FOR A CONCERT IN KYOTO.
SUUUURE... I KNOW YOUR MAIN REASON TO GO DOWN THERE IS AS AN IDOL GROUPIE.
WELL, YOUR FATHER AND I WILL BE BACK ON THE 28TH.
My taxi's here.
SO ENJOY YOUR CHRIST-MAS, 'KAY?
BYE-BYE!
バタン
"ENJOY MY CHRIST-MAS"...?

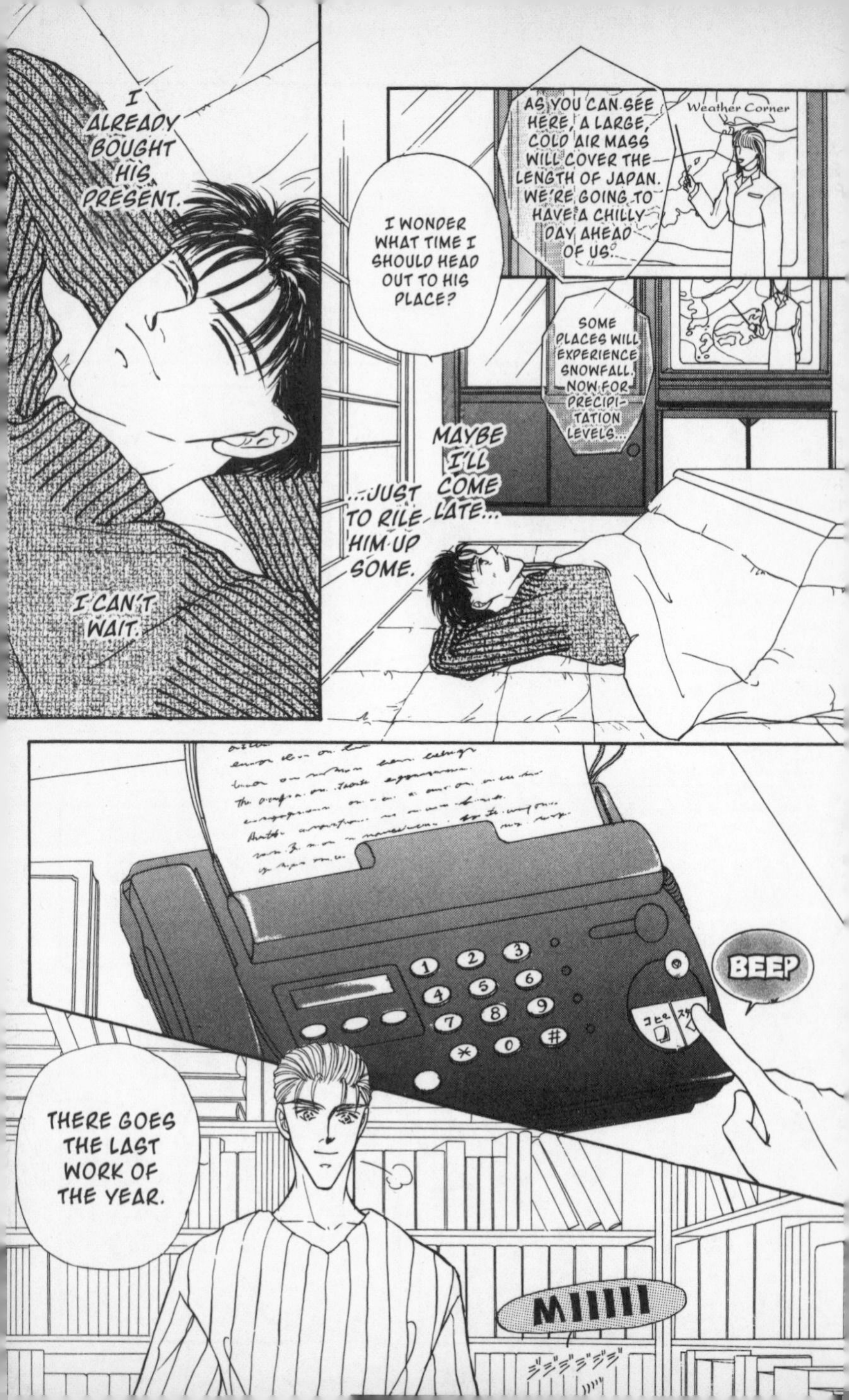
Weather Corner
AS YOU CAN SEE HERE, A LARGE, COLD AIR MASS WILL COVER THE LENGTH OF JAPAN. WE'RE GOING TO HAVE A CHILLY DAY AHEAD OF US.
I WONDER WHAT TIME I SHOULD HEAD OUT TO HIS PLACE?
SOME PLACES WILL EXPERIENCE SNOWFALL. NOW FOR PRECIPITATION LEVELS...
MAYBE I'LL COME LATE...
...JUST TO RILE HIM UP SOME.
I ALREADY BOUGHT HIS PRESENT.
I CAN'T WAIT.
BEEP
THERE GOES THE LAST WORK OF THE YEAR.
MIIIII

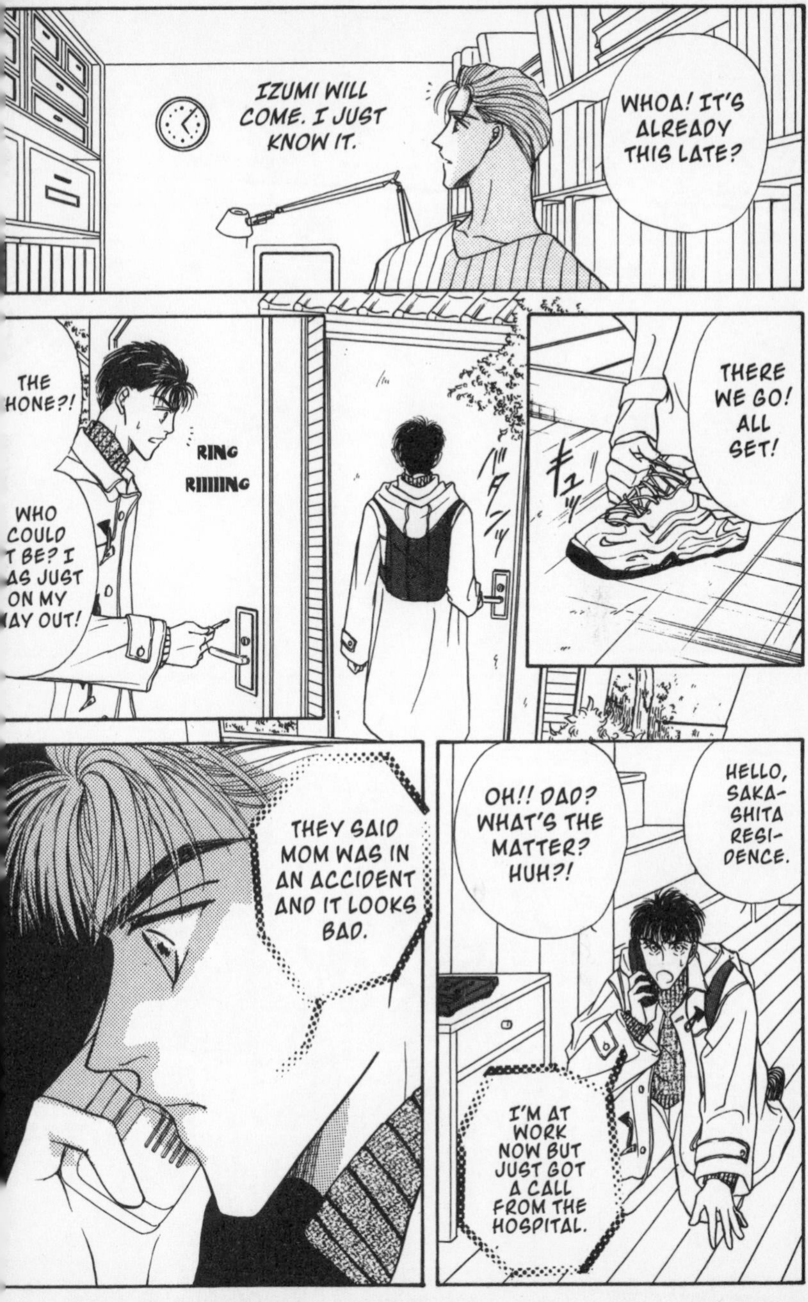
WHOA! IT'S ALREADY THIS LATE?
IZUMI WILL COME. I JUST KNOW IT.
THERE WE GO! ALL SET!
RING RIIIIING
THE HONE?!
WHO COULD T BE? I AS JUST ON MY AY OUT!
HELLO, SAKA-SHITA RESI-DENCE.
OH!! DAD? WHAT'S THE MATTER? HUH?!
I'M AT WORK NOW BUT JUST GOT A CALL FROM THE HOSPITAL.
THEY SAID MOM WAS IN AN ACCIDENT AND IT LOOKS BAD.

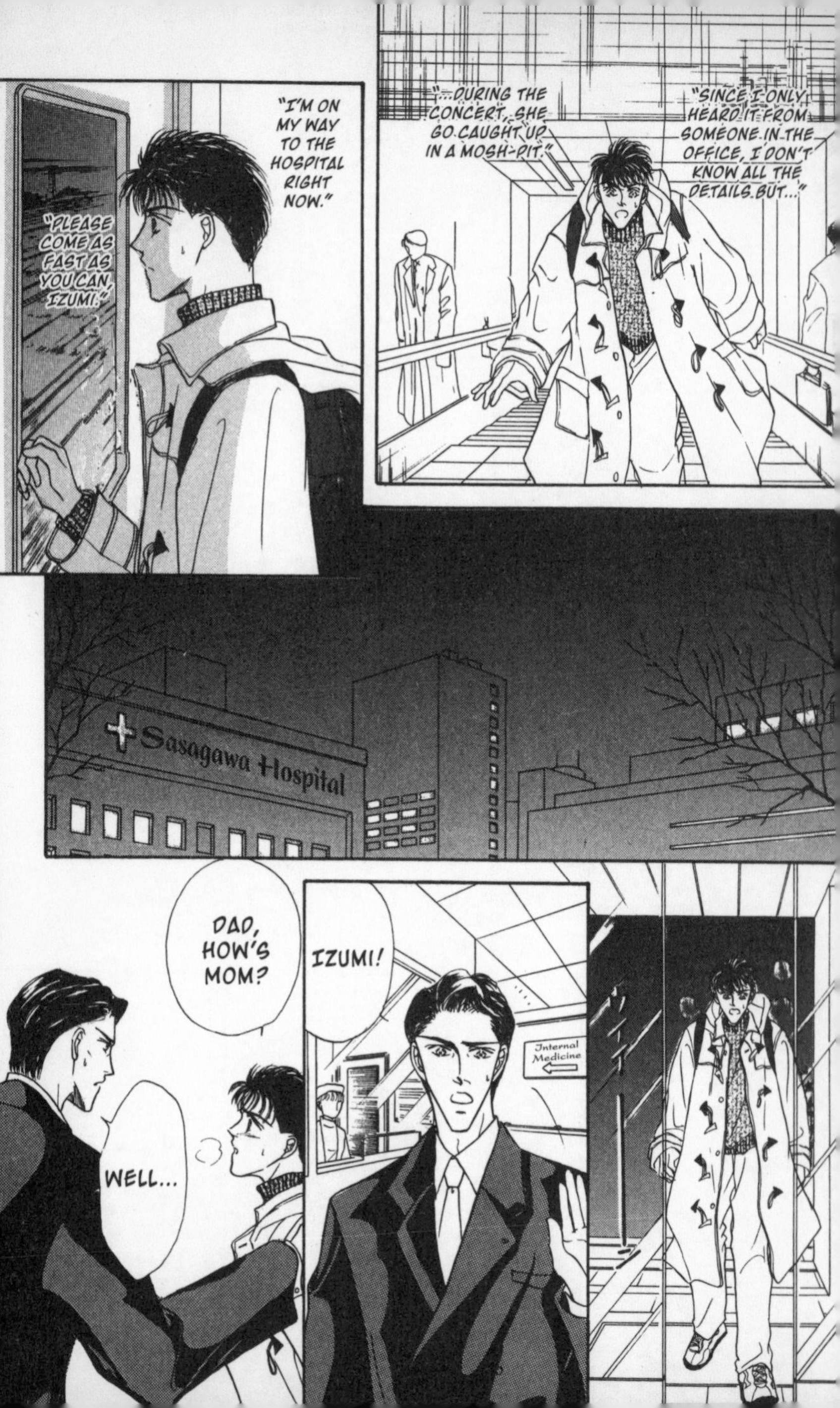
"SINCE I ONLY HEARD IT FROM SOMEONE IN THE OFFICE, I DON'T KNOW ALL THE DETAILS BUT..."
"...DURING THE CONCERT, SHE GO CAUGHT UP IN A MOSH-PIT."
"I'M ON MY WAY TO THE HOSPITAL RIGHT NOW."
"PLEASE COME AS FAST AS YOU CAN, IZUMI."
Sasagawa Hospital
IZUMI!
Internal Medicine
DAD, HOW'S MOM?
WELL...

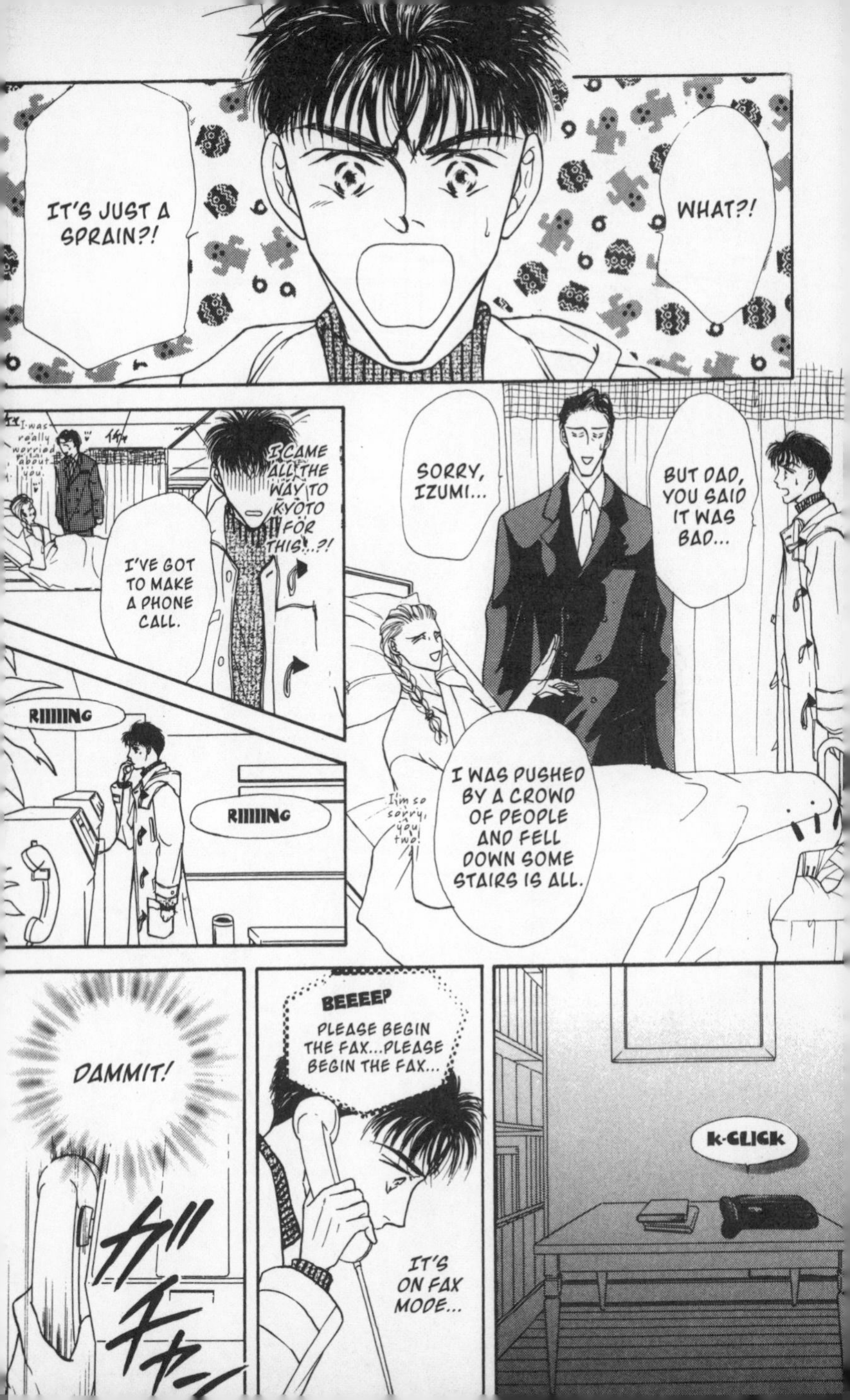
WHAT?!
IT'S JUST A SPRAIN?!
BUT DAD, YOU SAID IT WAS BAD...
SORRY, IZUMI...
I WAS PUSHED BY A CROWD OF PEOPLE AND FELL DOWN SOME STAIRS IS ALL.
I'm so sorry, you two!
I CAME ALL THE WAY TO KYOTO FOR THIS...?!
I was really worried about you.
I'VE GOT TO MAKE A PHONE CALL.
RIIIIING
RIIIIING
K-CLICK
BEEEEP
PLEASE BEGIN THE FAX...PLEASE BEGIN THE FAX...
IT'S ON FAX MODE...
DAMMIT!

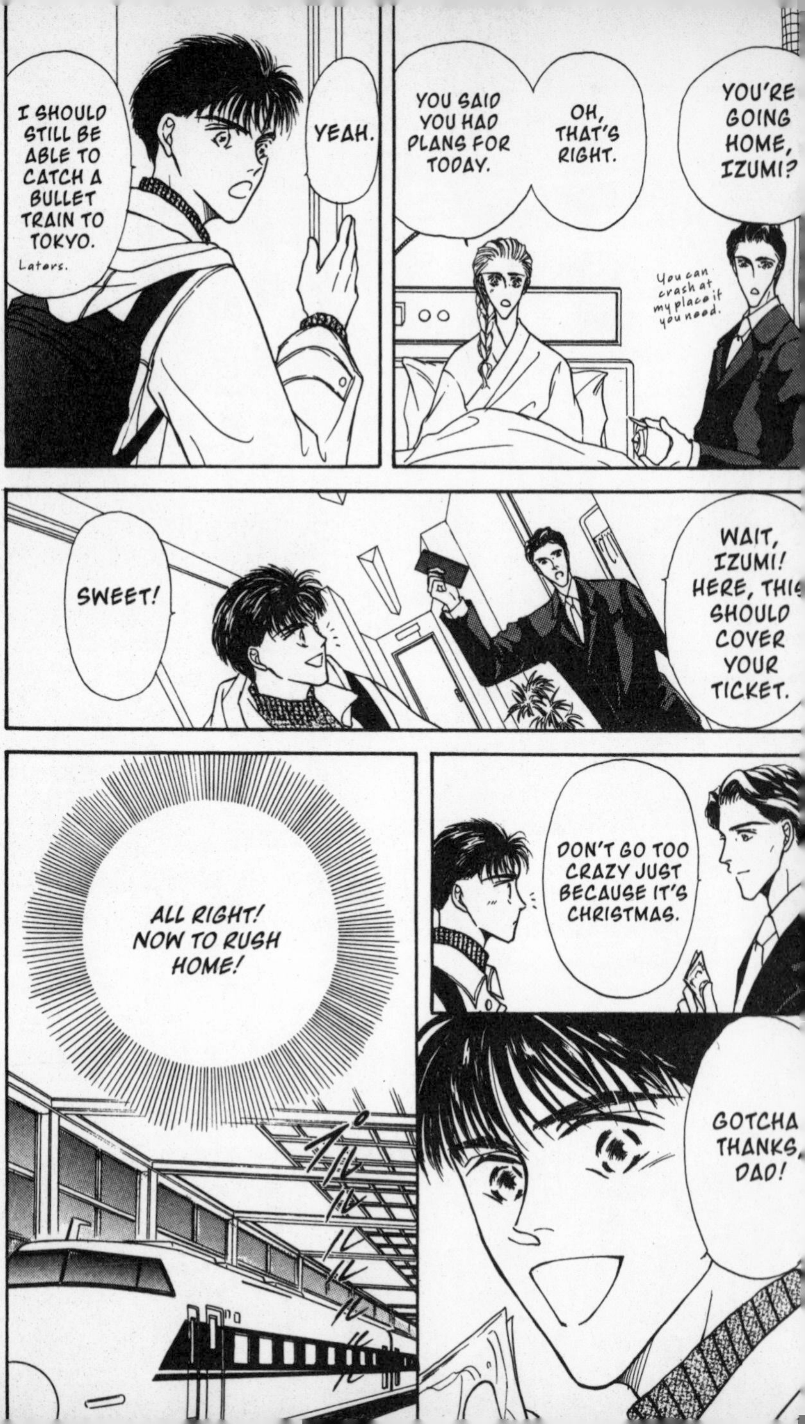
YOU'RE GOING HOME, IZUMI?
You can crash at my place if you need.
OH, THAT'S RIGHT.
YOU SAID YOU HAD PLANS FOR TODAY.
YEAH.
I SHOULD STILL BE ABLE TO CATCH A BULLET TRAIN TO TOKYO.
Laters.
WAIT, IZUMI! HERE, THIS SHOULD COVER YOUR TICKET.
SWEET!
DON'T GO TOO CRAZY JUST BECAUSE IT'S CHRISTMAS.
GOTCHA THANKS, DAD!
ALL RIGHT! NOW TO RUSH HOME!

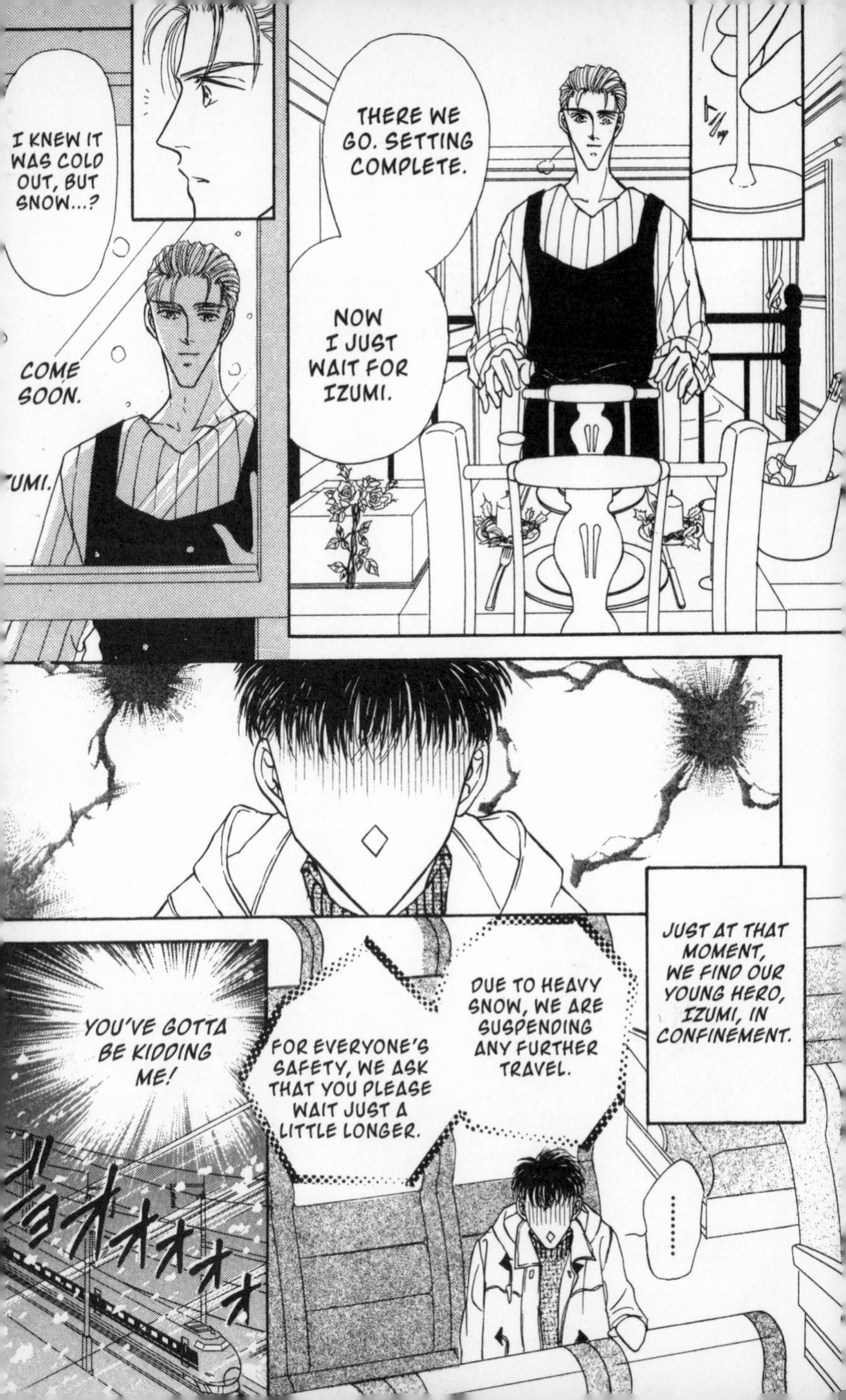
THERE WE GO. SETTING COMPLETE.
NOW I JUST WAIT FOR IZUMI.
I KNEW IT WAS COLD OUT, BUT SNOW...?
COME SOON.
ZUMI.
JUST AT THAT MOMENT, WE FIND OUR YOUNG HERO, IZUMI, IN CONFINEMENT.
DUE TO HEAVY SNOW, WE ARE SUSPENDING ANY FURTHER TRAVEL.
FOR EVERYONE'S SAFETY, WE ASK THAT YOU PLEASE WAIT JUST A LITTLE LONGER.
......
YOU'VE GOTTA BE KIDDING ME!

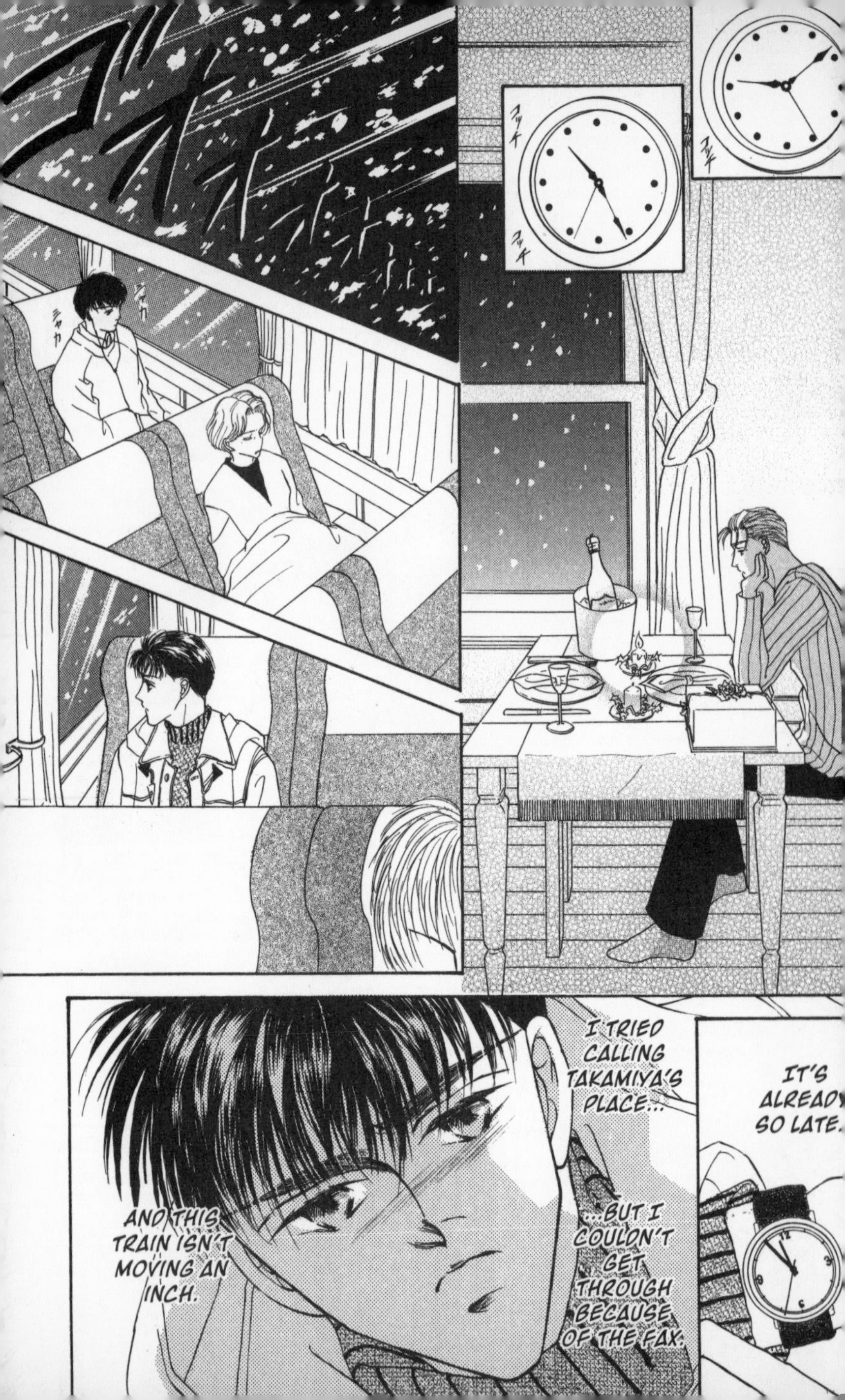
IT'S ALREADY SO LATE.
I TRIED CALLING TAKAMIYA'S PLACE...
...BUT I COULDN'T GET THROUGH BECAUSE OF THE FAX.
AND THIS TRAIN ISN'T MOVING AN INCH.

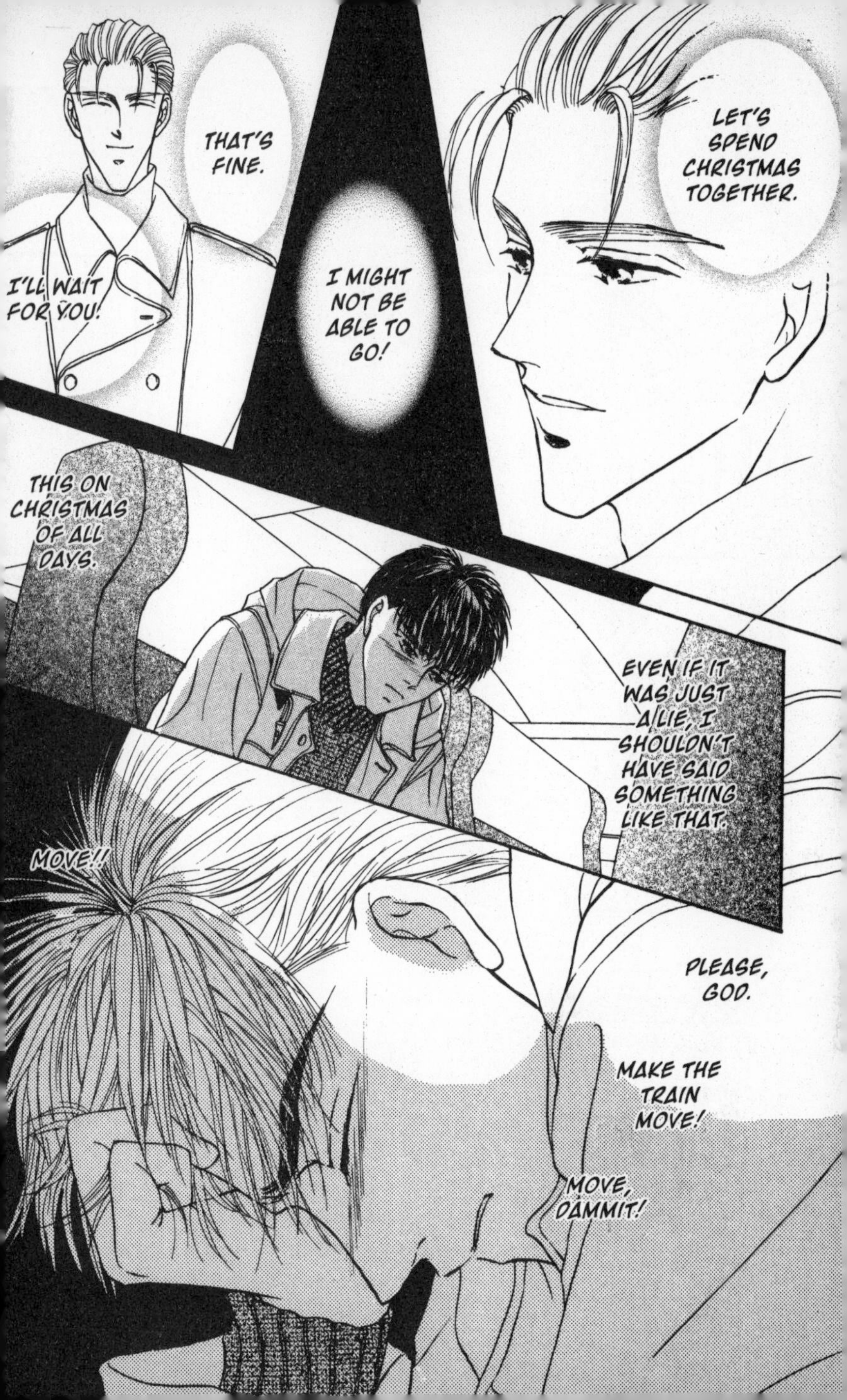
LET'S SPEND CHRISTMAS TOGETHER.
I MIGHT NOT BE ABLE TO GO!
THAT'S FINE.
I'LL WAIT FOR YOU!
EVEN IF IT WAS JUST A LIE, I SHOULDN'T HAVE SAID SOMETHING LIKE THAT.
THIS ON CHRISTMAS OF ALL DAYS.
PLEASE, GOD.
MAKE THE TRAIN MOVE!
MOVE, DAMMIT!
MOVE!!

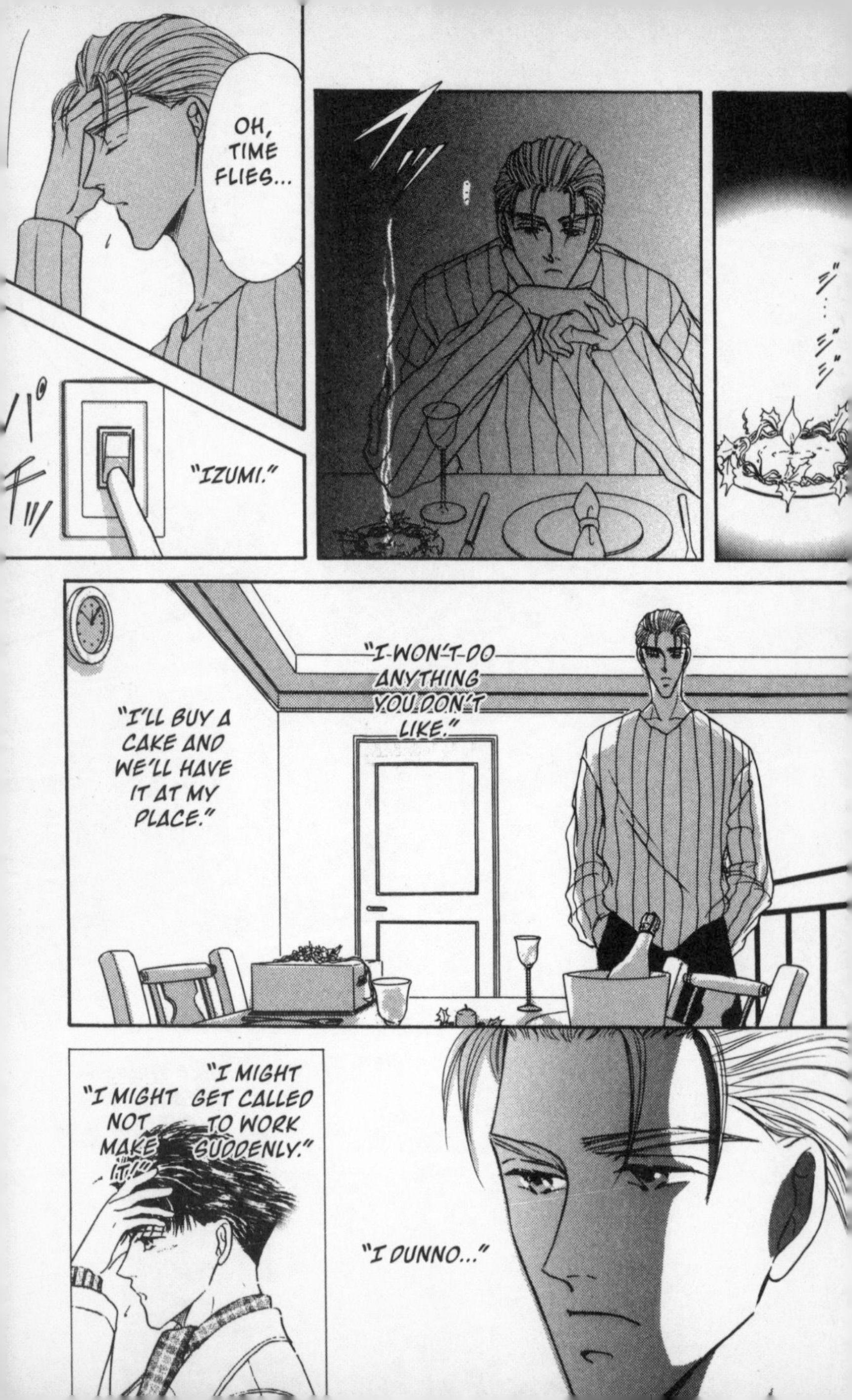
OH, TIME FLIES...
"IZUMI."
"I WON'T DO ANYTHING YOU DON'T LIKE."
"I'LL BUY A CAKE AND WE'LL HAVE IT AT MY PLACE."
"I DUNNO..."
"I MIGHT GET CALLED TO WORK SUDDENLY."
"I MIGHT NOT MAKE IT!"

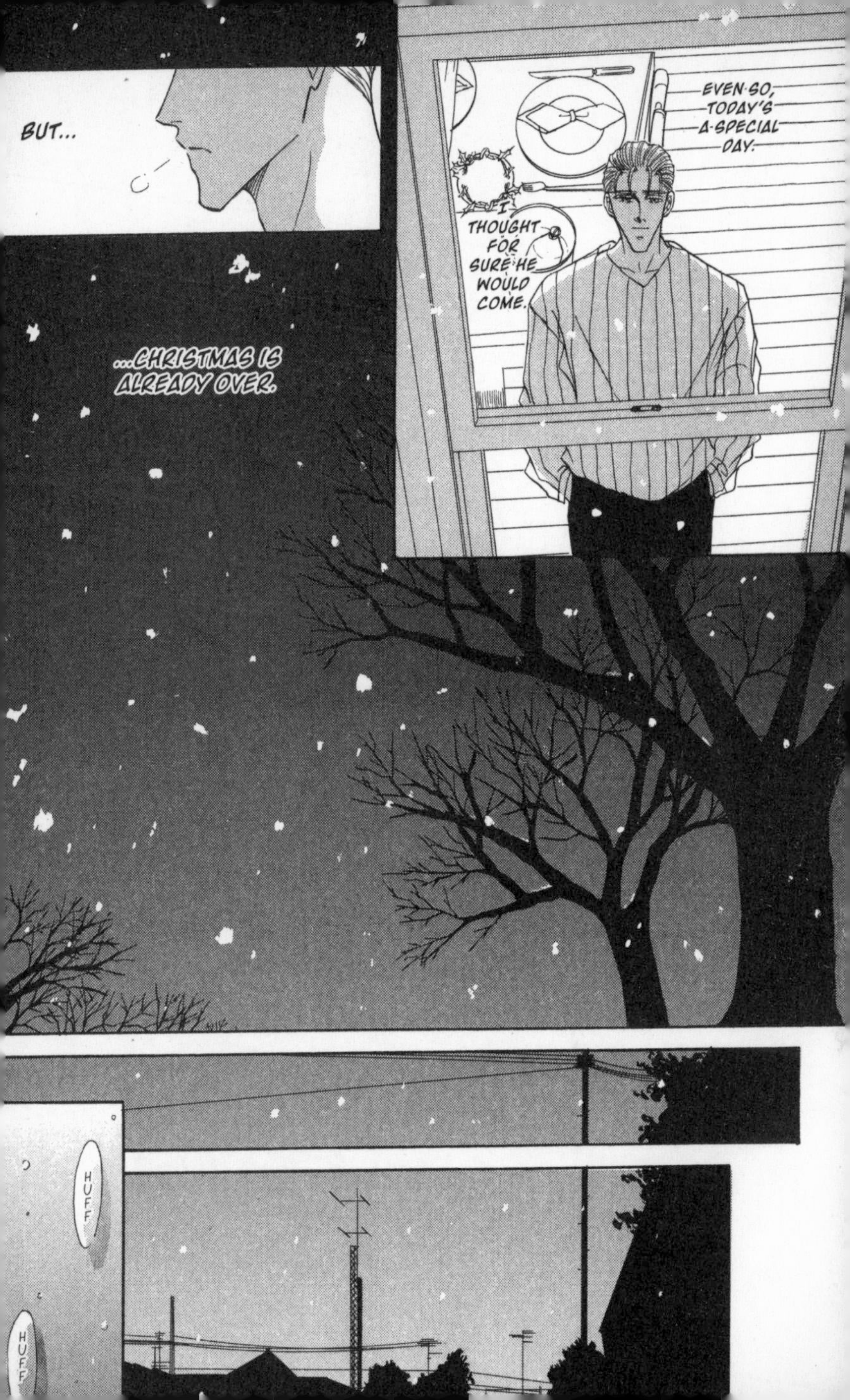
EVEN SO, TODAY'S A SPECIAL DAY.
I THOUGHT FOR SURE HE WOULD COME.
BUT...
...CHRISTMAS IS ALREADY OVER.
HUFF
HUFF

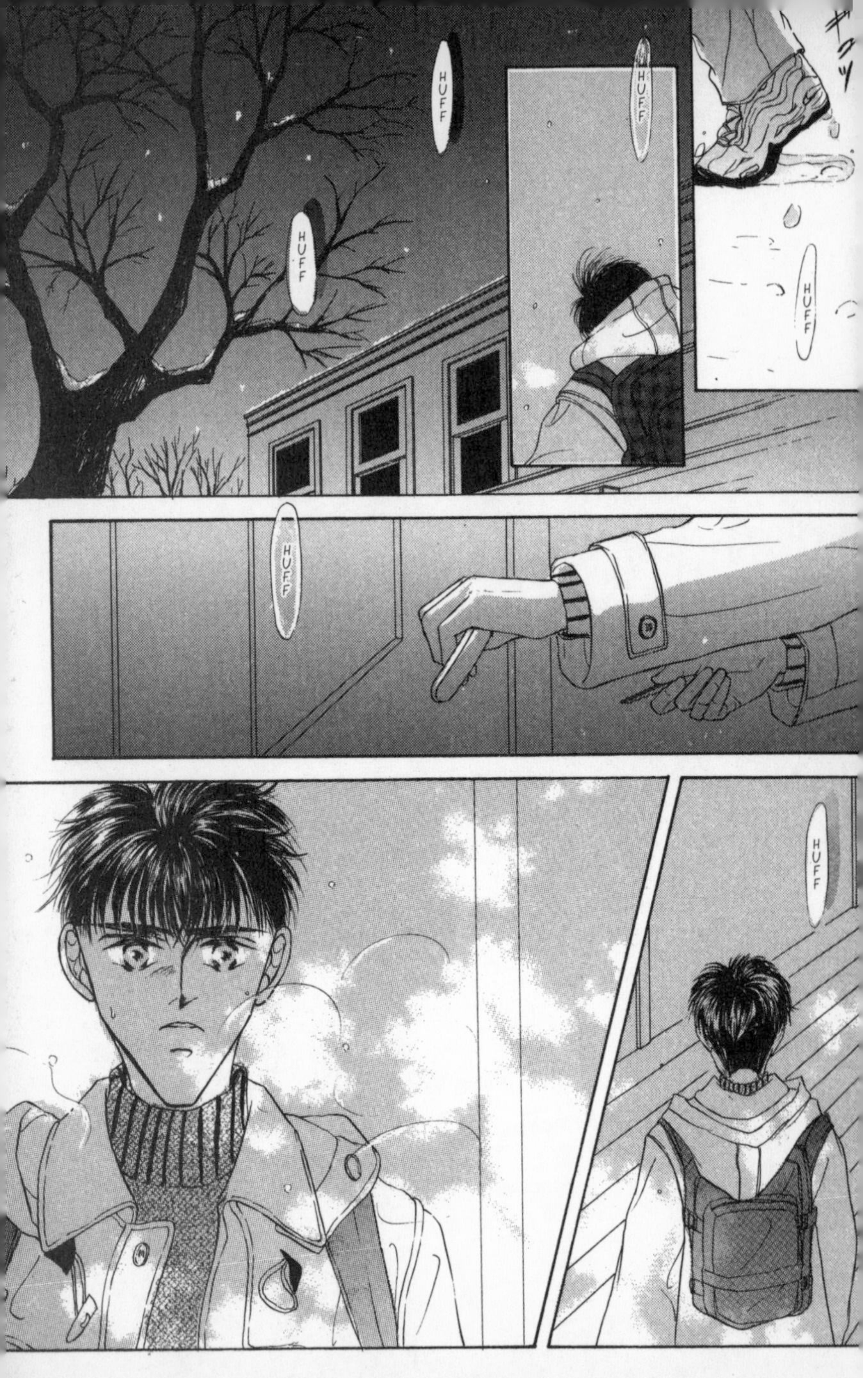
ギクッ
HUFF
HUFF
HUFF
HUFF
HUFF
HUFF

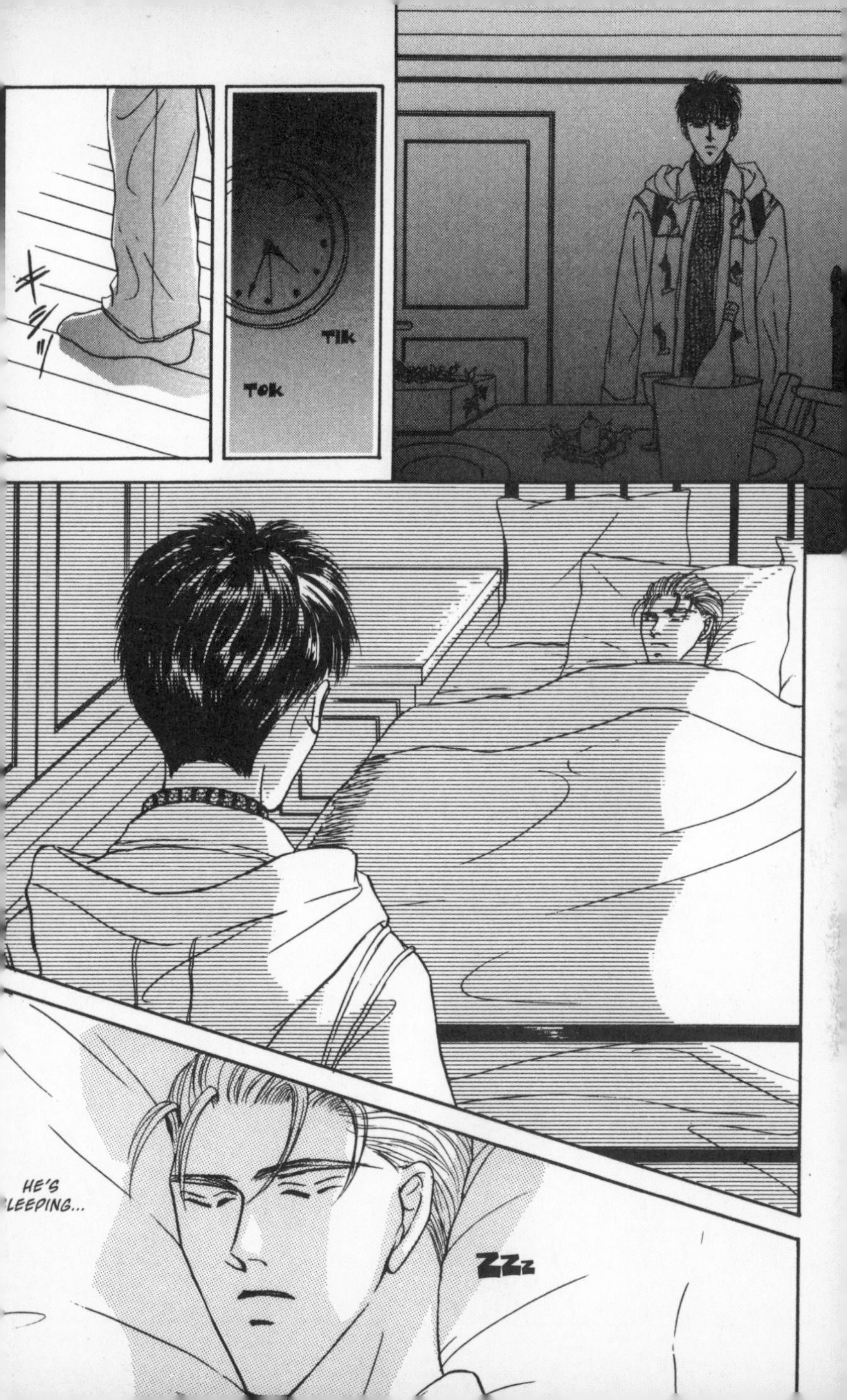
TIK
TOK
HE'S SLEEPING...
ZZz

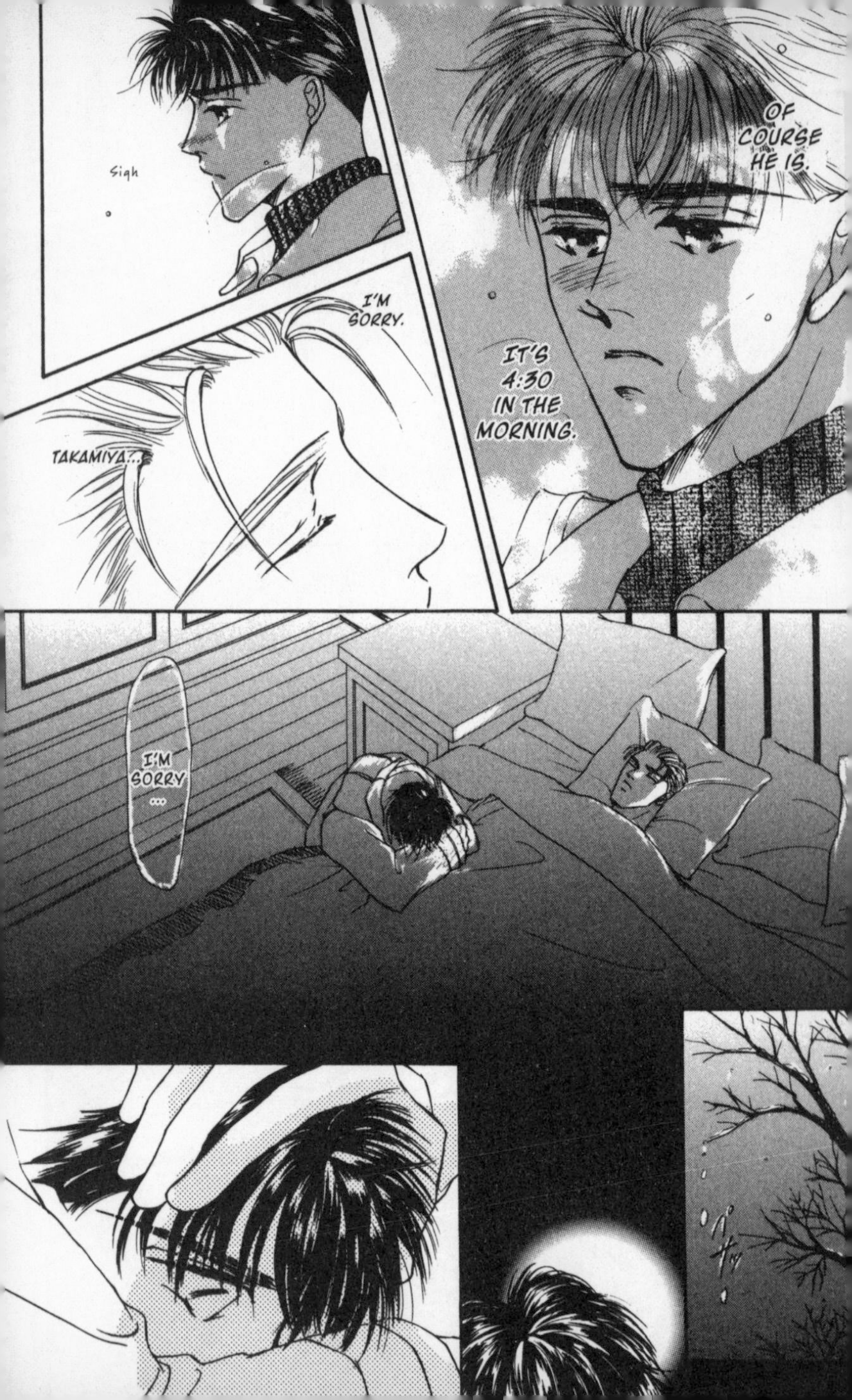
OF COURSE HE IS.
IT'S 4:30 IN THE MORNING.
Sigh
I'M SORRY.
TAKAMIYA...
I'M SORRY ...

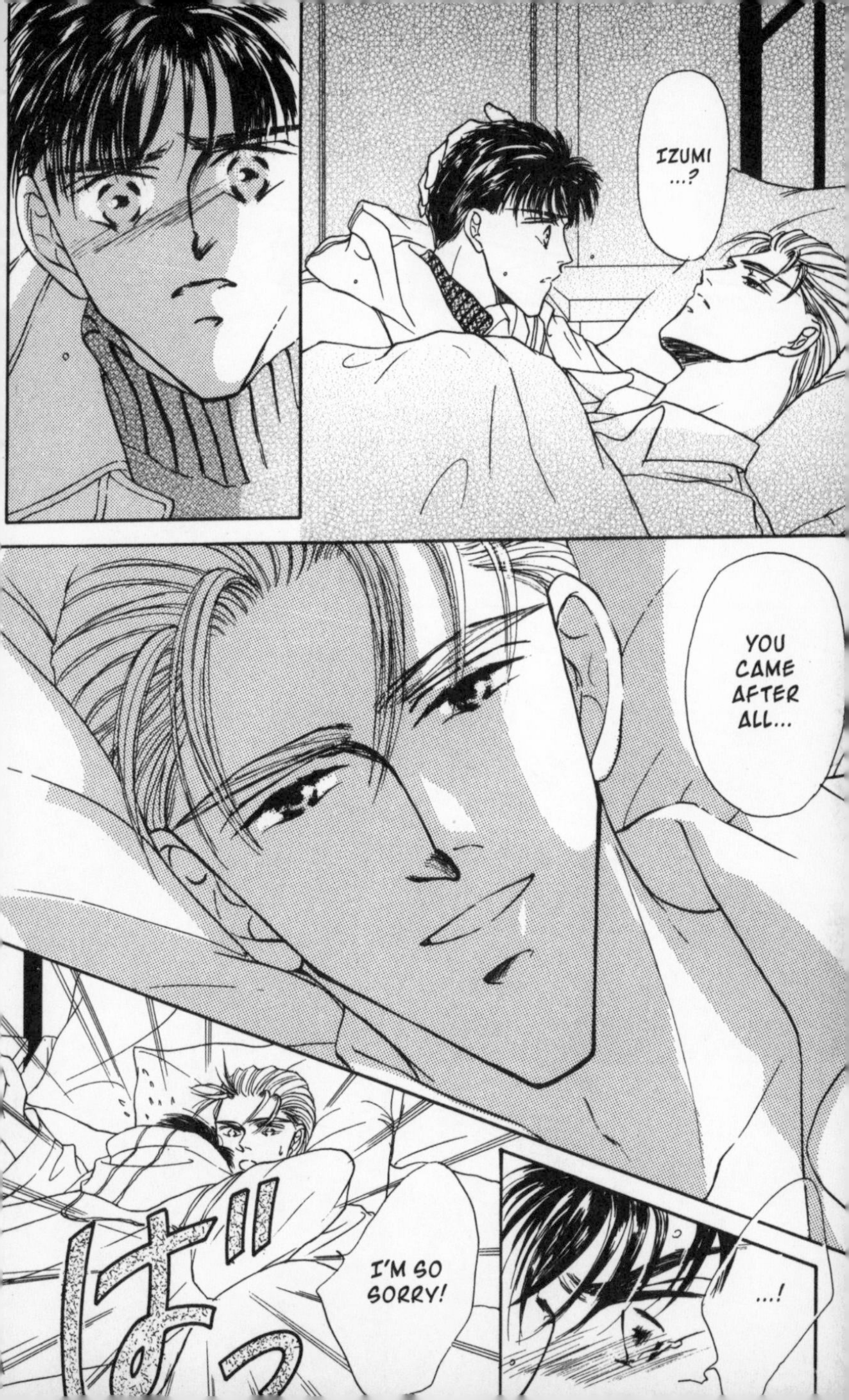
IZUMI ...?
YOU CAME AFTER ALL...
...!
I'M SO SORRY!
ばっ

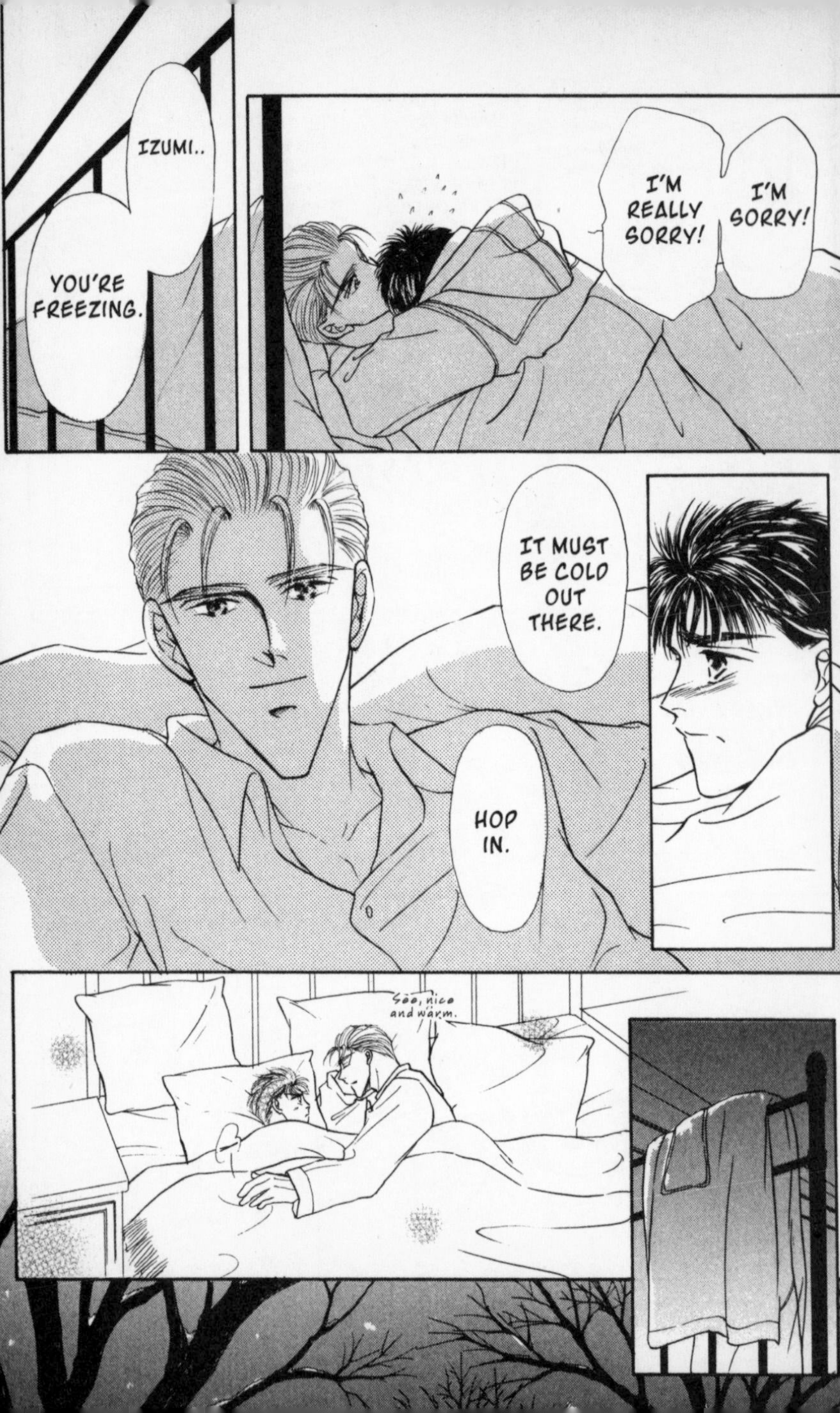
I'M SORRY!
I'M REALLY SORRY!
IZUMI..
YOU'RE FREEZING.
IT MUST BE COLD OUT THERE.
HOP IN.
See, nice and warm.

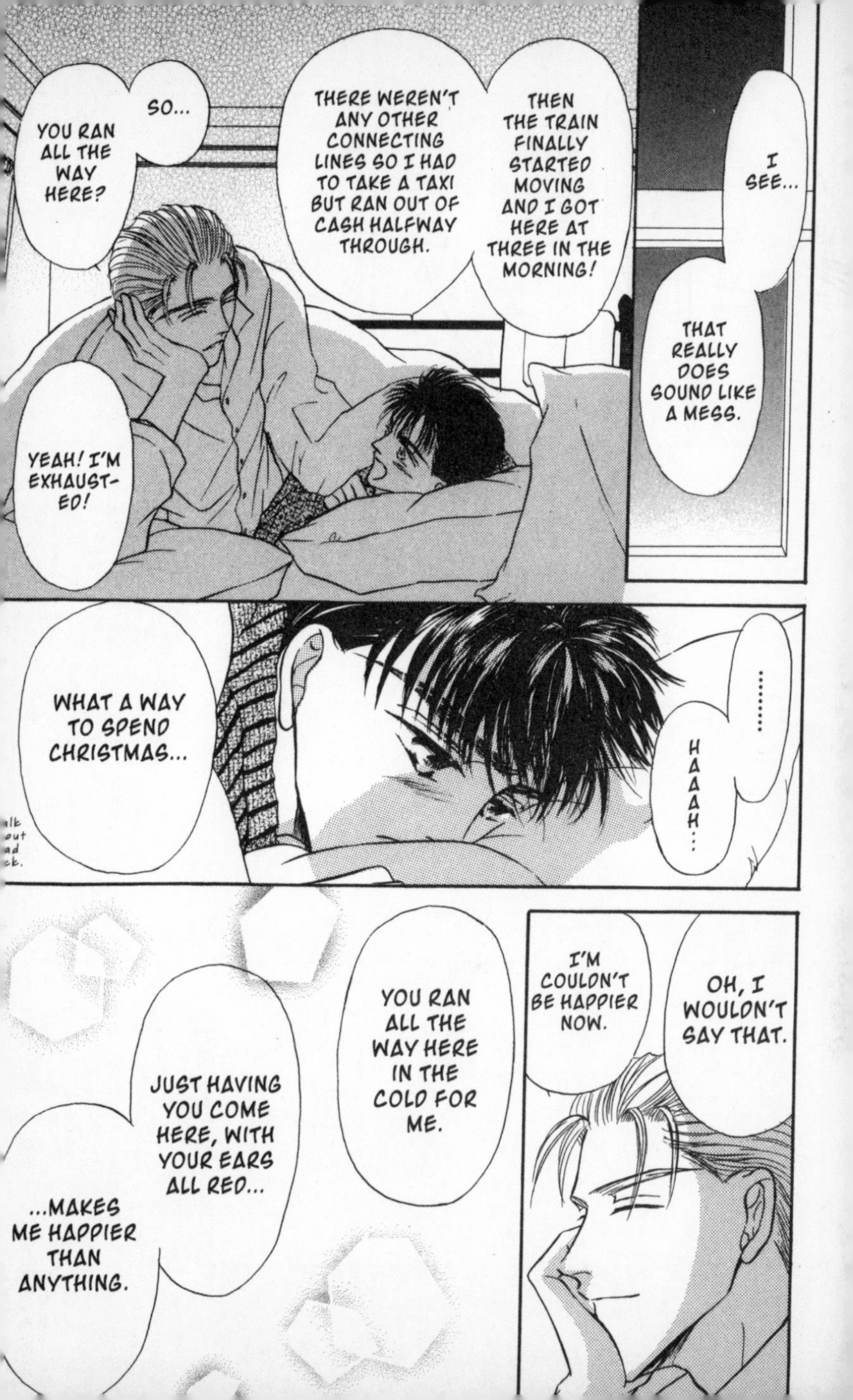
I SEE...
THAT REALLY DOES SOUND LIKE A MESS.
THEN THE TRAIN FINALLY STARTED MOVING AND I GOT HERE AT THREE IN THE MORNING!
THERE WEREN'T ANY OTHER CONNECTING LINES SO I HAD TO TAKE A TAXI BUT RAN OUT OF CASH HALFWAY THROUGH.
SO...
YOU RAN ALL THE WAY HERE?
YEAH! I'M EXHAUST-ED!
......
HAAAAH...
WHAT A WAY TO SPEND CHRISTMAS...
OH, I WOULDN'T SAY THAT.
I'M COULDN'T BE HAPPIER NOW.
YOU RAN ALL THE WAY HERE IN THE COLD FOR ME.
JUST HAVING YOU COME HERE, WITH YOUR EARS ALL RED...
...MAKES ME HAPPIER THAN ANYTHING.

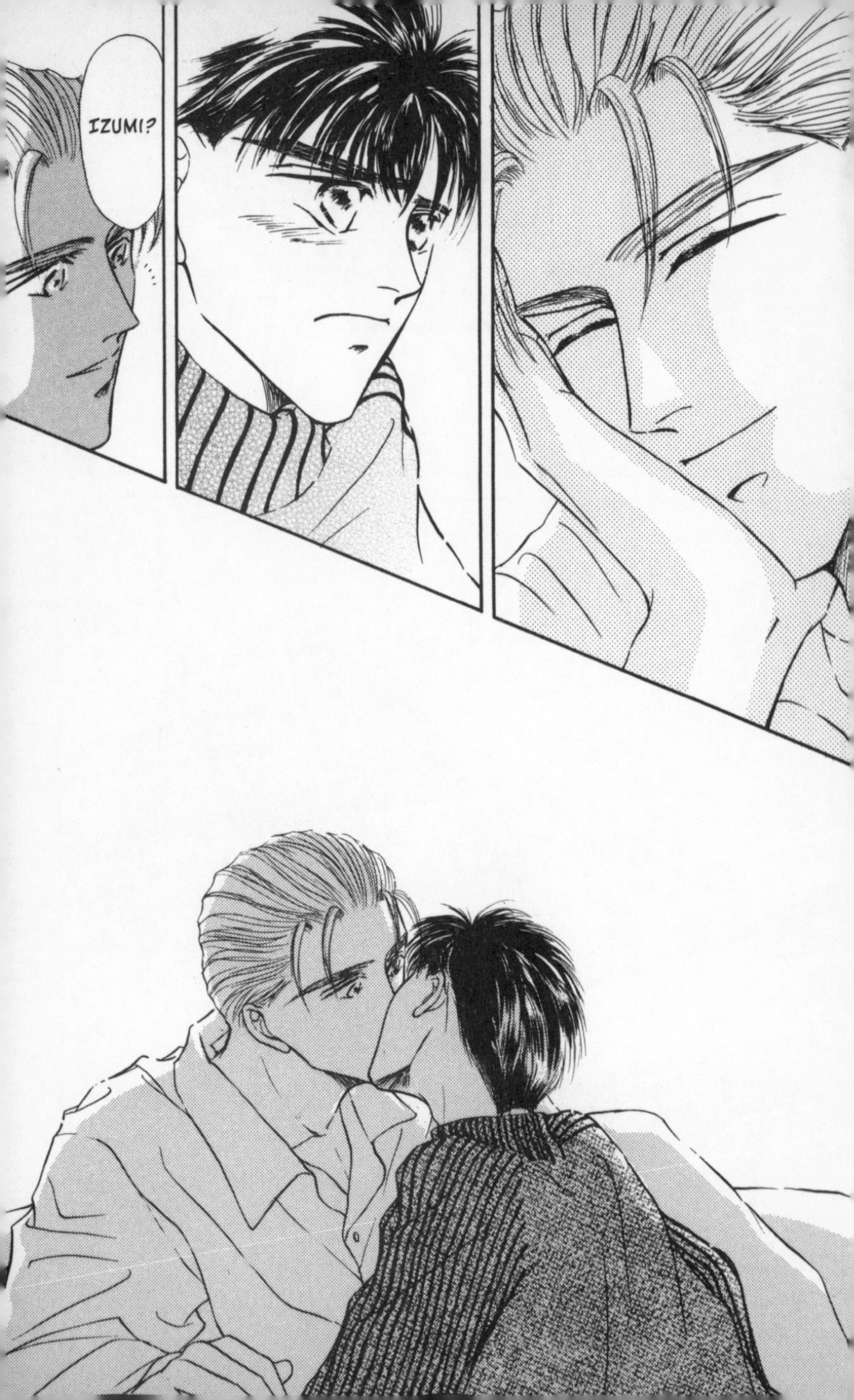
IZUMI?

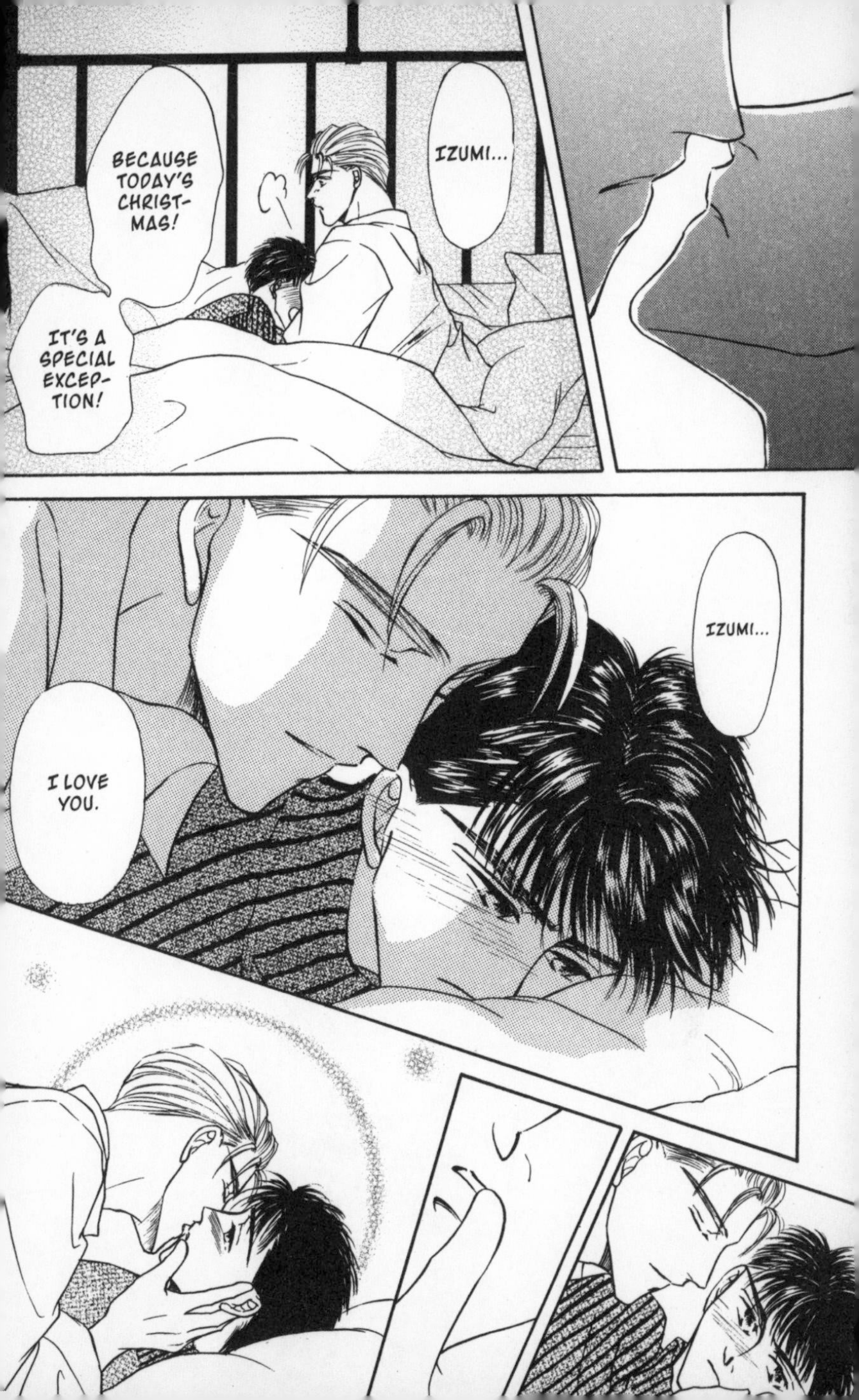
IZUMI...
BECAUSE TODAY'S CHRIST-MAS!
IT'S A SPECIAL EXCEP-TION!
IZUMI...
I LOVE YOU.

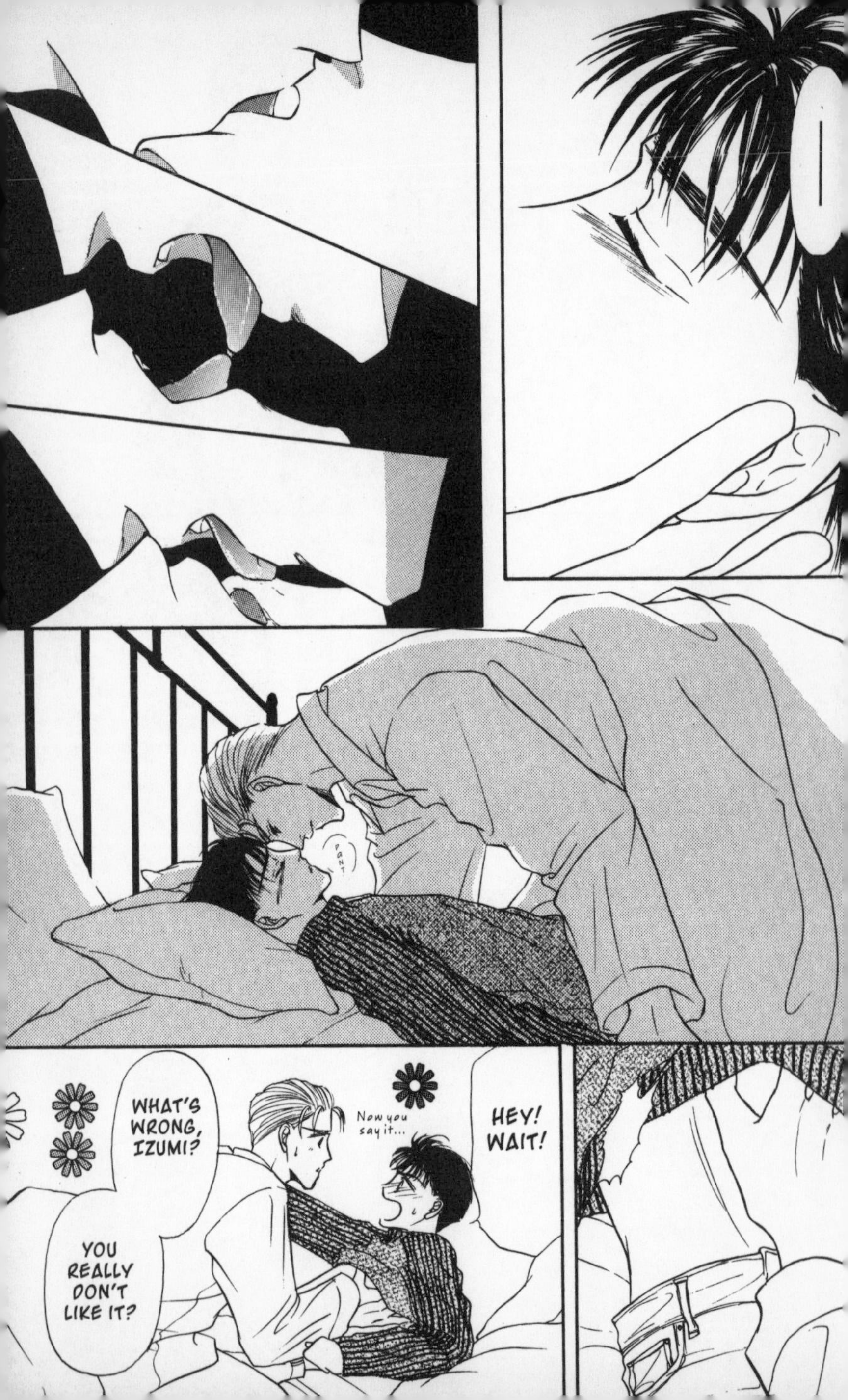
PANT
HEY! WAIT!
Now you say it...
WHAT'S WRONG, IZUMI?
YOU REALLY DON'T LIKE IT?

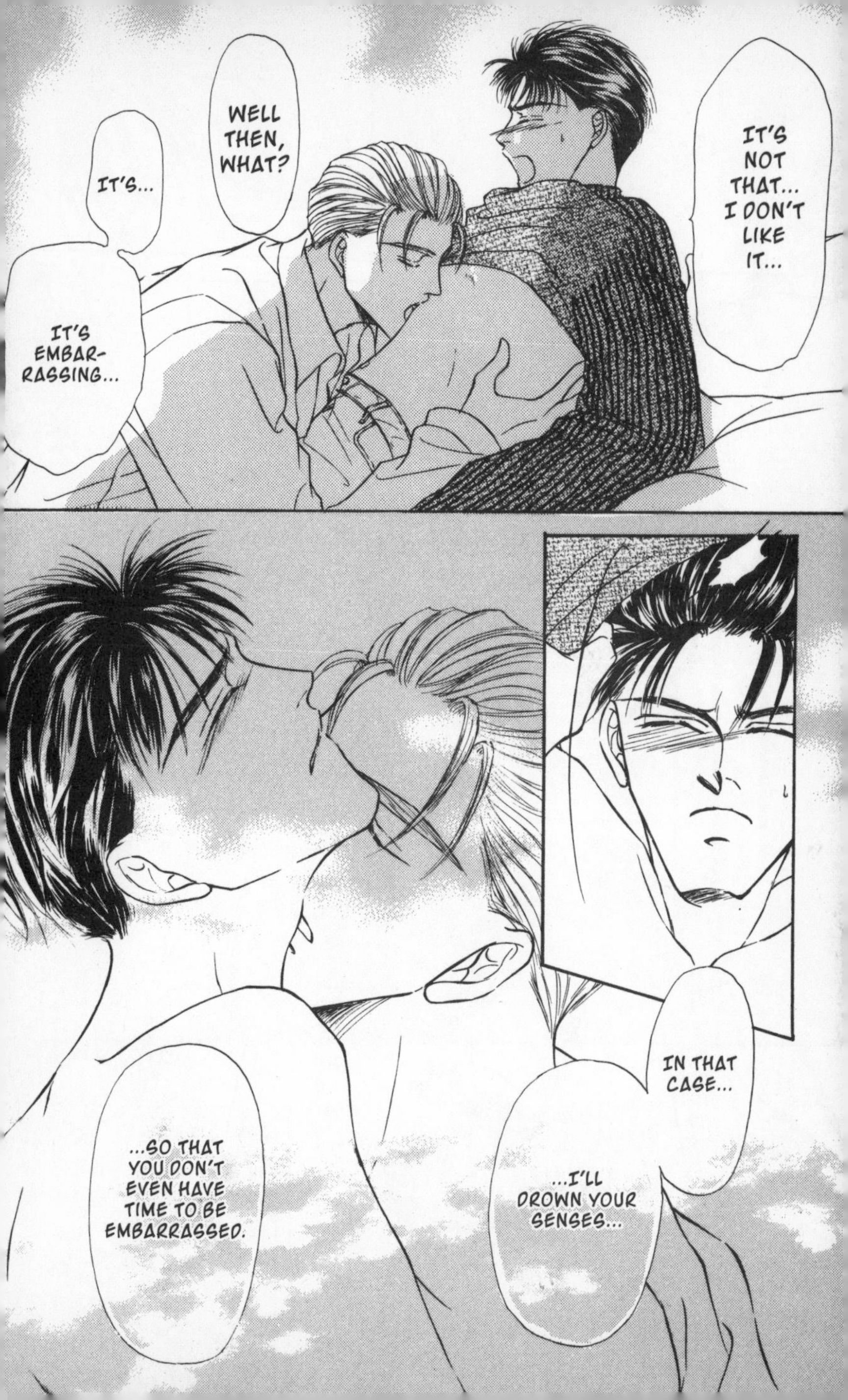
IT'S NOT THAT... I DON'T LIKE IT...
WELL THEN, WHAT?
IT'S...
IT'S EMBARRASSING...
IN THAT CASE...
...I'LL DROWN YOUR SENSES...
...SO THAT YOU DON'T EVEN HAVE TIME TO BE EMBARRASSED.

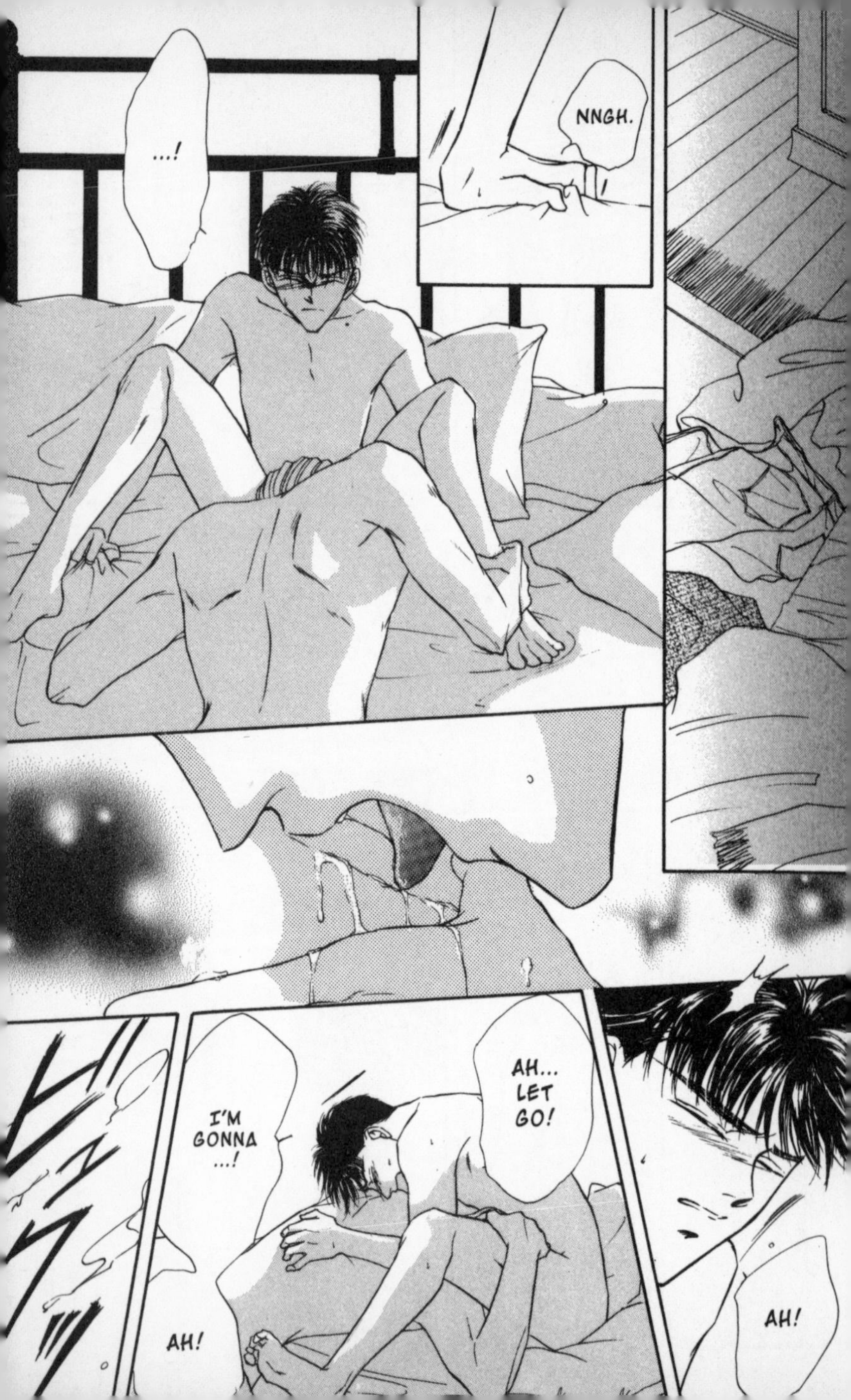
NNGH.
...!
AH!
AH... LET GO!
I'M GONNA ...!
AH!

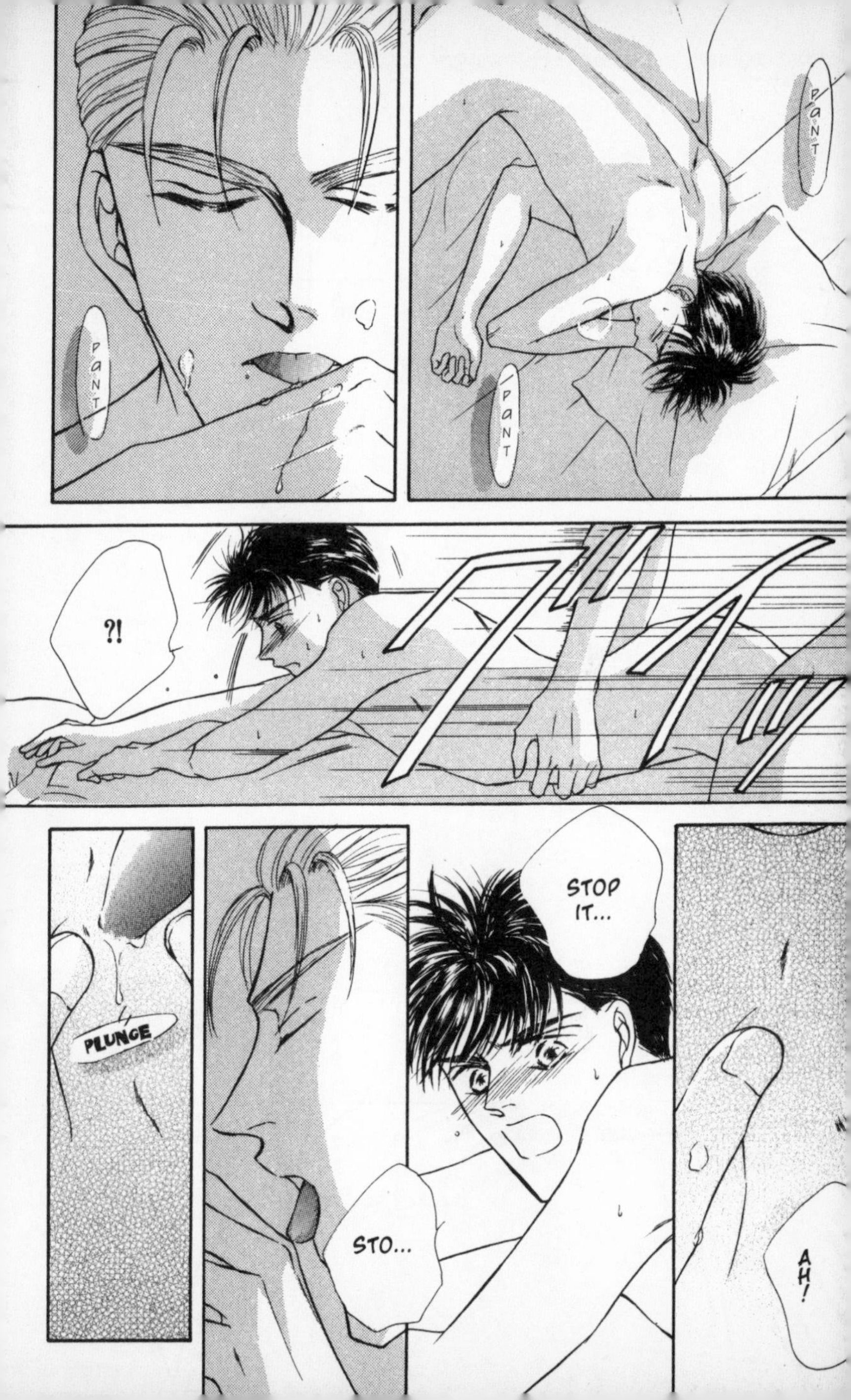
PANT
PANT
PANT
?!
AH!
STOP IT...
STO...
PLUNGE

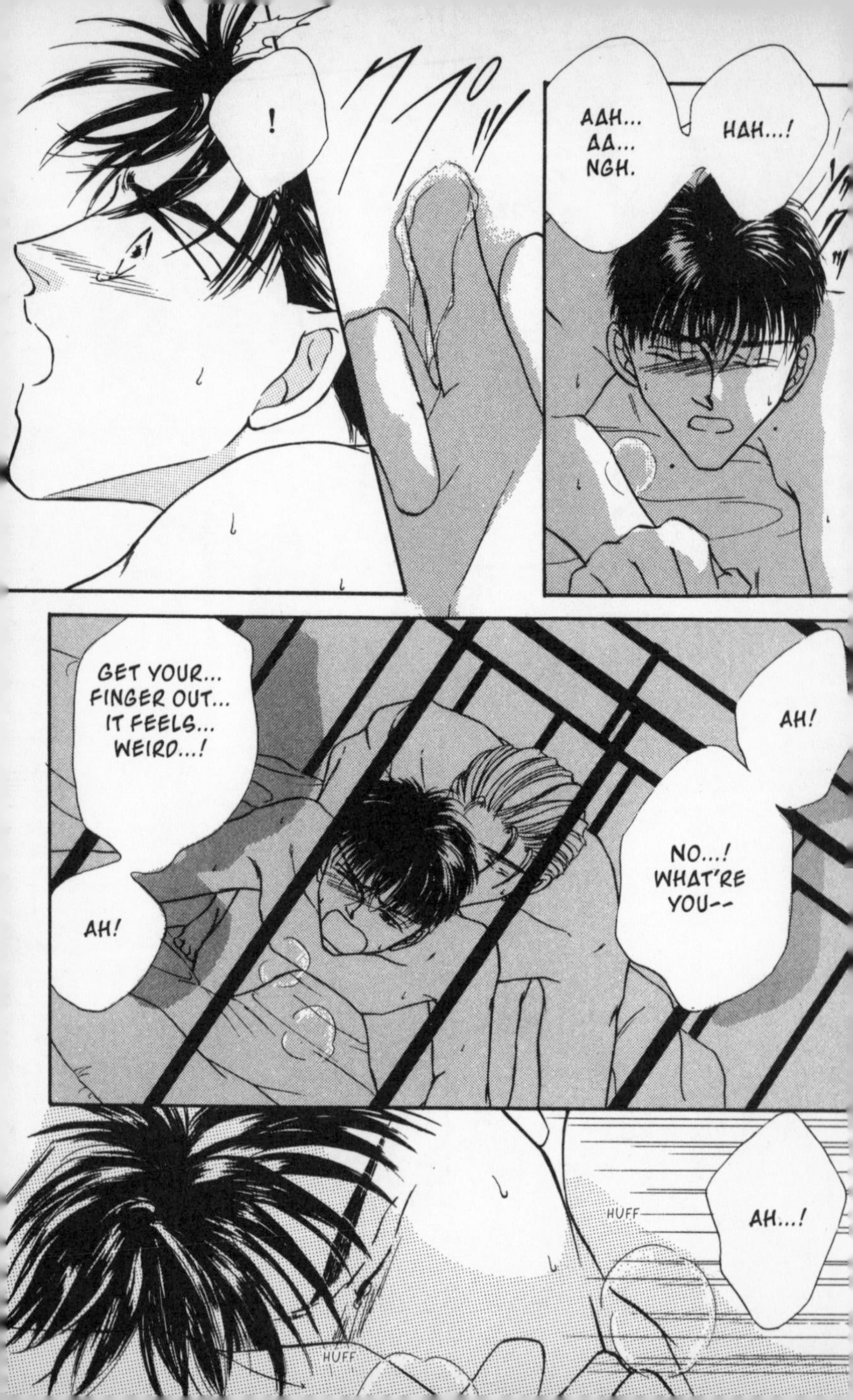
HAH...!
AAH... AA... NGH.
!
AH!
NO...! WHAT'RE YOU--
GET YOUR... FINGER OUT... IT FEELS... WEIRD...!
AH!
AH...!
HUFF
HUFF

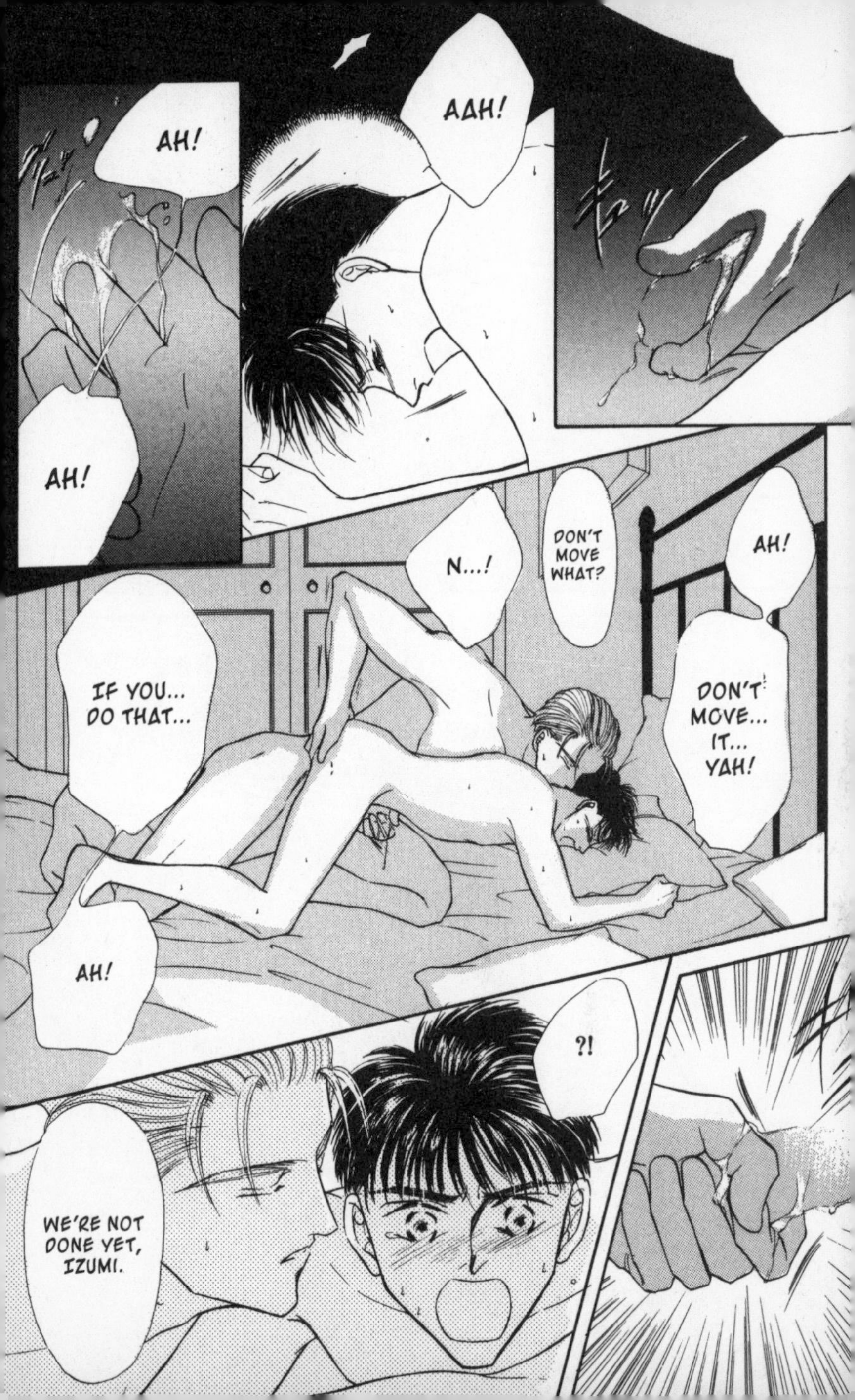
AAH!
AH!
AH!
AH!
DON'T MOVE... IT... YAH!
DON'T MOVE WHAT?
N...!
IF YOU... DO THAT...
AH!
?!
WE'RE NOT DONE YET, IZUMI.

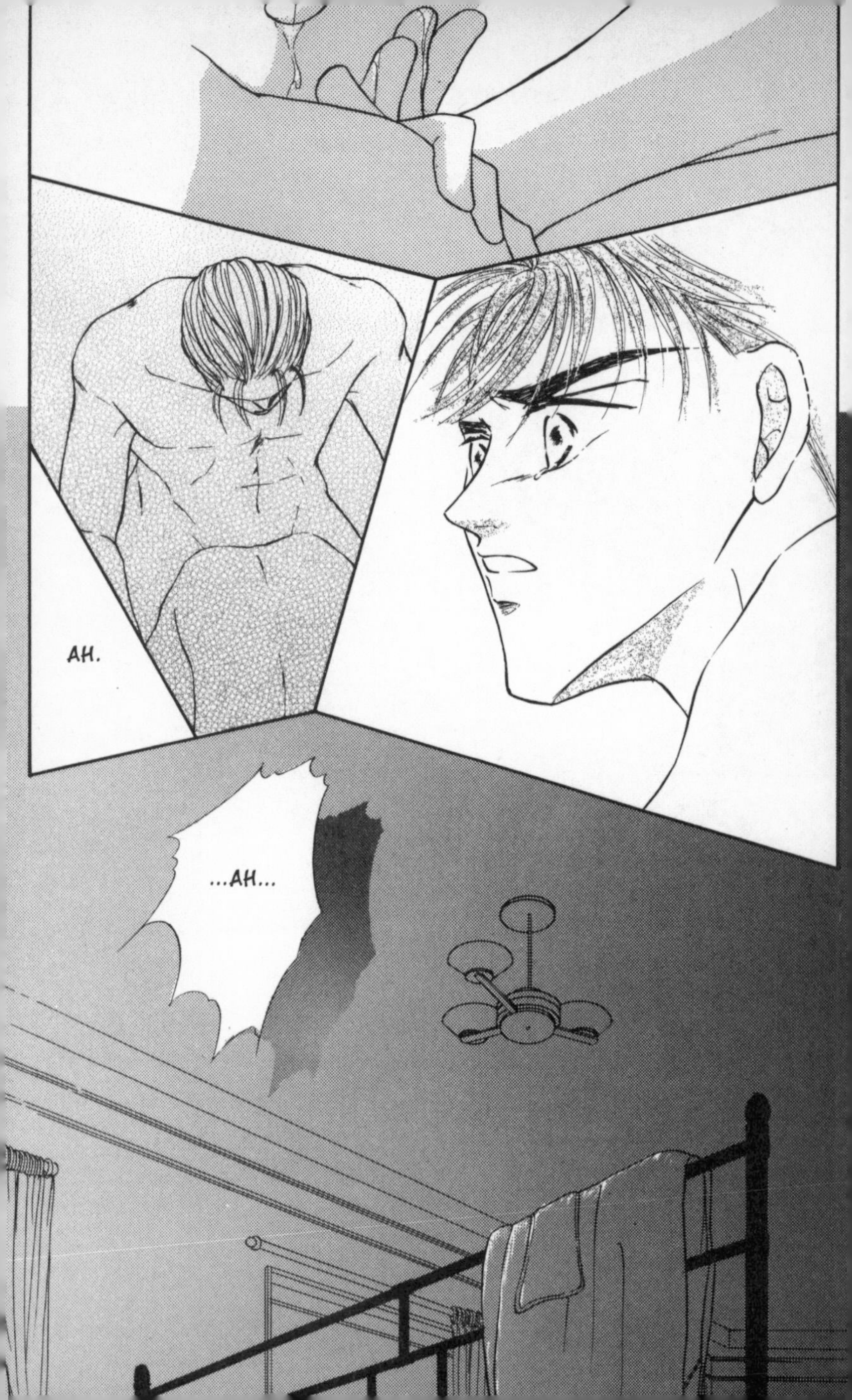
AH.
...AH...

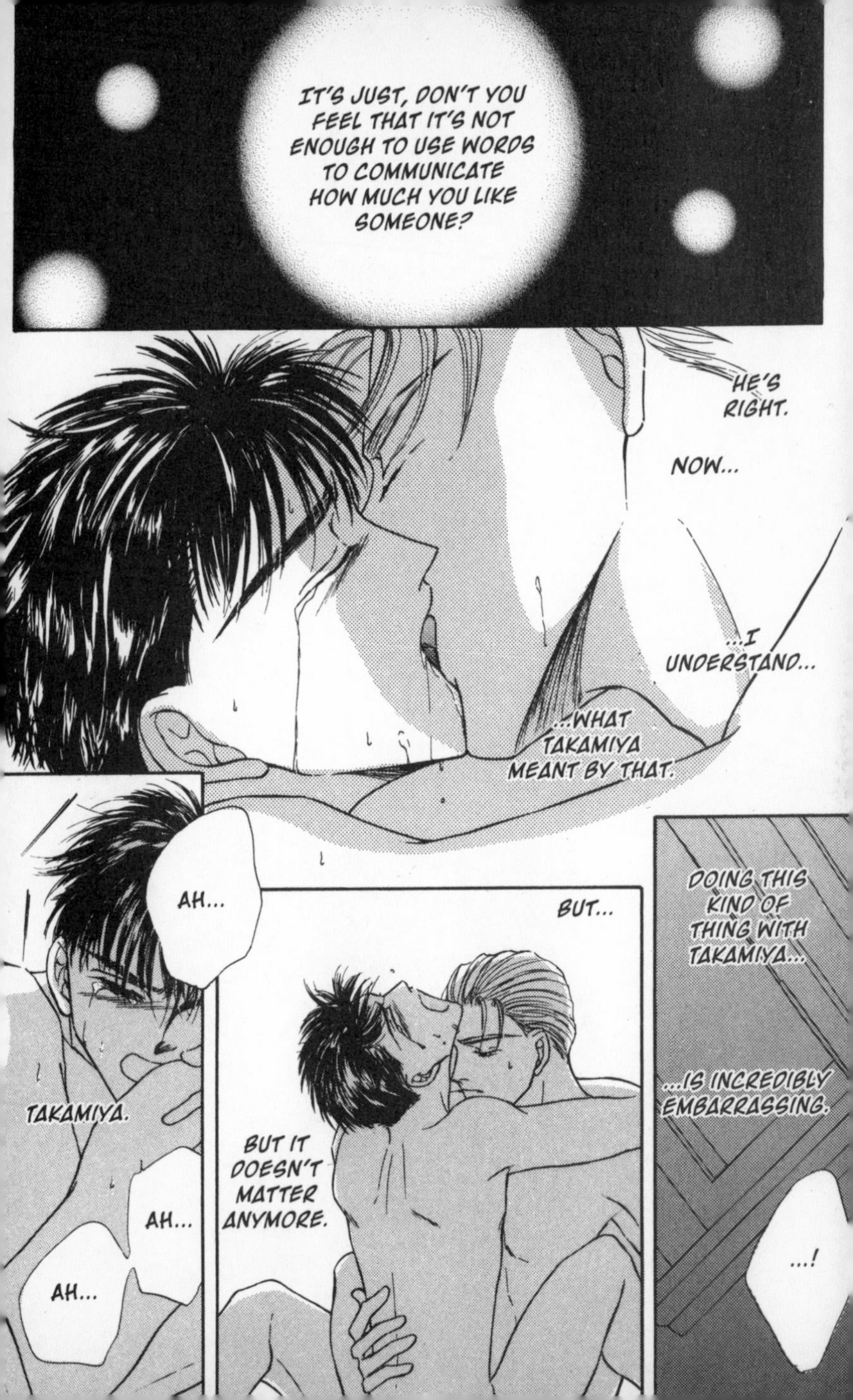
IT'S JUST, DON'T YOU FEEL THAT IT'S NOT ENOUGH TO USE WORDS TO COMMUNICATE HOW MUCH YOU LIKE SOMEONE?
HE'S RIGHT.
NOW...
...I UNDERSTAND...
...WHAT TAKAMIYA MEANT BY THAT.
DOING THIS KIND OF THING WITH TAKAMIYA...
...IS INCREDIBLY EMBARRASSING.
...!
BUT...
BUT IT DOESN'T MATTER ANYMORE.
AH...
TAKAMIYA.
AH...
AH...

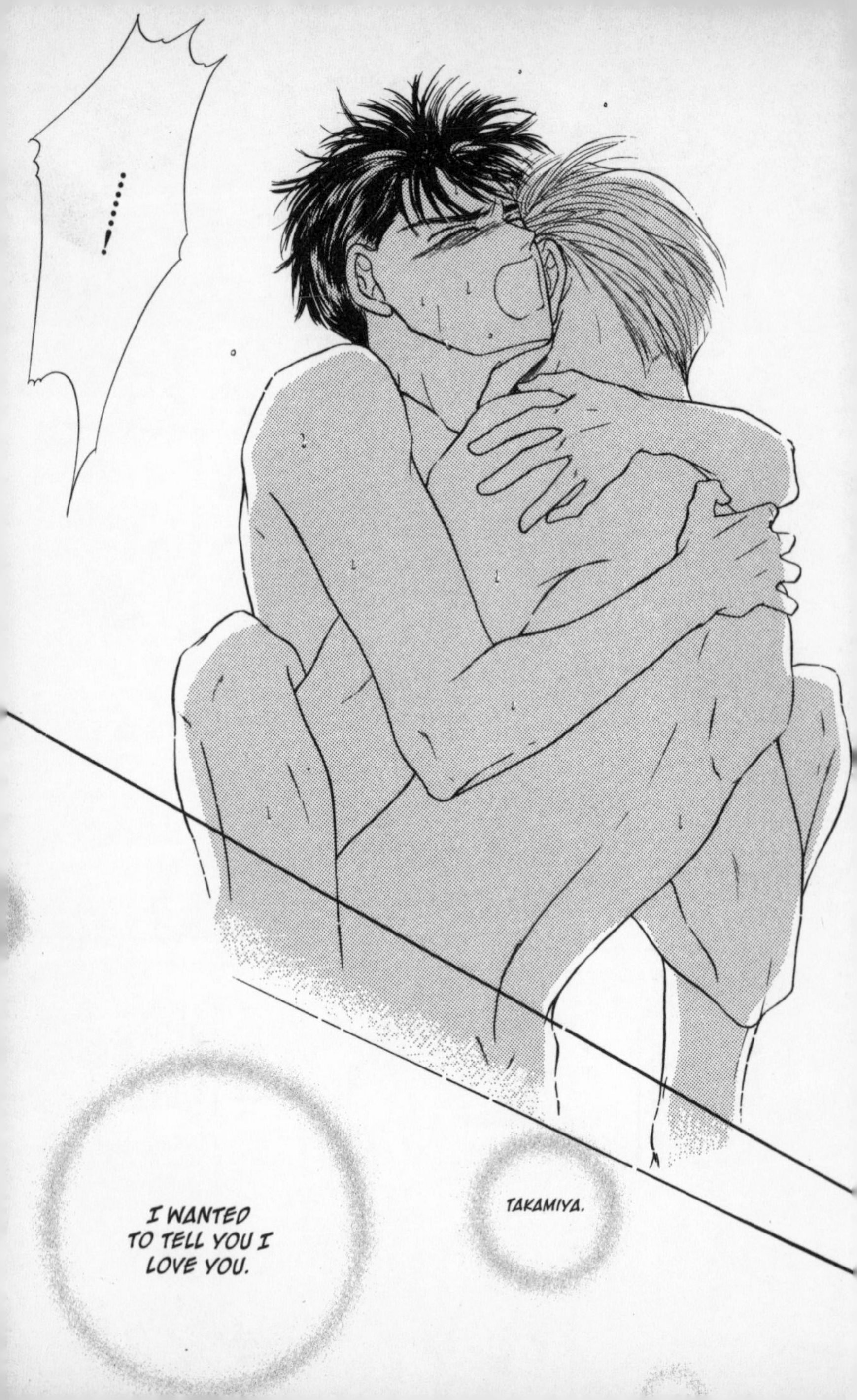
......!
TAKAMIYA.
I WANTED TO TELL YOU I LOVE YOU.

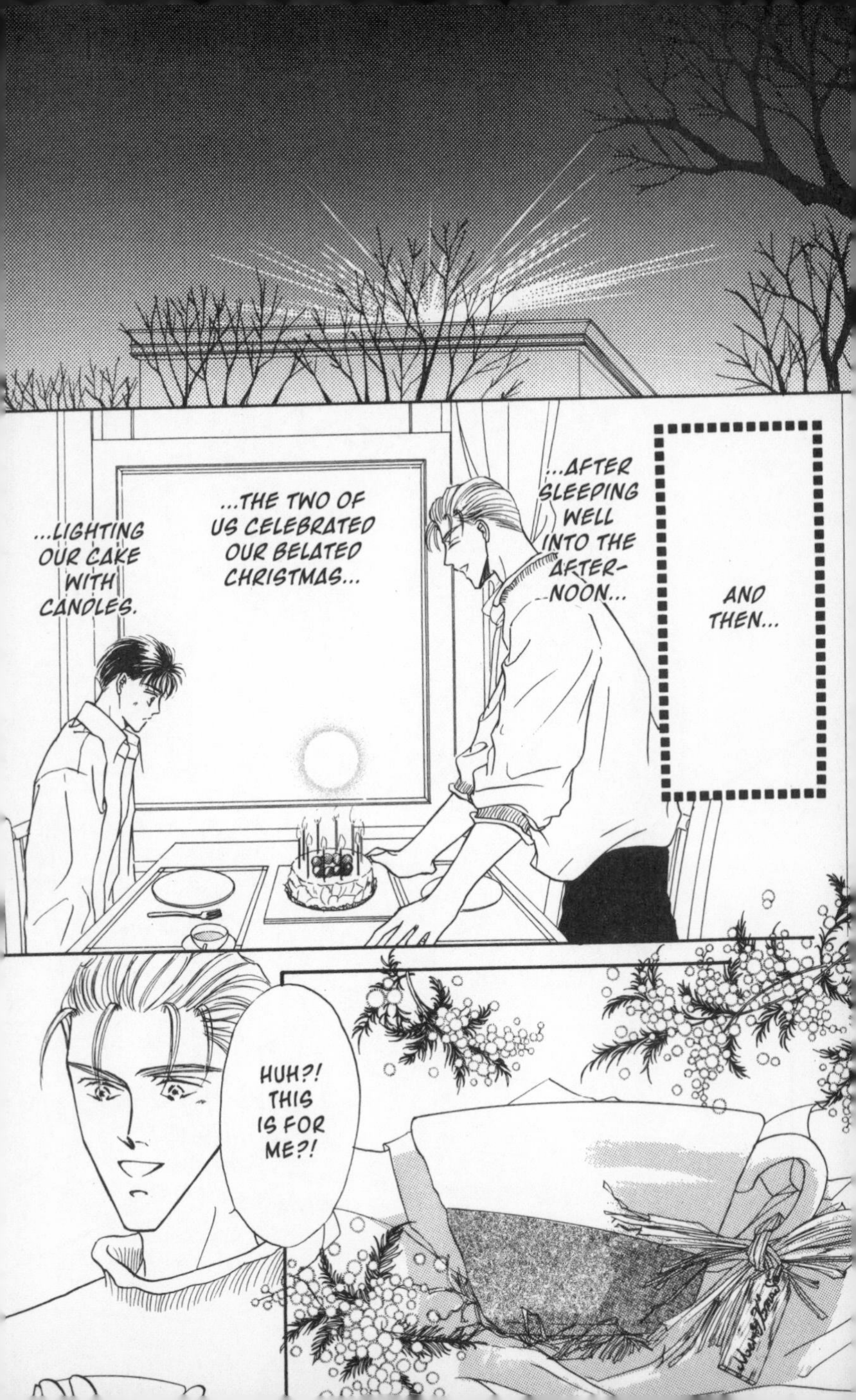
AND THEN...
...AFTER SLEEPING WELL INTO THE AFTER-NOON...
...THE TWO OF US CELEBRATED OUR BELATED CHRISTMAS...
...LIGHTING OUR CAKE WITH CANDLES.
HUH?! THIS IS FOR ME?!

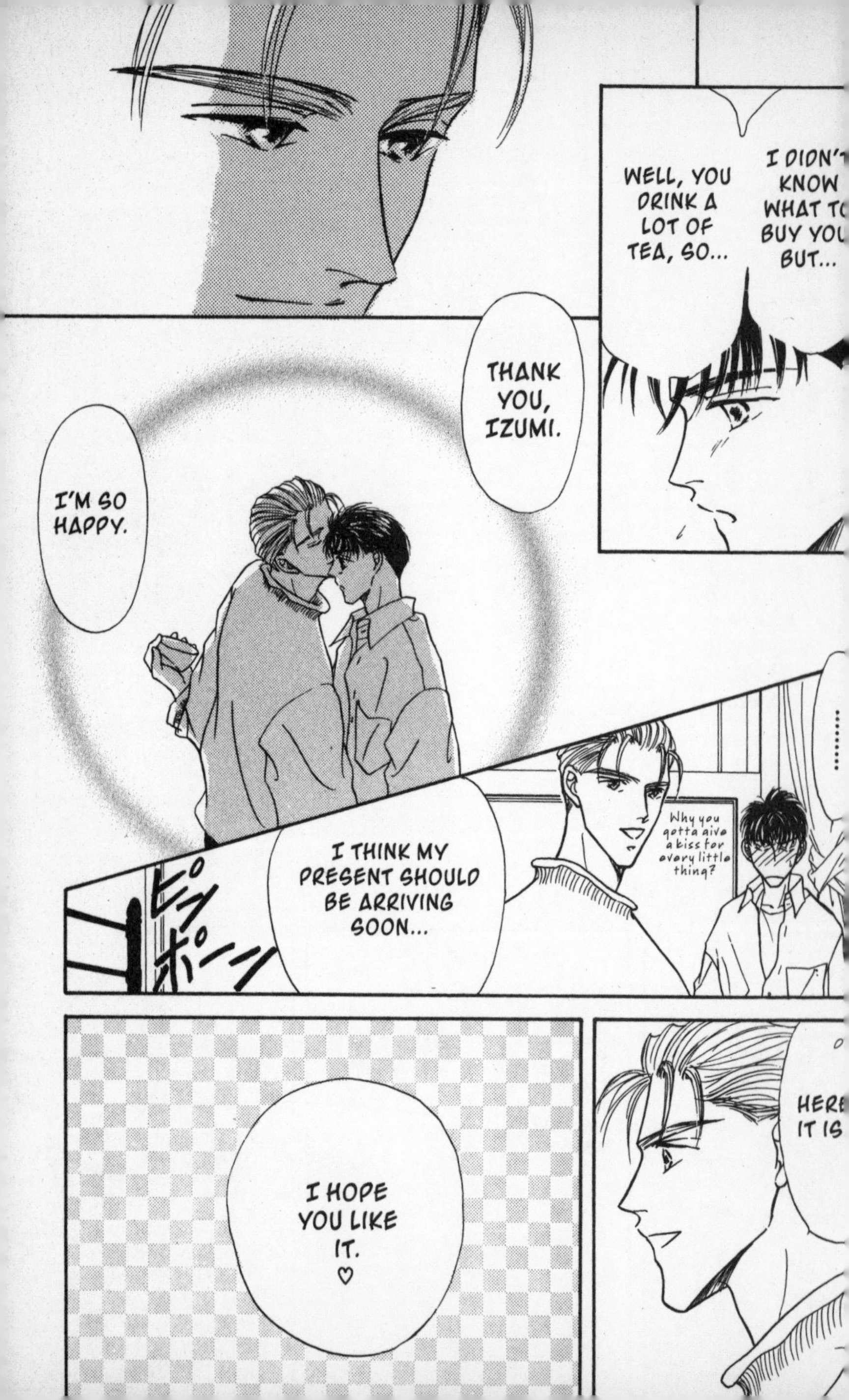
I DIDN'T KNOW WHAT TO BUY YOU BUT...
WELL, YOU DRINK A LOT OF TEA, SO...
THANK YOU, IZUMI.
I'M SO HAPPY.
......
Why you gotta give a kiss for every little thing?
I THINK MY PRESENT SHOULD BE ARRIVING SOON...
ピンポーン
HERE IT IS
I HOPE YOU LIKE IT. ♡

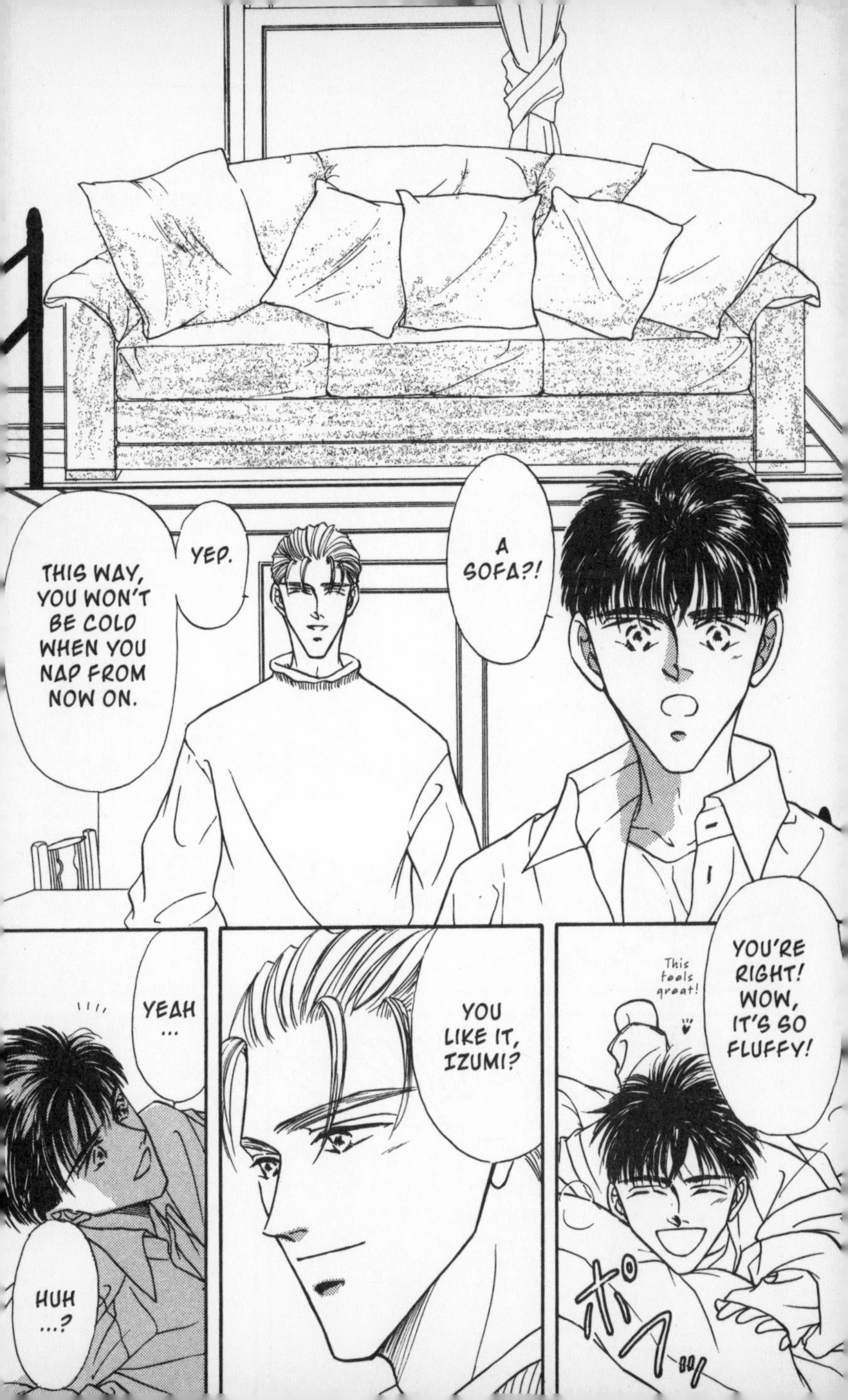
A SOFA?!
YEP.
THIS WAY, YOU WON'T BE COLD WHEN YOU NAP FROM NOW ON.
YOU'RE RIGHT! WOW, IT'S SO FLUFFY!
This feels great!
YOU LIKE IT, IZUMI?
YEAH ...
HUH ...?

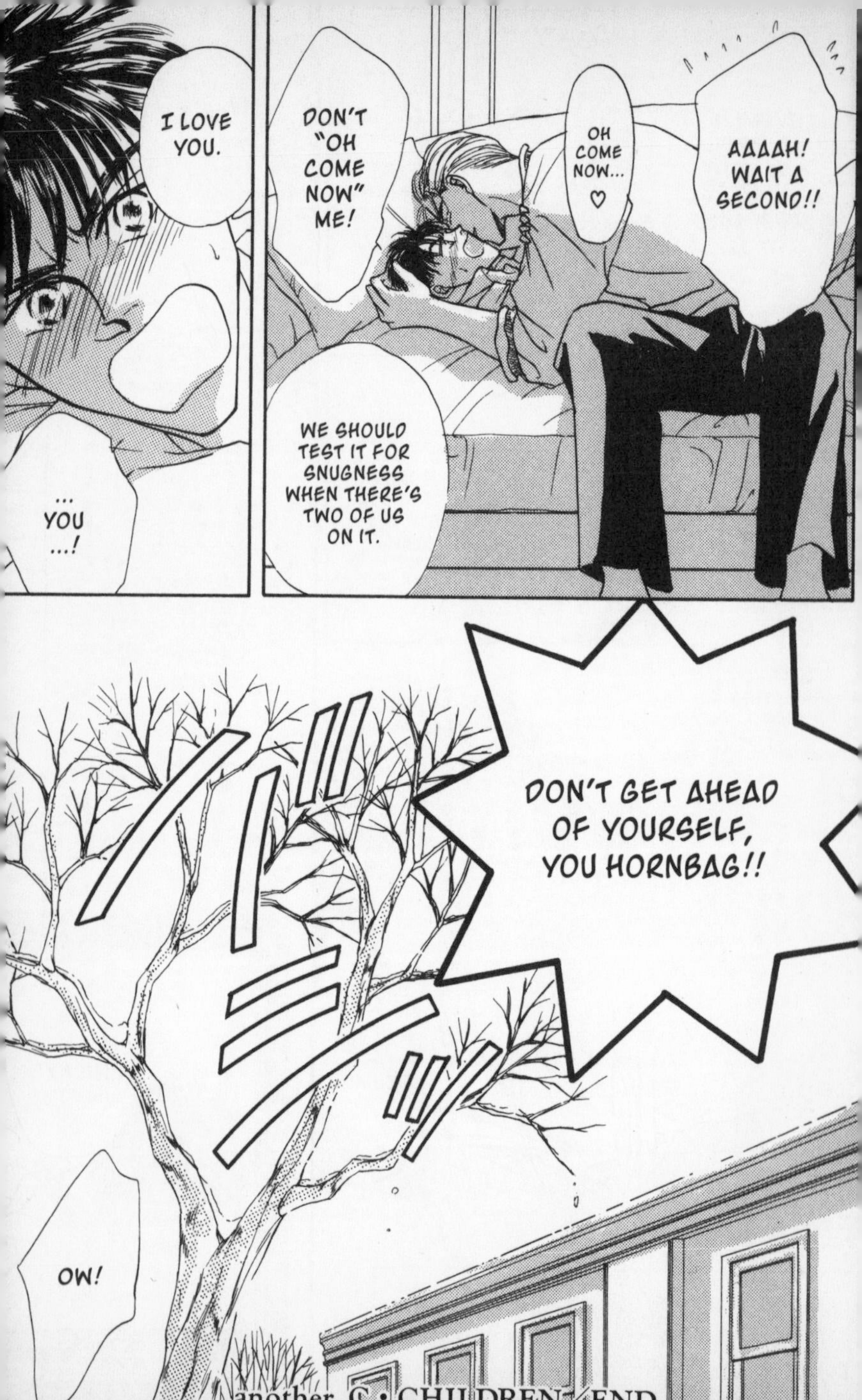
AAAAH! WAIT A SECOND!!
OH COME NOW... ♡
DON'T "OH COME NOW" ME!
WE SHOULD TEST IT FOR SNUGNESS WHEN THERE'S TWO OF US ON IT.
I LOVE YOU.
... YOU ...!
DON'T GET AHEAD OF YOURSELF, YOU HORNBAG!!
OW!

another C • CHILDREN / END

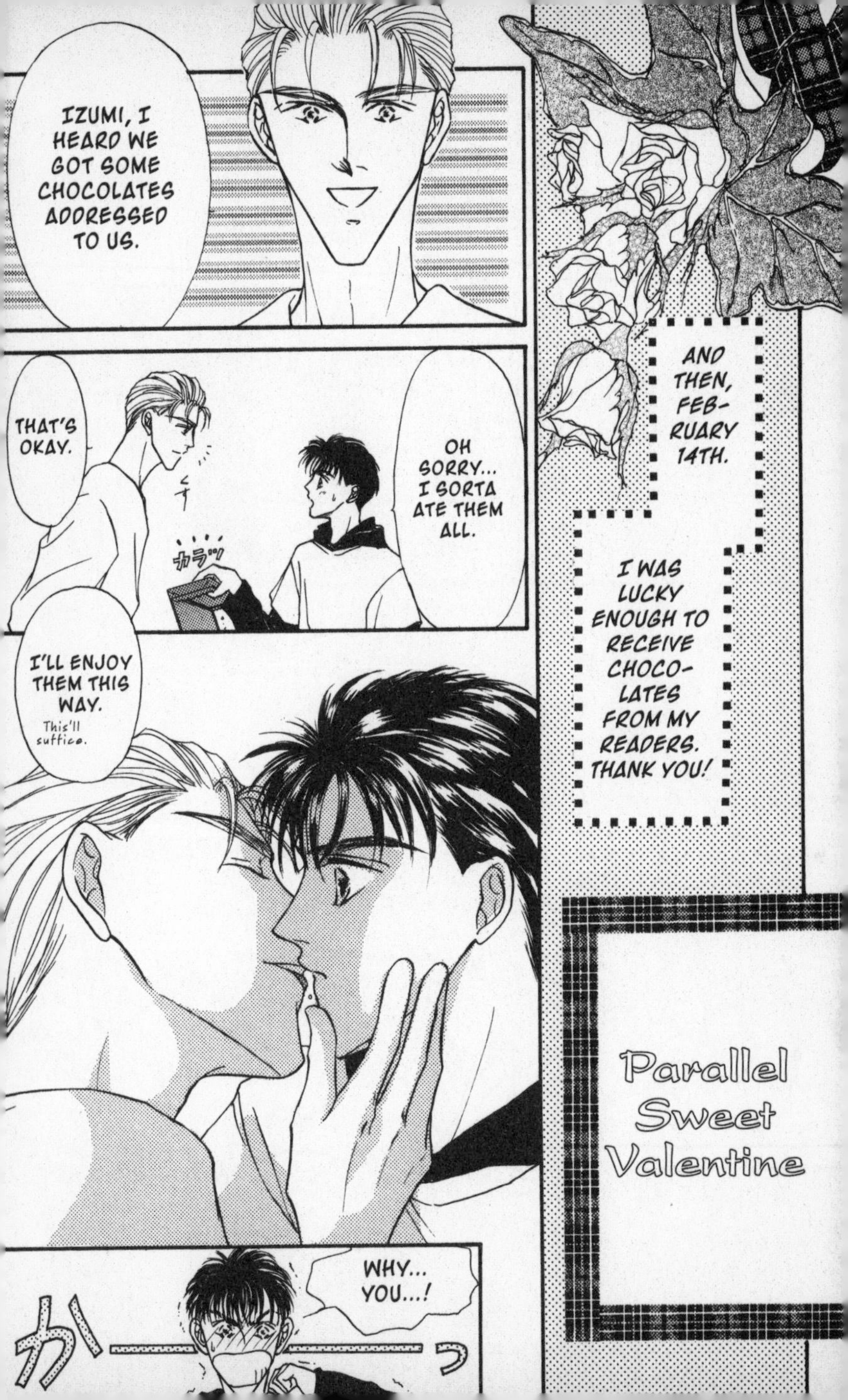
AND THEN, FEB-RUARY 14TH.
I WAS LUCKY ENOUGH TO RECEIVE CHOCO-LATES FROM MY READERS. THANK YOU!
Parallel Sweet Valentine
IZUMI, I HEARD WE GOT SOME CHOCOLATES ADDRESSED TO US.
OH SORRY... I SORTA ATE THEM ALL.
カラッ
くす
THAT'S OKAY.
I'LL ENJOY THEM THIS WAY.
This'll suffice.
WHY... YOU...!
か――っ

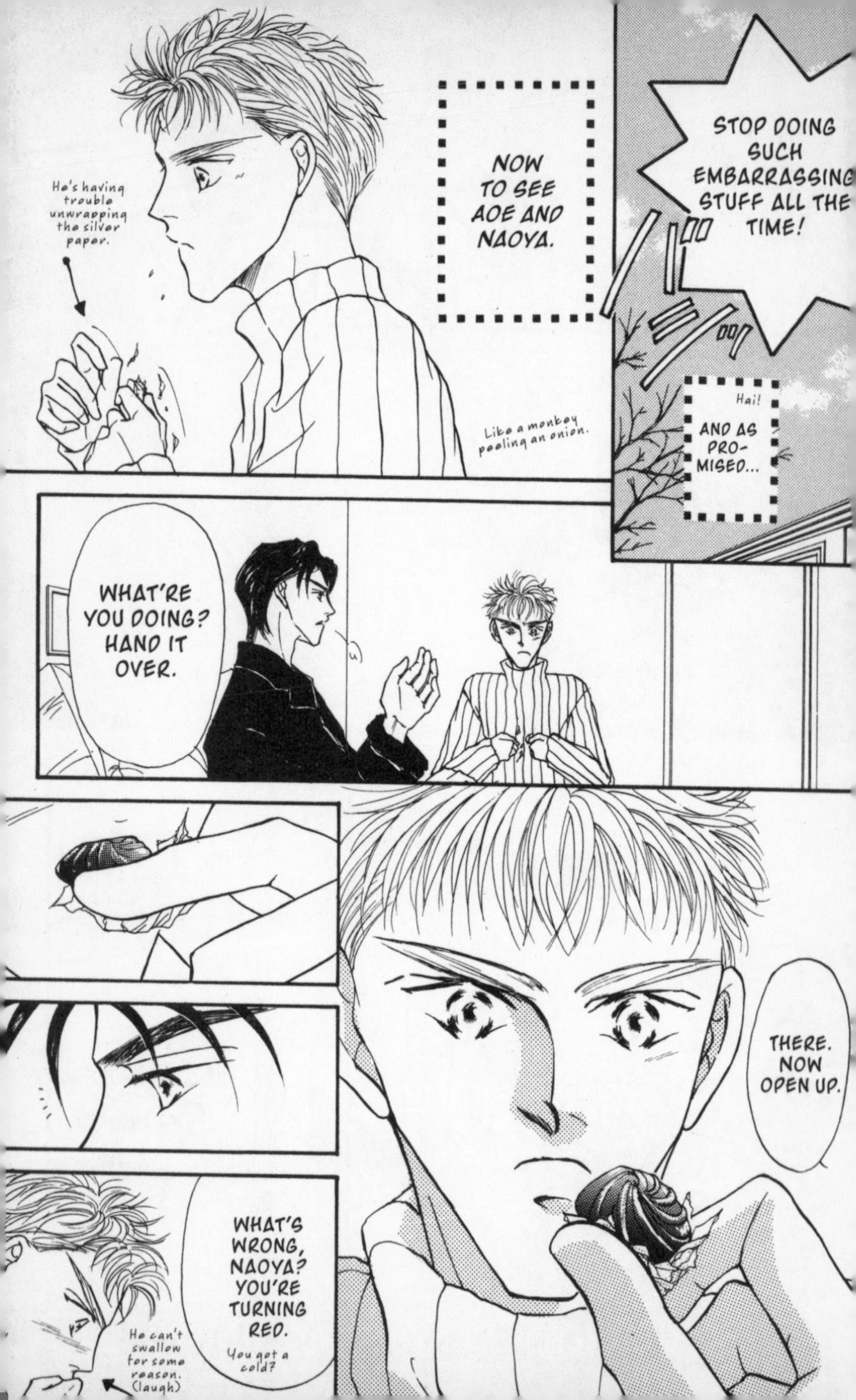
STOP DOING SUCH EMBARRASSING STUFF ALL THE TIME!
Hai!
AND AS PRO-MISED...
NOW TO SEE AOE AND NAOYA.
Like a monkey peeling an onion.
He's having trouble unwrapping the silver paper.
WHAT'RE YOU DOING? HAND IT OVER.
THERE. NOW OPEN UP.
WHAT'S WRONG, NAOYA? YOU'RE TURNING RED.
You got a cold?
He can't swallow for some reason. (laugh)

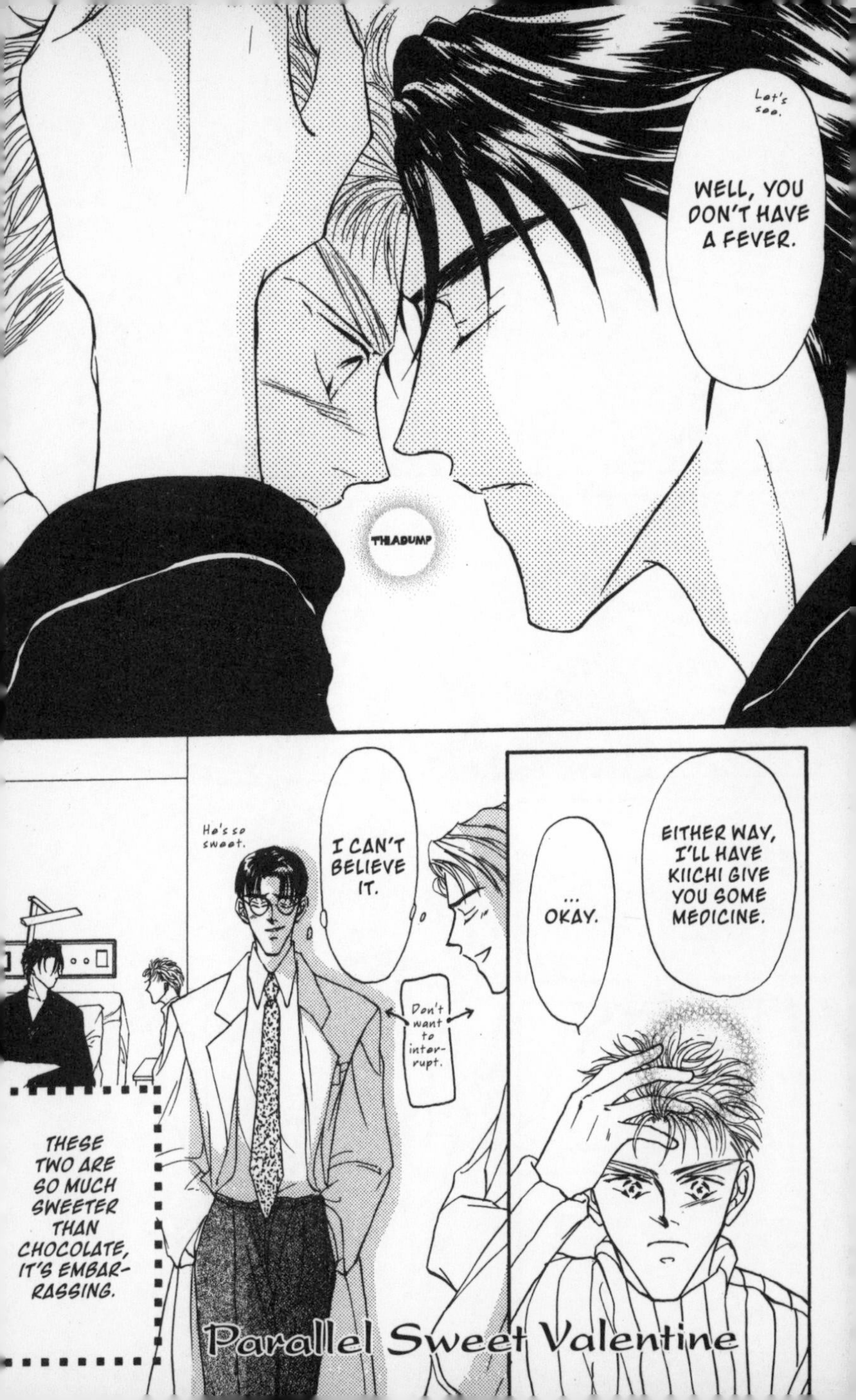
Let's see.
WELL, YOU DON'T HAVE A FEVER.
THADUMP
EITHER WAY, I'LL HAVE KIICHI GIVE YOU SOME MEDICINE.
... OKAY.
I CAN'T BELIEVE IT.
He's so sweet.
Don't want to inter-rupt.
THESE TWO ARE SO MUCH SWEETER THAN CHOCOLATE, IT'S EMBAR-RASSING.
Parallel Sweet Valentine

LOVE MODE

Yuki Shimizu

3

青 BLU

Now that Izumi has found happiness with Takamiya, it's time for the other "Izumi" to do the same. Blue Boy's number one hasn't been doing too well lately. But with his health improving, it may be time for him to find a love all his own. His chance may come when a young man named Arashi moves in next door. Will Izumi be able to find true love and bury the pain in his heart? There's also some wacky moments when Aoe brings Naoya home to introduce him to the family... Things just keep getting hotter and hotter with volume three of Love Mode.

LOVE MODE VOL. 2
Created by Yuki Shimizu

ISBN: 1-59816-011-7

First Printing: March 2006
10 9 8 7 6 5 4 3 2 1
Printed in Canada

青 BLU

BOYS' LOV

Earthian Vol. 1

Angels walk among us—they are scattered across the globe helping humans in crisis. Chihaya and Kagetsuya travel tirelessly, dealing with an array of characters and their hopeless problems. But when a growing legion of angels is plagued by the Black Cancer, it's up to Chihaya and Kagetsuya to find the fallen Lord Seraphim, who may have the key to the salvation of their celestial kind.

Wild Rock Vol. 1

BLU hits boys' love fans with a hot one-shot volume from fan-favorite creator Kazusa Takashima. Meet Emba and Yuuen, two very different heirs to warring clans, who meet and fall in love. Two side stories feature the respective clan leaders as tempestuous youth and introduce Yuuen and Emba's niece, the adorable little Nava.

Shinobu Kokoro: Hidden Heart

Follow the sizzling sessions with a young ninja-in-training as his master teaches him the secrets of the clan with a little hands-on instruction! Meanwhile, two shinobi take their relationship to new heights when a tragic separation leaves one of them caught between a rock and a hard place.

Hisae Shino is an unemployed anime voice actor who also has to support his son Nakaya, a sophomore in high school. The sweet and naive Shino will take any job he can get—even if it means boys' love radio dramas! When he gets paired up with the super-cool Tenryuu, the two bond...to a degree that Shino never intended!

Price: $9.99
Available in stores April 2006

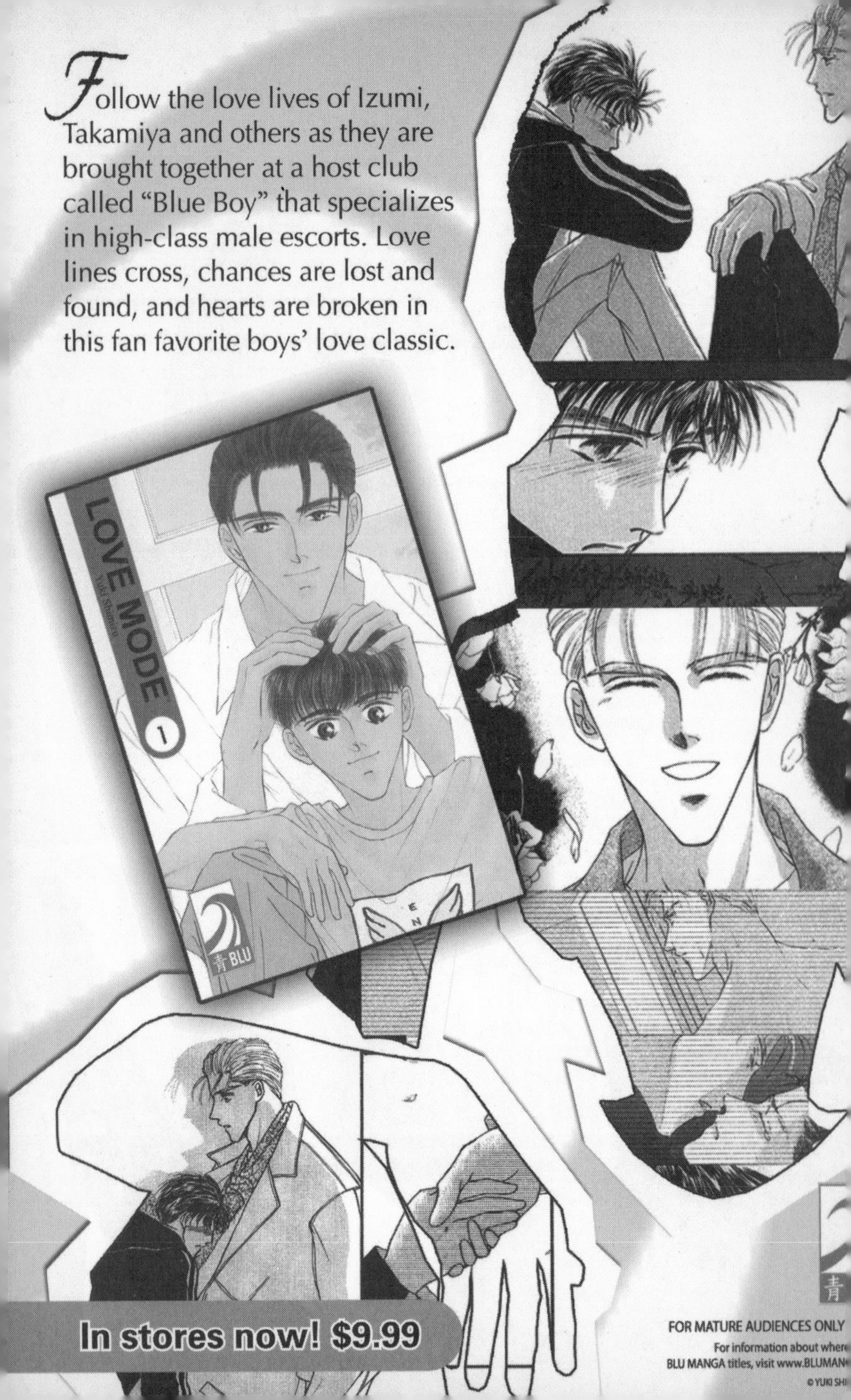
Follow the love lives of Izumi, Takamiya and others as they are brought together at a host club called "Blue Boy" that specializes in high-class male escorts. Love lines cross, chances are lost and found, and hearts are broken in this fan favorite boys' love classic.
LOVE MODE
1
青 BLU
In stores now! $9.99
FOR MATURE AUDIENCES ONLY
For information about where
BLU MANGA titles, visit www.BLUMAN
© YUKI SHI

stop

blu manga are published in the original japanese format

go to the other side and begin reading